MENANDER 'MISOUMENOS'
OR 'THE HATED MAN'

Introduction, Translation, and Commentary

BULLETIN OF THE INSTITUTE OF CLASSICAL STUDIES
SUPPLEMENT 143

EDITOR: GREG WOOLF

The cover image shows a mosaic pavement of Apollo and Daphne.
Roman, Antioch on the Orontes, The House of Menander, Turkey.

© Princeton University Art Museum/Art Resource NY/Scala,
Florence. Reproduced with permission.

ISBN 978-1-905670-97-0 (hardback)

© 2021 Institute of Classical Studies, University of London.

All rights reserved. No part of this publication may be reproduced, stored in a
retrieval system, or transmitted, in any form or by any means, electronic, mechanical,
photocopying, recording, or otherwise, without the prior permission of the publisher.

The right of the contributors to be identified as the authors of the work published here has
been asserted by them in accordance with the Copyright, Designs, and Patents Act 1988.

Menander *Misoumenos*,

or *The Hated Man*

edited with introduction, translation, and commentary
by
William Furley

Acknowledgements

I owe a debt of gratitude to some friends and colleagues who gave up their time to look at my efforts: Horst-Dieter Blume, Mark de Kreij, two anonymous readers for the Institute of Classical Studies (one in particular for their detailed and helpful comments). Responsibility for remaining mistakes is entirely mine, of course. Thanks also to Daniela Colomo at the Sackler Library for constant help with making the relevant papyri available which are held in their collection (Papyri Oxyrhynchi). To the British Library Reading Room for giving me access to P.Oxy. 2656 and allowing me to photograph it. To the Institute of Classical Studies for their continuing support. Principally of course to Menander, for continuing, albeit sometimes grudgingly, to make his texts available to us. And on a personal level to my wife Inga, who likes Menander (in Russian translation!) and whose care, loving support and encouragement mean everything.

I dedicate this work to the staff of the Royal Free Hospital, Hampstead, and its subsidiaries, who saw me through serious illness between 2015-2020. This book would not have been finished without them. With Hesiod: ὡς δ᾿ ὅτ᾿ ἀνὴρ ἀσπαστὸν ὑπεκπροφύγηι κακότητα / νούσου ὕπ᾿ ἀργαλέης …

London, Summer 2021

Contents

List of Figures xi

Abbreviations xiii

1 Introduction   **1**

1.1 The state of play 1

    1.1.1 What do we know? 2

    1.1.2 What do we not know? 4

    1.1.3 The puzzling middle section 9

    1.1.4 The scene of action 10

1.2 What is the play about? – Thrasonides 11

1.3 Other Characters 15

    1.3.1 Krateia 15

    1.3.2 Demeas 16

    1.3.3 Kleinias 17

    1.3.4 Getas 17

    1.3.5 Chrysis 18

1.4 Pictorial evidence 19

1.5 Legal Framework 20

1.6 Staging 22

1.7 Dating 24

1.8 Metre 26

1.9 Transmission of the Text 29

    1.9.1 Antiquity 29

    1.9.2 Modern Age 30

1.10 Technical points about this edition 32

2 Greek Text   **35**

Manuscripts 35

The cast 36

Act One 37

viii   *CONTENTS*

Act Two 42
Act Three 46
Act Four 53
Act Five 58
Unplaced papyrus fragments 61
Unplaced book fragments 63

3   Composite Readings   **67**
Lines 1-45 68
Lines 51-54 72
Lines 85-100 72
Lines 401-492 73
Lines 501-559 73
Lines 560-578 78
Lines 611-622 80
Lines 644-665 81
Lines 677-700 83
Lines 751-814 84
Lines 959-974 87

4   Translation   **89**
Act One 89
Fr. 2 91
Act Two 92
Act Three 95
Act Four 101
Act Five 106
Miscellaneous unplaced fragments 108

5   Commentary   **111**
Act One 111
Scene One: Thrasonides and Getas 111
Scene Two: Delayed prologue 142
Scene Three: Thrasonides and Getas? 144
Act Two 146
Scene One: ?? 146
Scene Two: Thrasonides and Getas 147
Scene Three: Demeas and Syra 147
Act Three 154
Scene One: Getas' secret mission 154

CONTENTS ix

Scene Two: Syra and Demeas 169
Scene Three: Recognition (1) 171
Act Four 183
Scene One: Drama indoors 183
Scene Two: Kleinias and Getas 195
Scene Three: Thrasonides' monologue 197
Act Five 213
Scene One: Getas and ?? 213
Scene Two: ?Sham suicide and Recognition (2) 213
Scene Three: Happy Ending 215
Book Fragments 220
Bibliography 223
Index of Main Passages Cited 233
Index of Greek words 238

List of Figures

1.1	Sir Eric Turner	1
1.2	Mytilene mosaic	20
1.3	P.Oxy. 2656	31
5.1	P.Oxy. 3370	127
5.2	P.Oxy. 4025	196
5.3	End of *Misoumenos*	219

Commonly used abbreviations

For details see Bibliography

Bl = Blanchard (2016)

CGCG = van Emde Boas *et al.* (2019)

CGF = Austin (1973)

DELG = Chantraine (1968)

GEW = Frisk (1970)

GG = Smyth (1976[10])

G-S = Gomme & Sandbach (1973)

HPP = Henry *et al.* (2014a)

K-A = Kassel & Austin (1983-2001)

K-Th = Koerte & Thierfelder (Third edition 1953-1955)

Kühner-Gerth = Kühner & Gerth (1966)

LSJ = http://stephanus.tlg.uci.edu, based on: Henry George Liddell, Robert Scott, Henry Stuart Jones, Greek-English Lexicon, 9th edition, Oxford (Clarendon) 1940

Mayser = Mayser (1906)

Chapter 1

Introduction

1.1 The state of play

Although to date no less than sixteen ancient manuscripts have been found bearing large or small portions of *Misoumenos*, the play as we have it today is in tatters. The most sizeable manuscript O^3, P.Oxy. 2656, which was deciphered and published by Eric Turner in the nineteen-sixties (1965 and 1968), is rubbed, torn, holed and lacerated in large measure and intact only in small (Turner, 1965).[1] It is to the credit of Turner's inspirational patience and skill that we owe the rediscovery of at least sizeable portions of the play, and a rough idea of the overall plan. Although O^3 gives us much, it also withholds much. The ink traces of letters on its fibres sometimes resemble the fast vanishing footprints of shore birds in wet sand. This manuscript is, as it were, the clothes donkey on which many other fragments are hung.

Figure 1.1: Sir Eric Gardner Turner (1911-1983) ©National Portrait Gallery

Throughout this edition the reader is requested to bear this in mind. The text is far from complete, and no amount of poring over it or wishing it otherwise will alter that at present. Arnott's *ars nesciendi* must be applied in large measure. On the other hand, the purpose of this edition is to push things as far as they can go, without fantasizing and without inventing. Very uncertain restorations are given in grey print to mark them more clearly than simple brackets, which are sometimes ignored by a reader, particularly an inexperienced one. Dots under letters have their

---

[1] For the sigla used in this edition, designed to tally with Blanchard, see the beginning of the chapters 'Text' and 'Composite Readings'.

CHAPTER 1. INTRODUCTION

usual papyrological significance, which is to indicate that ink traces in one or more manuscripts are consistent with the letter given, but not proof. The reader is referred to the chapter 'Composite Readings' for a close analysis of which letters can be read in which manuscripts, when more than one go to make up our knowledge of the reading of any particular line. Here the dots and brackets are given scrupulously. The reader will find that not all the dots have been transferred from the chapter 'Composite Readings' to the main text; I have omitted them when a reading seems sufficiently determined to bridge small uncertainties in individual letters. However, most of these dots have been retained.

Given all these disparate sources, we now have a number of quite lengthy passages of *Misoumenos* more or less complete. For example, that holds for the first fifty or so lines of text in which we are introduced by the playwright to Thrasonides and his trouble in love, and his servant, or batman, Getas. We also have a good sized middle portion including the recognition scene between Demeas and Krateia, the heroine of the piece, the girl who has conceived a strong dislike for the soldier. And, perhaps most importantly, we have a sizeable portion of Thrasonides' mournful soliloquy when he is weighing the issue of whether to go on living or not. In this he considered, among other things, the possible accusation which might be levelled against him, that in all his woes he is only considering his point of view, and not that of Krateia. His doubts and musings in this speech, are, I believe, quite unique in ancient literature, comparable in moment – although in a comedy by name – with Medea's fraught deliberations whether she should really kill Jason's children by her or not.[2] The speech is an expression of Thrasonides' despair which will probably grip most modern hearts. And there is the final scene in which everything turns out all right and Thrasonides is finally accepted by Krateia: clichéed, no doubt, but nevertheless the drama has been so intense that one feels real relief that Krateia has relented. If this play were complete, it would, one feels, be one of Menander's best. Surely that is the reason why so many ancient manuscripts have been found bearing lines of the play. It must have been popular in antiquity indeed, if so many scraps survived in Egypt alone.

1.1.1 What do we know?

We know that Krateia conceives a disliking for Thrasonides. That is the basis of the whole drama, and emerges at the beginning when Thrasonides explains to Getas why he is pacing about in the street outside his own front door, reluctant to go in because he is not welcome. In lines 31-2 he tells Getas the reason for his unhappiness: the 'prisoner of war' (i.e. Krateia) is doing him an injury (ἐλεῖν᾽ ὑβρίζομαι). She has conceived a hatred (43 μῖσος) for him; the epithet going with that hatred is lost, but in view of a similar passage in Aristainetos (1.22.14) I suggest ἐξαίσιον, 'terrible',

---

[2] Cf. Giacomoni (1998).

1.1. THE STATE OF PLAY

or 'unholy'.[3] Getas jokes that Thrasonides is like a 'magnet' in repelling Krateia so violently. The conversation between officer and batman continues, and before the text becomes illegible they resolve to try to discover what the reason for Krateia's disposition might be.

In the above exchange we have also learned that Thrasonides acquired Krateia as a prisoner of war (37 αἰχμαλώτου and 636-7). When Demeas, her father, arrives at Kleinias' house, he has come from Cyprus. When he recognizes Krateia, as she comes out of Thrasonides' house, he comments:

> Arriving from Cyprus I see here as first of my family members this girl.
> It is clear that our common enemy, war, has scattered members of the family every which way.[4]

Regardless of the question where Demeas is now speaking – Athens? – a natural way of taking this would be that Demeas' family members had been living in Cyprus and were now scattered by the events of war through the Greek world. When we put this remark together with the fragment which has Thrasonides' achieving successes as a mercenary officer in Cyprus (fr. 2), we may be correct in assuming that Thrasonides acquired Krateia in Cyprus, where she had fallen victim to war and had been offered up for sale on the slave market. Thrasonides had bought her there.[5]

Demeas had not been expecting to find her. A passage of Simplicius cites this development in *Mis.* to illustrate chance events:

> 'As when we say that the guest (or 'stranger') came by chance and, having paid the ransom for the prisoner of war, as Demeas in Menander's play [did for] Krateia, left (or 'released')…'[6]

---

[3] Austin, followed by most editors, suggested νέον.

[4] Lines 632-35. Cf. Katsouris (1980).

[5] The situation is comparable to that in *Sik.* 5ff., where it is related in the prologue that a military commander (9 ἡγεμών τις) bought Philoumenē on the marketplace in Mylasa after her family had been captured by pirates (2 ὡς δ᾽ ἐγκρατεῖς ἐγένοντο σωμάτων τριῶν) in Caria.

[6] Simplicius (*In Aristotelis physicorum libros commentaria* 9.384.15 Diels): ὅταν λέγωμεν ὅτι ἀπὸ τύχης ἦλθεν ὁ ξένος καὶ λυτρωσάμενος τὸν αἰχμάλωτον, ὡς ὁ παρὰ Μενάνδρῳ Δημέας τὴν Κράτειαν, ἀπῆλθεν ἢ ἀφῆκε (γράφεται γὰρ ἀμφοτέρως, ὥσπερ καὶ ἀντὶ τοῦ λυτρωσάμενος τὸ λουσάμενος). Arnott suggested changing τὸν sc. αἰχμάλωτον to τὴν, but the point is general, not specifically referring to Krateia yet. ἀφῆκε as a reading seems a little redundant after λυτρωσάμενος. The variant reading λουσάμενος must be wrong, unless λυσάμενος (thus Ross) is meant. Ross (1936, 530) comments that Simplicius' intertext here (Menander's *Misoumenos*) is likely to be mistaken as it is more probable that Aristotle was referring to Plato's imprisonment in Aegina and his being ransomed ᾽κατὰ τύχης᾽ by a certain Annikeris of Cyrene (Diog. Laert. 3.20; so already Diels with relevant passages). But Ross could know nothing of *Misoumenos* at that time, so his statement 'the allusion cannot be to the *Misoumenoi* (*sic*) of Menander' is without justification. See below, note on 432-3.

4   CHAPTER 1. INTRODUCTION

The important phrase here is ἀπὸ τύχης: Demeas had clearly not sailed deliberately from Cyprus to the setting of our play with a view to discovering Krateia. It
seems he was invited by Kleinias as his guest (there is mention of a letter: 417 and
425) and there accidentally discovered from Kleinias' old housemaid Syra that a girl
called Krateia was living next door. Incidentally, it does not seem likely that Demeas in the play 'sailed off again' (ἀπῆλθεν) having ransomed Krateia; a wedding
concludes the play as we have it. Demeas may have *wanted* to sail off again with
Krateia, but it seems that the reconciliation between Krateia and Thrasonides, which
we know happened at the end of the play, made that unnecessary.

1.1.2   What do we not know?

Having set out the above points which emerge clearly from surviving portions of text
– the estrangement of Thrasonides and Krateia, the chance arrival of Demeas and
recognition of Krateia, finally the reconciliation of the young couple and preparations
for their marriage – one can revisit a number of these points to show what, and how
much, is still uncertain. The reader should be reminded that the ancient audience, or
reader, would *not* have been in the same position of uncertainty. For one thing, the
play would have existed in its entirety so all details of plot and dialogue would have
been present. Second, there would very probably have been a prologue in which
a character 'in the know' would have filled the audience in at an early stage on all
elements of the plot which may at first have eluded the characters themselves.[7] For
example, Thrasonides may not have known why Krateia had taken a disliking to
him until quite late in the action,[8] but the audience will certainly have known the
background to the lovers' quarrel. So for this play we, the modern reader and scholar,
are in a much worse position to enjoy and evaluate this play than the ancient recipient.
If only a third of, say, *Othello* had survived we would be groping in the dark when
we tried to guess at the plot from surviving islands of action.

The worst uncertainty in *Mis.* is the reason for Krateia's hatred of Thrasonides.
We learn early on in the play that Krateia has conceived an 'abnormal' (reading
ἐξαίσιον in line 43) hatred of the soldier and Thrasonides' batman Getas teasingly
runs through a number of reasons why she might not like him: his soldier's pay is
modest; he's not *that* terribly bad-looking; he might be getting on in years a bit (91-
94). To Getas' mocking suggestions Thrasonides reacts with irritation but does not
give any reason himself. In line 95, unless the line was spoken by Getas, he says that
'we must discover the real compelling reason' (sc. for Krateia's mood). It seems at
this point that Thrasonides is truly ignorant of the reason. All he knows is that the girl
shuns him. In lines 50-56 he describes how he was lying in bed with the girl at night

---

[7] On the missing prologue of *Mis.* cf. Sisti (1973-74); Jacques (1974).   [8] In lines 709-10 he is still
claiming ignorance of why she rejects him.

1.1. THE STATE OF PLAY 5

and she did not stop him going out in the wind and rain: a sure sign that she did not care for him.

Boorish lover?

A number of ancient comments on the play indicate that it was Thrasonides' soldierly boasting, traditionally an attribute of the type of *miles gloriosus*, which put the girl off. The lexicon of Photius (σ 429) defines a word in Menander's *Mis.*, σπαθᾶν, as τὸ ἀλαζονεύεσθαι, 'boasting', but without context. Epictetus, in describing Thrasonides' abject behaviour in the face of Krateia's rejection of him (book fr. 1 of our play), says: τί δὲ προφέρεις σου τὰς στρατε‹ί›ας; 'Why do you parade your military campaigns?' With most detail, the late classical rhetor Choricius (5th/6th c.) says it was his blustering, boasting military manner which alienated him from Krateia. The whole passage runs:

> You can see from comedy, what an overweening and aggressive thing, what a boast, a soldier is. If one of you cares to imagine Menander's Thrasonides, he knows what I mean. He (Menander) says that the man suffered from a military unpleasantness and this put his lover off him. And 'hate' indeed has become eponymous for Thrasonides' drama.[9]

In the play itself there is one hint: a small fragment of O[5], probably to be placed toward the end of act one, has Getas saying to Thrasonides: 'My God! That's a very martial pose you're striking...' (lines 4-5 Ἄπ]ολλον· καὶ μάλα στρατιωτ[ικῶς] /[...] νῦν ὁρᾶις). Perhaps Getas is referring to a tactic, or approach, which Thrasonides now wishes to employ against Krateia, but unfortunately the context is not certain.

It is worth mentioning here that Lukian *Dial. meretr.* 13 tells the story of one Leontichos returning from the wars against the Gauls and in Paphlagonia and telling tales of prowess to his girlfriend Hymnis. She, however, is disgusted and walks off. The friend Chenidas tells him he has the choice

---

[9] Choricius Rhet. *decl.* 42.1.1, p. 509.8ff. Foerster-Richtsteig: Ἔχεις ἐκ τῆς κωμωιδίας παραλαβών, ὡς ὑπέρογκόν τι καὶ σοβαρὸν καὶ ἀλαζονεία στρατιώτης ἀνήρ. Εἴ τις ὑμῶν φαντάζεται τὸν Μενάνδρου Θρασωνίδην, οἶδεν ὃ λέγω. στρατιωτικὴν γάρ φησιν ἀηδίαν νοσοῦντα τὸν ἄνθρωπον εἰς ἀπέχθειαν αὐτῶι κινῆσαι τὴν ἐρωμένην. See Kraus (1971a, 2). It is, however, possible that Choricius is being too literal-minded and has misunderstood Getas' jibe at 90-92. See commentary *ad loc.* Zagagi (1994, 31) comments: 'On the face of it, this does not fit what we know of the play. But if we assume that it relates to the way Thrasonides *appears* in certain stages of the plot to the other characters, above all to Krateia, rather than to his *real* personality in the play, we may conclude that here we have a similar ambivalent approach to the character of the soldier as we had in *Perikeiromene*.' Traill (2008, 26) suggests that Choricius had not even read the play, as φησιν indicates an intermediate source ('someone-or-other says'). But this is wrong: Menander himself is subject of φησιν.

ἑλοῦ τοίνυν θάτερον ἢ μισεῖσθαι ἀριστεὺς εἶναι δοκῶν ἢ καθεύδειν μετὰ Ὑμνίδος ἐψεῦσθαι ὁμολογῶν, 'so choose between being hated while enjoying the reputation of a war-hero, or sleeping with Hymnis whilst conceding that you were lying.'

He says that's a difficult choice, but nevertheless prefers to admit he was lying in his *alazoneia*, in order to get Hymnis back. The names are all different in *Mis.* but the theme looks familiar, including the key-word μισεῖσθαι and mentioning sleeping with Hymnis, as Thrasonides recounts of himself and Krateia in lines 50-56. We know that Lukian frequently takes from Menander, particularly in the *Dialogues of Courtesans*, so there may be an echo of *Mis.* here.[10]

Against the theory of a boorish, repugnant Thrasonides, however, one should recall that Chrysippos quoted Thrasonides in this play as an example of how love is not a question of *erōs* (Thrasonides has plenty of that) but of *philia* (Thrasonides restrains himself out of respect for the girl's feelings).[11]

As to jealousy, which might spark boorish behaviour or boasting by the rebuffed lover, there are only exiguous traces in the play (cf. generally: Fantham (1986)). Gregory of Nazianzus (*Carmina de se ipso* 1176.5) mentions φθόνος, envy, of men like Thrasonides and comments that he displayed 'uncouth' behaviour (ἀγροικία) (see commentary on line 953). This is not necessarily *alazoneia*, but might be an attribute of the *miles gloriosus*. Later in the play, when Getas sees Demeas embracing Krateia (his daughter) he thinks that he has caught the man 'he was looking for' (619 τὸν ζητούμε[νον]). Now that looks as if Getas thought Thrasonides might have had a rival in love, and this 'other man' was the reason why she had cooled toward him. Without any context we encounter some form of the Greek for 'jealousy' in line 953 (ζηλοτυπ[ ). These are sparse testimony indeed to a jealousy theme in the play. Nevertheless we should keep the following in mind: (1) ancient testimonia attest loutish, boasting behaviour by Thrasonides in the play, possibly caused by jealousy; (2) neither Thrasonides nor Getas has any idea what is putting Krateia off him by about line 100 when the action is well under way; they might suspect a rival lover. Could we put these remarks together to conclude that jealousy led Thrasonides to display boorish, blustering behaviour toward Krateia, rather in the manner of Polemon in *Perikeiromene*, who 'loses it', to use a modern expression, when he thinks his girlfriend has been caught kissing another man? I doubt that Thrasonides assaulted Krateia, but he might have boasted of his prowess on the battlefield. There is plenty of space at the beginning of act two, for example, for an illustrative scene of lovers-at-loggerheads. If I happen to be right with a conjectural supplement to lines 609-10,

---

[10] Otto Ribbeck, *Alazōn*, Leipzig 1882, believed this work had *Mis.* as its source, but, as Kraus (1971a) says, this is too simplistic. To be fair, Ribbeck had hardly any of *Mis.* to go on then.   [11] Diog. Laert. 7.130 = *St. V. Frg.* III nr. 716, cf. Kraus (1971a, 3).

1.1. THE STATE OF PLAY

Krateia herself complains about aggressive behaviour on the part of Thrasonides toward *her*.

The brother's sword

Now Reinhold Merkelbach (1966) set in motion a theory which, in abbreviated form, runs as follows.[12] Krateia recognized among the war trophies which Thrasonides brought back from war in Cyprus the sword which belonged to her brother. She concluded that her master had killed her brother: what more reason could she need to loathe and despise him?

If that is correct we are to imagine the following sequence: Thrasonides and Krateia were getting on fine until Getas arrived back with the war spoils on the day before the play begins. Krateia saw the brother's sword (among all else), came to the dire conclusion that her brother had been a victim of Thrasonides, and immediately turned against him. That very night Thrasonides experienced the 'cold shoulder' and exited his house to wander around miserably outside in the wind and rain, where Getas meets him.

But how likely is it that Krateia inspected the spoils on the very evening Getas arrived back, when Thrasonides had not even had a chance to talk to Getas by the time the play commences? Moreover, in lines 29-32 Thrasonides explains to Getas that he had had no chance to explain what the cause of his misery was because the latter only arrived the day before (31 ἐχθές). Now that surely means that Thrasonides had been 'suffering dreadfully' (29 [ἀ]τυχῶ δεινῶς) at the hands of the 'prisoner of war' (Krateia) *before* Getas arrived home. And that can only mean that Krateia had cause to reject him in love *before* she had seen any of the war spoils. So the 'brother's sword' cannot have been the original reason for Krateia's dislike of Thrasonides.

But there *is* an important sword in the play, and its recognition is key. We hear at two points (578-80; 677-81) that *Demeas*, Krateia's father, has recognized a sword in Kleinias' house, which actually belongs next door, in Thrasonides' house (Getas has deposited Thrasonides' spoils of war there). He looks long at this sword (578-580) and recognizes it as 'one of his own' (592-3 my supplements). From this he deduces that Thrasonides has come into possession of this weapon belonging to Demeas' family. Perhaps the sword had passed into the hands of Demeas' son and its possession now by Thrasonides would be a pointer to the sad fate of its owner.

Following the recognition between father Demeas and daughter Krateia, a badly damaged passage shows the two discussing the death of a close family member (645-59). 'I know it well. He is dead … and by the hand of the person who should least have done the deed' (648-49). In my reconstruction the words are spoken by Demeas; in this I am following the explicit notice of O[3]; others put the words into Krateia's

---

[12] And picked up by Kraus (1971a, 9) and most subsequent scholars.

8   CHAPTER 1. INTRODUCTION

mouth. Then comes a very badly preserved line; I guess that in it, Demeas tells Krateia
that she has become the war trophy of this person (Thrasonides). Now if the missing
person they are discussing is Krateia's brother, as scholars have thought in the train
of Eric Turner, the implication would be that Krateia is co-habiting with the soldier
who slew her brother. That would be explanation enough why she hated him, but
the revelation comes relatively late in the play; in its earlier stages Krateia may have
had other reasons for spurning the soldier, as we have seen. In this passage there
is no mention of any sword, but that is not necessary because Demeas has already
recognized the sword and drawn his conclusions from it. It is these conclusions which
he reveals to Krateia in this scene.

How sure can we be that there was any brother involved in the plot? Krateia's
brother is *nowhere* mentioned explicitly in the surviving fragments, nor does he appear in flesh and blood, as it were, unless the truncated lines 948ff. are attributable to
him, as Geoffrey Arnott has suggested. Where Hunt thought he could read ἀ]δελφό[
on fr. 4 of O^{1v}, the placing of the fragment by Turner (1968, 34) shows that something else stood there. In line 642 I see the letters]φο.[which might conceivably be
part of ἀδελφός (or of many other things!). On the other hand, although scepticism
is a good critical tool, *someone* close to Krateia and Demeas has died, and a brother
looks like a good candidate. Otherwise a mother might be a possibility, but it does not
seem likely that Demeas' recognition of a family sword in the possession of an 'enemy'
would point to a mother's death. When Demeas recognizes his daughter for the first
time he says that war has 'scattered some members of my family (τῶν οἴκοι τινάς) in
all directions'. He does not say 'my children', which would include Krateia and her
brother, but only 'my family members'. Nor does the end of the play (as we have it)
clarify matters. Of course in the original play it did: any possible reason for Krateia's
reservations about Thrasonides were cleared away by the end of the production.

Ursula Treu (1974) believes that a remark in Clemens (*Strom.* 2.15.62.2), although not explicitly attributed to *Mis.*, may in fact reflect our play as, a little later
in 2.15.64.2, he does indeed mention the play. The first passage runs ὥσπερ ὁ τὸν
ἀντίπαλον ἀφεὶς καὶ ἀποκτείνας οἰκεῖον ἀντὶ πολεμίου, which seems to mean
'like the man who released his adversary and killed a relative instead of an enemy'.
This might reflect Thrasonides' killing of Krateia's brother (the οἰκεῖον) whilst releasing an enemy (the ἀντίπαλον, whoever he might have been). The later passage
cites Thrasonides as an example from comedy of passion: τὸν γὰρ κωμικὸν ἐκεῖνον
Θρασωνίδην ἄλλη σκηνὴ «παιδισκάριόν με» φησὶν «εὐτελὲς καταδεδούλωκεν»,
'another play has that comic figure Thrasonides [crying out] "A cheap slave-girl has
enslaved me!"' The phrasing of the first reference is, however, anything but unequivocal, and we note that the second passage mentions 'a different play',[13] seemingly

---

[13] σκηνή means 'stage' but here apparently (and uniquely), by metonymy, play. Blanchard translates

1.1. THE STATE OF PLAY

ruling *Mis.* out for the former quote. So far, the elusive brother evades capture.

Some have wondered whether the mysterious Kleinias was in fact Krateia's brother (Blanchard, 2016, 223-27). However, neither Krateia nor Demeas has recognized him, the former as his neighbour for some period of time, the latter as his house guest. The only explanation for this situation would be that Krateia and her brother were separated as infants and grew up separately, as is the situation in *Sikyonioi* and *Perikeiromenē*. However, Demeas' remark that he has come from Cyprus, where war has scattered his family, combined with fr. 2, in which Thrasonides is said to have acquitted himself bravely there, points rather to a recent separation of Demeas' family. Demeas seems to be an old *xenos*, guest-friend, of Kleinias: it seems very unlikely that Kleinias is his son in disguise, as it were.

So, tentatively, I advance a revised sequence. Thrasonides took Krateia with him when he left camp in Cyprus, having bought her on the slave market. He intended to treat her well, but she never took to him. She was repulsed by his soldierly bragging and arrogance.[14] Thus, when Getas arrives back home considerably later with the spoils, he encounters a master who is being 'dreadfully humiliated' (36 ἐλε[ίν'] ὑβρίζομαι) by the girl, and is thoroughly downhearted. When the master even begins to have suicidal thoughts, demanding a sword to end his life (book frr. 1 (Epictetus) and 3) Getas moves all the weapons and other spoils of war next door to Kleinias' house. There Krateia's father *Demeas* subsequently recognizes one sword as a family heirloom and comes to the conclusion that the man who it now belongs to (Thrasonides) must have been responsible for the death of his family member. When Demeas and Krateia meet and recognize each other in act three, Krateia's dislike of Thrasonides is compounded by the realization that she is cohabiting with her brother's slayer. Father and daughter become absolutely resolute in their determination to free her from the soldier's clutches. The sword of the brother was indeed a token, a *gnōrisma*, but one recognized by Demeas, not Krateia.

1.1.3 The puzzling middle section

With the publication of P.Oxy. 5198 (O^{11}) we now have, admittedly with many conjectural readings, a new section of continuous text 532-75. The latter half of this (557-75) is relatively stable now, given the combined readings of three manuscripts (see Chapter 'Composite Readings'). It is a monologue delivered by Getas in which he

---

'scène', but this meaning would be quite unprecedented, but greatly favourable to Treu's theory if it could be maintained.

[14] Horst-Dieter Blume points out to me (*per litt.*) that Thrasonides' behaviour in the first scene of the play, when he miserably walks up and down the street in front of his own front door, is anything but bullish and show-offish. That is correct. However, he might have offended the girl with military boasting before the night described in lines 50-56, and then, realizing the error of his ways when the girl shunned him, taken to despondent wandering the streets at night.

10   CHAPTER 1. INTRODUCTION

seems to be describing the goings-on in an inn in which his master is carousing. So far
so good. Before that, however, comes a new section of text, 532-56, which involves
a three-way dialogue between Syra, Kleinias' servant, and Chrysis, an hetaira, with
Getas (I think) conducting some secret business of his own, observed and commented
on by the two women. What exactly Getas is doing is open to question. I would like
to think this is the scene in which he secretes Thrasonides' spoils of war, including the
swords, in the neighbour Kleinias' house. Some lines point clearly in this direction,
but they require partial restoration, so we may fall foul of *petitio principii*. I have
restored lines 553-4 to say (Syra speaking): 'there are such beasts, one of whom may
trick us by smuggling into the house, but not any more, god willing'. If correct, or
nearly correct, Syra would be commenting on Getas' smuggling Thrasonides' spoils
of war into Kleinias' house. Let us hope that something like that is happening in this
scene; at the very least we must assume that such a scene happened before Demeas
can have recognized the sword among other war trophies in lines 677-79.

After the serving women's departure Getas launches into a description of what
was happening in the inn (?) where he left his master. Although, as I said, much of
the text is established, the content is very mysterious. Without here going into detail,
it seems certain that there is some plot against Thrasonides implicated in these lines.
Menander does not elsewhere indulge in skullduggery, so it is highly unlikely that
anything resembling a crime mystery is intended here; nevertheless, some danger to
Thrasonides seems to be indicated by Getas. There is a singer in Getas' description
who sings a skolion (I think) to the drinking party, and there is a fat man present
who resembles a pig. All very mysterious and we will not get to the bottom of the
mystery unless more text is discovered. What seems certain is that an inn plays a
part in this play, as in *Perikeiromene*, and probably provides a third, central door
of the *skēnē*. Getas comments at the end of the narrative: 'Why should I invite this
man to dinner after he has invited my master?' with an implied 'no chance!' It
seems that Thrasonides is attending some kind of carousing in an inn to which he
has been invited. The dubious character had approached Thrasonides, then backed
off, as if changing his mind (569). Could it be that fr. 6 (Orus fr. 35) arranged by
Blanchard as 'They hate Thrasonides, father, but they have not killed him' (μισοῦσι
μὲν / Θρασωνίδην, ὦ πάτερ, ἀπεκτάγκασι δ' οὔ), fits in here: that there was a
plot against Thrasonides' life? If ὦ πάτερ is correct, Krateia must be the speaker.
Again, *ars nesciendi* must prevail.

1.1.4   The scene of action

We look – almost – in vain for positive markers of the city which provides the scene
of the play. In line 42 Thrasonides swears by Athena, if the supplement [μὰ τὴν
Ἀθ]ηνᾶν is correct, and Athena is the patron goddess of Athens. Otherwise, not-

1.2. WHAT IS THE PLAY ABOUT? – THRASONIDES 11

Cyprus is almost all we can say, as Demeas has come from there.[15] Perhaps something can be made of the fact that Getas, in charge of the spoils, has arrived some time after Thrasonides: clearly the distance between theatre of war and scene of theatre was not that short, but this is scarcely hard evidence. Menander's plays *not* set in Athens are usually quite well marked: *Perikeiromene* in Corinth, *Leukadia* at the famous cliff, for example. The story of the play one might call universally human; certainly not typical of, or confined to, any particular locality. Unlike a modern thriller, where the setting – whether Hong Kong, for example, or Dubai, or Moscow – is essential for mood- and society-setting, Menander's plays rarely rely on local colour for their effects. That is certainly true of this play, and there is no reason on extant evidence *not* to imagine the action in Athens.[16] I would imagine the neutral setting to be deliberate. Menander wanted his play to be produced around the Greek world, not just in Athens.

1.2 What is the play about? – Thrasonides

It will be clear from the above that we only know partially what this play is about. From the extant portions it is clear that this is one of Menander's love dramas in which a couple is split by real or perceived events which make their love untenable. In *Epitrepontes*, for example, it is the (wrongly) perceived sexual relations, with ensuing pregnancy, of Pamphile which alienates the husband (in fact the man responsible for the pregnancy). In *Perikeiromene* it is the perceived infidelity of Glykera which enrages Polemon to the point of cutting off all his girlfriend's hair. In the present play Krateia turns against Thrasonides, that much is clear, and above the pros and cons of the predominant explanation – Thrasonides has killed her brother – are weighed up.

Krateia's disaffection for Thrasonides puts her in the driving seat, as it were, and him in the position of abject supplicant. One of the lively scenes is that in act four in which Getas relates the dialogue inside between Demeas, the father, and Thrasonides, the rejected lover. Time and time again Thrasonides begs for Krateia's hand from Demeas, but the father can only reply with 'free my daughter!' Demeas is, in Getas' words, like the proverbial donkey who does not respond to music.

---

[15] The formula of the marriage ceremony at the end of the play can hardly be used as evidence of Attic custom, as it is found at the end of the Corinthian play *Perikeiromene*, too.

[16] Although Susan Lape (2003, 191) points out, correctly it would seem, that: 'If the play was set in Athens, or if Thrasonides was an Athenian by birth, as seems likely, the buying and selling of Krateia would have been prohibited by law. On Lycurgus's initiative, sometime between 338 and 324, the Athenians passed a law forbidding any citizen or inhabitant of Athens to buy a free person captured in war ([Plut.] *Vit. X Orat.* 842a)'. However (192) she concludes that Menander deliberately suppresses the law to make the play less concerned with legal than ethical issues. She seems, therefore, to prefer the hypothesis that the scene is Athens.

In the relations between Krateia and Thrasonides the conventional tables are turned. In Greek society generally women were powerless politically and legally against their *kyrioi*, masters. Menander loves to create a situation where these relations are reversed. So, here, the brave soldier Thrasonides, whose prowess on the battle-field is undeniable, is defeated by the stubborn antipathy of his young lover. The latter is not even his social equal: far from being a young citizen girl, she is in reduced circumstances: a prisoner of war, bought on the slave market by Thrasonides as his property. True, he goes down on bended knee to her, promising her her freedom, worldly goods, the treatment due a wife (37-39); nevertheless the irony of their mis-matched situations underpins the comedy. The slave girl is mistress over her male master, who is reduced to effeminate tears by her cold heart. This seems to be a typical feature of Menander's 'soldier plays' (*Mis., Perik.*): a man's superiority on the battle-field is no use to him in matters of the heart, if his lady-love turns against him.[17] The motif is brought out touchingly in Thrasonides' great 'suicide speech' in act four. Here he explicitly contrasts his valour in battle with his impotence now in his emotional life. It is one of the great speeches of introspection in Greek literature.[18] He asks himself:

> 'What life is left to you now? Where is that emblem of valour? If only one could charge full tilt at the emotions – is that asking too much? – If one only could? With your eye on rape and pillage you may be brave then (sc. in battle); well, become brave now by hard thinking.' (807-11)

The remark 'If only one could charge full tilt at the emotions' is not easy to interpret. Does he mean: if only he could use his military valour against Krateia's recalcitrant mood now? Or rather: if only he could draw on his bravery now in order to finish off his pathetic life by suicide? Perhaps the latter, as he goes on to say that he should now leave as his legacy to Krateia the shame of having shunned the lover who had treated her so well (812-14). Here he is clearly thinking of suicide, and what message that will leave for Krateia. If I am right about the positioning of O^9, it looks probable that Krateia (and Demeas?) witness this great speech of Thrasonides, unknown to him. That would also make sense, as otherwise Krateia would be unaware of her lover's despair.

So this play is definitely about what we call nowadays relationships. At the end we know things turned out all right: regardless of whether the elusive brother of Krateia turns up or not, we have enough of the final scene to see Thrasonides receive the

---

[17] The term *miles amatorius* was coined for such figures by Hoffmann & Wartenberg (1973, 34). Cf. Bonollo (2019, 89-92).

[18] Bonollo (2019, 90) talks of 'una profondità introspettiva che non troviamo in nessun altro soldato menandreo'.

1.2. WHAT IS THE PLAY ABOUT? – THRASONIDES

joyful news from Getas that Krateia – and Demeas – have changed their minds and she is now prepared to have him as husband. The fact that the couple can now marry proves that not only has Krateia recognized her father (and he her) but that her status has changed from servant to citizen daughter eligible to marry. This more or less proves that Demeas and Thrasonides call the same city *patris*, whether this is Athens (probably) or elsewhere.

The important journey, however, as in all plays by Menander, is the emotional one, or perhaps one should say, psychological. Despite the fragmentary state of preservation of the play, we can see Thrasonides' inner journey from being offended by Krateia's refusal to sleep with him to abject despair and determination to kill himself and finally joy when he hears that she will have him. I think this is *katharsis* in a way not intended by Aristotle.[19] For this is a comedy. Menander takes his characters to the brink, and then, just when things seem insoluble, pulls a narrative rabbit from the hat which changes everything for the better. Thrasonides in this case has experienced emotional defeat in a way never experienced on the battlefield:

> A cheap little slave girl has enslaved me – which none of my enemies ever managed (book fr. 1 παιδισκάριόν με καταδεδούλωκ' εὐτελές, / ὃν οὐδὲ εἷς τῶν πολεμίων οὐπώποτε).

The audience will have known all along that Thrasonides did *not* kill Krateia's brother (let us hope he existed). His despair will have looked to them, to a degree, funny. Getas certainly makes fun of his master's predicament, at least in the first act, although by the time we have reached act four, Getas seems to have become dismayed by the stubbornness of Krateia and Demeas, and sympathetic to his master's cause.

All along the journey, as far as we can trace it, it is Thrasonides' psychology which interests Menander. In the opening speech we see him pacing about in the street, at night, in a rainstorm, outside his own house. The important point here is that he *could* go inside and join Krateia, but he does not wish to, because he knows he is not welcome. A brute of a man would never find himself in this humiliating position.[20] He would simply take what he wanted from the girl who was his property, and sleep quietly. Not so Thrasonides. He is deeply unhappy that the girl whom he wanted to convert from captive of war to mistress of the house does not return his affection. Some lines later he tells Getas that he would be the happiest man if she would only call him 'darling' (88-89), whilst if she spurns him he will experience φιλονικίαν πόνο[ν] μανί[αν, jealousy, pain, madness, an asyndetic chain of emotional stress of great intensity (87).

---

[19] Zagagi (1994, 33) calls it the 'redeeming process undergone in Menander's comedies by professional characters such as the soldier and the hetaira'. [20] See above on Chrysippos' comment, p. 6.

14   *CHAPTER 1. INTRODUCTION*

Later in the play, when he hears from Getas that the girl's father has turned up, he dashes across from the inn to his own house, where Krateia and her father are, and comments that his life is now on the line. Either the father will make him the happiest man on earth by accepting him as groom, or the most unhappy by rejecting him. He says he can no longer live in uncertainty but must know the truth. As he goes into the house he says that his 'soul intimates something bad' (668 μαντεύεθ' ἡ ψυχή τί μου, Γέτα, κακόν). This is Thrasonides' inner voice speaking prophetically to him as it were from the *adyton* of an oracle. Nor is he wrong. The conversation which ensues between Thrasonides, Demeas and Krateia inside is reported by Getas in a highly lively manner, with imitation of voices, lively proverbs and (no doubt) vivid gesturing by the actor playing Getas. Getas reports in monologue form Thrasonides' agony when Demeas is deaf to his pleas. Later Thrasonides himself appears and begins his 'confession speech' after he has been refused by prospective bride and father of the bride. He sees how others might see him: 'Someone may perhaps have called me petty-minded, seeing me make such a fuss about everything' (757-8). A new papyrus (O^{12}) allows us to follow his thoughts further. 'Let me remain strong, make a stone of my heart, keep my malady invisible to people round me. But how will I keep my [unhappiness] in and bear it more lightly? Drunkenness will one day strip off the bandage despite my best intentions' (761-66). It is a brilliant metaphor: drink will one day, like a clinician's hand, peal off the bandage and expose the wound underneath. Thrasonides realizes that it will not be possible to disguise his wounded heart. However much he may try to bear his misery stoically, all attempts will be futile.

We cannot follow the whole of his speech but lines **798-814** have been nearly completely restored by the combined efforts of scholars. Here we read how Thrasonides imagines Krateia's nurse reprimanding him for being too egoistic in his relationship with Krateia. 'She has suffered all manner of things', Simiche says. 'You only think of her from your point of view'. 'This is your own fault!' Thrasonides realizes that the past has, in some way, destroyed the present. He wonders whether he should let her go, then dismisses this thought as Krateia will only pour scorn on his pitiful state without her. Then he recollects his valour on the battle field and wishes it were of use to him on the battle-field of the emotions. He views his life from above, as it were, contemplating his misery and decides that suicide is the logical course.[21] He will leave this last rebuke to Krateia: that she spurned the lover who treated her well.

The play has a happy end, of course, as it must. But Menander has led his main character an agonizing dance. Like the surgeon who lifts the dressing to reveal the wound underneath, Menander has shown the inner emotional life of Thrasonides in

---

[21] Or, if the supplements of **814-16** hit the mark, feigned suicide.

1.3. OTHER CHARACTERS

relentless manner. Like Krateia, who stonewalls against his pleas, the play itself shows Thrasonides no pity. He is taken to the brink and saved only by the genre's convention of a happy end. One does not feel that he has truly been saved from himself. It is the pitiless exposure of his misery that one remembers.

One might speculate that this is Menander railing against the realities of mercenary warfare in his time. Rather than fighting only to defend and secure their *polis* now soldiers go gallivanting off to some corner of the Macedonian empire to fight for a foreign sovereign for the sole purpose of enriching themselves.[22] Thrasonides has been successful in this: he has secured much booty and bought himself a pretty captive girl whom he hopes to keep as partner. This plan fails dismally, however. The girl takes against him, probably precisely because of his military arrogance, and all his valour and success on the battlefield fail him in love. The plot *might*, then, support what one might call an 'anti-imperial agenda'. This is no way of living: to fight as a mercenary for *lucrum*. It might, *e contrario*, be supporting the good old family values of democratic Athens as an independent *polis*, as Lape (2003) would argue. Without mentioning Macedon, without hinting there is any political agenda, we are at least free to speculate that there *is* a political dimension to Thrasonides' near-tragedy.[23]

1.3 Other Characters

1.3.1 Krateia

Krateia is a young girl, presumably, who has entered Thrasonides' household, as we have seen, as a bought prisoner of war (636 αἰχμάλωτος).[24] It would appear that Krateia had lived with her father, and perhaps brother (and mother?) on Cyprus before the family fell victim to the turbulences of war. We do not hear much from Krateia in the play apart from a few lines in the recognition scene, when she recognizes her father. About her most expressive line, and it is incomplete, is line **609** when Krateia enters, saying 'I couldn't bear it ...', although what it is she could not bear has to be supplemented. Perhaps Thrasonides' martial blustering. Her other remarks in this scene are quite conventional, except perhaps **657-8** in which she says she must

---

[22] For an example of such enrichment see Plut. *Life of Demetrios* 7.4: Demetrios orders his troops to take from Babylon all they could carry. On the subject in New Comedy see Alan Sommerstein in Meineck & Konstan (2014, 234).

[23] But one could object that Athens was an imperial city herself in the fifth-century and hardly treated subject states – such as Melos – democratically.

[24] Zagagi (1994, 40) points out, correctly, that 'As to the actions of the girl herself – to judge by the few relevant fragments in our text – it again appears to have been Menander's intention to upset the stereotype. The complete freedom which the playwright allows her towards her captor – before and after he sets her free – is in total contrast to what we know of the attitude to prisoners-of-war in ancient times'. Bonollo (2019, 92-94) fruitfully compares Krateia to Tekmessa in Soph. *Aias*.

consider how best to live now that it has emerged that her master Thrasonides has turned out to be the killer of her brother (?). In the 'suitor' scene reported by Getas in act four, in which Thrasonides begs for Krateia's hand, we do not hear anything directly from Krateia, only from Demeas who has now reverted to being her *kurios*. At one point Krateia 'looks askance' when Thrasonides pleads with her (706). So Menander has employed much the same tactic with Krateia as he does with Glykera in *Perikeiromene*. He keeps her largely in reserve and builds the picture of irresistible attractiveness through her lover's devotion and submissiveness to her. She says just enough to keep the action going, remarks which are largely τὸ εὐπρεπές, 'what is seemly', in a particular scene. She does not take any active part in any extant scene except for the recognition. If there was a scene in which Thrasonides boasted to her of his valour and prowess, or even sought to intimidate her, then no doubt we would have seen her expressing some revulsion, or at least boredom. She may have worn the mask of the *pseudokorē* or perhaps *pallakē*. Her dress can be seen in the Mytilene mosaic (below), illustrating a scene in the fifth act, in which Krateia no doubt had a speaking part. Her name, being so closely connected with κράτος, strength, indicates her strength of character and bearing in denying Thrasonides. Incidentally, there is a woman named Krateia on a vase depicting Kabiros in the Mysteries of the Theban Kabiroi: see Albert Schachter in Cosmopoulos (2003, 131 and fig. 5.9).

1.3.2 Demeas

Demeas is Krateia's father, so fairly advanced in years, called an old man of sixty years, with white hair, when Getas first encounters him (620-21 γέρων οὗτός γε πολιὸς φαίνε[ται,/ ἐτῶν τις ἑξήκονθ'). We first see him in act two engaged in long conversation with Syra, Kleinias' maid. Unfortunately the section is badly damaged and we only get glimpses of what seems to be a para-tragic conversation in which Demeas tells the old woman something of his troubles. It does emerge that he has travelled from Cyprus (432 supplemented) bearing a letter (γράμματα 417, 425) which may have come from Kleinias, his host at the locality of the play. To Syra's question whether he has come intending to ransom certain 'bodies', he replies with an emphatic 'no' (433). This is the first occasion on which he hears that a Krateia is living next door to his host, Kleinias (442). Like his namesake in *Sam.* he is not afraid to show his emotions in the recognition scene and when discussing the fate of another family member (Krateia's brother?) in act three. In act four we only see him indirectly through Getas' report. In it he staunchly defends his daughter's virtue against the man he thinks has killed her brother. He is clearly a vigorous sixty-year old, one not inclined to cede to Thrasonides' pleas. He may have had the mask of *hegemōn presbutēs*, but it is impossible to be certain. He may be the central figure in the Mytilene mosaic.

1.3. OTHER CHARACTERS

1.3.3 Kleinias

Kleinias is probably a young man like his namesakes in *Theoph.*, Terence's *Andria* and *Heautontim.* (cf. Lukian *Dial. Mer.* 10). He is giving a party at the end of act three and looking for a girl who is important to him (671-76). He is the host of *xenos* Demeas and in act four he is more interested in the whereabouts of his guest Demeas than in what Getas is telling him about Thrasonides' entreaties to Demeas to marry Krateia.

Above I argued against the position that Kleinias may be Krateia's brother. All signs point to the fact that Demeas' family was scattered by recent war in Cyprus. Kleinias repeatedly refers to Demeas as his 'guest' (ξένος) whom he wants to entertain to dinner. It is clear that he does not entertain any hopes that his guest will turn out to be his father. He has written a letter to Demeas inviting him to come (417, 425). I have supplemented in 434 κακότητος, (Demeas') misfortune, as the reason Demeas is sought, but there can be no relying on that.

Another idea about Kleinias, that he may be Thrasonides' rival in love, can be dismissed, in my opinion. He talks about searching all round town to find the girl he wishes to invite to dinner (671-2 καὶ τρίτη ἐμή τις, 'and thirdly my girl'). That description hardly suits Krateia who lives next door, and *is* next door. Moreover, when Getas thinks he has found Thrasonides' rival embracing Krateia – in fact it is her father Demeas – it shows that Getas has no idea who this rival is or what he looks like. He is simply τὸν ζητούμενον. This does not square with the character of Kleinias, whom Getas must know, being a neighbour.

Finally, Turner's idea (1965, 14-15) that Kleinias might be a half-brother of Krateia, 'the offspring of an irregular union between Demeas and some girl with whom he left his sword as a token and a gift to his son' (G-S 441). Apart from being too constructed, we can dismiss this half-brother because he is not the person whom Krateia laments in 648-9. Even if the half-brother is identified in the course of the play, that is not going to exculpate Thrasonides from having killed the person Krateia is lamenting in these lines.

So, *ars nesciendi* again: we do not know the whole truth about Kleinias' role in the play yet.

1.3.4 Getas

In fact Thrasonides' manservant Getas is one of the more colourful characters in the play. His language is vivid and expressive, anything but subservient. In the opening scene he joins his master reluctantly in the rain before their house in the middle of the night, comparing himself pejoratively to a dog: even a dog is not made to go outside in such weather (15-16). He keeps pace with his master who is striding up and down the street, soliloquizing with Night: 'he'll be the death of me', Getas pants. 'Isn't he oaken?' (sc. in his resilience to the elements). He is capable of teasing his master about his love pangs (90-100), commenting that his master is not *that* bad looking; true, his soldier's pay is on the meagre side ... actually his looks are very suave, he may be getting on in years a bit ... and so on. At this stage Getas is not taking his master's woes very seriously. It seems, however, that Getas is responsible for moving the master's swords next door to prevent him taking that route to suicide, a charitable gesture, surely. Later, in one of the key scenes on which Menander has expended much ingenuity, Getas reports on the conversation in Thrasonides' house between Demeas with Krateia and Thrasonides (act four). Getas' emotional reports on the exchanges within are interspersed with Kleinias' efforts to find his lost guest, Demeas. Kleinias does not seem interested in Getas' remarks, only on the whereabouts of Demeas. The scene is a masterpiece of comic technique. Getas' excitement and dismay is set off against the foil of Kleinias' indifference. By this time Getas seems firmly on the side of his master. He not only reports on the stubbornness of Demeas, he imitates his master's voice and peppers his remarks with proverbs. The actor playing Getas needed to master Menander's *tour de force* here.

Getas reports on another important scene indoors, too: the one in the inn when a fat musician seems to strike up a song (557-75: see above). He describes how someone may have wanted to make an attempt on his master's life. Unfortunately we need more text to understand what is going on here. Getas is hardly less than omnipresent in the play, rather like Onesimos in *Epitr.* or Daos in *Asp.* Even in the last scene when Thrasonides gets his bride, it is Getas who relays the good news to his master that 'they' (Demeas and his son?) have decided to give him Krateia's hand. Getas is the figure on the left in the Mytilene mosaic. Since as a group these mosaic scenes illustrate the titles of the plays, the scene here in act five obviously featured Getas, too.

1.3.5 Chrysis

Perhaps for reasons of economy, editors have come round to the view that the person called Chrysis in the third act, who is there depicted as engaged in conversation first with Getas, then with Syra, and Krateia's old nurse must be one and the same figure. It has been assumed that Chrysis is Krateia's *trophos*, resident with her in Thrasonides' house. However, recently Bonollo (2019) has argued convincingly that Chrysis elsewhere in Menander, comedy and comedy-like works such as Lukian's *Dialogues of Courtesans*, is uniformly an hetaira.[25] The most obvious case in Menander is Chrysis, Demeas' *pallakē* in *Sam.* Now, if the Chrysis in *Mis.* remains true to this comic tradition, she cannot be Krateia's elderly nurse. Bonollo suggests, in fact, that this role is probably to be assimilated with the Simiche mentioned by Thrasonides in

---

[25] Remarked upon by Blanchard (2016, 248 n. 4).

1.4. PICTORIAL EVIDENCE

act four. As a name, Simiche is also Knemon's old housemaid in *Dys.*[26] This would mean that we have two female characters where we thought we had only one: now there is an hetaira called Chrysis who plays an active role in act three, and an old nurse of Krateia who plays a non-speaking part, also in act three, when she accompanies Krateia to recognition of her father. Immediately the question arises what role an hetaira named Chrysis had in the play: was she perhaps the woman sought by Kleinias at the end of act three? Was she the focus of attention in a secondary 'love-interest' in the play, as Habrotonon is in *Epitr.*, and the 'daughter of Philinos' mentioned by Pataikos in line 1028 of *Perik.*?

1.4 Pictorial evidence

One of the Mytilene mosaics depicts act five of *Misoumenos*: ΜΕΙΣΟΥΜΕΝΟΥ ΜΕ Ε (= Μισουμένου μέρος ε'), it says at the top (see p. 20). The characters visible are discussed by Arnott (252-53),[27] who thinks they are most likely to be, from left to right, Getas, Demeas (or perhaps Krateia's brother) and Krateia. The character on the left has a scarf round his neck and he holds the ends in either hand, as if he were throttling himself. This *might* be interpreted as mimicry of Thrasonides' attempt at suicide (he could not find a sword to do that). The middle character might be Krateia's brother, showing that he was alive and well, so that Thrasonides was exculpated. Charitonidis *et al.* (1970, 107) think he might be an old man, or a soldier; Stephanou (2006, 320-26), on the other hand, thinks he may rather be a 'young man' ('Jüngling'). He would need to be a young man to qualify as Krateia's brother, who may well have been a soldier, or at least a fighting man, if Thrasonides was thought to have killed him fighting in Cyprus. Nothing surviving of our manuscripts contains a scene with this constellation of characters, so the mosaic clearly illustrates a missing scene, no doubt somewhere after 824, where there is a large gap; cf. Charitonidis *et al.* (1970, 57ff. and plate 8).[28]

Henry *et al.* (2014a, 108) have pointed out that Krateia in the mosaic is wearing what might be described as a 'grey' (blue-grey) chiton with black edges. In lines 542-44 there is talk of a 'grey *ephestridion*' (542-3 φαιὸν δ' ἔχει ἐφεστρίδιον) and in the next line there is talk of 'fringes', or 'edges' (544 τὰ κράσπεδ'); here any mention of black is missing. Could it be that the 'grey *ephestridion*' (a type of cloak worn by men and women) has come into the possession of Krateia by act five, and she is now wearing it?

---

[26] It is quite like Sophrone, Pamphile's nurse in *Epitr.*

[27] And see Webster (1973).

[28] For a cake-mould from Ostia (3rd. c. AD) which may depict the same scene see Webster (1969, 222 IT 80).

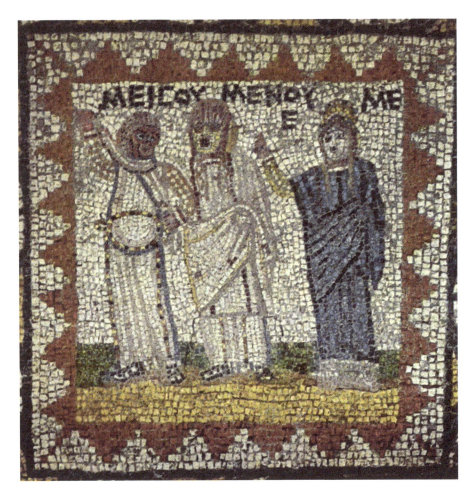

Figure 1.2: The Mytilene mosaic, from Act Five of *Misoumenos*

1.5 Legal Framework

As with so many of Menander's plays, there is a strict legal framework to the action which playwright and audience obviously knew about from living in the society.[29] Krateia is a prisoner of war (αἰχμάλωτος) purchased, apparently, for not much money (fr. 1 παιδισκάριον εὐτελές), by Thrasonides after the Cyprus campaign in which he was serving under 'one of the kings' (fr. 2).[30] This means that she was strictly his property, to be disposed of as he wished. In fact he brought her home and

---

[29] Cf. Turner (1979).
[30] It seems that Simiche came with Krateia as her old nurse. See above p. 11 for the law which forbade Athenians to buy free citizens captured in war as slaves.

1.5. LEGAL FRAMEWORK 21

set her up as 'mistress of the house', with all possible personal freedoms (37-40). He did not use her as a sex toy, as he refrained even from going to her when she made her dislike of him apparent. He wanted to be treated as a legitimate lover, and, it seems, he wanted to treat her as his 'official' concubine.[31] He is certainly depicted as having had sex with her at some stage, as he says that he acquired her as a virgin and was the first to be called 'her man' (707-8).[32] This ruled out any further marriage prospects for Krateia if she ever acquired her freedom, except to Thrasonides himself. Perhaps it was this which contributed to her hatred: she knew it was either this soldier as husband (potentially) or spinsterhood. Then Demeas sails into port, without the intention of ransoming anyone (432-3), and discovers that a Krateia is living next door to his host Kleinias. He also recognizes a sword belonging to the next door household as familiar. Having met up with Krateia and 'caught up' to a degree, the scene in act four recounted by Getas shows Demeas with his mind set on ransoming Krateia from Thrasonides, whilst the latter pleads for Krateia's hand.[33] Demeas has resumed his role as Krateia's *kyrios* (695), and now it is incumbent upon Thrasonides to secure Demeas' 'yes' to their marriage. For Krateia to marry Thrasonides in an official sense, as they do at the end of the play, both he and she must be free citizens, presumably of Athens. So, although Thrasonides acquired her as a prisoner of war in Cyprus, she must have been an Athenian girl all along. The official marriage agreement between Demeas and Thrasonides comes into force in 974-76. In this way the play has a trajectory from war and the spoils of war toward civic society with its conventions and arrangements. This might be viewed as a political statement (Lape, 2003), or as a kind of fairy-tale.

In *Perik.* Glykera simply ups and leaves Polemon when she is fed up with him; she is her 'own mistress' (497). This is not true of Krateia, who is Thrasonides' slave-girl, at least at present. A suppliant branch is mentioned at several points in the play, and we may guess that Krateia wants to lay a suppliant branch on an altar to obtain asylum from Thrasonides; however, the details elude us. When Demeas appears and father and daughter recognize each other, it becomes clear that Krateia is, in fact, the daughter of a free (?)Athenian. If the law of Lycurgus still applied that Athenians were not allowed to buy prisoners-of-war who were free citizens (above p. 11), then Thrasonides' ownership of Krateia would automatically be annulled. However, that does not not seem to be the case in act four, when Demeas repeatedly asks Thrasonides to ransom Krateia. On the other hand, in this scene Thrasonides treats him

---

[31] See Fantham (1975).

[32] Traill (2008, 32) sees this differently.

[33] For Krateia's status in the play see Traill (2008, 25-33). On p. 30 she writes: 'The two men see the situation so differently they can scarcely communicate with one another. Thrasonides wants to convert his informal "marriage" into a legitimate one; Demeas wants to rescue his daughter from enslavement as a soldier's concubine'.

22   CHAPTER 1. INTRODUCTION

as Krateia's *kyrios*, or guardian. He recognizes that he has legal charge of her and is his gateway to marrying her. Part of the fun for an Athenian audience in this scene may have been the legal *impasse* into which developments had led the trio. Demeas was her *kyrios* but Thrasonides her owner. It was a situation in which two things had to happen simultaneously – Thrasonides to release her, and Demeas to give her in marriage – as in spy films where an exchange of prisoners (for example over the Glienicke-Brücke in Berlin) must be exactly simultaneous. This simultaneity is precisely conveyed in Getas' words in lines **698-700**.

1.6   Staging

By the time Menander came to producing his plays the Theatre of Dionysos in Athens had undergone its Lycurgan renovation involving raising the stage (*logeion/proscenium*) to produce a raised platform for the actors approximately 2-3.2m. deep, 20m. wide and perhaps 2.5m. above orchestra level.[34] The wide stage allowed for three openings in the *skēnē*, which could represent three entrances, for example, two houses and a shrine in the middle (*Dys.*), temple (*Leuk.*), or two houses and a central inn, as we have in *Mis.*[35] Likewise the width of the *logeion* will have made 'walking scenes' such as we find at the beginning of *Mis.*, and in act four where Getas paces up and down, believable. When Demeas and Syra 'set off' from Kleinias' to Thrasonides' house in act three, at least there were a few metres to cover in which conversation could take place. Hughes (p. 222) comments that the wide stage will have appeared 'overwhelmed by vacancy' in New Comedy, but this is to ignore non-speaking characters such as Getas' helpers in the 'smuggling' scene, or the maid Simiche at various points. Since the stage represented an outdoor, not indoor, space, I think it will quite plausibly have created the impression of a street.

The first scene, fictionally by night, is clearly played in front of Thrasonides' front door, with the soldier pacing up and down, making gestures of despair, followed up and down later by Getas.[36] The speaker of the delayed prologue, whoever he or she was, may have appeared at stage level (Mastronarde, 1990, 288 n. 18), or perhaps on the roof of a house. If it was Polemos, as Turner guessed, he might have stood on Thrasonides' roof and praised the soldier at the end of his speech (see text and commentary). The third scene again seems to have been played by Thrasonides and Getas, followed by the first dance of the rowdy chorus.

In act two the action moved (after a sizable gap in our sources) to Kleinias' house, at which Demeas arrives from the side entrance leading to the harbour (probably the

---

[34] Hughes (2012, 222), Philippides (2019, 302).   [35] So already Webster (1973, 293); and *Theoph.*, *Encheir.* and *Perik.*, see Philippides (2019, 303 n. 7).   [36] Thrasonides was probably standing outside already when the play began (Frost, 1988, 81).

1.6. STAGING

Piraeus), and talks to Syra. That is all we know of this act.

In act three there is some business involving a suppliant branch which (probably) Krateia wants to lay on an altar, then the main action we can guess at in which Getas moves Thrasonides' war spoils to the neighbours' house (Kleinias), watched from the side by Syra and Chrysis, who remain hidden to Getas. Getas then enters from Kleinias' house and describes the strange (to us) goings on in the central inn, to which he returns to follow developments. Syra enters from Kleinias' house and she and Demeas make their way across to Thrasonides' house. Then, after Syra has departed – great excitement! – Krateia comes out of her door and is recognized and reunited with her father. Her nurse – Simiche in my reconstruction – accompanies her out of the house, but as a mute figure who can only nod or gesticulate. At some stage Getas appears (from the inn or from Thrasonides' house?) and challenges Demeas, who he suspects of being a rival suitor of Krateia. Having learned the truth he goes off to fetch Thrasonides (from the inn). At the end of the act Thrasonides is returning home with trepidation to see how Demeas will receive his proposal of marriage to Krateia, and Kleinias makes a short appearance to announce that the welcome dinner for Demeas is still short of a guest.

In act four Kleinias appears complaining that now Demeas has walked off before the dinner party; he goes across to Thrasonides' house to try and track him down, encounters Getas there, who relates in a frantic monologue with much quoted speech what has eventuated between Thrasonides and Demeas (impasse). To Getas' excited 'messenger speech' there is added a ludicrous aspect in Kleinias' attempts to attract his attention. The scene will have been one of the liveliest in the play. After some action we can barely follow in view of the lacunose state of the text, Thrasonides appears and begins his long rumination on his bad luck in love and determination either to do away with himself, or to pretend to. If O^9 belongs at lines 751-58, Krateia and her father eavesdropped on this suicidal monologue. This will have added an additional dimension to Thrasonides' prolonged monologue. Thrasonides' declaration of emotional bankruptcy is balanced and anticipated by Getas' furious account of the stone-walling by Demeas and Krateia. Getas anticipates precisely this despair in his master (722-24). Thus act four is the emotional climax of (what survives of) the play, featuring two powerful and extended monologues.

In act five a lot of text is unfortunately lost after line 829, in which at least two things must have played out. There must have been the scene illustrated by the Mytilene mosaic involving Getas, Krateia and ?, and, presumably, the appearance of Krateia's brother (again from the Piraeus) showing that he was not dead! The final scene shows everyone reconciled and the marriage ceremony between Krateia and Thrasonides well on its way.

As in Menander generally there is not much racy action, although the 'smuggling' scene in act three may have been quite dramatic. The subplot involving some

24 CHAPTER 1. INTRODUCTION

plot against Thrasonides may have taken place solely through reported speech, as Getas describes what was going on in the inn in act three. The suspense, pleasure and humour of the play derive more or less exclusively from the dialogues and monologues. There were at least two high points involving the latter: Getas' description of the altercation between Thrasonides and Demeas (and Krateia), and Thrasonides' monologue. Both of these are linguistically dense, syntactically abrupt and rapid, and contain much variation through quotation, figures of speech, and rapid changes in direction. They will have required supremely skilled actors to deliver them convincingly.

There are no stage directions in the extant manuscript fragments, unlike the αὐλεῖ, 'flute music', between lines 879-80 of *Dys.* But Menander's text usually makes it amply clear what is happening, broadly, on stage. Entrances and exits are marked by forms of the verbs ἐξ- or εἰσέρχομαι, 'I'm going out/in', or by comments on doornoise. Walking-up-and-down scenes, as at the beginning of the play and when Getas goes on a 'walkabout' outside Thrasonides' house, are marked in the text either by forms of περιπατῶ, 'I walk about', or by comments by others on the difficulties of keeping up. When Demeas embraces Krateia in act three, after recognizing his lost daughter, the text says ἔχω σε, 'I embrace you'. In the knocking-at-the-door scene played by Demeas and Syra in act three, markers in the text (however lacunose this is) make plain what is happening. In most surviving plays the arrival of the chorus for the first *entr'acte* is announced by a speaker at the end of act one. Thus the text comments on its own staging. One hardly has to read between the lines. This may have made it easier for Menander's plays to circulate in Greece. One really only needed the text to put on a new production, wherever that might be.[37]

1.7 Dating

The play's popularity in antiquity is attested by the fragments of a large number of manuscripts found in the Roman province of Egypt alone. It is unlikely for that reason to have been a very early play but rather one stemming from his mature period. Arnott (1996b) collects the references to warfare in Cyprus to conclude: 'These references may imply that Thrasonides was presented as a mercenary who had fought in support of one of the ten Cypriot kings when Ptolemy I was campaigning between 321 and 309 BC to bring the island under his control, and it seems likely that the play was written at some time during or shortly after that period'. Blanchard, on the other hand, suggests two possible interpretations of fr. 2 in which it is said that Thrasonides fought with distinction under 'one of the kings' in Cyprus. If these were

---

[37] It has been calculated that there were not enough performances of the Lenaia or Dionysia during Menander's lifetime to accommodate all (?)hundred-and-five plays he wrote. So some must have been *intended* for production abroad or in the Attic demes (Scafuro, 2014, 219-20).

1.7. DATING

the Cypriot kings whom Ptolemy subjugated by 312/311 then, Blanchard says, *Mis.* would have to be dated prior to that, perhaps in 312. Or the kings in question could be the diadochs who ruled Cyprus after that, perhaps Demetrios Poliorketes who siezed Cyprus from Ptolemy in 306, and had acquired the honorific title of 'King' (βασιλεύς) by then (Plut. *Life of Demetrios* 10.3). If Thrasonides was imagined fighting under this ruler, then *Mis.* would have to be dated after that date. I would tend to favour Blanchard's position. Another slight handhold might be the second production of Alexis' comedy *Krateia* in 306 BC: conceivably the play's title suggested a suitable name for Menander's heroine (see p. 172).

Plutarch (*Life of Demetrios* 16-17) gives a graphic account of Demetrios' defeat of Ptolemy in the battle for Cyprus at Salamis (306 BC). Much booty (λαφύρων 17.1.5) was taken, and many women (16.4.2), including the famous hetaira Lamia, who promptly captivated Demetrios. If our Thrasonides had fought on Demetrios' side (fictively of course) – after all, Demetrios has sailed to Cyprus from Athens – he would have had ample opportunity to acquire rich pickings (line 35 λαφύρων) and possibly the young woman Krateia, who would have had the status of an αἰχμάλωτος.

Apart from mentions of war in Cyprus, there are no contemporary references, no satirical remarks *ad hominem* such as we still find in *Samia* and which Sommerstein (2014b) uses to date this play relatively early. Likewise there are no visible tetrameters, such as we find in *Perik.*, which may also be a sign that they have, as it were, died out in Menander's art by this time. These last two observations would tend to place *Mis.* certainly in the middle period of Menander's writing, more probably relatively late (around the turn of the fourth/third century?). This, then, would have to be squared with the latter interpretation of fr. 2. Turner goes so far as to advocate a date in the early third century, for reasons of literary development (Turner, 1979, 126). There are passages of *Mis.*, for example, Thrasonides' 'suicide speech', which are so remarkable that Menander seems to have moved far from the norms of New Comedy as such and entered a mode we might call 'psychological drama'. If Plautus' *Curculio* is based on a Greek original, one sees how different Menander's play, with roughly the same historical background, is from that (Elderkin, 1934).

As for production date, Gomme and Sandbach (p. 744) suggested that the wintry storm evoked by Thrasonides in the first scene (13-14 χειμῶνος ὄντος...τρέμοντι) points to production in the winter festival of Lenaia (January), but this is too literal. The spectators had to imagine night (when it was day) – no reason why they shouldn't imagine winter (when it was spring)!

1.8 Metre

The metre of the entire (extant) play is the comic iambic trimeter.[38] There are no tetrameters as in *Dysk.* or *Sam.*, no extraneous metres such as the hexameters in *Theophoroumene*,[39] no indications of musical accompaniment to lines more sung than spoken (as in *Dysk.* after line 879). Since the trimeters of Menander have been excellently treated in other works,[40] I give here only a brief introduction to the subject for those unfamiliar with the comic trimeter.

Two iambs (⏑—) combine to form an iambic measure (metron), which is repeated three times in a trimeter:

$$\times - \cup - \mid \times - \cup - \mid \times - \cup \smallfrown$$

As will be seen, the first position of each metron is anceps (short or long) and the final position is long, even when a prosodic short syllable occupies the position ('brevis in longo').

The comic trimeter differs from the tragic in being freer with 'resolved positions', that is, when a double-short takes the place of a long, anceps or short. All positions in the comic trimeter can be resolved in this fashion except the last two. A fuller symbolic representation is, then:

$$\overset{\times}{\smile} \underset{\smile\smile}{} \overset{\times}{\smile} \underset{\smile\smile}{} \mid \overset{\times}{\smile} \underset{\smile\smile}{} \overset{\times}{\smile} \underset{\smile\smile}{} \mid \overset{\times}{\smile} \underset{\smile\smile}{} \cup \smallfrown$$

Comic trimeters are, however, rarely a riot of double-short positions. Resolution of two consecutive positions is as good as non-existent. And the so-called 'proceleusmaticus', meaning four short syllables comprising one iambic foot (⏑⏑⏑⏑ for ⏑—) does not seem to occur in Menander, although it does occasionally in Aristophanes.[41] In practice we very commonly find one or two double-shorts in a line of Menander, more rarely three and exceptionally four.

This comparative freedom of resolution means that rhythmic patterns quite alien – one would think – from the iambic alternation of short-long are admissible. Spondees (——) are possible when a long anceps stands before an unresolved long. Anapaests (⏑⏑—) are possible when an anceps or a short is replaced by a double-short. One anapaest can follow another, producing what is, strictly speaking, an anapaestic monometre. Even a dactyl (—⏝) is possible when a resolved long follows a long anceps. Resolution after a short leads to the so-called tribrach (three successive short syllables). In this apparent anarchy of rhythm the only secure anchor is the last two positions, which are, unfailingly, iambic.

---

[38] This section is taken, with suitable adaptation, from my edition of *Epitrepontes*.
[39] See Handley (1969).
[40] See esp. Handley (1965, 56-73), Gomme & Sandbach (1973, 36-39); more specialized studies: White (1909); Rubenbauer (1912).   [41] See Handley (1965, 57); Newiger (1961).

1.8. METRE

One would like, indeed, to know how these lines were spoken by the actors. Much as one tries to assimilate the truth that Greek metre was quantitative rather than accentual, one feels that a rhythm with rises and falls (what used to be called *arsis* and *thesis*, German 'Hebung' und 'Senkung') must have asserted itself, however subtly. Certainly the modern reader of Menander will find it easier if he maintains a kind of mental iambic rhythm as handhold through the plethora of double-shorts and other 'anomalies'.

Let us take some examples. Some lines consist of regular iambics. Lines 3 and 6, for example, spoken by Thrasonides, run:

$$——\cup—\,|\,——\cup—\,|\,\cup—\cup\widehat{\cap}$$
3 πλεῖστοι λέγονται φροντίδες τ' ἐρωτ[ι]καί—
6 πρὸς ταῖς ἐμαυτοῦ νῦν θύραις ἔστηκ' ἐγώ

But the first line of the play contains one resolution:

$$——\cup—\,|\,——\cup\underset{\smile}{\cup}\,|\,——\cup—$$
1 ὦ Νύξ—σὺ γὰρ δὴ πλεῖστον Ἀφροδίτης μέρος

and the second two resolutions:

$$\overset{\times}{\smile}—\cup—\,|\,——\cup\underset{\smile}{\cup}\,|\,——\cup—$$
2 μετέχεις θεῶν, ἐν σοί τε περὶ τούτων λόγοι

The pattern becomes more complicated in e.g. **24**, with three resolutions. This leads to an anapaest in the first foot, and a tribrach in the second and fourth feet:

$$\cup—\overset{\times}{\smile}—\,|\,\cup\underset{\smile}{\cup}\cup—\,|\,—\underset{\smile}{\cup}\cup—$$
τί βουλό]μενος; πότερα κελευσθε[ὶ]ς ὑπό τ[ινος

Or again in line **37** (tribrach, anapaest, dactyl):

$$\cup\underset{\smile}{\cup}\cup\underset{\smile}{\cup}\,|\,——\cup—\,|\,—\underset{\smile}{\cup}\cup—$$
ὑπὸ τίνος;] ὑπὸ τῆς αἰχμαλώτου· πριάμενος

In practice, there are, on average, one, or two resolved positions in a comic trimeter. This differs markedly from tragic practice (even later Euripides). In the so-called paratragic passages of Menander we find a much greater affinity with the tragic trimeter (far fewer resolutions). The opening address of Thrasonides in fact tends toward the paratragic mode, as befits his tragic view of himself, whilst the rhythm changes toward the comic as soon as Getas joins him (two resolutions common in each line). What really distinguishes the comic trimeter is its capacity to resolve *any* position in each line, except the last two. This makes it seem far more anarchic than the stately march of tragedy.

The comic trimeter does not fall so conspicuously into two halves, divided by a strong caesura after the fifth or the seventh position, as in the tragic trimeter. Frequently there is, technically, caesura in fifth or seventh position, but sometimes not.[42]

This information is probably sufficient for the reader to 'scan' the lines of *Misoumenos*. The editor is faced with more technical problems, in particular the prosodic treatment of double-short positions resulting from resolution. Menander has a marked tendency not to allow a so-called 'split anapaest', that is, word-break between the two short syllables of an anapaest or between the double-short and the long syllable. One can call this phenomenon a 'bridge': word end is not tolerated after one or both of the shorts in an anapaest. It would appear that the poet and his audience expected an anapaest to be, as it were, a sound-bite, a unit of sound and sense, and a word-break between the elements apparently destroyed this unity. In fact the rule is not absolute. Various small words combine with others to form a sense unit; here word-break is allowed within the anapaest. Nor is the rule absolute; it has been calculated that Menander's verse admits a split anapaest on average every 700 lines.[43]

The most interesting question is whether there was an aesthetic 'value' to such variations of metre. Did a double-short in a certain position add anything to the comic effect of a line, or to the ēthos of a speaker or his/her mood at the moment? Certainly we can recognize the para-tragic tone of certain lines by their adherence to tragic norms in the trimeter, as I just mentioned. If that is the case, the converse might also be true: the further the rhythm departed from the tragic norm, the more comic or potentially comic a line might be. Or it might be that the greater flexibility of the comic trimeter was intended to resemble the language as really spoken by average people, in contrast to the high-faluting tragic style. Handley's conclusion regarding the aesthetic effect of metrical variation is largely negative: we notice the tone of a certain passage by context rather than by its metre, even if, on occasion, the metre seems to match this perceived tone (1965, 59).

Metrical effects are never prolonged or sustained, however, in a speech by Menander. A line which impresses by its metrical licence is often followed by a regular iambic trimeter or an unremarkable sequence of trimeters. Similarly, there do not seem to be inherent distinctions between slaves and the free in the number of resolutions they speak with on average. Individuals are not characterized by a propensity to resolutions; nor are individual scenes distinguished by a greater frequency of certain metrical features. Where we can discern distinctions (in other plays) is in metre itself: the longer tetrameter tends to be used for hectic or climactic scenes. The longer, perhaps faster, lines cannot fail to be noticed by the listener. But in a play without metrical variety such as *Misoumenos* it seems the intention is rather to assimilate the verse of stage

---

[42] See Handley (1965, 57).

[43] For detailed exposition see Handley (1965, 63-66); Arnott (1957). Similar considerations apply to 'divided resolutions', that is, when a resolved long is divided between words.

1.9. TRANSMISSION OF THE TEXT

with spoken Attic idiom. Double-shorts are a sure way of breaking the monotony of regular iambics and of marking the genre's distance from tragedy. Conversely, those who try to supplement gaps in Menander soon realize that his apparently free rhythm is in fact anything but free. It gives the impression of freedom until one tries to imitate it. In short, Menander's rhythms maintain a delicate balance between formality and freedom. Perhaps the greatest attribute is their variety. Speech never becomes monotonously rhythmical; on the contrary there is constant play with the flexibility of the metre. This, combined with Menander's long periods, someties spread over several verses, gives an incredibly lively and speech-like impression. Rather than being a dance with repetitive steps it is more like a modern dance with endless variety and improvisation.

1.9 Transmission of the Text

1.9.1 Antiquity

Granted Menander wrote *Mis.* very approximately around 300 BC, we must imagine his play surviving through the next few centuries by a combination of written texts and public and private performances.[44] The survival of Menander's texts in antiquity is well described by H-D. Blume (1998) and Blanchard (2014). Aristophanes of Byzantium, author of the famous remark about Menander and Life,[45] seems to have been responsible for producing an Alexandrian edition of the plays.[46] *Mis.* was clearly one of the popular plays as witnessed by the scraps of sixteen copies which we have rediscovered from the Roman province of Egypt. A scene from *Mis.* decorates one of the panels of the late 3rd c. Menander mosaics in Mytilene. Clearly the play was well enough known then for the householder and his visitors to make something of the picture. There are at least five ancient quotations from Thrasonides' opening speech alone, proving it was well known. Scholars and sophists were still quoting from *Mis.* in late antiquity but the plays sank from sight in the era of Byzantine scholarship and did not share in the all-important transliteration into minuscule script which took place in this era. There is no medieval manuscript of Menander's works, at least none known to current scholarship, only a collection of Menandrean *apophthegmata*, or proverbs.[47] Menander lived on through the centuries as a bodiless name, as it were. His genre survived through the Latin imitations of Plautus and Terence, who were known and influential in the Renaissance. There is no specific adaptation of *Mis.* in

---

[44] Cf. Plut. *Comparison of Aristophanes and Menander. Mor.* 853-4 with Nervegna (2013, ch. 3).

[45] 'O Menander and Life: which of the two of you imitated the other?' ὦ Μένανδρε καὶ βίε, πότερος ἄρ' ὑμῶν πότερον ἀπεμιμήσατο; Syrianus *Comm. in Hermog.* II 23.   [46] See Pfeiffer (1978, 235ff.)   [47] See Jaekel (1964)) and more recently Pernigotti (2008).

Latin. Drago (1997) has advanced the hypothesis that a fictional letter of Aristainetos (1.17) has the *Mis.* as its intertext, but there are important differences. The lover in this letter complaining about a recalcitrant hetaira called Daphnis is not desperately unhappy like Thrasonides, but instead vows to be persistent and diligent in his erotic campaign. Nevertheless there are some interesting coincidences in language, indicating, I would say, that Aristainetos wrote his playful letter at least with *Mis.* in mind. The letter does not help us one bit in understanding more about the plot of the play.

1.9.2 Modern Age

Before 1965 *Mis.* was, apart from minor fragments, just a name. It was Turner's Herculean efforts deciphering and publishing P.Oxy. 2656 (O^3) which gave the play a backbone and some flesh which allowed other fragments to be inserted like pieces of a puzzle (Turner, 1965). This was followed by *The Oxyrhynchus Papyri* vol. XXXIII, London 1968, in which Turner cemented his edition of P.Oxy. 2656. To this was added P.Oxy. 2657 (O^4), belonging to *Mis.*, and collations of P. Berlin 13281 (B^1) and P. Berlin 13932 (B^2) by Colin Austin. Turner acknowledges the collaboration of Eric Handley and John Rea in the *BICS* supplement, and Colin Austin and R.A. Coles in addition in his edition for *P.Oxy.* The notes on O^3 and O^4 are full of the suggestions and conjectures of these scholars.

Turner was also the moving force behind the edition of the play's beginning (Turner, 1978), which combined at least three papyri (see chapter 'Composite Readings'). Turner conducted a London seminar on this section of text held at the Institute of Classical Studies in London in autumn 1977. Here Turner acknowledges the input from Colin Austin, Walter Cockle, Alan Griffiths, Eric Handley, F.H. Sandbach and M.L. West, a star-studded cast indeed. This publication produced, if not continuous text, then at least substantial portions, of the first hundred lines of the play. This publication was backed up by publication in the Oxyrhynchus series of P.Oxy. 3368-3371 (O^{5-7}). Here other names are acknowledged. In addition to the ones previously named we find W.S. Barrett, Hugh Lloyd-Jones, and Peter Parsons. We can see what skill and expertise were combined in this edition. I had tutorials with the 'two Erics' in the earlier 'seventies at University College London, just before the seminar mentioned. Their rooms were always full of framed papyri, on loan from various museums. I like to think now that some of them were from *Mis.* and that in this very period Turner and Handley were ruminating on the play. It was presumably in good measure Turner's work on this play which earned him the knighthood.[48]

Colin Austin collected all the papyrus texts of comedy in Austin (1973), a chalcenteric feat including everything that was then known of *Mis.*, all in meticulous detail.

---

[48] It is worth reading the beginning of Turner's 1979 paper for his 'personal confession of faith' (p. 106) in Menander and his art.

1.9. TRANSMISSION OF THE TEXT

Figure 1.3: Papyrus Oxyrhynchi 2656 (O³): lines 690-706 of the play. Courtesy of the Egypt Exploration Society.

He was still calling the play *Thrasonides* at that stage, following the colophon in O³ (*Misoumenos* has to be supplemented).

Some important work was done by Margaret Maehler (wife of Herwig) on Thrasonides' soliloquy in act four when P.Oxy. 3967 (O⁸) was published. This could be combined with the readings of O³ to produce quite full sense. This was followed up by a paper produced by Eric Handley in 1996 in which he produced what he called 'stochastic restorations and conjectures' on this section of text. Handley says that 'they are not for publication in this form, whether by me or by anyone else', but in fact they have entered the scholarly tradition, and I discuss (some of) them in this edition.

Sandbach included in his revised OCT of Menander (Oxford 1990) the new discoveries for the beginning of *Mis.* as an appendix to the main text, and used the awk-

32   CHAPTER 1. INTRODUCTION

ward numbering of lines A1-A100. Francesco Sisti's 1985 edition[49] took over this numbering system but incorporated the new discoveries of text at the beginning of the play in the proper order. The edition is quite conservative, but collects knowledge of the play's text to date in an inclusive manner. The commentary is quite brief, but the *apparatus* impresses with its wealth of detail.

Most anglophone people who wanted to read *Mis.* will have turned to Geoffrey Arnott's second volume of the complete Menander, published in the Loeb series in 1996. Arnott supplies a useful introduction, a text restored in good measure with quite full *apparatus* for this series, translation and running commentary on how the action of the play is to be understood.

Since then the most important discovery of text has come from Oxyrhynchus again, in the form of several fragments of text from the middle part of the play, P.Oxy. 5198 and 5199 ($O^{11,12}$), published by W.B. Henry, P.J. Parsons and L. Prauscello. O^{11} joins O^3 and O^{10} and the Berlin parchment fragments to fill out much of what we did not know from 532-55.[50]

Prior to this one the most up-to-date edition has been that by Alain Blanchard in the third volume of the Budé series (Paris 2016).[51] Blanchard collects information about the text impressively, giving the reader a full *apparatus* and, like Arnott, translation (in French of course) and useful notes on what is happening and how difficulties are to be understood. Blanchard (2014, 251) is of the opinion that *Mis.* may have been one of a triad in the editorial process, preceded by *Perikeiromene* and followed, perhaps, by *Thrasyleōn*, whose common theme is 'the suffering man'.

Colin Austin was working on a new OCT when he died. The work is being continued by Peter Parsons and Lucia Prauscello in Oxford. Likewise Rudolf Kassel in Cologne was said to be working on the full Menander text for the series begun by himself and Colin Austin (*Fragmenta Comicorum Graecorum*).[52] These are complete works, no doubt including *Mis.* The more Menander is discovered, the greedier one becomes for further discoveries of text, in the hope of filling in gaps: fragments stimulate curiosity much more than a total blank.

1.10   Technical points about this edition

- My line numbering matches that of Blanchard except between 768-919; O^{12} contains traces of five more lines following 767, which we did not know about

---

[49] Menandro *Misumenos*. Edizione critica, traduzione e commento a cura di Francesco Sisti, Geneva 1985.   [50] Unfortunately not quite enough to make the overall sense clear.   [51] In the bibliography as Blanchard (2016).   [52] Before his sad demise in 2020. Whether this work will be continued by a successor, I do not know.

1.10. TECHNICAL POINTS ABOUT THIS EDITION   33

before. I thought, rather than numbering them 767a,b,c etc., it was better to use continuous numbering.

- Conjectures in the text which are very much open to doubt are printed in grey print (apart from the normal square brackets indicating missing letters or text). I do not retain the grey when printing the lemma in the commentary.

- End- and middle-sigma are used in the main text, lunate sigma in the chapter containing 'composite readings' as here it is more than usually uncertain whether a particular sigma stood at the end of a word or not.

- In the *apparatus criticus* I usually give the lemma or *variae lectiones* without the dots and brackets which belong to an accurate transcription of the word in question. These are, of course, given in the main text, so the reader must refer to this to know what is the state of transmission. I follow this policy in the *apparatus* in the interests of greater clarity and readability. The same applies to the index of Greek words, in which whole words are given, with brackets only included when the reading is largely supplemented. In the commentary, on the other hand, the lemma is taken directly from the main text. Unattributed supplements go back to Eric Turner (1965 and/or 1968).

- The masks beside the text are miniatures from genuine model masks of New Comedy, mainly from Lipari. There is no way of knowing which masks the characters actually wore, so the faces have been chosen for their general suitability (age, sex, social status).[53] They are not only intended to show exits and entrances on stage, but also to remind the reader in a general way of the conventions of New Comedy. I do not include masks to indicate exits at the end of acts, as it was the convention that the stage was cleared at these points in the play. One may take the 'exit masks' here as read.

- I have seen the originals of all papyri except I+K, B^1, B^2, O^1 and P. Strasb. WG 307. In the case of these I have worked from good photographs except for O^1, of which the black-and-white photo which P. Parsons kindly lent me is only of reasonable quality.

- References to fragments of Greek comedy are to Kassel-Austin (K-A) where possible, otherwise to Kock (e.g. Antiphanes) or Koerte-Thierfelder.

---

[53] As Brown (1987, 185) says: 'So the Lipari masks help us to visualise the staging of Menander's comedies in a general way, but perhaps they do not help us so visualise more precisely the staging of a particular comedy.'

- The translation aims to give some idea of the flow of Menander's verse by using free English verse. Although I try to keep all of Menander's words, some compromises have to be made to rhythm and 'sound'.

- In the commentary I retain the division of acts into three scenes which I developed for *Epitrepontes*, but am aware that others see this quite differently.[54]

---

[54] Scafuro (2014, 222-23) says the idea 'makes sense'.

Chapter 2

Greek Text

Manuscripts[1]

- I+K = *PIFAO* inv. 89[v] lines 1-17 + P.Köln 7.282 v.,[2] lines 18-30[3]

- B[1] = P.Berlin 13281, lines 567-578, 611-622

- B[2] = P.Berlin 13932, lines 532-544, 560-572

- O[1] = P.Oxy. 1013, lines 644-665 (frr. 1-5 verso), 677-700 (frr. 1-4 recto)

- O[2] = P.Oxy. 1605, lines 919-932, 948-974

- O[3] = P.Oxy. 2656, lines 501-814 (806 Bl), 959-996

- O[4] = P.Oxy. 2657, lines 401-492 + letters from 17 other lines

- O[5] = P.Oxy. 3368, lines 1-18, 34-45, 51-68, 85-100, fr. C (? end of Act One) (241-247 Bl)

- O[6] = P.Oxy. 3369, lines 12-54, 78-94

- O[7] = P.Oxy. 3370, lines 30-43

- O[7b] = P.Oxy. 3371, with play's title

- O[8] = P.Oxy. 3967, lines 793-829 (784-821 Bl)

---

[1] For simplicity's sake I adopt and extend Blanchard's numeration. This conflicts with Sandbach's in the OCT of course. [2] Photo *ZPE* 6 pl. 1, *ZPE* 8 pl III, P.Köln7, pl. 1a, Turner (1973, pl. 3), *LDAB* 2657 [3] Photograph *ZPE* 8, 1971, Taf. III

- O^9 = P.Oxy. 4025, ?lines 751-757 (= fr. 3 Arnott, fr. 11 Blanchard)
- O^{10} = P.Oxy. 4408, lines 552-559
- O^{11} = P.Oxy. 5198 fr. 1, lines 523-554, fr. 2 (placed conjecturally) lines 509-522
- O^{12} = P.Oxy. 5199, lines 753-772 (753-766 Bl)
- S = P.Strasb. WG 307 verso col. i.30-col. ii.3 = fr. com. adesp. *1036 K-A, ?lines from the end of the prologue

The cast

In order of appearance in the surviving fragments:

 Thrasonides, the mercenary soldier

 Getas, his servant

?? Speaker of the Prologue, a goddess?

 Syra, Kleinias' housemaid

 Demeas, Krateia's father

 Chrysis, ?an *hetaira*

 Krateia, Thrasonides' concubine

 Kleinias, Thrasonides' neighbour, probably a young man

?? Krateia's brother

Non-speaking parts:-

- a cook (μάγειρος)
- Simiche, Krateia's old nurse

Act One 37

The scene

This is, as is conventional in New Comedy, a street, probably in Athens but not conspicuously, with three house façades with their doorways. In the centre an inn, flanked by the houses of Thrasonides and Kleinias respectively.

ΘΡΑΣΩΝΙΔΗΣ ἢ ΜΙΣΟΥΜΕΝΟΣ

Act One

(ΘΡΑΣΩΝΙΔΗΣ)

⌐ὦ Νύξ—σὺ γὰρ δὴ πλεῖστον Ἀφροδίτης ┐ μέρος   ⊤ I+K, O⁵
μετέχεις θεῶν, ἐν σοί τε περὶ τούτων λόγọι
πλεῖστοι λέγονται φροντίδες τ' ἐρωτ[ι]καί—
⌐ἆρ' ἄλλον ἀνθρώπων τιν' ἀθλιώτερον
ἑόρακας; ἆρ' ἐρῶντα δυσποτμώτερον; ┐   5
⌐πρὸς ταῖς ἐμαυτοῦ νῦν θύραις ἕστηκ' ἐγώ, ┐
ἐν τῶι στενωπῶι περιπατῶ τ' ἄνω κάτω
ἀμφοτερ⟨ίσ⟩ας μέχρι νῦν μεσούσης σου σχεδόν,
⌐ἐξὸν καθεύδειν τήν τ' ἐρωμένην ἔχειν. ┐
⌐παρ' ἐμοὶ γάρ ἐστιν ἔνδον ἔξεστίν τέ μοι   10
καὶ βούλομαι τοῦθ' ὡς ἂν ἐμμανέστατα
ἐρῶν τις, οὐ ποῶ δ'· ┐ ὑπαιθρίωι δέ μοι   ⊤ O⁶
χειμ[ῶνος ὄν]τος ἐστὶν αἱρετώτερον
ἑστη[κέναι] τρέμοντι καὶ λαλοῦντί σοι.

ΓΕΤΑΣ

τὸ δ[ὴ λεγόμ]ενον, οὐδὲ κυνί, μὰ τοὺς θε[ούς],   15
νῦν [ἐξι]τητέον ἐστίν· ὁ δ' ἐμὸς δεσπότης
ὥσπερ θέρους μέσου περιπατεῖ φιλοσο[φῶν
τοσαῦτ'· ἀπολεῖ μ'· οὐ δρύϊνος; οὐκ ἐᾶι μ' ὕ[πνον   ⊥ O⁵

---

1 Σ Theocr. 2.20c   4 -5 ἀνθρώπων I+K, O⁵, Plut. *Mor.* 525a: -ον edd. pl.   ἆρ' ἄλλον Handley: τίνα ἄλλον Plut. Σ C², Ἄπολλον Plut. cett. codd.   5 ἔρωτα cj. Diggle   6 Apoll. *de constr.* 2.107 p. 209.5 Uhlig   8 ἀμφοτερίσας Furley, vel ἐπ' ἀμφοτέρας Sandbach 1990: ἀμφοτερας O¹⁹: ἀμφοτεράκις Arnott: ἀφ' ἑσπέρας Austin   9 Σ Eur. *Phoin.* 478, Σ Ar. *Ach.* 1164b, Char. *Kall.* 4.7.7   εξωκαθειδειν et fin. εχει O⁵   10 Plut. *Mor.* 524F-525A = fr. 336   14 suppl. Rea   15 in. suppl. Austin   16 O⁵: ἐξιτητὸν corr. West coll. Alciphr. 2.27.1   17 suppl. Handley   18 τοσαῦτ' Barigazzi: τοσοῦτ' al.   οὐκ ἐᾶι suppl. dub. Sisti   ὕπνον dub. Sisti

38 CHAPTER 2. GREEK TEXT

	λαβεῖν δ]ιατρίβων γ᾽ ἐγκραγ[ὼν] πεσ[ὼν χαμαί.	
Θρ	τίς νῦν ἀνακρο]ύσει τὴν θύραν;	
Γε	⌞ὦ δυστυχής,	20
	τί οὐ καθεύδεις; σύ μ᾽ ἀποκναίεις περιπατῶν·⌟	
	εἰ μὴ καθε]ύδεις· περίμεν᾽ εἴ μ᾽ ἐγρη[γ]ορὼς	
	ὁρᾷς.	
Θρ	Γέτα,] σὺ δ᾽ αὐτὸς ἐξελήλυθας;	
	τί βουλό]μενος; πότερα κελευσθε[ὶ]ς ὑπό τ[ινος	
	τῶν ἔνδον] ἢ τὸ τοιοῦτον ἀπὸ σαυτοῦ π[οι]ῶν;	25
(Γε)	μὰ Δί᾽ οὐκ ἐ]κέλευον οἱ καθεύδοντες.	
(Θρ)	Γ[έτα,	
	παρῆσθας, ὡς] ἔοικε, κηδεμὼν ἐμός.	
(Γε)	⌞εἴσελθε κἂν νῦν, ὦ μακάρι·⌟ ἐν πα[ντ]ὶ γὰρ	
	ἦσθας μακ]άρι[ο]ς.	
(Θρ)	τίς; [ἀ]τυχῶ δεινῶς, Γ[έτα·	
Τ I+K, O⁷	πέπονθα γὰρ] τὰ μέγιστ᾽ ‹ἔγωγ᾽›· ἀλλ᾽ οὐδέπω	30
	σχολὴ καθο]ρᾶν σ᾽· ἐχθὲς γὰρ εἰς τὴν οἰκίαν	
	τὴν ἡμετέ[ρα]ν ἐλήλυθας σὺ διὰ χρόνου.	
Τ O⁵ (Γε)	ἐν στρατο]πέδωι γὰρ [ὤ]ς ‹σ᾽› ἀπῆρα καταλιπὼν	
	ἦσθ᾽ εἰκό]τως εὔψυχος, [ὅτ]ι δὲ τάττομ[αι	
	ἐπὶ τῆς π]αραπομπῆς τ[ῶ]ν λαφύρων, ἔ[σχ]ατος	35
	ἥκω. τί δὲ τὸ λ]υποῦν σε;	
(Θρ)	ἐλε[ίν]᾽ ὑβρίζομαι.	
(Γε)	ὑπὸ τίνος;]	

---

19 λαβεῖν διατρίβων Austin   al. leg. suppl. Furley: ἐγκατέλιπ᾽ ἐσπουδακῶς
Austin, Blanchard   20 -21 Choerob. *in Theodos. can.* p. 176.40-177.3 Hilgard +
Lex. Seg. α p. 125.19-22 Bachmann = fr. 9 K.-Th.   τίς νῦν ἀνακρούσει suppl.
Furley   22 εἰ μὴ Furley: ἢ καὶ καθεύδεις Sandbach   περιμένει μ᾽ ἐγρηγορὼς
[ἔνδον τις;] Parsons ap. Turner   23 ὁρᾷς. Γέτα Sandbach   διαυ Π, corr. Handley σὺ δ᾽ αὐ-   24 τί βουλόμενος; Sandbach   ὑπό τινος Barrett: ‹ο›ὔποτε
Austin   25 τῶν ἔνδον Barrett   26 μὰ Δί᾽ Handley, οὐκ (tum οἶμ᾽) Sandbach
27 παρῆσθας Sandbach, vel ἐπῆλθες possis   28 Schol. Patm. in Dem. p. 10 (ubi
κἂν leg.), cf. Σ Isokr. 3.41, κἂν O⁸: καὶ νῦν O⁶   fin. γὰρ edd.: Π γε hab. vid.
29 ἦσθας Sandbach tum μακ]άριος Rea: in. καιρῶι Koenen:]αρχος leg. Turner,
unde [ὔπ]αρχος Handley: χιλίαρχος R.F. Thomas   μακάριος. (ΘΡ) τίς; dist.
Gronewald: ἀτυχῶ Gronewald   Γέτα fin. Furley: πάνυ Arnott: παθών
Lloyd-Jones: τ[ρέμων] Turner   30 πέπονθα γὰρ Furley: Γέτα Gronewald: ἤδη
κάκ᾽, ὦ Γ. Arnott: ἔα με σημῆναι olim Turner   ‹ἔγωγ᾽› ins. Furley   31 σχολὴ
καθ- Turner e.g.: καιρὸς Arnott   33 [ἐν στρατοπέδ]ωι ut vid. O⁷:]πεδου O⁶ leg.
suppl. τοῦ στρατοπέδου Turner: στρατόπεδον dub. Sisti   ὡς ‹σ᾽› ins. Furley:
ὡς Turner   34 ἦσθ᾽ Gronewald   [ὅτ]ι δὲ τάττομ[αι] O⁶ suppl. Turner: ω]ς
δ᾽ ὑδρ[εύ]σομα[ι O⁷ leg. suppl. Furley   36 ἥκω Belardinelli, Gronewald, vel ἥκον
possis: πάντων Austin: Μυσῶν Turner   τί τὸ λυποῦν Austin, δὲ add. Parsons
υβ\Ρ/ιζομαι O⁶

Act One   39

(Θρ)	ὑπὸ τῆς αἰχμαλώτου· πριάμενος	
	δούλην, π]εριθεὶς ἐλευθερίαν, τῆς οἰκίας	
	δέσποιν]αν ἀποδείξας, θεραπαίνας, χρυσία,	
	ἱμάτια δο]ύς, γυναῖκα νομ[ί]σας—	
(Γε)	εἶτα τί;	40
	γυνή σ᾽ ὑβ]ρίζει;	
Θρ	καὶ λέγειν αἰσχύνομαι,	
	μὰ τὴν Ἀθ]ηνᾶν.	
Γε	ἀλλ᾽ ἔμοιγ᾽ ὅμως φράσον.	
(Θρ)	ἐξαίσιόν] με μῖσος—	
(Γε)	ὤ, Μα[γ]νῆτις εἶ;	⊥ O[7]
	μισεῖ σ᾽· ἄτοπ]α γὰρ ὑπονοεῖς.	
(Θρ)	ἦ 'νθρώπινον	
	ἢ κατὰ τρόπο]ν {τ᾽ εἶναι} τόδ᾽ ἐστίν;	
(Γε)	οὐδὲ κ[υ]ρία	45 ⊥ O[5]
	] ... [.] . αν . [.] πάλαι σφόδρα	
	] .. [ ]στ᾽ εἶναι γὰ[ρ	
	] πειρώμ[εθα	
	] . [.] ... [	
(Θρ)	] ⌐τηρῶ τὸν Δία	50
	ὕοντα πολλῶι⌐ νυκτὸς [οὔσ]ης, ἀστραπάς,	⊤ O[5]
	βροντάς, ἔχων αὐτὴν δὲ κατάκειμαι.	
(Γε)	εἶτα τί;	
Θρ	κέκραγα «παιδίσκη, βαδίσαι γάρ», φημί, «δεῖ	
	ἤδη με πρὸς τὸν δεῖν᾽», ἐπ›είπας ὄνομά τι.	⊥ O[6]
	πᾶσ᾽ ἂν γυνὴ δήπ[ο]υ [τόδ'] εἴποι· «τοῦ Διὸς	55
	ὕοντος, ὦ τάλαν; [πρὸς ἄνθρω]πόν τινα;	

38 δούλην Furley: αὐτὴν Austin: εἶτα π. Brown cum interp. post πριάμενος: περιθεὶς Handley   39 suppl. Turner   40 ἱμάτια Austin, δούς Turner   41 γυνή suppl. Turner coll. Ap. *Synt.* 1.41: (Γε.) ἐλείν᾽ ὑβ]ρίζει; Austin ap. Turner, Blanchard   42 μὰ τὴν Ἀθηνᾶν Furley vel ἀπηγχόμην ἄν Lamagna: ἀπειχόμην vel ἀπεσχόμην ἄν Sisti: οὐκ ἂν ᾠόμην Gronewald: ὄφιν, λέαιναν (post Handley) Arnott (ἔχιν Cartledge (2016b, 16))   43 ἐξαίσιον cj. Furley coll. Aristainetos 1.22.14: μισεῖ νέον cj. Austin.   Μαγνῆτις, εἰ Furley: Μαγνῆτι σὲ mal. Turner   44 μισεῖ σ'; Furley: μισεῖν (post σε) Turner   45 in. leg. suppl. Furley: οἴει τὸ τυχόν Arnott: [δοκεῖ καλό]ν τ᾽ εἶναι τόδ'; Turner e.g.   κυρία suppl. Turner   46 πάλαι leg. suppl. Furley   48 πειρώμεθα leg. suppl. Furley   50 -51 Nonius Marc. IV p. 619-20 Lindsay   51 οὔσης suppl. Handley   fin. βροντάς in init. vs. subsequ. transp. Handley   54 ἐπείπας West, Austin: ὑπείπας Arnott: ‹μ'›. «εἶπας ὄνομά τί;» Handley, Turner: τὸν δεῖνά γ᾽ Sisti   55 δήπου τόδ᾽ Furley: δὴ ταῦτά γ᾽ edd.   56 πρὸς ἄνθρωπόν τινα; Austin, West: μέθες τρόπον τινά Handley (τρόπον iam Turner), vel ἄνες possis

40   CHAPTER 2. GREEK TEXT

		σκότ[ους τε]αϲτα[»	

(Γε)   ηδ[

          ε[

          […]   60

          […]

          […]

          […]

          …[

(Θρ)   του[65

(Γε)   εν[

          ο..[

⊥ O[5]   ἀχ.[

[gap of nine lines]

⊤ O[6]   (?Θρ)   φήϲων μο[

               ὁ τοῖχος ου.[

               ερειϲεαυτ[80

               οὐκ εἰκότ[ως

     Γε   ὦ τᾶν, τα.[

               τρόπον τε[

     (?Θρ)   ὑπερεντρ[υφῶϲα

⊤ O[5]   αὕτη ᾿ϲτί· [πρ]όϲεχ᾿, ὦ φιλ[τάτη, τὸν νοῦν ἐμοί·   85

               παρορωμένωι δὲ πε[ριβαλεῖϲ παραχρῆμά μοι]

               φιλονικίαν πόνο[ν] μανί[αν

(Γε)   τί, ὦ κακόδαιμον;

(Θρ)   ἀλλ᾿ ἔγωγ᾿ ἂν «φί[λτατε»

               κλη[θ]εὶς μόνον θύϲαιμι πᾶϲι τοῖϲ θε[ο]ῖ[ς.

(Γε)   τί [ο]ὖν ἂν εἴη τὸ κακόν; οὐδὲ γὰρ ϲφόδρ᾿ εἶ   90

               ἄκρως ἀηδὴς ὥϲτε γ᾿ εἰπεῖν· ἀλλά ϲο[ι

               τὸ μικρὸν ἀμέλει τοῦ ϲτρατιωτικοῦ [νοϲεῖ·

               ἀλ[λ᾿] ὄψιν ὑπεράϲτειος· ἀλλὰ μὴν ἄγ[εις

⊥ O[6]   τ[ῆς] ἡλικίας ..να..ιτ᾿ ἔτη ποθέν .[

(Θρ)   κακῶς ἀ[π]όλοιο· δεῖ τὸ πρᾶγμ᾿ εὑρεῖν [ὅ τι   95

               ἐϲτίν ποτ᾿, αἰτίαν ἀναγκ[αί]αν τινὰ

               [δεῖ]ξαι.

(Γε)   μιαρ[ὸ]ν τὸ φῦλόν [ἐϲ]τι, δέϲ[π]οτ[α.

---

57 ϲκότους τε vel ϲκότου leg. suppl. e.g. Furley: ϲκ.π̣τ̣[leg. Turner   84 suppl. e.g.
Furley   85 suppl. e.g. Turner   86 suppl. e.g. Turner   88 «φίλτατε» vel φίλτατος
Furley: φιλοφρόνως Lloyd-Jones   90 οὖν Furley: νέον Sisti   92 πικρὸν corr.
Lamagna   fin. νοϲεῖ Furley: βλάβη S. West   93 ἄγεις Turner, ἄγαν possis   94
τῆς Turner: ἐφ᾿ (ἐπι scr.) Arnott

Act One   41

(Θρ)   ἂν μ]ὴ παρῆι[ϲ]—

(Γε)   σὺ δέ γ᾽ ἃ διηγεῖ, δέσπ[οτα,
          οὔτε γ᾽] ὁμοθυμεῖ πρὸς [σὲ] ϲυκάζει τέ [ϲε
          αὐτό]νομο[ϲ· ο]ὐκ ἀεὶ γ[ὰρ ε]ὔλογος τέ τ[ιϲ   100   ⊥ Ο⁵
          [γυνή]

(a few lines missing, then probably the delayed prologue, to which the following
fragments, conjecturally, belong.)

Fr. 2 (7)

Σ in Hom. *Od.* 17.442 ὅτι ἀεὶ πολλοὺς εἶχεν ἡ Κύπρος βασιλεῖς ἐν ταύτῳι φησι καὶ
ὁ Μένανδρος ἐν Μισουμένωι ὡς ἐν παρεκβάσει·

                              ἐκ Κύπρου λαμπρῶς πάνυ
          πράττων· ἐκεῖ γὰρ ὑπό τιν᾽ ἦν τῶν βασιλέων.

Fragmentum dubium: P.Strasb. WG 307 verso col. i.30-col. ii.3 = fr. com. a-
desp. *1036 K-A

          ἀγαπᾶτε τοῦτον πάντες ὃς ἔχει τἀγαθὰ   ⊤ S
          ἅπαντ᾽ ἐν αὑτῶι· χρηστός, εὐγενής, ἁπλοῦς,
          φιλοβασιλεύς, ἀνδρεῖος, ἐμ πίστει μέγας,
          σώφρων, φιλέλλην, πραΰς, εὐπροσήγορος,
          τὰ πανοῦργα μισῶν, τὴν [ἀλ]ήθειαν σέβων,   5
          ἐπιστάμ[ενος
          τιμᾶν θεο . . . [
          αὑτὸν κυβε[ρνᾶν   ⊥ S

5 [ἀλ]ήθειαν leg. Furley: [δ᾽ ἀ]ληθ- edd.   6 ἐπιστάμ[ενος τὸ δίκαιον, ἐμμένειν
νόμοις e.g. Austin-Stigka   7 τιμᾶν θεοὺ[ς καλῶς τε διάγειν τὸν βίον e.g. Austin-
Stigka   8 αὑτὸν κυβε[ρνῶν κἀρετὴν ἀσκῶν ἀεί e.g. Austin-Stigka.

(about **140** lines missing, including the following small fragment of O⁵, which
seems to come from a conversation between Thrasonides and Getas; Getas(?)
sees thieves approaching which seems to mark the entry of the chorus, about
to sing and dance the first *entr'acte*. Sandbach, following Turner, placed the

---

99 οὔτε γ᾽] ὁμοθυμεῖ Furley: . . . .]ομόϲαι τε in. Turner   πρός τι Turner   101
suppl. e.g. Furley

fragment after line 99. If the fragment marks the first ΧΟΡΟΥ, then that is impossible.)

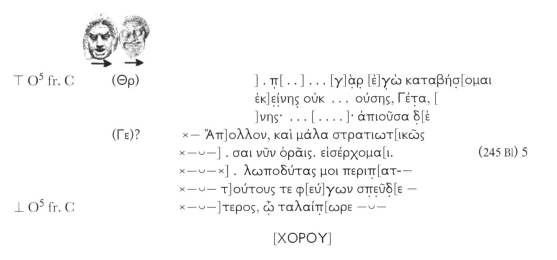

⊤ O⁵ fr. C   (Θρ)   ] . π[. .] . . . [γ]ὰρ [ἐ]γὼ καταβήσ[ομαι
                             ἐκ]είνης οὐκ . . . οὔσης, Γέτα, [
                             ]νης· . . . [. . . .]· ἀπιοῦσα δ[ὲ
         (Γε)?   ×— Ἄπ]ολλον, καὶ μάλα στρατιωτ[ικῶς
                        ×—∪—] . σαι νῦν ὁρᾶις. εἰσέρχομα[ι.   (245 Bl) 5
                        ×—∪—×] . λωποδύτας μοι περιπ[ατ-—
                        ×—∪— τ]ούτους τε φ[εύ]γων σπεῦδ[ε —
⊥ O⁵ fr. C   ×—∪—]τερος, ὦ ταλαίπ[ωρε —∪—

[ΧΟΡΟΥ]

Act Two

(here there is a gap in our sources of approximately one hundred and fifty lines. Perhaps in the first scene there was an encounter between Thrasonides and Krateia in which he displayed boastful, boorish comportment.)

⊤ O⁴   ]ν
                     ] . [   ]ις
                                        ]
                               ]εκ . . [. . .]τομου
                               ] . τους λογίζεται   405
                               γ]εγεν{ν}ημένον
                               ] . π' ὑπονοεῖς

---

1 (fr. C) fin. suppl. dub. Furley   4 in. χρηστῶς, e.g. possis   fin. Furley: -[ικόν] Turner, al.   7 (fr. C) φεύγων Turner   σπεῦδ[ε leg. suppl. Furley: ἐκλύτ[ως Turner   8 vel ὦ ταλαίπ[ωρος] poss.   406 Turner: -γεννη- Π   407 ὑπονοεῖς Sisti: ὑποτιθεὶς possis

Act Two   43

(Γε)   ] . δέσποτα
(Θρ)   εἰ]σιών, Γέτα
                              ]ικακ[. .] . ονους   410
                              ] ἀφεὶς δὲ σοῖς
                              ] . ἀνεω[ι]γμένον
                              ἄν]οικτον τοῦτ᾽ ἐμοί
                              νομ]ιζε[
                              ]ιας. εἰ δέ τις   415
                              ]α . . ηκεν γέ μοι

(ΔΗΜΕΑΣ)

                              ἐκεί]νης γράμμα[τ]α
                                δε]ῦρ᾽ ἄγω
                              ]τί βούλεται;
                              ἐ]κ[εί]νην τὴν θύραν   420
                              ]τ[ὴ]ν οἰκίαν
(ΣΥΡΑ)

                              ] . ος γὰρ ἂν κόψαντί σοι
(Δη)   ]ης ἕστηκ᾽ ἐγώ
                              ]α:
(Συ)   οὑτοσί, ξένε.
(Δη)   παρ᾽ ἐκεί]νου γράμματα   425
(Συ)   ]δὸ[ς] ταυτί.
(Δη)   λαβέ.
(Συ)   ἐπε]ράνω, ξένε;
(Δη)   ] . . ὀκτώ γ᾽ ἡμέρας
                              ] πιαῖνον πάθας
                              ] . οὐκ ἔχω λέγειν.   430
                              ]β . α.
(Συ)   ποδαπὸς εἶ, ξένε;
(Δη)   ἐγώ; παρ[ὰ Κύπρου.
(Συ)   σώμα]τ᾽ οὖν λυτρούμενος
          ἥκεις πυ[θόμενος;

---

410 μόνους leg. Turner   411 Furley:] . φεις . . . ις leg. Turner   413 ἄνοικτον τοῦτ᾽
Furley: π . . εμοι al.   416 Furley: ηχεν al.   417 περὶ Arnott, al. dub. Turner   418
δε]ῦρ᾽ ἄγω Turner   420 in. ἐκείνην Turner   423 in. vel]ηγ   424 ουτοσει Π, corr.
Turner   425 ἐκείνου dub. Turner   426 τ[[ι]]αυτι Π leg. Furley   427 ἐπε]ράνω
Furley   428 ὀκτώ γ᾽ dub. Furley   429 πιαῖνον πάθας Furley: fin. σέβας dub.
Austin: σ‹π›άθας dub. Turner: σὺ βάς Borgogno   432 suppl. Turner, Handley

44   CHAPTER 2. GREEK TEXT

(Δη)	μὰ τὸν Ἀ]πόλλω, ᾽γὼ μὲν οὔ,	
	ἀλλ᾽ ἕνεκα [τῆς ἐμοὶ κακότη]τος γενομένης	
	ζητοῦσί μ[ε] . ἀνύεται	435
	<u>αὕτη δὲ π[</u> .	
(Συ)	] φής:	
(Δη)	τοῦτό μοι	
	συμπρᾶξ[ον.	
Συ	]μαι τόδε, γέρον,	
	<u>ἄλλοις πα[</u>	
Δη	ἰ]χνεύων πάλιν	
	<u>ἐὰν δ᾽ αμ[</u>	
(Συ)	--	
(Δη)	]̣νη	
	<u>σ̣ωτὴρ κ[εκλήσει</u>	440
(Συ)	<u>τί τοὔνομ᾽ [ἐστί</u>	
(Δη)	<u>Κράτ‹ε›ιαν [</u>	
(Συ)	<u>ἔστιν πα̣[ρὰ γείτοσι</u>	
(Δη)	–	
(Συ)	<u>οὗτος γὰρ ι̣[</u>	
(Δη)	ὦ Ζεῦ τ̣ρ̣[ο]π̣[αῖε	445
	ἀπροσδόκ[ητον	
	<u>ἡμῖν ἃ δ[εῖ</u>	
	<u>ἐὰν κα . [</u>	
	ἀ]γορεύετ᾽ ον[	
	] . άντων ἀρκ[	450
	] ἰδίοις πάρεστ[ι	
	. . [ ]ν[.] . . αρπ[	
	<u>λ̣ . .</u>	
(Συ)	εὔξ̣ας̣[θαι,] γέρ[ον,	
	ανεμ[. . .] . [.]ε . . . [. .] . . σι[	
	. . π̣λ . [. .]α . . λ . . μοι . . . [	455
	κ]ἀ̣π̣ε̣ῖ̣[τ]α̣ θεῶν ἃ δ[εῖ	
	π . . . [.]δος . . . [	
	πως [. .] . ρα . . . [	

---

433 πυθόμενος Furley, al. Turner   434 τῆς ἐμοὶ κακότητος e.g. Furley   435 με Furley   437 τοδ᾽ε Π   440 dub. Turner   442 κρατιαν Π   443 παρὰ γείτοσι e.g. Furley   445 τροπαῖε Turner: ὕπ[α]τ[ε nisi hiat. poss.   447 δεῖ Furley e.g.   448 leg. Furley: .μονη α[al.   449 Arnott   450 πάντων possis   451 ἰδίοις Furley: ἰδίωι al.   453 εὔξασθαι γέρον Turner, fin. et Σύρα possis   454 ἀνέμ[ωι vel ἀνέμ[οις Furley: ἐμελ- Turner   455 .πλο̣.[Blanchard   456 tent. Furley

Act Two 45

Κρά[τεια] . μφ[
τ . . [. . .] . . . . . . [460
τὴ[ν . . . .]ς[. .] . εν . . νγ . [
αὐτ[.]δ . κ[. .] . . . συμ[
παι . . . . . . πάλιν δου[
καὶ πάξ:

[Δ]ημ   . . υλλ[.]ν του[
(Συ)   μὰ Δ[ία, τ]ὰ τουπι . . ωι· ἀλ[465
(Δη)   τρο[παὶ] δύ' ἑκατέρωθε[ν
(Συ)   καὶ τοῦτο φοβερ[ὸ]ν ἐκπ[
(Δη)   φέρ', εἰς τὸ πρόσθεν εἰ γεν[ήσει
εἰς τὴν ὁδόν. γελοῖον ε[ἰ
εἴσω λαβόν[τα] τουτονὶ δ.[470
(Συ)   ἀλ‹λ›' εὐθὺς αὐτῶι τὴν ἀν[
ὅπου 'στὶ μηδὲ τόνδ' ἐ . [
ποίει τὸ σαυτοῦ πρῶτον [
καλῶς· ἐγὼ δὲ σὺν βρα[χέως ποήσομαι.
(Δη)   πῶς οὖν:
(Συ)   [. . .]ἀπάτην [475
εὑρεῖ[ν] μὲν ἀ[ν]απαυσαντ[
ἀλλ' εὖ παθὼ[ν τ]ὴν χάριν [
[α]ὐτὴν γυναῖκα π[ροσ]δρ[αμὼν
καὶ [γ]ὰρ πο[ή]σεις εἰ[. .] . . [
ὑμ . [.] . . ἔνειμας . [. . .] . [480
(Δη)   μὰ τ[οὺ]ς θεούς, κτ[–
(Συ)   τρεπ[ό]μενος εὐ[
(Δη)   ὁρᾶν [.] . . . ρκ' . . [
δειν[ὸν] λαβὼν [
(Συ)   κακο[ῦ γὰ]ρ ἀνδρὸς [485
. [. . . . . .]το πραξ[
]μι παντὸ[ς

---

459 Κρά[τεια Austin, -ειαν ἀμφ[possis   460 ὅτ' ἔστ' Furley   464 καὶ πάξ: Furley
465 μὰ Δία Turner, al. Furley   466 τροπαί Furley: τρόποι? Turner   467 φοβερὸν
Turner, ἐκπ[ονεῖν] possis   468 suppl. e.g. Furley: Γέτα, τὴν παρθένον vel γεραιά,
τὴν κόρην Austin   474 fin. e.g. Furley   475 ἀπάτην leg. Furley: ἐρῶτα τὴν suppl.
Turner:]ωτατην Sandbach   476 εὑρεῖν μὲν Furley: εὕροιμεν Turner spat. brevius:
εὕροις μὲν possis   477 τὴν suppl. Furley   478 in. αὐτήν, fin. π[ροσ]δρ[αμών cj.
Turner   479 leg. suppl. Furley, εἰ[δέναι χρή e.g. possis   480 in. ὑμῖν vel sim., tum
ἀπένειμας possis   482 dubit. Furley   484 leg. Furley: αναιτων Turner   485
suppl. Furley: κάκι[στ]ος ἀνδρῶ[ν Coles   486 leg. Furley, e.g. κακὸν τὸ πρᾶξαι
possis: τοπραξ al.

46 CHAPTER 2. GREEK TEXT

```
                    ]ο̣ν εὑρὼν [
                    ]γυναικ.[
                    τὴ]ν χάριν [                        490
                    ]ν λέγωμ[εν
⊥ O⁴                ] . [
```

(gap of approximately 8 lines including *entr'acte*)

[ΧΟΡΟΥ]

Act Three

? ⟶

Τ O³

```
                                          ]οποι
                                          ὁ]λίγον
                                          ]α . . . ον
                                          ]νπ . . . μ . ι
                                          π]άλιν προσδο̣[κ-      505
                                          ] . ω[
                                          ἐγέ]νετ᾽ ἄρα
                              ].[     ] . [ . . ] . ν
                              ]α .
        Γ̣ε̣                            ξί[φ-
                              ].χα[                          510
                              ]ρω[ . . . . . . . . ]τ[
                                ] . . [ . . . . ]αμ[ . . ] . . . [
                                      ] . . μενα
        (?Γε)                         ]μεθα
        π . . . χ . [                        ]α̣·         515
        . ι[ . . . ] . . [ . . . ] . ι[ . . . ]ο . [ . . ]αυ̣[ . ] . [
        . . ] καί τιν᾽ α . α[ . . . . ] . [ . . . ] . . [ . . ]μ[
        __] . ωϲ .
        (?Ϲυ)         ὁδὶ μὲ̣ν̣ [εἰ]ϲιὼν τὸ κα̣[κὸν] ειν[ . ] . μ[
                      ϲ]ὺ δ᾽ ἥτις εἴπαϲ᾽ . . [ . . . . . . . . ]χει[
        (?Χρ)         οὐκ ἂν δυναί[μην         ] . νον[        520
                      εἶναί με . [
```

---

488 εὑρὼν leg. Furley: ευρον al.   491 Furley   505 vel προσδέ[χου Turner   507 Turner   509 ξίφος suppl. Austin coll. fr. 1 εἶτα ξίφος αἰτεῖ   514 fin. leg. Furley: ἐλήλυθα Austin   518 in. e.g. ἴσως   ὁδὶ κτλ. leg. suppl. dub. Furley, sed ?ειν[contra metr., totus v., ut vid., longior, vide 'Composite Readings'.   519 ϲ]ὺ vel ο]ὐδὲ   521 in. θ]εῖναι poss.

Act Three   47

ἱ]κετηρίαν [

..] . ρ[. . .]λα[. . . .] . . . [   ]αγ[   ] . [⊤ O[11]

. . . [. . .] . τ[   ]

Γε   γι[ν-   ] . . . [

                                      ]αν[το]ῦ ξέν[ου   525

___.]αυ[. . . . .] . αν.

(??)   [   ]λε . [. . .] . . . . εωμ[

.] . . [. . . .] . ρενθ[   ] εὐθὺc [. .]δ[   ] . . . [

ὁδ᾿ [ὑπερ]πέπαικ[ε   ] λό[γ]ους τουτ[-

.] . [ca. 8   ].ωνω σφόδρ᾿ αυτη[

τ[.] . [. . . .] . ν περι . . [   ] . . ς ἐξαίφνη[ς   530

α[. .] . . . [. .]γηc[θ]ήcει τοῖς φίλ[οις

___ἱκετηρίαν;

(Συ)   τί λέγου[c]α;

Χρ   «ἐμοὶ μαχεῖ, τάλαν;»   ⊤ B[2]

«μ]ὰ Δί᾿ ἀλλ᾿ ἐκεί[νωι]», φησί. «δεινὸν γὰρ βίον

ζῆι κ[α]ὶ ταλαίπωρόν τιν᾿·» οὐ γάρ; μακάριον

αὔτη γε καὶ ζηλωτὸν ὅσα γ᾿ οὕτως ἰδεῖν.   535

αὐ]τὴ δ᾿ ἄμ[ει]νον οἶδε τά γ᾿ ἑαυτῆς πολύ.

?(Γε)   τοῦτ᾿ ε[ἰ]κ[ός] ἐστιν τὸν τράχηλον τουτονί

  . . .] . μ᾿ ἀ[νενε]γκεῖν μοι τὸν ὑποκαθήμενον;

Χρ   τί] τοῦτο; τ[ο]ῦτο τίς πότ᾿ ἐστιν; ἔστι γὰρ

παρά τινος οὗτος ὁ ψιθυρισμός, οἶδ᾿ ἐγώ.   540

ἀπαλλάγηθ᾿ ἐ[ν]θένδ᾿. ἐγὼ δ᾿ ἀναλή[ψο]μαι·

Συρ   ἴσθι δέ μ᾿ ἕτ[οιμον], μακαρία.

(?Γε)   φαιὸν δ᾿ ἔχει

ἐφεστρίδιον.

Χρ   δηλόνοτι ταῦθ᾿ ὅταν λέγηι

ὑφα]σμά[τω]ν τὰ κράσπεδ᾿.

Γετ   ἐν δ᾿ αὐτῶι μό[νον   ⊥ B[2]

        ±12   δα]κτύλιον [καὶ χ]ρυσία   545

ἐ[ν] δ᾿ ἄξον[ες . .]η\δὲ/παρ[. . . .] . εμ[

___φίλων τε . [.]ειθε[

---

524 Γετ leg. Blanchard: *n.p.* Γλύκερα? HPP   525 fin. Turner   527 εὐθὺς vel εὐρύς
leg. Furley   528 ὁδ᾿ ὑπερπέπαικε cj. Furley: πεπαικ[iam leg. Arnott   530 τις Furley
531 θήσει HPP in *comm.*   535 δὲ vel γε Austin   536 αὐτή Henry: αὔτη δ᾿ Turner
πολύ Furley ex B[2]: ἐγώ Henry   537 suppl. dub. Furley   538 ἀνενεγκεῖν μοι Furley:
cett. HPP   542 in. (vel ἑτοίμην) leg. et suppl. Furley   μακαρία· φαιὸν Parsons
ap. Green & Edwards (2015)   543 ἐφεστρίδιον Parsons ibid.   544 ὑφασμάτων
vel τῶν εἱμάτων e.g. Furley   545 suppl. HPP   546 ἐν δ᾿ ἄξονες Furley:]δεῖξον
Austin

48   CHAPTER 2. GREEK TEXT

[Χρ]υς   τί] βούλετ[αι ◡—
                  ὁ τοιοῦτο[ς οὖν;]
(?Γε)   πρῶτον [τάδ᾽] εἰσενέγ[κατε
                  θαἰμάτ[ι]α, π[ρὸς] δὲ ταῦτ[α καὶ λαβρ]ώνια.
                  ἔπειτα πρὸς κ[ο]τύλας ἄπ[ειμι κ]αταλιπ[ὼν   550
                  τὴν γῆν κροτοῦσαν· κ[   ]σαντο[
⊤ O¹⁰   σ]πείσονθ᾽ ἕ[ως] τρέπωσ[ι]ν ε[ὶς] ἔρανόν [ποτε.
(Συ)   ἐσ]τὶν τ[ο]ιαῦτα θηρί᾽ ὧν παρεισφορῶν
⊥ O¹¹   ε[ἴ]σω τις ἡμᾶς λανθάνει, νῦν δ᾽ οὐκέτι,
                  ἂν οἱ θεοὶ θέλωσιν.
        Χ^{ΡΥ[Σ]}   ἀπίωμεν, Σύρα.   555
                  ἐ]γὼ [συν]άχθομαι δέ, νὴ τὴν Ἄρτεμιν.
                  ἡμεῖς . . . ισκ . . [. .].
        Γετ   μετὰ τίνων πίν[ε]ι ποτὲ
                  ὁ δε[σπότ]ης; ἐντ[αῦ]θ᾽ ἄπιστον οὐδ[ὲ ἕν·
                       ]εν . [   ]ιμα[. . .]ἄρχοντά [πως
⊥ O¹⁰   κατέλειπον. ἠισ᾽ ἄν[θ]ρω[πος ἐπιεικῶς] παχ[ὺς   560
                  τὴν ὄψιν, ὗς ἄνθρωπ[ος . .] . [. . .] . . [
                  τὰ γύναι᾽, ἵν᾽ ἔξωθεν θεωρε[ῖν ἐδέδοτο
                  –ἆρ᾽ οὗτός ἐστι Μυσό[ς];– ‹εἶτα σχὼν› λύρα[ν
                  ἠισέν ποτ᾽ αὐτῶν θάτερος σθεν[αρώ]τε[ρον
                  –τὸν ἄνδρ᾽ ὁρᾶν πάρ᾽, ὦ πολυτίμητ[οι θε]ο[ί–   565
                  «πλουτεῖν ἀμ[έμπ]τως», τοῦτο δὴ τὸ τοῦ λόγου,
⊤ Β¹   πίνων δικαίοις ἦισεν ἀνθρώποι[ς. σύ γε
                  ἀγαθὸν ἄκουσμ᾽ ἥκεις πρὸς ἡμᾶς· ἀλλὰ τί
                  τοιαῦτα κάμπτεις καὶ πάλιν στέλλει διδοὺς

———————————————————————————————————

547 ἔπειθε vel ἐπείθετο sim. possis   τί Furley   548 leg. suppl. Furley   549
λαβρώνια HPP   πρός suppl. Furley   550 κοτύλας HPP   καταλιπών
Henry, ἄπειμι Furley: Henry e.g. ἄγει   552 σπείσονθ᾽ Turner: ἃ] πέπονθ᾽ possis   553 ἐστὶν τοιαῦτα Turner   θηρί᾽ ὧν Furley (i.e. θηριαων): θηρίων Gonis
παρεισφορῶν Furley, παρεισφέρων iam Gonis in comm.: παρεισφρέων HPP   554
εἴσω τις ἡμᾶς Gonis   556 συνάχθομαι Gonis in comm.: [[συη]] post]γω in O³ eras.
557 ἡμεῖς ??   ἐκειν- ? Furley   558 ὁ δεσπότης; ἐνταῦθ᾽ leg. suppl. Furley
     δ
ουθ[O¹⁰: οὐδὲ ἕν Austin: leg. Gonis: ιουφ Turner   559 ἄρχοντά πως e.g. Furley: ἔρχεται πάλιν Austin   560 ἠισ᾽ Austin, ἄνθρωπος Mette, ἐπιεικῶς e.g. Furley
562 in. suppl. Turner   ἔξωθεν θεωρεῖν Austin: ἔξωθ᾽ ἐπιθεωρεῖν Merkelbach
ἐδέδοτο vel εἴχομεν e.g. Furley   563 Μυσός leg. suppl. Furley in O³: δοῦλος (v.l.?)
Turner in Β²   εἶτα σχών suppl. e.g. Furley: καὶ contra metr. ms.: ‹ὃς› κελεύεται
Cartlidge (sc. δοῦλος)   564 σθεναρώτερον leg. suppl. Furley: σαφέστερον Turner
565 ὁρᾶν πάρ᾽ Furley: ὁρᾶις γάρ Austin   566 πλουτεῖν ἀμέμπτως leg. suppl.
Furley: ἐπὶ πᾶσιν in. leg. Austin, ἀγαθοῖς Handley: ὄντως Turner, Handley   569
in. leg. suppl. Furley: παθὼν ἀνακάμπτεις Wilamowitz (μαθών Austin): ἐνθάδ᾽ ἔτι
vel ἐνθάδε τί (sic) dub. Sisti

Act Three 49

τὰς συμβολὰς, εἰ μή τι κακὸν ἡμᾶς ποεῖς; 570
λῆρος· κελεύσω τοῦτον ἐπὶ δεῖπνον πάλιν
τὸν δεσ[π]ότην καλέσαντα; φανερῶς ἐστι γὰρ
μιαρός. β]αδιοῦμ᾿ εἴσω δὲ καὶ πειράσομαι
κρύπτω]ν ἐμαυτὸν ἐπιθεωρῆσαί τι τῶν
ποιουμέ]νων ἔνδον λαλουμένων θ᾿ ἅμα. 575 →

Συ ἀτοπώ]τερον τούτου, μὰ τὼ θεώ, ξένον
οὐπώπο]τ᾿ εἶδον. αἲ τάλας, τί βούλεται;
ἐν τῶι γὰ]ρ οἴκωι τὰς σπάθας τῶν γειτόνων ⊥ B¹
τ . [. . . α]ὑτὰς εἰς μέσον
]νο[. .] . [πολ]ὺν [χ]ρόνον 580
] . . . η . [. .]εν ταύτ[ας] [φ]ράσαι
] . . ν εἰ βούλεται
] . αλλα[. .] . . . .
[Δη] δεῖξ . [.]
(Συ) τ]αύτας θήσεται
] ἡμίσεις.
Δ[η] καλῶς· 585
] . . . νησ . ι . .
(Συ) ἐγώ
] . εἶδον.
Δη εὖ [γὰ]ρ ἂν
] τὴ]ν θύραν κόψασά μοι.
(Συ) αὐτὸς μὲν οὖν σὺ] κόπτε· [τί] μ᾿ ἐνοχλεῖς, τάλαν;
(Δη)] . . [.] . . . [. .]
(Συ) [λά]β᾿. ἀπ̣οτρέχω· δέδ‹ε›ιχά σοι· 590
] . . . [. . ἐ]κκάλει κα[ὶ δ]ιαλέγου
] . . . . [. . .] . [.]α . α . [.] .
[?Δη] ὧν τ[υγ]χάνω
σπαθῶν] ἐναργ[ῶ]ς τὴν ἐμὴν ταύτην ὁρῶ;
(?Συ) τί οὐ δὲ κ]όψει̣ς τὴν θύραν;
(Δη?) [κό]ψ[ας] δ᾿ ἔτι

---

573 μιαρὸς Arnott: κακός, φαῦλος poss.   574 κρύπτων Wilamowitz: παράγων
vel εἰσφρῶν Sandbach   578 in. suppl. Edmonds   579 in. σκοπεῖ e.g. Webster, ἰδών
Mette   581 ταυτ[[ην]]ας O³   582 τῶν σπ]α̣[θ]ῶ̣ν suppl. Mette   584 ΓΡΑ O³ in
marg.   585 ἡμίσεις dub. Furley   587 fin. leg. et suppl. Furley (ρ[.]ν Turner): ἂ̣ν̣ [γὰ]ρ
εὖ Kassel   589 suppl. Sandbach   590 λάβ᾿· ἀποτρέχω Sandbach   δέδειχα corr.
Handley   591 Handley   592 suppl. dub. Turner   593 leg. suppl. Furley   594 τί
οὐ δὲ κόψεις Furley: κόψει Turner   δ᾿ ἔτι Turner, vel δὲ τί possis

50 CHAPTER 2. GREEK TEXT

μ[. . . . .]σάμην ἔγωγέ φι[±4-5]νονθ᾽ ὅλως. 595

(Συ)]τ . ϲ[. . ,] τάλαν, . ν . [. .][. . . . . .]ς· καλοῦ.

(Δη?) ὄντ[ως] ποησ[ἡγ]ησάμην

. . .] . [ ]ι̣[ ]ποτέ

. . . . .]ϲ[. . .]κ̣ . .

(Δη?)] . θελ[ω]ν̣ . . . . . .] . ν προ . [. .]

]ερ[. . . . .] . π[ρό]σω 600

]ρ̣[ ]τισε

] . . . λ[ἐλευ]θέρα.

(Συ)]τ[ ] τὼ θε[ώ

. υ[ ] . . [.] . [ ] . . [ ]σ̣α̣το,

⌞ἐνθύμιόν μοι τοῦτο γέγονεν ἀρτίως⌟ 605

. [.] . . [. . .]κ̣α̣μ̣[. .]τοσωστ[. . . . . .]ς̣ οὐδ̣[ὲ ἕν.

Δη ‾π]ρόσ[ειμ᾽ ἐ]γώ. παῖ, παῖδε[ς]. ἐ[π]ανάξω· ψ[οφεῖ

‾αὐτῶν προϊών τις εἰς τὸ πρ[όσθ]ε[ν τῆς θύρας.

ΓΥΝ̣[Η] [ΚΡΑ]ΤΕΙΑ

οὐκ ἂν [δυ]ναίμην κ[α]ρτερ[εῖ]ν̣ τὸν γενόμενον

‾τ[ό]τ᾽ ἔ[ντο]νον. τί ταῦτ[α] φ̣[ήις; οὐ μανθάνω. 610

Τ Β¹ Δη ὦ Ζεῦ, τίν᾽ ὄψιν οὐδὲ προσδ[οκωμένην

‾ὁρῶ;

(Κρ) τί βούλει, τηθία; τί μοι λαλεῖς;

‾πατὴρ ἐμός; ποῦ;

(Δη) παιδίον Κράτεια.

(Κρ) [τίς

‾καλεῖ με; πάπ‹π›α· χαῖρε πολλά, φίλτατ[ε.

(Δη) ‾ἔχ̣ω σε, τέκνον.

(Κρ) ὦ ποθούμενος φαν[είς, 615

‾ὁρῶ σ᾽ ὃν οὐκ ἂν ὠιόμην ἰδεῖν ἔτι.

Γε ἐξῆλθεν ἔξω. παῖ, τί τοῦθ᾽; αὕτη τί σ[οι,

ἄνθρωπε; τί ποεῖς οὗτος; οὐκ ἐγὼ ᾽λε[γον;

---

595 ἔγωγέ φημι Austin   ὄνθ᾽ ὅλως dub. Turner   596 τάλαν leg. Furley: τοπασαν Turner   597 leg. suppl. Furley   600 πρόσω Furley   601 fin. e.g. ἐφρόντισε   603 μὰ vel νὴ τὼ θεώ possis   605 Lex. Sym. p. 410 Bühler s.v. ἐνθύμημα   606 fin. dub. Furley (ουθ[εν Π ?)   607 in. leg. suppl. Furley   609 οὐκ ἂν δυναίμην Turner   καρτερεῖν Handley   μοι γενόμενον e.g. Furley: ἔνδον γ᾽ ἔτι Kraus (1971a, 8)   610 ἔντονον e.g. Furley: ἐκεῖνον vel ἐλεῖνον Austin (contra metrum) fin. e.g. Furley   611 προσδοκωμένην suppl. Wilamowitz   613 suppl. Jensen   615 φανείς suppl. Wilamowitz   617 suppl. Handley

Act Three   51

ἐπ’ αὐτοφώρωι τόνδε τὸν ζητούμε[νον
ἔχω. γέρων οὗτός γε πολιὸς φαίνε[ται,   620
ἐτῶν τις ἑξήκονθ’, ὅμως δὲ κλαύ[σεται.
τίνα περιβάλλειν καὶ φιλεῖν οὗτος [δοκεῖς;   ⊥ Β[1]

Κρ	_οὑμὸς πατήρ, Γέτα, π[ά]ρ[εστιν.
[Γε]	[τίς λόγος

οὕτω γελοῖος; οὐ νο ... [
_τίς εἶ; πόθεν θ’ [ἥκεις;   625

Δη	αὐτὸς πορε[υθεὶς

ταύτης.

(Γε)	ἀληθῶς σο[ί], Κ[ράτεια, γὰρ πατὴρ

ὅδ’ ἐστὶν ὁ γέρων;

(Κρ)	λάμ[βαν’ αὐτὴν μάρτυρα.
[Γε]	τί τοῦτο; καὶ σύ, γράιδιο[ν, τοιαῦτά γε

λα]λεῖς; πόθεν, βέλτιστε, [νῦν π]α[ρ]ελ[ήλυθας;   630
_οἴκοθεν;

Δη	ἐ[βο]υλόμην ἄν.
Γε	ἀλλὰ [τ]υγχάνε[ις

ἀπόδημος ὢν ἐκεῖθεν;

Δη	ἐκ Κύπρου παρ[ὼν

ἐνταῦθα πρῶτον τῶν ἐμῶν ταύτην ὁρ[ῶ.
καὶ δῆλον ὡς ἔσπαρκε τῶν οἴκοι τινὰς
_ὁ κοινὸς ἐχθρὸς πόλεμος ἄλλον ἀλλαχῆι.   635

Γε	ἔχει γὰρ οὕτως· αἰχμάλωτος γενομένη

α]ὕτη πρ[ὸ]ς ἡμᾶς ἦλθε τοῦτον τ[ὸ]ν τ[ρ]όπον.
δ]ραμὼν δέ σοι τὸν δεσπότην ἤδη καλῶ.
. [. . . . . .] . . . . [.] . [. .] . [.]α

Δη	οὕτω πόει .

. . .] . . [. .] . [.] . πο . . . ουμ[. . . .] . . . [640
. [   ] . . . ιτ . κα . [. . . . . .] . ων . [
]ἱ]κετη[ρ]ίαν . . . [. .]φο . [. . . .] . αρη . [Τ Ο[1]
. [   ] . . . ι[. . . . .]ιτ . [.] . αι . [
ε[   ] . . [

(?Κρ)	]φαίνεται[. . .] . [. . .] . . [645

ἡμ]εῖς πάτρ[ας] ἦμεν.

---

619 -622 suppl. Wilamowitz   623 πάρεστιν, τίς λόγος Sandbach   624 e.g. νοῶ
Furley   627 γάρ, Κράτειά, σοι πατήρ suppl. e.g. Sandbach   628 suppl. e.g. Arnott
629 fin. suppl. e.g. Furley   630 λαλεῖς iam Austin (1966, 296)   νῦν παρελήλυθας
Furley   631 ἀλλὰ τυγχάνεις Turner, Sandbach: ἀλλ’ ἐτύγχανες Kassel   636
[[ε]]γενομενη Π   645 φαίνεται leg. Furley

52 CHAPTER 2. GREEK TEXT

⊥ O¹ (Δη?) ὅτε τηλ . [. . . . [
ὅ]δ᾽ οὐκέτ᾽ ἐστί.
(Κρ?) τίς λέγει σοι τὸν λόγο[ν;
(Δη?) εὖ οἶδ᾽] ἀπόλωλε.
(Κρ) οἴμοι τάλαινα τῆς ἐμ[ῆς
Τ O¹ ἐγὼ τύ]χης· ὡς οἰκτρά, πάπ‹π›α φίλτατε,
π]επόνθαμεν. τέθν[η]κε;
Δη ὑφ᾽ οὗ γ᾽ ἥκιστ᾽ ἐχρ[ῆν. 650
[Κρ] οἶσ]θα‹ς› σὺ τοῦτον;
(Δη) οἶδα, καὶ σύν[οισθά γε
ἀλοῦσ᾽ ἅμιλλά [τ᾽] οὖσα τοῦ[δ᾽ εἰ]λη[μμ]έ[νου.
διὰ τί, Κράτεια—
(Κρ) φέρ[ε, τί εἶπας ἀρτίως;
ὁ τοῦτο πράξας εἶ[λεν ἐμέ γε;
(Δη) οὕτως ἔχει.
(Κρ) ἀλλά, πάτερ, ε[ ] . α 655
ἄπαντ᾽ ἀ[. . . . . . .]υκ[. . .] . [. .] . [. . . . .] .
βουλευτέ[ο]ν νῦν ἐστ[ιν·] ἀλλ᾽ ἧι κά‹μ›ὲ δ[εῖ
ζῆν εὐπρε[π]ῶς μετὰ τ[ο]ῦ[τό γ᾽ ἐνθυμητέον.
(Δη) ὢ τοῦ παραδόξου καὶ ταλαιπώρου [βίου.

Θρ πατὴρ Κρατείας, φή‹ι›ς, ἐλήλυ[θ]᾽ ἀρ[τίως; 660
νῦν ἢ μακάριον ἢ τρισαθλιώτατον
δείξεις με τῶν ζώντων ἁπάντων γεγονότα.
εἰ μὴ γὰρ οὗτος δοκιμάσει με, κυρίως
δώσει τε ταύτην, οἴχεται Θρασωνίδης·
⊥ O¹ ὃ μὴ γένοιτ᾽. ἀλλ᾽ εἰσίωμεν· ο[ὐ]κέτι 665
τ]ὸ τοιοῦτον εἰκάζειν γάρ, εἰδέναι δέ, δεῖ

---

646 in. leg. suppl. Furley   τηλοῦ vel τηλουρός Handley, cum θανὼν possis 647
τὸν λόγον Turner: ταῦτα δή leg. possis   648 εὖ οἶδ᾽ suppl. Sandbach, Krateia ded.
Sisti   ἀπόλωλε leg. Furley   ἐμῆς Turner 649 ἐγὼ Webster, τύχης, πάπ‹π›α
suppl. corr. Turner   650 not. pers. ΔΗ supra ὑφ᾽ transpos. Merkelbach, Mette
τ O³, γ᾽ corr. Austin   651 in corr. Turner   fin. Furley (συνῆν ἐγὼ Mette):
συνώικισα Sisti   652 ἀλοῦσ᾽ et ἄμιλλά τ᾽ Turner: ἀμίλλαι Austin: ἐλοῦϲαμιμο . .
[vel ἀλ-) O¹ teste Hunt   τοῦδ᾽ εἰλημμένου cj. Furley   653 φέρετε κλάδους e.g.
Webster   654 suppl. Furley   655 ε[ἰσίωμεν] cj. Webster, vel e.g. ἔνδον   657 ἀλλ᾽
ἧι κάμὲ δεῖ Arnott: ἀλλ᾽ ἧι κάμ᾽ ἔδει / ἔζην· τί πρέπει Sandbach   658 ζῆν εὖ O¹
teste Hunt, εὐπρεπῶς Furley   661 τρισαθλιώτατον van Leeuwen (1919)

Act Four 53

        ἡμᾶς. ὀκνηρῶς καὶ τρέμων εἰσ[έρχ]ομ[αι.
        μαντεύεθ' ἡ ψυχή τί μου, Γέτα, κακόν.
        δέδοικα. βέλτιον δ' ἀπαξάπ[αντα τ]ῆς
        οἰήσεως.
ΓΕᵀ   πῶς; ταῦτα θαυμάσαιμι δ' [ἄν.   670

ΚΛΕΙΝΙΑΣ (+ Μάγειρος)
        ξένος ἐστὶν εἷς, μάγειρε, κἀγὼ καὶ τρίτη
        ἐμή τις, εἴπερ νὴ Δί' εἰσελήλυθεν.
        ἀγωνιῶ γὰρ καὐτός. εἰ δὲ μή, μόν[ος
        ὁ ξένος· ἐγὼ γὰρ περιδ[ρα]μοῦμαι τὴν [πόλιν
        ζητῶν ἐκείνην πᾶσαν· ἀλλὰ πάραγε [σὺ   675
        καὶ τοῦ ταχέως, μάγειρε, φρόντισον πάνυ.

        ΧΟΡΟΥ

Act Four

Κλ   τί φῄς; ἐπιγνοὺς τὴν σπάθην τὴν κειμέν[ην   ⊤ Ο¹
        ἔνδον παρ' ἡμῖν ὤ‹ι›χεθ' ὡς τοὺς γείτονας
        τούτων ἀκούσας οὖσαν αὐτ[ήν]; πηνίκα
        ἔθεντο δ' οὗτοι δεῦρο τα[ύ]την ἢ τ[ί]νο[ς   680 ⊥ Ο¹
        ἕνεκα πρὸς ἡμᾶς, γραῦ; [τ]ί π[λ]είστων κε[ι]μ[ένων
        μόνη 'στὶ λήψεως [ἐκείνη; γνοῦσα γὰρ
        εὔδηλος εἶ. ψοφεῖν [δὲ προ]ίων φαίν[ε]τα[ι   ⊤ Ο¹
        αὐτῶν τις, ὥστε πάντ' ἀκούσομαι σαφῶ[ς.
Γε   ὦ Ζεῦ πολυτίμητ', ὠμότητος ἐκτόπου   685
        ἀμφοῖν ἀπανθρώπου τε, νὴ τὸν Ἥλιον.
(Κλ)   ξένος τις εἰσελήλυθ' ἀρτίως, Γέτα,
        ἐνθάδε πρὸς ὑμᾶς;
Γε   Ἡράκλεις, αὐθαδίας·
        ἐρῶντος ἀξίου τ' ἀπ' ἀν]θ[ρ]ώπου λαβεῖν

---

669 ἀπαξάπαντα Turner: ἀπαξάπαν γε τῆς cj. Arnott   679 -680 suppl. Turner
681 τί πλείστων κειμένων leg. suppl. Furley, -ειστων iam leg. Coles   682 μόνη
'στί Furley: μόνης τί al.   al. e.g. Furley   683 Sandbach: ἐψόφηκ[ε· προ]ϊὼν φ-
Turner   687 εισεληλυθεν Π   689 suppl. e.g. Furley

54 CHAPTER 2. GREEK TEXT

<pre>
          γυναῖκ[α.
Κλ   ἀκούει δ᾽ οὗτος οὐδὲν ὅ]τι λαλῶ.   690
(Γε)   φ[   ]
Κλ   ] Δημέας
            . [   ] . [. .]
Γε   ἐκεῖ]νος μ[η]δὲ γρῦ
            .].[.   «   ]σα [κ]αὶ γ[ά]ρ, Δημέα,
            φ[ιλῶ Κρά]τει[α]ν αὐτός, ὡς ὁρᾶις, ἐγώ,
            σὺ δ᾽ εἶ πατ]ὴρ ‹καὶ› κύριος.» ταυτὶ λέγει   695
            ἐλεινὰ κλάων, ἀντιβολῶν. ὄνος λύρας.
(Κλ)   σ]υμπεριπατήσω καὐτός, ὡς ἐμοὶ δοκῶ.
Γε   ἓν τοῦτο δ᾽ εἴρει· «τὴν ἐμαυτοῦ σ᾽ ἀξιῶ
            ἥκω[ν] ἀπολυτροῦν ὧν πατήρ.» «ἐγὼ δέ γε
            αἰτῶ γυναῖκά σ᾽ ἐντετυχηκώς, Δημέα».   700
Κλ   ἔνδ[ον] μ[έ]ν ἐσθ᾽ ἄνθρωπος εἰσεληλυθώς·
            τοὔν[ο]μα λέγει γὰρ οὑτοσὶ τὸν Δημέαν.
Γε   ὦ ['Ηρ]άκλεις· ἀνθρωπίνως ἂν οὐ λάβοι
            τὸ συμβεβηκός; ὖς ὄρει, τὸ τοῦ λόγου.
            ἀλλ᾽ οὐχὶ τοῦτο δεινόν, ἀλλ᾽ αὕτη πάλιν   705
            ὑ[φο]ρᾶι βοῶντος· «ἀντιβολῶ, Κράτεια, σέ,
            μή μ᾽ ἐγκαταλίπηις· παρθένον σ᾽ εἴ[λ]ηφ᾽ ἐγώ,
            ἀ]νὴρ ἐκλήθην πρῶτος, ἠγάπησά σε,
            ἀγ]απῶ, φιλῶ, Κράτεια φιλτάτη· τί σοι
            λυ]πηρόν ἐστ[ι] τῶν παρ᾽ ἐμοί; τεθνηκότα   710
            πεύσει μ᾽ ἐάν μ᾽ ἐγκαταλίπηις.» οὐδ᾽ ἀπόκρισις.
(Κλ)   τί ποτ᾽ [ἐ]στὶ τὸ κακόν;
Γε   βάρβαρος, λ[έ]αινά τις
            ἄν[θρωπος.
Κλ   οὐ]χ ὁρᾶις με, κακόδαιμον, πάλαι;
(Γε)   ἀπρο[σδόκη]τον.
(Κλ)   οὐχ ὑγιαίνει παντελῶς.
Γε   ἐγὼ μὲν [αὐτήν], μὰ τὸν Ἀπόλλω τουτονί,   715
            οὐκ ἂν ἀπ[έ]λυσ᾽. Ἑλληνικὸν καὶ πανταχ[ῆ
</pre>

⊥ Ο[1]

---

690 suppl. e.g. ante λαλῶ Furley (ιλαλω Ο[10]): πῶς τουτὶ λάβω Arnott (]τιλ..ῶ κλεινΟ[1])   692 ἐκεῖνος suppl. Arnott   693 suppl. Handley   694 suppl. e.g. Sandbach   695 σὺ δ᾽ εἶ suppl. e.g. Sandbach, πατὴρ καὶ Turner   696 ἐλεινὰ Furley (ἐλεεινά iam Kumaniecki): ἅπαντα Sisti   697 συμ- Wilamowitz   698 εἴρει dub. Turner, edd.: ἔρρει olim Furley (tum Blanchard)   704 ὄρει edd. pl.: ὀρεῖ (< ὀρεύς) Kells, Turner   705 αλλα ταυτη παλιν Ο[3]   706 ὑφορᾶι βοῶντος Furley, ἀφορᾶι λέγοντος iam Austin, edd. pl.   κρατια Ο[3]   707 -λειπης Ο[3], corr. suppl. Turner   713 fin. γετα del., πάλαι s.l. Ο[3]

Act Four   55

γιν[όμε]ν̣ον ἴσμεν. ἀλλ’ ἐλεεῖν ὀρθῶς ἔχει
τὸν ἀ̣[ν]τελεοῦνθ’. ὅταν δὲ μηδ’ ὑμεῖ[ς ἐ]μέ,
⌊οὐδὲ λόγον ὑμῶν οὐδ’ ἐπιστροφὴν ἔχω.⌋
«οὐ̣[κ ἔστι] σοι;» τί δ’; [ο]ὐθὲν ἄτοπον, ὡς ἐγὼ   720
δο̣[κῶ.] βοήσεται δὲ καὶ βουλεύσεται
κ̣[τα]νεῖν ἑαυτόν. στὰς βλέπει δὲ πῦρ ἅμα,
οὐ̣[δὲ̣] κ̣α̣τ̣ά̣κει[τ]α̣ι, δράτ̣τ̣εταί ⟨τε⟩ τῶν τριχῶν.

ΚΛ   ἄν̣[θρωπε], κ̣αταꭓ̣όψεις με.

Γε   χαῖρε, Κλεινία.
π[όθεν πάρ]ε̣σθ’;

ΚΛ   οὑμός τι θορυβεῖν φαίνεται   725
ἐν]δὸ̣[ν παρε]λθὼν φ . [. .] . ε̣ι . ὡς ὁ ξένος
                ‥[

(?)   ‥[

                        ] ‥[
                        ] . ο̣ι δευτερ . [730
                    ] . ν̣ου καλ . . . [
τα‥[   ] . [.] ‥ [   ] ‥ [   ]ν[
‥[   ]ἔγωγε:

Γε   εἰσ . . . . . . , Κ[λε]ινία
ΚΛ̣   ουκ[. . . . . . ‥] . α . δυ̣ . [. . . .] πρὸς θεῶν·
εὐεργ[ετ‥‥] . ρ . [‥] . [Δ]ημέα[ς̣:]

[Κ]λ   . η . αρ ‥   735
‥εγ . [. . . .] ‥ ἐξ[έρ]ꭓ[ετα]ι, Γέτα[

(?Γε)   . . . . ‥] . [. . . .]με[. . .] . . . μὲν ‥ [
. [. . . . . . ‥] . . . [
‥ [. .] . [   ] . επ[. . .] ‥ γ’[. .] . νος[

(?ΚΛ)   ἐγὼ [‥] . . . [. ἀ̣]ϕ̣ῆ̣κε̣ γὰρ   740
[Γε]   . ε . . . . [. . . . . . ‥]νο[μί]ζεται
(ΚΛ)   εἰσέρχο[μαι . . . .] ‥ [. . .]που σϕ[ό]δρα
(Γε)   τὸ μὲν̣[. . . . . . ‥‥] . . . . ν [‥] . ρ̣ι̣σ̣τα . ο[
‥ [. . . . . ‥‥] ‥ [. . . . . ‥]] ‥ βι̣ο̣[
[ο]ὔ ϕησι [‥] . [. . . .] δια . [745
‥]λ . ꞓ . . ο[. . . . . . ‥] . σ . α[. . . . .] . [
‥] . α[.]ι̣[‥] ‥ [. . . . . . ‥] . αꞓ[‥] . [

---

719 Et. magn. 58.43-45 Gaisford, Et. gen. 1.416.1-3 Lasserre-Livadaras   721 δοκῶ
Mette   βουλευ\ϭ/εται O³   722 κτανεῖν Webster   723 οὐδὲ κατάκειται, ⟨τε⟩
Furley, ⟨γε⟩ al.   724 ἄνθρωπε Turner, χαῖρε Handley   725 πόθεν Handley   726
in. ἐνδὸν παρ- suppl. Austin e.g.   734 δυοῖν possis   πρὸς Blanchard, Furley   735
[Δ]ημέα Turner   736 ἐξέρχεται Furley   740 fin. ἀϕῆκε vel παρῆκε possis   741
fin. suppl. e.g. Furley

56 CHAPTER 2. GREEK TEXT

		. .] . . τ[. .] . . [. . . . .] . . . τα . [.] κατὰ τὸ μ̣[
(Κλ?)		‗πό[ει] δὲ τ[οῦ]το πρ[ὶν π]ες[εῖν] ἐμπειρίαι.
(Γε?)		‗γ . [.]λ̣[. . . . .]α[.]ι̣[. . .] κ̣α̣ὶ πλά̣νης γεν[-. 750

Τ Ο⁹	(Θρ?)	.] . .ι[.] . . [. . .]τὴν [ἀργ]ίαν, α . . . . . ε παῖ;[
	(?)	. . . .] . α[. . . .] . . . . . Κρά]τειαν ἐξαγε[
Τ Ο¹²		κ̣[.]ι̣ . α[. . . . . δ]ακρύει, Δημέα
		‗.]ι . [. . . . . .]α[. . . .] . . [.]αι [μονό]νουχι μικρὰ Κλε[ινι-

	(Κρ)	.] . ι[. . . . .] ἑα̣υ̣τόν, τάλα[ν.[755

	(Δη)	‗εν . . [. . . . .] . . . . . τα δεῦρο, θυγάτριο[ν.
⊥ Ο⁹	(Θρ)	ὅλ]ως με μικρόψ[υ]χον εἶπέ τι[ς], τυχόν,
		ὁ]ρ̣ῶν ἀλύονθ᾽ ὧ[δε] πολ[λ]ὰ πρ[άγ]ματ[α·
		εἰ δ᾽ ἐς μέσον γ[. . . . .] π[ερ]ι̣φέρ[ε]ι̣[ς καὶ νοεῖς,
		ἑτέροις τί τοῦτ᾽ [ἄ]ν αὐ . . . . . ελ[. . . .; ὅμως 760
		ἔστω στέγειν με καὶ λίθον ψυχὴν φ[ορε]ῖ̣[ν
		ποεῖ⟨ν⟩ τ᾽ ἄδηλον τοῖς συνοῦσι τὴν νόσ[ον.
		δυνήσ[ομα]ι . [. . . .]ι̣ς̣ο̣ι . . ., Γέτα; τίνα
		τρόπον κ̣αθέξω τ̣ο̣ῦτο καὶ ῥᾳ̣[ον] φέρω;
		⌊ἀπαμφιεῖ γὰρ τὸ κατάπλαστον τοῦτό μου 765
		καὶ λανθάνειν βουλόμενον ἡ μέθη ποτέ.⌋
		ἀσχημονήσω δ᾽ ἡνίκ[
		. . .]ι . . [ἔ]φθαρμ̣αι δ᾽ . . . [
		] . . [. . . .] . . [. .]ςθ᾽ ον . . [
		ἀλλ᾽ ἐμφανίζω[770
		] . . . . κ̣ακὸν [] . [
⊥ Ο¹²		. . .]υτον ο̣ . . [] . . α̣α[

---

748 fin. vel κατὰ τὸ μ̣[749 πρὶν πεσεῖν ἐμπειρίαι e.g. Furley, ἐμπειρία iam Turner
750 κ̣α̣ὶ πλά̣νης Coles ap. Turner, fin. e.g. γένοιτό γ᾽ ἄν.   751 τὴν μωρίαν vel
ἀργίαν e.g. Furley   fin. ἄπληστε παῖ Turner   752 suppl. Parsons: fin. περὶ Ο³
leg. Coles ap. Turner   754 μονόνουχι suppl. Furley: οὐχί al.   756 θυγάτριον
Austin   757 ὅλως vel ἴσως in. e.g. Furley   εἶπέ τις edd.   758 in. ὁρῶν . . . ὧδε
suppl. Henry   πολλὰ πράγματα Turner   759 εἰ δ᾽ ἐς μέσον Turner, al. Furley
e.g.   760 ἑτέροις τί τοῦτ- Turner, ἂν αὐ Furley   761 ἔστω στέγειν Sandbach:
ἔστω· στέγειν e.g. Turner: ἔστ᾽ ὥστ᾽ ἔχειν Handley   φορεῖν Furley: φέρειν edd.
763 Γέτα; suppl. dub. Furley   764 suppl. Turner   765 -766 Synagōgē cod. B α
1600 Cunningham = Suda α 2891 = Phot. α 2245   767 δ᾽ ἡνίκ᾽ ἂν dub. Henry   768
leg. suppl. Furley   772 vel]υτο νο-

Act Four   57

(Between the last traces of O^{12} and first legible traces of page D horizontal fibres fr. A, parts a + b, of O^3 at least one verse is missing, perhaps more. Here, until line **919**, the line numbering must depart from Arnott and Blanchard, because they do not reposition the fragment of O^3 according to the evidence of O^{12}. Blanchard acknowledges the traces of O^{12} but relegates them to a note.)

<pre>
                    ] . [   ] . . [
[. . . .]κ . [   ] . [775
. . . [. .] . [. .] . [. .] . [
ἐ[γ]ὼ γὰρ ἔτι τοῦτ' οὔ[πο]τ' ἀ[
ἀγαπωμένη παρ' ἐ[μ]ο[ῦ   (770 Bl)
οὐχ ἡρμόσαμεν αὐτο[
ὀδύν[ας ἐ]νέγκα[ς] εὖ θ' . [. . . .] . [780
εἴπηι προσελθὼν . π . . . τυλη[
ἔστιν, Κράτειά, σοι καθίζεσθ[αι ‿—
λυπρὰ κατ[αδ]έσματ' α[-   (775 Bl)
ἐγώ τε τ . . [. . . . . . τ]οῦτο[
εἴπα[ς] ἔκλα[ιον . .] . . . α[785
ἀ]λλ' ἄψατ' ο[. . . .] . [. .]α βρόχ[
ἔτι βέλ[τιον
ἄπασι[.] . [(780 Bl)
ἀλλ' ὥσπ[ε]ρ ϊ . . . . [ἀ]λλὰ τί;
. . . . . . [   ]έχει   790
.] . . . [   ]εδυν
      ]υ προς[   ] . [   ]ια[
      ] . τοκ . [. . . . .] . . [. .]ιαν[(785 Bl) ⊤ O^8
[± 6   ]εἴ πως εἴρ[ηκ . [. . . .] . . . . [
. . .] κρίνηι γὰρ εἰ τὴν α[ἰτί]αν . . . . [795
. .] . γὰρ φράσαι . . . τον [. .] . ο . ωτ . [
ἐ]ξῆλθεν ἐκ [.] . . . . συν . [. . . . .] . . . . . . [
ὀργῆι σ', ἐλεεινός. Σιμίχ[η 'ξ]ελήλ[υθεν.   (790 Bl)
τί] φήις; «πέπονθ' ἄπα[ν]θ'»; ὑπὲρ ταύτης λαλ[εῖς;
μ]έλει τ' ἐμοὶ ταύτης δι' ἐμαυτόν; μὴ λέγε.   800
</pre>

---

777 ἔτι, οὔποτ' ἀ[Furley   778 παρ' ἐμοῦ Furley   780 vel ἐνέγκασ' leg. suppl. Furley: νκα[ms.   781 ἐπὶ κοτύληι ? Furley   783 leg. suppl. Furley, vel λυγρὰ in. possis   784 inter lin. postea script.   786 fin. βρόχ- possis   787 suppl. Furley   794 vel εἶπ' ὡς εἴρ[ηκ- 795 κρινη γὰρ εἰ leg. Furley, fort. ἀποκρινῆι (fut.): κρινεῖ τὴν αἰτίαν Maehler   796 in. ἅμα possis   797 Furley: ἐξῆλθ' Turner, ἔνε[[κ]]ˈχ' leg. Blanchard   798 ὀργῆι σ' Handley, Arnott: ὀργῆς Turner   Σιμίχη 'ξελήλυθεν dist. Handley, 'ξελήλυθεν leg. suppl. Maehler   799 «τί» φῆις «πέπονθε;» dist. Handley   ἄπανθ' corr. Maehler   λαλεῖς suppl. Turner

58 CHAPTER 2. GREEK TEXT

ἄπαν ἀτύχημα τοῦτ'· ἐκεῖ[νον μὴ] ψέγω·
ο]ὐκοῦν ἕν ἐστι τοῦτό σοι, τὸ κωλύ[ει]ν
ταύτην ἀπολαβεῖν τοῦτ[ον· ‹ἀλλὰ› παντ]αχοῦ   (795 Bl)
οὕτως ἔχει. πρόσθεν γενό[μενα ἀπ]ώ[λ]ε[σε
τὸ ζῆν. ἀφήσεις; ἀλλ' ἐρεῖ· «θέλ[εις, τά]λαν,   805
οἴκτωι τὸ μισοῦν ὡς σεαυτὸν [ἐλ]κ[ύσαι;]»
καὶ τίς ὁ βίος σοι; ποῦ τὸ τῆ[ς σ]ωτ[ηρ]ία[ς
ἐ]πίσημον; εἴ τις ὁμ[ό]σε ται[ς ὀ]ργαῖς [τρέχ]οι –   (800 Bl)
πλεονεξία τοῦτ' – εἴ[περ; ἁ]ρπάσαι βλ[έ]πων
ἴσως ἰταμὸς εἶ τότε· λογισμῶι νῦν γενοῦ   810
εὔψυχος. ἀ[πό]ρως ζῆις, ὀδυνηρῶς, [ἀσ]θενῶ[ς –
ὄν[ε]ιδος αὐτῆι τοῦτο καταλιπεῖν σε δεῖ
ἀθάνατον. εὖ παθοῦσ' ἐτιμωρήσατο   (805 Bl)
τὸν τἀγάθ' αὐτῆι δόντα· πῶς ο[ὐ]κ ἔ[σ]τι μοι
αὐτὸν κτα]νεῖν με προσποου[μένωι μόνον   815
τὸν παῖδα π]έμψαι τοῦτον εἰ[ς τὴν οἰκίαν·
          ]εν.δ[. .]ησθαι[.]εσ[
      ] γὰρ [. . ἐσ]τιν οὕτω [(810 Bl)
        ] . [   ]ωσηκ . . . [
          τ]ύχοις ἂν εἰ[820
          ]τισπα[.]η[
          ] ἀνοσιωτ[ατ-
          ]ησιν τιν . [(815 Bl)
          κ]αὶ τρισαθλ[ι-

      [ΧΟΡΟ]Υ

⊥ O³

Act Five

---

801 ἄπαν Furley: ἐμόν et ἐκεῖνον leg. suppl. Maehler, μὴ Handley   802 ἕν ἐστι
Handley: ἔνεστι Turner, Maehler   τὸ (vel τι) κωλύειν leg. suppl. Maehler   803
τοῦτον suppl. Maehler et ἀλλὰ add. m. c.   πανταχοῦ Austin: πολλαχοῦ Turner
804 γενόμενα ἀπώλεσε (script. plen.) Furley: γενόμεν' iam Maehler   fin.
ἀνατρέπει cj. Handley   805 θέλεις Furley: θέλξεις H.Maehler: ἐρεῖς, ἕλξεις Handley   τάλαν dub. M. Maehler: ἅπαν Handley   806 sic div. edd. pl.: post μισοῦν
dist. Maehler   ἑλκύσαι Furley: ἀσχαλᾶις cj. M. Maehler   808 leg. suppl. Handley (ὀργαῖς iam dub. Maehler)   809 εἴπερ Handley   810 ex τότε τῶι λογ- corr.
M. Maehler   γενοῦ Maehler   811 ζῆις Maehler: ζῆθ' Handley   ἀσθενῶς M.
Maehler   812 αὐτῆι et καταλειπειν O³ vid. hab.   813 ἐτιμωρήσατο leg. suppl.
Maehler   815 suppl. e.g. Furley: κτανεῖν vel ἀνελεῖν με προσποούμενον iam M.
Maehler   816 suppl. e.g. M. Maehler   821 πάθηι vel σπά[θ]η possis

Act Five   59

(Γε?)   ] . αυτὸν ν[825
                                  ὀδύ]νηρον . [
                                  ] τὸ φάρμ[ακον
                                  ]εστ[(820 Bl)
                                  ]ρ.[⊥ O⁸

(Gap of about 98 lines probably including the following fragments. In this gap must have fallen the scene illustrated in the Mytilene mosaic, as it is clearly marked 'act five'. From line 919 we can return to Blanchard's line numbering, as the number of lines missing (for example between 829 and 919) is approximate.)

                                  ]εις   ⊤ O²
                                  ]   920
                                  ]ς
                                  ]ν
                                  ]θη
                                  ]
                    ]] . [925
                                  ]ν κακόν
                                  ]
                                  ]αι
                                  ]
                                  ]   930
                                  ]παρῆν
                                  ] .   ⊥ O²

                    (gap of between 11 and 17 lines)

(?ΚΡΑΤΕΙΑΣ ΑΔΕΛΦΟΣ)
                    οὐκέτ[ι   ⊤ O²
                    Θρασω[νιδ
                    τί τάνα[950
                    καλῶς [
                    οὐ παιδ[
                    ζηλοτυπ[
                    ἃ νῦν λε[γ
                    εἰς τοὔρ[γον   955

---

826 suppl. Furley   949 fr. 6 pot. ibi colloc. μισοῦσι μὲν / Θρασωνίδην, ὦ πάτερ, ἀπεκτάγκασι δ' οὔ.

60 CHAPTER 2. GREEK TEXT

		διακοσι[-
		νὴ Δία, τ[
	Γε	ἀναγε[.] . [
		ἀπὸ τῆς [θύ]ρας, ἄνθρ[ωπ', ἄπιθι.
	(Θρ)	τί τοῦτο παῖ;
		φαίνει γὰρ ἀγαθὸν ν[ῦν ἐπαγγελῶν τί μοι. 960
	(Γε)	διδόασί σοι γυναῖκα [τὴν ἐρωμένην.
	(Θρ)	προσευξάμην ταῦ[τ' . . . [
	(Γε)	οὕτως ἀγαθὸ[ν] γέ[νοιτό σοι
	(Θρ)	οὐκ ἐξα[π]ατᾶ‹ι›ς δὲ [
		πῶς εἶπεν;
	(Γε)	Ἡρ[άκλεις, 965
	(Θρ)	τὰ ῥήματ' αὐτά μοι [πατρὸς τοῦ Δημέου
		λέγων τάχα τρέχ' εἰ[ς ἐμοῦ
	(Γε)	ἔλεγεν «θυγάτριον, [ἄνδρα βούλει τόνδ' ἔχειν;»
		«ναί», φησι, «πάπ‹π›α, βούλ[ομαι· πρὶν γὰρ κακὰ
		ἤκουσ'· ἃ δ' ἤκουσ' ἀ[ν]α[λελύσθαι νῦν δοκεῖ.» 970
		ἐκπλεῖ γελῶσά γ' ἠπί[ως
	(Θρ)	ἀγαθὰ λέγεις.
	(Γε)	ἐφήδομ'. ἀ[λλὰ τὴν θύραν
		ψοφεῖ τις αὐτῶν.
	Δη	πρ[ὸς σὲ νῦν ἐξέρχομαι.
	[Θρ]	καλῶς ποιῶν.
	(Δη)	παίδ[ων ἐπ' ἀρότωι γνησίων
		δίδωμι τὴν ἐμὴν θυγατέρα [σοι γαμεῖν 975
		καὶ δύο τάλαντα προῖκ' [ἐπ' αὐτῆι.
	(Θρ)	λαμβάνω]
		μόνον ἀπόδος σύ, Δημέ[α, τὴν παῖδ' ἐμοί.
		πάντας γὰρ ἀντε[ιρημένους ταύτηι λόγους
		ἀπὸ ταὐτομάτου [τὰ γ]εν[όμεν' ἐξέλυσε νῦν.
		δεῖπνον ξένια κ[αὶ 980

---

959 ἄνθρωπ' suppl. Turner, ἄπιθι e.g. Arnott, τί τοῦτο παῖ; Sisti   960 φαίνει Handley   fin. suppl. e.g. Furley   961 τὴν ἐρωμένην cj. Furley e.g.   962 ταῦ[τ' leg. suppl. Furley   963 ἀγαθὸν γένοιτο Turner, σοι Furley   966 suppl. e.g. Furley   967 τρέχεις Turner: τρέχ' ει[Arnott: εἰς ἐμοῦ Furley   968 suppl. e.g. Furley: [τοῦτον ἂν βούλοι' ἔχειν] Arnott e.g.   969 suppl. e.g. Furley   970 ἀναλελύσθαι (Blume *per litt.*) vel ἀνατετράφθαι suppl. e.g. Furley   971 ἐκπλεῖ et ἠπίως leg. suppl. Furley   972 ἐφήδομ'. ἀλλὰ Furley (ἐφήδομαι iam Turner)   973 suppl. e.g. Webster   974 suppl. Webster   977 τὴν παῖδ' cj. Furley: τὴν θυγατέρ' (sic iam Sandbach) ἐμοί Blanchard, *contra metr.*   978 suppl. e.g. Furley   979 suppl. e.g. Furley

Unplaced papyrus fragments

ἀλλ’ εἰσί[ωμ]εν … [
γε[.] .. […..] .. [
πα . [
ἐπ’ αὔρ[ιον
.] . [.]οπ[….. .]α[985
ἐστ’ ἔνδο[ν

(Δη)   σὺ πρ[ό]φ[ερε] τ[ο]ί[ν]υν.[
εἶ[έ]ν· μετέμελ’ αὐτ[ῆι
παιδάριον, ἅψας δᾶι[δας ἡμῖν ἐκδίδου,
στεφάνους τ’ ἔ[.] …… .. [990
καὶ μηδέπω δειπν[
προσμείνατ’ ἐπ … [
ὑμᾶς ν … [..] . λ .. · μ[ειράκια, παῖδες καλοί,
ἄνδρες πρεπόντως πά[ντες ἐπικροτήσατε·
ἡ δ’ εὐπάτειρα φιλογέ[λως τε παρθένος   995
Νίκη μεθ’ ἡμῶν εὐ[μενὴς ἔποιτ’ ἀεί.

MENANΔ[POY
Θρασωνί[δης ἢ Μισούμενος]
εὔνοιαν τῶι ἀναγ[ιγνώσκοντι καὶ]
τῶι γράφ[οντι]   ⊥ O³

Unplaced papyrus fragments

1. O⁴ (Turner)

A very thin sliver of O⁴ remains unplaced:

1] . [/ 2]δεκ[/ 3]ων[/ 4]υκ[/ 5] … [/ 6] . φ . [/ 7] … [/ 8]ειν[/
9] .. ς[/ 10] … [/ 11]ψ . [/ 12]ςυν[/ 13] . εδ[/ 14]φοι[/ 15] . μα[/
16]ισν[/ 17]χοι[

2. O⁸ fr. 3

[   ] . [
[   ]οςη . [
[   ] . οιν . [

---

987 leg. suppl. Furley: οὐ προφέρετε Turner

```
[          ]ϲ δυ̣ο̣[
[        σπ]άθην [                              5
[        νο]μίζω[
```

3. O¹¹ fr. 2

Although fr. 2 of O¹¹ is conjecturally placed in Composite Readings (lines 509-24), this position is by no means certain, and it may be worth repeating the readings here, including possible supplements.

```
]ϲτεθ̣[
]ο̣η . ε . [
] . . τηδ̣[
]κατη[
]αντ . [                                        5
] . λον . [
] . . ρε̣ν̣ . [
      χρ
] ἀ̣τυχῷ[
] ἐγῷδα δ[
] κ̣ακὸν [                                      10
ο]ὕτωϲ ἔ̣[χει
]α̣τον:[
      γ . .
] . :τί̣   ϲυ̣[
] παϲι τ[
] . . . . ϲ[                                    15
        ] . [
```

4. O¹¹ fr. 3

```
      ?n.p.
]ρ̣ϲ̣ι̣ . [
]το̣υτ[
] . κειν[
]περανα[
]νεϲτ᾽ ε[                                       5
]ϲτι̣ . α[
] . ο[[τ̣ι̣. ]]π̣[] . [
] . ει[
] . [
```

Unplaced book fragments   63

5. Fragmentum dubium: P. Berol. 8450

×—◡—]πρὸς ἐμαυτὸν[
×—◡—τ]ὴν Χρυσίδ᾽[
×—◡—] τοῦτον εἰ[
×—◡] . ἐκείνην [
×—◡—]ν· τίνα γὰρ α[5
×—◡]εστ᾽ ἐλευθ[ερ
×—◡— τρ]ίχας τ᾽ ἐτιλ[λ-
×—◡—]ν πρώ[η]ν ε[
×—◡—]ε· καὶ τ[.]δε.[
     ]ι γὰρ κ[α]τῆλ[θε   10
     ] ἀνάγ[κ]ας [
     διδα]σκαλο[.] δε[
     ] γὰρ ἐκ[.] . δ[
     ] ἀτυχει[.] τα[
     ]τωϲ[. .]λ . [15
     ] και[. .]ο[
     ]ουτω[
     ]ετο[
     ]υλε[
     ]πα[20
     ]ϲϲ[

Miscellaneous unplaced book fragments

1. Epictetus *Dissertationes ab Arriano digestae* 4.1.19; cf. Clemens (*Strom.* 2.15.62.2)

 ἀλλ᾽ εἰ σὺ αἰσχύνῃ τὰ σαυτοῦ ὁμολογεῖ⟨ν⟩, ὅρα ἃ λέγει καὶ ποιεῖ ὁ Θρασωνίδης, ὃς τοσαῦτα στρατευσάμενος, ὅσα τάχα οὐδὲ σύ, πρῶτον μὲν
ἐξελήλυθε νυκτός, ὅτε ὁ Γέτας οὐ τολμᾷ ἐξελθεῖν, ἀλλ᾽ εἰ προσηναγκάζετο ὑπ᾽ αὐτοῦ, πόλλ᾽ ἂν ἐπικραυγάσας καὶ τὴν πικρὰν δουλείαν ἀπολοφυράμενος ἐξῆλθεν. εἶτα, τί λέγει;

    παιδισκάριόν με, [φησίν], καταδεδούλωκ᾽ εὐτελές,
    ὃν οὐδ⟨ὲ⟩ εἷς τῶν πολεμίων ⟨οὐ⟩πώποτε.

τάλας, ὅς γε καὶ παιδισκαρίου δοῦλος εἶ καὶ παιδισκαρίου εὐτελοῦς. τί
οὖν ἔτι σαυτὸν ἐλεύθερον λέγεις; τί δὲ προφέρεις σου τὰς στρατε⟨ί⟩ας; εἶτα
ξίφος αἰτεῖ καὶ πρὸς τὸν ὑπ᾽ εὐνοίας μὴ διδόντα χαλεπαίνει καὶ δῶρα τῇ

64　　　　　　　　　　　　　　*CHAPTER 2. GREEK TEXT*

μισούσῃ πέμπει καὶ δεῖται καὶ κλαίει, πάλιν δὲ μικρὰ εὐημερήσας ἐπαίρεται·
_____

1 καταδεδούλωκ᾽ corr. Salmasius: καταδεδούλωκεν Arrian　　2 οὐδὲ εἷς corr. Κο-
ραῒς p. 404: οὐδεὶς Arrian　　οὐ- add. Meineke

2. (7). Schol. in Hom. *Od.* 17.442 see p. 41.

3. (12) Pollux 10.145.5-146.2
ὅτι δὲ καὶ τὴν σπάθην ἐπὶ τοῦ ξίφους εἰρήκασιν … καὶ ἐν τῶι Μισουμένωι
Μένανδρος, ὅταν λέγηι

　　　ἀφανεῖς γεγόνασιν αἱ σπάθαι

4. (4) Ps.-Justinian Mart. *De mon.* 5.107CD p. 142 Otto
Ἐν Μισουμένωι δὲ πάλιν ἀποφαίνων περὶ τῶν εἰς θεοὺς παραλαμβανο-
μένων τὰς γνώμας, μᾶλλον δὲ ἐλέγχων ὡς οὐκ ὄντας, ὁ αὐτὸς Μέναν-
δρος·

　　　εἰ γὰρ ἐπίδοιμι τοῦτο, κἂν ψυχὴν <πάλιν>
　　　λάβοιμ᾽ ἐγώ· νυνὶ γάρ – ἀλλὰ ποῦ θεοὺς
　　　οὕτω δικαίους ἔστιν εὑρεῖν, ὦ Γέτα;

　　　1. πάλιν add. Bentley CV

5. (10) Schol. in Aristoph. *Thesm.* 423 = Sud. λ 64
Μένανδρος Μισουμένωι (Μισουμέναις Sud.)·

　　　Λακωνικὴ κλείς ἐστιν, ὡς ἔοικέ, μοι
　　　περιοιστέα

καί φασιν (καί φασιν om. Sud.) ὅτι ἔξωθεν περικλείεται μοχλοῦ παρατιθε-
μένου (περι- Sud.) ἤ τινος τοιούτου, ὥστε τοῖς ἔνδον μὴ εἶναι ἀνοῖξαι.

6. (13) Orus fr. 35 καὶ ἀπεκτόνασιν, οὐκ ἀπεκτάγκασιν. Μισουμένωι· **πάτερ
μὲν Θράσωνι, ἀπεκτόνασι δ᾽ ου.**
Lex. Seg. α p. 126.21-22 Bachmann s.v. ἀποκτίννυσιν (…) καὶ ἀπεκτόνασιν,
οὐκ ἀπεκτάγκασι. Μισουμένωι· **πάτερ μὲν Θράσων᾽, ἀπεκτάγκασι δ᾽ οὔ.**
Suda α 3000 vel 3372· ἀπεκτάγκασι, καὶ ἀπεκτόνασι· **μισοῦσι μέν, ὦ πάτερ, Θράσωνα, ἀπεκτάγκασι δ᾽ οὔ.**
Text corrected by Dobree (p. 277):

Unplaced book fragments 65

μισοῦσι μὲν
Θρασωνίδην, ὦ πάτερ, ἀπεκτάγκασι δ᾽ οὔ

7. (14) Phot. σ 429 **σπαθᾶν**· Μένανδρος Μισουμένωι· τὸ ἀλαζονεύεσθαι.

8. Phot. ε 893 **ἐνερόχρως**· νεκρόχρως· Μένανδρος Μισουμένωι.

9. Photius α 2519 (cf. *Lexica Segueriana* α page 125.24; *Suda* α 3362, line 1) Μένανδρος <Μισουμένωι>. **<Ἀπόκνιζε>**· ἀπόσκαλλε, ἀπότιλλε.

Fragmentum dubium

Hermeias ad Platonis *Phaedrum* p. 33.16 Couvreur

οὐπώποτ᾽ ἠράσθης, Γέτα;
(Γε.) οὐ γὰρ ἐνεπλήσθην.

Chapter 3

Composite Readings

The purpose of this section is twofold. On the one hand it aims to unburden the *apparatus* at points in the text where multiple papyri permit a reconstuction of continuous text; on the other it aims to facilitate understanding of this reconstruction for the reader. They can see for themselves which letters come from which papyri, where they overlap, where there are still gaps etc. It should be emphasized that the readings given below do not constitute a re-edition of the papyri. They do not supplant or replace the authoritative publication of these papyri in any way. Nevertheless, I have checked the originals of the papyri wherever possible, and good photographs wherever not, and have tried to form my own judgement as to which letters can be read. For this reason readers will find minor discrepancies between some of the readings given below and those printed in the papyrological editions. Where there are discrepancies these represent places, of course, where readings are difficult and doubtful. At such points certainty does not exist, and we must all be cautious. I have tried to steer a course between respect for the original publications and a certain independence of judgement. One can make serious mistakes by adopting others' readings without checking them oneself, as the slightest error in the original publication – for example, a misplaced or missing square bracket – if reproduced, perpetuates the illusion of a certain reading where there is none. Finally, I hope setting out the fragments like this will allow others to share the fun of reconstructing Menander from a diversity of traces on papyrus. Establishing a text at such points is like walking on the smallest of stepping stones through a worryingly deep river.

I use the manuscript sigla as given at the beginning of the text. I use lunate sigma instead of the conventional two sigma shapes used in the main text (which make reading somewhat easier).

- I+K = *PIFAO* inv. 89^v lines 1-17 + P.Köln 7.282^v
- B^1 = P.Berlin 13281, lines 567-578, 611-622

CHAPTER 3. COMPOSITE READINGS

- B^2 = P.Berlin 13932, lines 532-544, 560-572

- O^1 = P.Oxy. 1013, lines 644-665 (frr. 1-5 verso), 677-700 (frr. 1-4 recto)

- O^2 = P.Oxy. 1605, lines 919-932, 948-974

- O^3 = P.Oxy. 2656, lines 501-814 (806 Bl), 959-996

- O^4 = P.Oxy. 2657, lines 401-492 + letters from 17 other lines

- O^5 = P.Oxy. 3368, lines 1-18, 33-45, 51-68, 85-100, fr. C (? end of Act One) (241-247 Bl)

- O^6 = P.Oxy. 3369, lines 12-54, 78-94

- O^7 = P.Oxy. 3370, lines 30-43

- O^{7b} = P.Oxy. 3371, with play's title

- O^8 = P.Oxy. 3967, lines 793-829 (784-821 Bl)

- O^9 = P.Oxy. 4025, ?lines 751-757 (= fr. 3 Arnott, fr. 11 Blanchard)

- O^{10} = P.Oxy. 4408, lines 552-559

- O^{11} = P.Oxy. 5198, lines 523-554

- O^{12} = P.Oxy. 5199, lines 753-772 (753-766 Bl)

Lines 1-45

$\begin{cases} \text{I+K} \\ \text{O}^5 \end{cases}$
I+K   ]πλειστον αφροδειτης με[
O⁵   ω νυξ cυ γαρ δη πλειστον αφ[...]ειτης μερος

I+K   ]ν: εν coι τε περι τουτων λο[
O⁵   μετεχειc θεων· εν coι τε π[..]ι τουτων λογοι

I+K   ]νται φροντιδεc τ ερωτ[
O⁵   πλειcτοι λεγονται φροντιδ.[...]ρωτ[.]και

I+K   ]ωπων [[τινα]] αθλιωτατο[
O⁵   αρα αλλον ανθρωπων[.....]θλιωτερον

I+K   ]ρωντα δυςποτμωτατο[
O⁵   εορακαc αρα ερωντα[...].οτμω[..]ρον

5

Lines 1-45 69

$\{$ I+K   ]αυτου νυν θυραις εστηκ[
   O⁵   προς ταις εμαυτου ν̣[.]ν θυραις εστηκα̣ εγω

$\{$ I+K   ].ω περιπατω τ᾽ ανω κατ[
   O⁵   εν τω στενωπω περιπατων τε α[.]ω κ̣α̣τ̣ω

$\{$ I+K   ]εχ̣[.]ι νυν μεσουσης σου c[[α]]\X/[
   O⁵   αμφοτερας μεχρι ν̣[.]ν μεσουσης c[.]υ σχεδο̣ν̣

$\{$ I+K   ]ειν την τ ερωμενην εχει[
   O⁵   εξω καθευδειν την τε ερωμενην εχει

$\{$ I+K   ]ε̣c̣τιν ε̣νδον εξεcτιν τε[10
   O⁵   π̣α̣ρα μοι γα[.] εcτιν ενδον εξεcτιν τε μοι

$\{$ I+K   ]τουτ[[θ]] ωc αν εμ[μ]ανεcτ[
   O⁵   και βουλομαι τουτο ωc αν εμμανεcτατα

$\{$ I+K   ]ιω δε· υπαιθρι . [.] . εμοι
   O⁵   ερω[. . .]· ουτω ωδε υπαιθριω δε μοι
   O⁶   ] . . . [

$\{$ I+K   ]τοc εcτ[.]ν̣ αιρετ̣[.]τ[. .]\ερ/οc
   O⁵   χειμ̣[. . . . .] εcτιν αιρετωτερον
   O⁶   ] . . οc ε[. . . .] αιρετωτερο̣ν[

$\{$ I+K   ]μοντι και λα[. . .]υτ[.] cοι
   O⁵   ̲ε̲c̲τ̲[. . . . . .]ρ̣εμ̣οντ[.] και λα̣λουντι cοι
   O⁶   ]τ̣ρεμοντ̣ι [.]αι λαλουντι co[

     $\{$ I+K   ]ενον ου[.] . . [. . . .]ατουcθ[
γετας   O⁵   το δ[. . . . . .]ενον ουδε [. . . . . .]τω θεω[15
     O⁶   ]ενον ουδε κυνι μα το[

$\{$ I+K   ]ν εcτιν· . [
   O⁵   νυν̣[.] . . [.] . ητεον εcτ[. . . . .]δε[.]ποτης
   O⁶   ον εcτιν ο δ εμο̣c δεcπο̣ . [

$\{$ I+K   ] . . [
   O⁵   ω . περ θε . ουc μεcο[. . . . . . .] . . .
   O⁶   ]υc μεcο̣υ περιπατει φιλο̣c . [

$\{$ I+K   ] . . . ου̣ . [
   O⁵   τοc[] . . τ̣ . · . πο̣λε̣ι [
   O⁶   ]ει· ου δρυϊνοc . . . . . υπ . [

CHAPTER 3. COMPOSITE READINGS

{
I+K   ]οιεν . [
O⁶   ]ιατριβων[]εγκα . . . . πες[

{
I+K   ]ν θυρα[
O⁶   ] . . . . την . [.].αν ὦ .υϲτυχηϲ   20
      γ

{
I+K   ]κναι[
      Γε
O⁶   ].ειϲ ϲὐ μ᾽ . [.]οκναιειϲ περιπατω
(T)   τί οὐ καθεύδειϲ; ϲύ μ᾽ ἀποκναίειϲ περιπατῶν

{
I+K   ]εριμεν[
O⁶   ]υδειϲ· περ[.]μεν ει μ᾽ εγρη[.]ορωϲ//

{
I+K   ]οϲ εξελ[
O⁶   ]υδι αυτοϲ [. .]εληλυθαϲ

{
I+K   ] . τερα κ[
O⁶   ]μεν . ϲ πο[. .]ρα κελευϲθε[.]ϲ υπο τ .

{
I+K   ]ουτον α[
O⁶   ]η το τοιουτο[.] απο ϲαυτου π[. .]ων   25

{
I+K   ]οι καθευ[
O⁶   ]κελευον οι [.]αθευδοντεϲ: . ετα

{
I+K   ] . εμων [
O⁶   ] εοικε κηδ[.]μων εμοϲ [

{
I+K   ] . καρι[
O⁶   ]αι νυν ω μ[.]καρι[.] εν πα[. .]ι γαρ
T   εἴϲελθε κἂν νῦν, ὦ μακάριε

{
I+K   ]τυχ . [
O⁶   ] . ριοϲ . ιϲ: . [.]υχω δεινωϲ [. . . .]:

{
I+K   ]\ϲ/τα\:/α[
O⁶   ]τα μεγιϲτ᾽[. .]λ᾽ ουδεπω . . [30
O⁷   ]α μεγιϲτ αλλ . ου . . πω

{
O⁶   ]ραν ϲ᾽ εχθεϲ [.]αρ ειϲ την οικιαν
O⁷   ] . εχθεϲ γαρ ειϲ τη . οικια .

---

21 (T) Choerob. in Theodos. can. p. 176.40-177.3 Hilgard; Lex. Seg. α p. 125.19-22 Bachmann   28 Σ Patm. in Dem. p. 10; Σ in Isokr. 3.41

Lines 1-45

71

$\left\{\begin{array}{l}O^6 \\ O^7\end{array}\right.$

    ] την ημετε[. .]ν cυ δια χρο[.]ου

    ] . εληλυθαc cυ δια [.] . [

$\left\{\begin{array}{l}O^6 \\ O^7\end{array}\right.$

    ]πεδου γαρ [. .]απηρα . αταλιπων

    ]ωι γαρ . . . . ηρα κα[.]α̣λιπω̣[

$\left\{\begin{array}{l}O^5 \\ O^6 \\ O^7\end{array}\right.$

    ]ωc ε.ψυχοc [

    ] . ωc ε . ψυ . [. . .]ι δ . τ̣αττομ[

    ]ευψ . [. .] . . δ huδρ[. .] . ομαι

$\left\{\begin{array}{l}O^5 \\ O^6 \\ O^7\end{array}\right.$

    ] . ραπομπηc τ[

    ]ραπομπη̣[. . .] . λαφυρων ε . . ατοc   35

    ]μ . [. . . .]νλ̣[.]φυ̣ [.] . . . [

$\left\{\begin{array}{l}O^5 \\ O^6 \\ O^7\end{array}\right.$

    ]υπουν c' ε . [. . . .] . υβ\ᴩ/ι . . [

    ] . υπουν c' ε . [. . .] υβ\ᴩ/ιζομαι:

    ] . ου . [. . . .] . . [.]α υβ[. .] . . μ[

$\left\{\begin{array}{l}O^5 \\ O^6 \\ O^7\end{array}\right.$

    ] υπο τηc αιχμαλω̣το[.] π̣[

    ] υπο τηc αιχ[. . .]ωτου πριαμενοc

    ]ο̣ τηc α[. . . .]λω̣το[. .] πρ[.]αμ̣[

$\left\{\begin{array}{l}O^5 \\ O^6 \\ O^7\end{array}\right.$

    ]εριθειc.ελευθερ . [. . . . .] . [

    ]ρ̣ιθειc ελευ[. . .]ια[] τηc οικιαc

    ] . c̣ ελ̣ . . θερ̣[. .]ν [. . .] . [

$\left\{\begin{array}{l}O^5 \\ O^6 \\ O^7\end{array}\right.$

    ]ν απ . . . [. .]ξαc̣ . θερ̣ . . [.] . ν̣αc̣ χρ . [

    ] . ν αποδειξα . θεραπαιναc χρυc̣ια

    ]ποδειξαc· θ[

$\left\{\begin{array}{l}O^5 \\ O^6 \\ O^7\end{array}\right.$

    ] . . . [. . .] . . . . c : ειτα τι

    ]υc γυναικα νομ[.]cαc: ειτα τι̣   40

    ]υναικα νο[

$\left\{\begin{array}{l}O^5 \\ O^6 \\ \\ O^7\end{array}\right.$

    ] . ιcχυνο̣μ̣[

    ] . ιζει: και λεγειν α̣ . cχυνομαι̣

        θρ̄

    ]κ̣αι λεγειν [

$\left\{\begin{array}{l}O^5 \\ O^6 \\ \\ O^7\end{array}\right.$

    ] . . [.] . ωc . . α̣co̱ν̱

    ]ηναν: αλλ εμοιγ' ομωc φρα̣[. .]ν:

        γετ

    ]αλλ ε[

72 CHAPTER 3. COMPOSITE READINGS

$\begin{cases} O^5 \\ O^6 \\ O^7 \end{cases}$
　　　　　　　　　　]ν . . . . [
]με μεισος: ω μα[.]νητις . .
　　]μει[

$\begin{cases} O^5 \\ O^6 \end{cases}$
　　　　　　　　] . νθρωπινον
]α γαρ υπονοεις ηνθρωπιν . .

$\begin{cases} O^5 \\ O^6 \end{cases}$
　　　　　　　]τιν[]ουδ[] . . [
]ν τ' εινα . . οδ εστιν: ουδε κ[.] . ια
　　　　　　　　　　　　　　45

From here on O^6 is our only source; readings are those in the main text.

Lines 51-54

$\begin{cases} O^5 \\ O^6 \\ T \end{cases}$
ϋοντα πολλω νυκτος αστ . . πας βροντας
　　　　　　]ης αστρα[
ϋοντα πολλῶι [

$\begin{cases} O^5 \\ O^6 \end{cases}$
εχων δε αυτην κατακειμαι ειτα τι
　　　　　　]ατακειμ . [

$\begin{cases} O^5 \\ O^6 \end{cases}$
κεκραγα παιδισκη βαδισαι γαρ φημϊ δει
　　　　　　]δισαι . . [

$\begin{cases} O^5 \\ O^6 \end{cases}$
ηδη με προς τον δεινα ειπας ονομα τι
　　　　　] . [

O^5 continues until **68**, then O^6 takes over at **78**, with a gap of approx. nine lines inbetween.

Lines 85-100

$\begin{cases} O^5 \\ O^6 \end{cases}$
. . . . . στι[. .]οσεχ ω φι . [
αυτη εστ . [
　　　　　　　　85

$\begin{cases} O^5 \\ O^6 \end{cases}$
παρορωμενω δε π . [
παρορωμ[

$\begin{cases} O^5 \\ O^6 \end{cases}$
φι . . νικιαν πονο[.] μανι[
φιλ . . ικια . [

---

51 T Nonius Marc. IV p. 619-20 Lindsay s.v. *servare*

Lines 501-559 73

$\begin{cases} \text{O}^5 & \text{τι ω κακοδαιμον [] αλλ εγωγε αν φι[} \\ \text{O}^6 & \text{τι[.] κακ[} \end{cases}$

$\begin{cases} \text{O}^5 & \underline{\text{κ.η[.]εις μονον θυςαιμι παςι τοις θε[.] . [}} \\ \text{O}^6 & \text{κλ[} \end{cases}$

$\begin{cases} \text{O}^5 & \text{τι [.] . ν αν ειη το κακον ουδε γαρ ςφροδρα ει} \\ \text{O}^6 & \text{τι[} \end{cases}$ 90

[[...]] $\begin{cases} \text{O}^5 & \text{. . . ως αηδης ωςτε γε ειπειν· αλλα co[} \\ \text{O}^6 & \underline{\text{ακ[}} \end{cases}$

$\begin{cases} \text{O}^5 & \text{. . μεικρον αμ[.] . . [.] του ςτρατι . τικου [} \\ \text{O}^6 & \text{το . [} \end{cases}$

$\begin{cases} \text{O}^5 & \text{[. .] . . ψιν υπεραςτειος αλλα μ[[μ]]ην αγ[} \\ \text{O}^6 & \underline{\text{αλ[}} \end{cases}$ (ην above)

$\begin{cases} \text{O}^5 & \underline{\text{τ . . η . ικια . . []να . . ιτ ετι π . θεν . [}} \\ \text{O}^6 & \underline{\text{. [}} \end{cases}$

O^5 continues until line 100. For lines 241-247 (Bl) of O^5 = fr. C see main text. Then there is a gap of somewhat over one hundred and fifty lines.

Lines 401-492

See main text for readings of the sole manuscript O^4. Then a gap of approx. eight lines.

Lines 501-559

Here we encounter some difficulties because the sheet A-vertical-fibres was put together by Turner from two main fragments of O^3, and the join, as he says, is not necessarily at the correct point. Although the match of fibres looks quite good at the join, I believe line 518 for one shows that the join cannot be correct as any reasonable supplementation of what letters *can* be read leads to a line which is one or two syllables (metrical positions) too long. In the face of such uncertainty, however, I retain Turner's placement of the right fragment for simplicity's sake. In the transcription which follows, a vertical bar (|) indicates schematically the point where the fragments meet in Turner's restoration.

A second complication concerns fr. 2 of O^{11}. The editors of this papyrus (Henry *et al.*, 2014a) say that the fragment belongs above fr. 1 but at an uncertain distance.

There are $21 + \leq 8$ (i.e. max. 29) lines between the top of fr. 1 of O^{11} and the previous chorus break (ΧΟΡΟΥ) and fr. 2, itself 16 lines long, belongs in this gap, as it has no free lines corresponding to an *entr'acte*. In other words, although the exact position of fr. 2 above fr. 1 is uncertain, the margin of error is not that great. Now, if my supplements of line 518 in O^3 are not wide of the mark:

.] . ως. ὁδὶ μεν [εἰ]σιὼν τὸ κα[κὸν] ἐρ[εῖ.

we have a match between κακόν in this line and κακον in line 10 of fr. 2. Some will sigh here, and rightly: the construction is precarious and will not bear the weight of being incorporated in the main text. Nevertheless in this chapter of readings I include fr. 2 of O^{11} at said juncture, but emphasize that this is conjectural. To maintain this, I assume that fr. 2 overlaps with fr. 1 of O^{11} at the end by two lines (lines 523-4), that is, the bottom of fr. 2 stood to the right of the top of fr. 1.

O^3		|]οποι	
O^3		|]λ . γον	
O^3		|]α . . . ον	
O^3		|]υπ . . . μ . ι	
O^3		|]αλιν προσδο[	505
O^3		|] . ω[	
O^3		|]ν̣ε̣ταρα	
O^3	] .[|] . [. .] . ν		
O^3	Γε		
O^{11} fr. 2	]αξ̣ι̣ [|		
	]cτεθ[		
O^3	] .χα[|		510
O^{11}	]ο̣η̣c̣ . [		
O^3	]ρω[. . . . . | . .]τ[		
O^{11}	]: τη . . [		
O^3	] . . [. . . | .]αμ[. .] . . . [		
O^{11}	]τατη[		
O^3	|] . . μενα		
O^{11}	]αντ[		
O^3	|] . εθα		
O^{11}	]λλον[		
O^3 π . . . χ . [	|]α̣·		515
O^{11}	] . . ι̣εν . [		

Lines 501-559   75

$\begin{cases} \text{O}^3 \\ \text{O}^{11} \end{cases}$.ι[. . .] . . [. . .] . ι[. . .]ο . [. | .]αυ[.] . [

                                             χρ
                                       ]α̇τυχ . [

$\begin{cases} \text{O}^3 \\ \text{O}^{11} \end{cases}$.] και τιν᾿ α.α[. . . .] . [. . .] . . [. | .]μ[

                                       ]εγωδα δ[

$\begin{cases} \text{O}^3 \\ \text{O}^{11} \end{cases}$ ___ .] . ωc: ο . ιμεν[. .] . ιων . οκ̣ . [. . | .]ει . [.] . μ[

                                       ]κ̣ακον[

$\begin{cases} \text{O}^3 \\ \text{O}^{11} \end{cases}$ . .]υ δ ἥτις ειπα . . [. . . . . | .]χει[

                                       ]υτωc ε̣[

$\begin{cases} \text{O}^3 \\ \text{O}^{11} \end{cases}$ ουκανδ . ν . . [|] . νο̣υ̣[520

                                     ]α̣τονδ[

$\begin{cases} \text{O}^3 \\ \text{O}^{11} \end{cases}$ ειναι . ε . [

                                       υετ
                                     ].: τῆcτ[

$\begin{cases} \text{O}^3 \\ \text{O}^{11} \end{cases}$.]κετηρια̣ν [

                                       ]παcι τ[

$\begin{cases} \text{O}^3 \\ \text{O}^{11} \end{cases}$ [. .] . ρ̣[. . .]λα̣[. . . .] . . . [   ] . [

                                       ] . . . α̣c[

$\begin{cases} \text{O}^3 \\ \text{O}^{11} \end{cases}$ . . . [. . .] . τ̣[   ] . . . [

                                       ] . [

Notes

519 O³ fin. leg. Furley:]χρο̣υ̣[Turner

After this the placement of fr. 1 of O¹¹ ceases to be conjectural.

$\begin{cases} \text{O}^3 \\ \text{O}^{11} \end{cases}$ [. .] . ρ̣[. . .]λα̣[. . . .] . . . [   ] . [

                                       ]αγ[

$\begin{cases} \text{O}^3 \\ \text{O}^{11} \end{cases}$ . . .] . . .] . τ̣[   ] . . . [

                                   υε
                                  ]:γ̣ι̣[   ] . [

$\begin{cases} \text{O}^3 \\ \text{O}^{11} \end{cases}$ [   ] . . υξεν[525

                                   ]αν[

$\begin{cases} \text{O}^3 \\ \text{O}^{11} \end{cases}$ ___ [.]αυ[. . . . .] . αν: . . [.] . . [   ] . . . . εωμ̣[

                             ]λε . [. . .] . [

$$
\left\{
\begin{array}{ll}
O^3 & [.]..[....]] . ρενθ[....] .. [\quad\quad] ... [\\
O^{11} & \quad\quad\quad\quad] ευθυς [..]δ[
\end{array}
\right.
$$

$$
\left\{
\begin{array}{ll}
O^3 & ... [....] πεπαικ[\\
O^{11} & \quad\quad\quad\quad]λο[.]ους του . [
\end{array}
\right.
$$

$$
\left\{
\begin{array}{ll}
O^3 & [.] . [.... ...] . ωνως . οδ . [\\
O^{11} & \quad\quad\quad\quad] . σφοδρ᾿ αυτη[
\end{array}
\right.
$$

$$
\left\{
\begin{array}{ll}
O^3 & τ[.] . [....] . ν . ερι .. [.] . [..] . [\\
O^{11} & \quad\quad\quad\quad] .. ς εξαιφν . [
\end{array}
\right.
$$

530

$$
\left\{
\begin{array}{ll}
O^3 & α[..] ... [..]γης[\\
O^{11} & \quad\quad\quad\quad]ησει τοις φιλ[
\end{array}
\right.
$$

$$
\left\{
\begin{array}{ll}
B^2 & \quad\quad\quad\quad]:εμοὶ μαχεῖ τάλαν: \\
O^3 & \underline{\quad}ικετηριαν .. λεγου . [\\
O^{11} & \quad\quad\quad\quad]α:ε\overset{χρ}{μ}οι μαχ[
\end{array}
\right.
$$

$$
\left\{
\begin{array}{ll}
B^2 & \quad\quad\quad\quad]ι·δεινὸν γὰρ βίον \\
O^3 & .]α δι αλλ εκει[...]φ . [\\
O^{11} & \quad\quad\quad\quad] . ςι δεινον γ . [
\end{array}
\right.
$$

$$
\left\{
\begin{array}{ll}
B^2 & \quad\quad\quad\quad]ιπωρον τιν᾿:οὐ γάρ:μακάριον \\
O^3 & ζη . [.] . ταλαιπωρ.ν τ[.....] . [\\
O^{11} & \quad\quad\quad\quad] . ιν ου γαρ. μακ[
\end{array}
\right.
$$

$$
\left\{
\begin{array}{ll}
B^2 & \quad\quad\quad\quad]ηλωτὸν ὀντ᾿ οὕτω.ϊ .. ιν: \\
O^3 & αὕτη .. και ζηλω[..]ν [\\
O^{11} & \quad\quad\quad\quad]ωτον οςα γ ουτω [
\end{array}
\right.
$$

535

$$
\left\{
\begin{array}{ll}
B^2 & \quad\quad\quad\quad]νον οἶδε τά γ[.]εαυτη[.] . ολ. \\
O^3 & [..]τη .. μ[\\
O^{11} & \quad\quad\quad\quad]οιδε τα γ εαυτης . [
\end{array}
\right.
$$

$$
\left\{
\begin{array}{ll}
B^2 & \quad\quad\quad\quad]εμοντον ... αυ .. τουτονϊ \\
O^3 & [.]ουτ᾿ε .. κ[\\
O^{11} & \quad\quad\quad\quad]τραχηλον του . [
\end{array}
\right.
$$

$$
\left\{
\begin{array}{ll}
B^2 & \quad\quad\quad\quad]α .. εῖνα᾿ . [.....] . υποκαθημενῶ \\
O^3 & [..] . εμ᾿ α[\\
O^{11} & \quad\quad\quad\quad] . ν .. μοι τον υπο[
\end{array}
\right.
$$

Lines 501-559

$\left\{\begin{array}{l}\text{B}^2 \\ \text{O}^3 \\ \text{O}^{11}\end{array}\right.$

B²   ] . ο τίς ποτ' εϲτιν:έϲτι γὰρ
O³   [. .]τουτο . [.] . [
O¹¹   ] . ιϲ ποτ εϲτιν· εϲτ[

B²   ]ουτοϲ ο ψιθυριϲμόϲ οἶδ'εγω
O³   π . ρα τινοϲ ουτοϲ [540
O¹¹   ]ψιθυριϲμοϲ' οιδ εγω[

B²   ]ηθεν . . . . . εγώτ . . . γ . . νημι[. . .]ναι:
O³   απαλλαγηθ'έ[
                    θε
O¹¹   ]ὁ̇ν̇δε εγω δ α̣[[ᵛ.]]αλημ̣[

B²   ]παρ εμοῦ . . . . φειὸν δ' έχειϲ
                                    δ
O³   ∴ ϲθ . [[τ̄]]ε μ έτ
O¹¹   ] μακαρια· φαιον δ εχ[

B²   ]υ δῆλα . . . [. . . .]υπανλέγει
O³   . . . [. .] . τριδιο̣[
O¹¹   ]νοτι ταυθ οταν λεγη [

B²   ]μα[. . . . .] . . [. . .]υτω μο[
O³   [. . . . .]ϲμ̣[   ]ν τα κρ[
O¹¹   ] το κρα̣ϲπεδ̣ εν δ αυ[

O³   [. . . . .]τυλιον
O¹¹   ]κ̣τυ . [   ]ρυϲ . . [545

O³   . [.]δ . [.]ξον[. . . . . .]παρ[
O¹¹   ]ηπ̣[   ] . εμ[
            δε

O³   φιλων τε . [. . . .] . . υ̇C[
O¹¹   ]ειθε[   ]βουλετ[

O³   οτοιουτο[   ] . . [
O¹¹   ]πρωτο̣[   ]ιϲενε . [

O³   θαιματ[.]α̣ . [. . .]δετα̣[
O¹¹   ]ε̣ ταυτ[   ]ωνια . [

O³   επειτα προϲ̣[. .]τυ . . . . . [550
O¹¹   ]αϲ απ[   ] . ταλιπ[

O³   την γην . ρο̣το̣υ . αν· . . [.] . [   ] . . [
O¹¹   ]αν·κ[ϲ̣ . αντο̣[

$$\begin{cases} O^3 & [\,.\,]\pi\epsilon\iota\varsigma\text{o}\nu\theta'\,.\,[\,.\,.\,]\,\tau\rho\epsilon\pi\omega\,.\,[\,.\,.\,]\iota\,.\,[\,.\,.\,.\,.\,]\epsilon\rho\alpha\nu\,.\,.\,[\,.\,]\,. \\ & \underset{.}{\tau}[\\ O^{10} & \qquad\qquad\qquad]\,.\,.\,[\\ O^{11} & \qquad\qquad\qquad\quad]\epsilon\pi\omega\varsigma[\qquad\qquad\qquad]\epsilon\rho\alpha\nu[\end{cases}$$

$$\begin{cases} O^3 & [\,.\,.\,]\,.\,\underset{.}{\iota}\nu\,.\,[\,.\,]\,.\,\alpha\upsilon\,.\,[\,.\,.\,.\,]\,.\,\eta\rho\iota\omega\,.\,.\,.\,.\,[\,.\,.\,.\,]\,.\,.\,.\,[\\ O^{10} & \,.\,.\,.\,[\,.\,.\,.\,.\,.\,]\alpha\,\theta\,.\,.\,.\,.\,[\,.\,]\nu\,\pi\alpha\rho\epsilon\iota\varsigma\phi\,.\,.\,[\,.\,]\,. \\ O^{11} & \qquad\qquad\qquad]\,.\,\rho\iota[[::]][\qquad\quad]\,.\,\omega\nu \end{cases}$$

$$\begin{cases} O^3 & [\,.\,.\,]\omega\underset{.}{\tau}\underset{.}{\iota}[\,.\,.\,]\mu\alpha[\,.\,.\,.\,]\nu\theta[\,.\,]\,.\,\epsilon\,.\,\underset{.}{\nu}[\,.\,.\,]\delta\underset{.}{\text{o}}\underset{.}{\upsilon}\,.\,\epsilon\,.\,[\\ O^{10} & \,.\,.\,.\,.\,\tau\underset{.}{\iota}\varsigma\,\eta\mu\alpha\varsigma\,\lambda\alpha\nu\theta\alpha\nu\epsilon\iota\,\nu\upsilon\nu\,\delta\,\text{o}\upsilon\kappa\epsilon\tau\iota \\ O^{11} & \qquad\qquad\quad]\lambda\alpha\nu\,.\,[\qquad\quad]\,.\,\nu\delta[\end{cases}$$

$$\begin{cases} O^3 & \qquad\qquad\qquad\qquad\qquad\quad \overset{[\,.\,]PY}{[\,.\,]\,.\,\text{o}\iota\,\theta\epsilon\text{o}\iota\,\theta\epsilon\,.\,[\,.\,.\,.\,.\,]\,.\overset{\cdot}{\alpha}\overset{\cdot}{\pi}\overset{\cdot}{\iota}\,\omega[\,.\,]\,.\,[\,.\,]\,.\,\upsilon\rho\alpha\cdot} \\ O^{10} & \alpha\nu\,\text{o}\iota\,\theta\epsilon\text{o}\iota\,\theta\epsilon\lambda\omega\varsigma\iota\nu{:}\overset{\chi\rho\upsilon}{\overset{\frown}{\alpha\pi}\iota\omega}[\,.\,]\epsilon\nu\,\varsigma\upsilon\rho\alpha \end{cases}\qquad 555$$

$$\begin{cases} O^3 & [\,.\,]\gamma\omega\,[[\varsigma\upsilon\eta]]\,[\,.\,.\,.\,]\,.\,\theta\text{o}\mu\alpha\iota\,\delta\epsilon\,\nu\eta\,.\,.\,.\,[\\ O^{10} & \qquad\qquad\qquad\quad]\,.\,\delta\,.\,.\,.\,\eta\,.\,[\,.\,.\,]\,\alpha\rho\tau\epsilon\underset{.}{\mu}\iota\nu \end{cases}$$

$$\begin{cases} O^3 & [\,.\,.\,]\mu\epsilon[\,.\,.\,.\,.\,.\,.\,.\,]\,.\,.\,.\,.\,.\,.\,.\,.\,.\,[\\ (O^{10} & \,.\,.\,.\,.\,\varsigma\,.\,.\,.\,\iota\varsigma\kappa\,.\,.\,[\quad]\overset{\gamma\epsilon\tau}{\mu}\overset{}{\epsilon}\tau\,\alpha\,\tau\iota\nu\omega\nu\,\pi\iota\nu[\,.\,]\iota\,\pi\text{o}\tau\epsilon \end{cases}$$

$$\begin{cases} O^3 & \qquad\qquad\qquad\qquad]\iota\text{o}\upsilon\phi[\\ O^{10} & \,.\,\delta\,.\,[\,.\,.\,.\,]\,.\,.\,.\,\epsilon\nu\tau[\,.\,.\,]\underset{.}{\theta}\,\alpha\pi\iota\varsigma\tau\text{o}\nu\,\text{o}\upsilon\delta[\end{cases}$$

$$\begin{cases} O^3 & \qquad\qquad\qquad]\iota\underset{.}{\mu}\underset{.}{\alpha}[\,.\,.\,.\,]\,.\,\rho\chi\,.\,.\,.\,.\,.\,[\\ O^{10} & \qquad]\epsilon\nu\,.\,[\end{cases}$$

Lines 560-578

In this section we are again plagued by the uncertainties of the Berlin parchment B^2, which looks so promising, but is in fact very difficult to decipher owing to bleed-through and fading. I give predominately the readings of C. Austin, cited by E. Turner in P.Oxy. XXXIII.

$$\begin{cases} B^2 & \kappa\alpha\tau\acute{\epsilon}\lambda\epsilon\iota\pi\text{o}\nu\,\tilde{\eta}\varsigma\alpha\nu\,[\\ O^3 & [\,.\,.\,.\,.\,.\,.\,.\,]\,.\,\text{o}\nu\,.\,[\,.\,.\,.\,.\,]\rho\omega[\,.\,.\,.\,.\,.\,.\,]\,.\,[\,.\,.\,]\pi\alpha\chi[\end{cases}\qquad 560$$

$$\begin{cases} B^2 & \tau\eta\nu\,\acute{\text{o}}\psi\iota\nu\,\tilde{\upsilon}\varsigma\,\acute{\alpha}\nu\theta\rho\omega\,.\,[\,.\,.\,.\,.\,]\,.\,[\\ O^3 & [\,.\,]\,.\,\nu\,\text{o}\psi[\,.\,]\,.\,\upsilon\varsigma\,\alpha[\quad 13\text{-}14 \quad]\,.\,.\,[\end{cases}$$

$$\begin{cases} B^2 & \tau\alpha\,\gamma\upsilon\nu\alpha\iota'\,\iota\nu\,\acute{\epsilon}\xi\omega\theta\epsilon\nu\,\epsilon\pi\iota\theta\epsilon\omega\rho\epsilon \\ O^3 & [\,.\,.\,]\gamma\upsilon\underset{.}{\nu}\underset{.}{\alpha}\underset{.}{\iota}\,.\,.\,[\end{cases}$$

Lines 560-578 79

$\left\{\begin{array}{l}\text{B}^2\\\text{O}^3\end{array}\right.$

B² ἄρ’ οὗτος εστι δουλος και λύρ . [

O³ [. . .] . τος ε̣ς̣τ[.] μ̣υ̣ς . [. . . .]ει̣[. . .] . . [. .] . . [

B² ἦςε̣ν̣ π̣οθ᾽αυτῶν θάτεροῦς[
  (with τ above)

O³ [. . . .] . π̣οτε αυτ[. .] . . τ̣εροc cθ . . [. . .] . ε[

B² τὸν ἄνδρα . . . . ὁρᾶν ῶ πολυ

O³ [. . . . .] . . . . π̣αρ ω π . λ . τιμητ . . [. .]ο̣[565

B² . . . . . ειν . . [. . . . .]τοῦτο δη τ[

O³ [. . . . .]τωc τ̣ο̣υτ[.] δη το το[.] . . γου

B¹   ] . . [. .] . [.] . . . [

B² π\ι/νω\ν/ δικαίωc ἠ̣cεν ανθρώ[

O³ [. . . . .] . ιc ηιcεν α . θρωπ . . [

B¹   ] . [. .]υcμ᾽ηκεις προς ημας·αλλα τι

B² ἀγαθὸν ἀκουςμ᾽ήκεις προς . [

O³   ]μ᾽ηκει[. . .]ο̣ς ημαc·αλλα . ι

B¹   ] καμπτες καὶ παλιν στελλει διδους

B² . . . δε . . κα̣μπτε̣ς κα̣ὶ π̣α̣λιν στελ[

O³   ] . τ̣εις κ . ι . [. .]λ̣[.]ν στελλει δι[

B¹   ]ολ̣ὰ̣c·ει μη τι κακον ημας ποεις

B² τας cυμβολας ει μη . . κ[.]κὸν η[.]ᾶc[570

O³   ] . . [   ]κο̣ν̣ ημας ποεις·

B¹   ]λευ\c/ω τουτον επι δειπνον παλιν

B² λῆρ̣ος κελεύcω [. . .]τον επι δεῖπ[

O³   ] . τ[.] . τ̣ον ε̣ . . δειπνο̣ν παλι . [

B¹   ]οτην καλεσαντα· φανερως εστι γαρ

B² τὸν δεc[. .]την[. . . . .]α·φ[

O³   ]τ̣ην . [.]λ̣ε̣c̣α̣ν[.]α φανερωc εστι γαρ

B¹   ]αδιουμ̣᾽ εicω δε και πειρασομαι

O³   ] . . ι̣ο̣[. .]᾽ εicω δ̣ε̣ [. .]ι πε[ι]ραcο . [.]ι

B¹]ν εμαυτον επιθεωρησαι τι των

O³   ] . ι των

B¹   ]νων ενδον λαλουμενων θ᾽ αμα·   575

O³   ] . . [.]θ[.]μα

80 CHAPTER 3. COMPOSITE READINGS

B¹   ]τερον τουτου μα τω θεω ξενον
O³   ] . [. . .]νον

B¹   ]τ᾽ ειδον· αι ταλας· τι βουλεται
O³   ]ι̣β[. .]λ̣εται

B¹   ]ρ̣ οικωι τας σπαθας των γειτονων
O³   ] . [. . . . .]ων γειτονων

For lines 579-610 our sole witness is O³

Lines 611-622

]α̣ς̣   B¹   ω[.]ε̣υ τιν᾽ οψιν ουδε προσδ[
Δ̣Η-   O³   . ζε[. . .] . οψ̣ι̣ν ουδε π̣[

B¹   ορω: τι βουλει τηθια τι μοι λαλεις
O³   . [.] . . . . [.] . λ[. .]τηθεια· τι̣ . [

] . . .   B¹   πατηρ εμος·που:παιδιον κρατεια[
       O³   πα̣τηρ εμο[

] . ε   B¹   καλει με:παπα χαιρε πολλα φιλτατ[
      O³   __. λει μ . πα̣π[

B¹   __.]χω σε τεκνον: ω ποθουμενος φαν[615
O³   [.]χω ς̣ε̣[

B¹   ορω σ᾽ ον ουκ αν ωιομην ιδειν ετι
O³   ορω σ᾽ ον̣ . υ[.] . . [

Γετ   B¹   εξηλθεν εξω. παι τι τουθ᾽· αυτη· τις[
Γετας   O³   εξηλθεν εξω π̣[

B¹   ανθρωπε τι ποεις ουτος· ουκ εγ̈ωλε[
O³   ανθρωπε τι ποεις [

B¹   επ αυτοφωρω τονδε τον ζητουμε[
O³   επ αυ . [.]φορω τ̣ο̣ν̣δε τον̣ . . . [

B¹   εχω· γερων ουτος γε πολιος φαινε[620
O³   [.]χ̣ . γερων ο[. . .]ς̣ γε̣ . . [

Lines 644-665   81

$\left\{\begin{array}{ll} B^1 & \text{ετων τις εξηκοντα· ομως δε κλαυ[} \\ O^3 & \text{[.].[.].[..]c εξηκονθ[..].c[} \end{array}\right.$

$\left\{\begin{array}{ll} B^1 & \text{τινα περιβάλειν και φιλειν ουτος[} \\ & \text{λλ·/ .} \\ O^3 & \text{....].εριβαλει .[...].[} \end{array}\right.$

From 623-644 we rely exclusively on O^3.

Lines 644-665

Next we come to the fragments of O^{1v} which overlap with the trunk of O^3. Here I only have a black and white photograph to work with, and, exceptionally, have not seen the original (apparently it is in Cairo). Accordingly I have not really been able to check the readings of these fragments properly. I have omitted here Turner's fr. 2 of O^1 verso (line 648?), as it does not seem to fit. There is a gap of 1-2 lines between fr. 1 and fr. 3 of O^1 verso.

Frr. 1, 2, 3, 4, 5 verso (See Turner (1968, 34)).

$\left\{\begin{array}{ll} O^{1v} \text{ fr. 1} & \text{]..[} \\ O^3 & \text{ε[±13]..[} \end{array}\right.$

$\left\{\begin{array}{ll} O^{1v} & \text{]...πα[} \\ O^3 & \text{........ ....]φ...νου[...].[...]..[} \end{array}\right.$ 645

$\left\{\begin{array}{ll} O^{1v} & \text{].πάτρ[} \\ O^3 & \text{[..]εικ[..]ι[...].μεν: οτε τηλο.[.]...[} \end{array}\right.$

$\left\{\begin{array}{ll} O^{1v} \text{ fr. 2} & \text{....]κέτι[} \\ O^3 & \text{[.]δουκ[..].cτι· τις λεγει coι τ.ν λ...[} \end{array}\right.$

$\left\{\begin{array}{ll} O^{1v} & vac. \\ O^3 & \text{]απ.λω.α:....ι.αλαινα της εμ[} \end{array}\right.$

$\left\{\begin{array}{ll} O^{1v} \text{ fr. 3} & \text{[.....]χη...[ ].φι...[} \\ O^3 & \text{]ως οικτρα παπα φιλτατε} \end{array}\right.$

$\left\{\begin{array}{ll} O^{1v} & \text{.].πονθαμεν: τ[.....].: ύφ ου [} \\ O^3 & \text{........]ν.τεθ[.]ηκε: } \overset{ΔΗ}{\text{ύφ}} \text{ ου τ ηκιστ' εχ[} \end{array}\right.$ 650

$\left\{\begin{array}{ll} O^{1v} & \text{[...]θα cὺ τοῦτον.[ ]και cυν.[} \\ O^3 & \text{]οιδα κ..cυν[...]...[} \end{array}\right.$

82   *CHAPTER 3. COMPOSITE READINGS*

$\begin{cases} O^{1v} \\ O^3 \end{cases}$ ἁλοῦςαμ . . . . . [   ]τ[
                     ] . ουςα του[. . . .]λι[. . .] . . [

$\begin{cases} O^{1v} \\ O^3 \end{cases}$ δια τι κρατεῖα φ . ρ[
  [vac.]

$\begin{cases} O^{1v} \\ O^3 \end{cases}$ ο τοῦτο πράξας ἐ . [
  ο τουτ[

$\begin{cases} O^{1v} \\ O^3 \end{cases}$ ἀλλὰ πάτερ ε[
   . [   ] . α   655

$\begin{cases} O^{1v} \\ O^3 \end{cases}$ απαντ᾽α[
   . . [. .]τ᾽α[. . . . . .]υκ[. . .] . [. .] . [. . . . .] .

$\begin{cases} O^{1v} \\ O^3 \end{cases}$ βουλευτε[
  β . υ . ευ[.] . [.]ν νυν εστ[. .]αλλη κα[.]εδ[ ] . [

$\begin{cases} O^{1v} \\ O^3 \end{cases}$ ζήν . . πρε[
   . ζ[.] . [.] . . [.] . . μετο . . [.]υ[.] . . . [ ] . [

Θρ $\begin{cases} O^{1v} \\ O^3 \end{cases}$ ω του παρα[
   . . [.]υ παραδοξου και ταλαιπ . . ου[ ] . . . [

$\begin{cases} O^{1v} \\ O^3 \end{cases}$ πατηρ κρατειας [. .] . . [. . .] . αρ[
  πατηρ κρα[.]ειας φης εληλ[.]θ᾽ . . [660

$\begin{cases} O^{1v} \\ O^3 \end{cases}$ νυν η μακαριον ῇ τρὶςαθλίῳ . . . . [
  νυν η μακαριον η τρισαθλιω . . . ον

$\begin{cases} O^{1v} \\ O^3 \end{cases}$ δειξεις με των ζώντων ἁπάντων γεγ[
  δειξεις με των ζοντων . παντ[. . . .]γονοτα

$\begin{cases} O^{1v} \\ O^3 \end{cases}$ εἰ μὴ γαρ οὗτος δοκιμάσει με κυρι . [
  ε[. . .] γαρ ουτος δοκιμα . . ι . κυ . ιως

$\begin{cases} O^{1v} \\ O^3 \end{cases}$ δώσει τε ταυτη . οἴχεται Θραςωνίδ[
  δ[. .]ει τε ταυτην οιχετα . [. . . . .]ης

$\begin{cases} O^{1v} \\ O^3 \end{cases}$ ὃ μὴ γένοιτ᾽. αλλὰ εισίωμεν· . . κετι[
  ο μη γενοιτ᾽ αλλ εισιωμεν . . κετι   665

For the verses **666-676** we are again reliant on O^3 alone.

Lines 677-700

To this section belong frr. 1, 2, 3, 4 of O^{1r} (See Turner (1968, 36)).

$\begin{cases} \text{O}^{1r} \text{ fr. 1} \qquad\qquad\qquad]νκειμ[\\ \text{O}^3 \quad τι φης ἐπιγνους την σπ . θην την . ει . ε . [. . \end{cases}$

$\begin{cases} \text{O}^{1r} \qquad . . . .]γείτο[\\ \text{O}^3 \quad ενδον παρ ημιν ωχεθ' ως . ους γειτονας \end{cases}$

$\begin{cases} \text{O}^{1r} \text{ fr. 2} \quad . . . .]νίκα [[\\ \text{O}^3 \quad τουτων ακουσας ουσαν α . . . . πηνικα \end{cases}$

$\begin{cases} \text{O}^{1r} \text{ fr. 2} \quad . . . .]ἠ . . . . [\\ \text{O}^3 \quad εθεντο δ ουτοι δευρο τ . [. .] . . η τιν . . [\end{cases}$ \qquad 680

$\begin{cases} \text{O}^{1r} \quad vac. \\ \text{O}^3 \quad ενεκα προς ημας γρα . [.] . [.] . . . ων . . . . [\end{cases}$

$\begin{cases} \text{O}^{1r} \quad vac. \\ \qquad\qquad ηστι λημψεων.[\\ \text{O}^3 \quad μον[[ωνεπειλη . ο . [. . . . . .]ατ . . . . [\end{cases}$

$\begin{cases} \text{O}^{1r} \text{ fr. 4+3} . . . .]ει . . . [. . . . .] . . . ιων φ[.] . [\\ \text{O}^3 \quad . . δηλο . . . ψοφει . . [. . . .]ιω . φαιν[.]ται \end{cases}$

$\begin{cases} \text{O}^{1r} \quad . . . .] ὡστε πάν[. .]κούσομαι σαφω[\\ \text{O}^3 \quad \underline{α}.των τις· ωστε π . . τ' . . ουσομαις[.]φ . [\end{cases}$

ΓΕΤ $\begin{cases} \text{O}^{1r} \qquad\qquad\qquad]τητος εκτόπου \\ \text{O}^3 \quad ω ζευ πολυτειμητ' ωμοτητος εκτοπ[\end{cases}$ \qquad 685

$\begin{cases} \text{O}^{1r} \qquad\qquad\qquad] . [.]νὴ τον ηλιον: \\ \text{O}^3 \quad \underline{α}μφοιν απανθρωπ . υ . ε νη τον η . . . . \end{cases}$

$\begin{cases} \text{O}^{1r} \text{ fr. 3} \qquad\qquad] . ως γέτα \\ \text{O}^3 \quad ξενος τις εισεληλυθεν αρτιως γε[\end{cases}$

$\begin{cases} \text{O}^{1r} \qquad\qquad\qquad]λεις αυθαδιας: \\ \qquad\qquad\qquad\qquad\qquad γετ \\ \text{O}^3 \quad . νθαδε προς ϋμας: ἠράκλεις· αυθαδιας \end{cases}$

$\begin{cases} \text{O}^{1r} \qquad\qquad\qquad] . [.]ώπου λαβεῖν \\ \text{O}^3 \quad . [\qquad\qquad\qquad] . [\end{cases}$

$\begin{cases} \text{O}^{1r} \qquad\qquad\qquad]τι λ..ω^{κλειν} \\ \text{O}^3 \quad \underline{γ}υναικ[\qquad\qquad]ι λαλω \end{cases}$ \qquad 690

84 CHAPTER 3. COMPOSITE READINGS

$\left\{\begin{array}{l} O^{1r} \\ O^{3} \end{array}\right.$

$\left\{\begin{array}{ll} O^{1r} & \text{]: δημεας}^{κλειν} \\ O^{3} & φ.[\qquad\qquad]ας \end{array}\right.$

$\left\{\begin{array}{ll} O^{1r} & \text{]. c ουδε γρῦ} \\ O^{3} & .[\qquad\quad].[\qquad].οсμ[.].εγρυ \end{array}\right.$

$\left\{\begin{array}{ll} O^{1r} & \text{]ρ' δημέα} \\ O^{3} & [.].[\qquad\quad]cα[.]αι.[...].[.]ε̣α \end{array}\right.$

$\left\{\begin{array}{ll} O^{1r} & \text{]. c .. ᾶc εγὼ} \\ O^{3} & .[\qquad\qquad]τ..[...].α̣υτος.[...]...εγω \end{array}\right.$

$\left\{\begin{array}{ll} O^{1r} & \text{]τη̣c κ̣[.]ρ̣.ο̣[.] ταυτι λέγει} \\ O^{3} & [\qquad\qquad]ηρ κυριος ταυτι λεγει \end{array}\right.$ 695

$\left\{\begin{array}{ll} O^{1r} & \text{]. α κλάων αντιβολων όνος λύρας:} \\ O^{3} & \underline{\quad}.[.....]κλαων αντιβολων ονο̣. λυρας \end{array}\right.$

$\left\{\begin{array}{ll} O^{1r} & \text{]περιπατήcω καυτòc ὼс εμοῖ δοκεῖ:} \\ O^{3} & \underline{\quad}[.]υμ[...]ιπατηcω κα̣υτος ως εμοι δοκω \end{array}\right.$

γετ $\left\{\begin{array}{ll} O^{1r} & \text{]τουτο δε ειρηκε τη[..]μαυτοῦ c αξιῶ} \\ O^{3} & εν τ̣[..].ο δ' ειρ̣ει την εμαυ[...]c' αξιω \end{array}\right.$

$\left\{\begin{array}{ll} O^{1r} & \text{..]ω τ' απολυτροῦν αγωων πατήρ· εγὼ δέ γε} \\ O^{3} & ηκω[..] απ̣ο̣λυτρουν ων π....[....]γε \end{array}\right.$

$\left\{\begin{array}{ll} O^{1r} & \text{]ῶ γυναῖκα c' εντετυχ}^{\backslash ηκ/}\text{ωc δημέα:} \\ O^{3} & αιτω̣ [..].αικα c' εντετυχηκω[.] δη[..]α: \end{array}\right.$ 700

Until line 750 O^{3} is our sole authority, luckily in quite good condition some of the time.

Lines 751-814

$O^{3} + O^{9}$

$\left\{\begin{array}{ll} O^{3} & [.]..ι̣[.]..[...].η.[....].αν....c.ε παι̣[\\ O^{9} &].[\end{array}\right.$

$\left\{\begin{array}{ll} O^{3} & [....]cα̣[....].........[...]περι[\\ O^{9} &]τειαν εξαγε[\end{array}\right.$

$\left\{\begin{array}{ll} O^{3} & κ.ι.α[.........]...ε...ι.[....].ε̣.[\\ O^{9} &]κρυει δημε̣[\end{array}\right.$

Lines 751-814

85

$\begin{cases} O^3 \\ O^9 \end{cases}$
  O^3 [.].[.]....α[....]..[.]αι[........ ...].α..[
  O^9]νουχι μικρα κλε[

$\begin{cases} O^3 \\ O^9 \end{cases}$
  O^3 [.]..[.... .....].....ον ταλαν   755
  O^9]..εαυτον ταλαν

  O^3 ενκ.[.....]..........δε[..]ο[..]γατριο[
  O^9]τα δευρο θυγ[

... O^3 ..]..με.εικρ..[.]χον ει..τι[..]υχον
  O^9].....[

  O^3 [..]...α...νθ'.[..].ολ.απ.[.].ματ[
  O^{12}]λυονθ ω[

  O^3 ει δ' εc.εcον.......... φε....[
  O^{12}]c μεcον μ[

  O^3 ετεροι... τουτ..αυ.....ελ.[760
  O^{12}]οιc τι του

  O^3 .cτω cτ..ειν μ. και λιθον.υχην φ[...]ι.
  O^{12} [vac.]

  O^3 ποει τ' αδηλον τοιc cυνουcι την νο.[.].
  O^{12} [vac.]

  O^3 δ.νηc[...]..[.....]:::...[...]..[.]τιν.[
  O^{12} [vac.]

  O^3 τροπον[..]θε.[...].υτο και.....ερω.
  O^{12} τ[.]οπον καθεξ...

  O^3 απαμφ[..]ι[.]αρ τ[...]ταπλαcτον τουτο μου   765
  O^{12} .παμφιεcει γαρ το κα.[

  O^3 [-vac.-]
  O^{12} και λανθανειν βουλο[

  O^3 [vac.]
  O^{12} αcχη[.]ονηcω δ.νικ[

  O^3 [....]κ.[   ].[
  O^{12} ...]ι..[.]φθαρμαι δ'

Four more lines are traceable in O^{12} (see main text) before we arrive at the top of Turner's page D (horizontal fibres: Fr. A), where O^8 joins in.

$\left\{\begin{array}{l} O^3 \\ O^8 \end{array}\right.$
$\begin{array}{l} [\qquad\qquad] . \text{τοκ} . [. . . . .] . . [. .]\text{ι}\underset{.}{\alpha}\underset{.}{\nu}[\\ [\qquad\qquad\qquad\qquad] . [\end{array}$

$\left\{\begin{array}{l} O^3 \\ O^8 \end{array}\right.$
$\begin{array}{l} [\quad 7\text{-}8 \quad] . \text{c ε}\iota\rho[.] . [. . . .] . . . . [\\ [\quad \pm 6 \quad]\text{ειπ}\underset{.}{\omega}[\qquad\quad] . . [\end{array}$

$\left\{\begin{array}{l} O^3 \\ O^8 \end{array}\right.$
$\begin{array}{l} [. . . . .] . \rho\iota\nu\eta\,\gamma . \underset{.}{\rho}[. . . . . . .] . \underset{.}{\varepsilon} . . [\\ [\qquad\qquad]\rho\,\varepsilon[.] . \tau\eta\nu\,\underset{.}{\alpha}[. . .]\alpha\nu[\end{array}$ 795

$\left\{\begin{array}{l} O^3 \\ O^8 \end{array}\right.$
$\begin{array}{l} [. . .] . \rho\,\phi\rho\alpha\underset{.}{\varsigma}\alpha . . . . . \underset{.}{\text{ο}} . . [. .] . \underset{.}{\text{ο}} . \omega\tau[\\ [. .] . \,\gamma\alpha . \,\phi[.] . \text{c}\alpha\iota . [. .]\tau\text{ον}[\end{array}$

$\left\{\begin{array}{l} O^3 \\ O^8 \end{array}\right.$
$\begin{array}{l} [.]\underset{.}{\xi}\underset{.}{\varepsilon}\lambda\theta\varepsilon[.]\nu\underset{.}{\nu}\underset{.}{\varepsilon}\overset{.}{\kappa} . . [. . . . .]\lambda . . . . . [\\ [\qquad] . \lambda\theta\varepsilon\nu \qquad\qquad \text{c}\upsilon\nu . [\end{array}$

$\left\{\begin{array}{l} O^3 \\ O^8 \end{array}\right.$
$\begin{array}{l} \text{οργη cε} . [. .]\iota\nu\text{οc} . . . . \lambda\eta\lambda . [. .] . [\\ [\qquad]\text{c} . \varepsilon\lambda\varepsilon\varepsilon\iota\nu\text{ο}[.]\,\text{cιμι}\chi[\end{array}$

$\left\{\begin{array}{l} O^3 \\ O^8 \end{array}\right.$
$\begin{array}{l} [.] . \phi\eta . \,\pi\varepsilon\pi\text{ον}\theta\,\alpha . \alpha . . . \text{υπερ ταυτ} . . \lambda\alpha\lambda . [\\ [\qquad] . \underset{.}{\text{c}} \pi\varepsilon\pi\text{ον}\theta' . \pi[. .]\tau\alpha\,\theta'\,\upsilon . [\end{array}$

$\left\{\begin{array}{l} O^3 \\ O^8 \end{array}\right.$
$\begin{array}{l} [.]\varepsilon . \varepsilon\iota . \varepsilon\mu\text{οι τ}\underset{.}{\alpha}\underset{.}{\upsilon} . . . . . \varepsilon[.] . \upsilon\text{τον μ} . . . \varepsilon\gamma\varepsilon \\ [\qquad]\varepsilon\iota\,\tau\,\varepsilon\underset{.}{\mu}\underset{.}{\text{ο}} . \,\tau\alpha[. . .]\text{c δι εμ}[\end{array}$ 800

$\left\{\begin{array}{l} O^3 \\ O^8 \end{array}\right.$
$\begin{array}{l} [.] . . . \text{ατυχημα τ}\underset{.}{\text{ο}}\underset{.}{\upsilon}\text{τ} . . . [6\text{-}8]\,\psi\varepsilon\gamma\omega \\ [\qquad]\nu\,\text{ατυχημα}\,\tau . . \tau\,\varepsilon\kappa\varepsilon[\end{array}$

$\left\{\begin{array}{l} O^3 \\ O^8 \end{array}\right.$
$\begin{array}{l} . \upsilon\underset{.}{\kappa}\underset{.}{\text{ο}}\upsilon\nu\,\varepsilon\nu\varepsilon\text{cτι τ}\underset{.}{\text{ο}} . \tau . . . [. .]\omega . . [.] . \nu \\ [\qquad]\text{ο}\underset{.}{\upsilon}\nu\,\varepsilon\nu\,\varepsilon\text{cτι τουτο cοι}\,[\end{array}$

$\left\{\begin{array}{l} O^3 \\ O^8 \end{array}\right.$
$\begin{array}{l} \tau\alpha\overset{.}{\upsilon}\tau\overset{.}{\eta}\overset{\kappa}{\nu} \cdot \,\text{απολαβ}\underset{.}{\varepsilon}\underset{.}{\iota}\nu\,\tau . . . \tau . [. . . .]\alpha\underset{.}{\chi}\underset{.}{\text{ο}}\underset{.}{\upsilon} \\ [\qquad]\tau\eta\nu\,\text{απολαβειν τουτ}[\end{array}$

$\left\{\begin{array}{l} O^3 \\ O^8 \end{array}\right.$
$\begin{array}{l} \text{ουτωc εχει προ}\underset{.}{\text{c}}\theta\varepsilon\nu\,\gamma\varepsilon\underset{.}{\nu}\underset{.}{\text{ο}}[\pm 5] . \omega . . . \\ [\qquad]\omega\text{c εχει τ} . . \rho\text{οcθεν γεν}[\end{array}$

$\left\{\begin{array}{l} O^3 \\ O^8 \end{array}\right.$
$\begin{array}{l} \text{το ζην αφηcειc αλλ ερε}\underset{.}{\iota}\,\theta\varepsilon\lambda[4\text{-}5] . . . [\\ [\qquad]\eta\nu . \alpha\phi\eta[. . .]\underset{.}{\text{c}}\,\alpha\underset{.}{\lambda}\lambda\,\varepsilon\rho\varepsilon\iota . . . [\end{array}$ 805

$\left\{\begin{array}{l} O^3 \\ O^8 \end{array}\right.$
$\begin{array}{l} \text{οικτω το μιcουν ωc cεαυτ}\underset{.}{\text{ο}} . . . . . [\\ [\qquad]\rho\omega\,\text{το μ}[. .]\text{ο}\underset{.}{\upsilon}[.] . \text{c cεα}[.] . [\end{array}$

$\left\{\begin{array}{l} O^3 \\ O^8 \end{array}\right.$
$\begin{array}{l} \text{και τιc ο βιοc cοι} \cdot \,\text{που το τη}[. .] . [.] . [. . .]\underset{.}{\alpha}[\\ [\qquad] . [\qquad]\tau\text{ο τη}[3\text{-}4] . . . [\end{array}$

Lines 959-974   87

$\left\{\begin{array}{l}\text{O}^3\\\text{O}^8\end{array}\right.$ επιcημον· ει τιc ο . . cε τ . ι . [. .] . . α[.] . . [.]οι
$\phantom{\left\{\right.}$ [ ] . τα[. . .]ργαιc [

$\left\{\begin{array}{l}\text{O}^3\\\text{O}^8\end{array}\right.$ πλεονεξια τουτε . . . . . ρπαϲαι[. .]πων
$\phantom{\left\{\right.}$ [ ]α[. .]αϲαι βλ[

$\left\{\begin{array}{l}\text{O}^3\\\text{O}^8\end{array}\right.$ ïcωc ïταμοc ει τοτε[[μ̣]]ογιcμ . . [. .] . . [.] . . .   810
$\phantom{\left\{\right.}$ [ ]ω λο[. . . .]ω νυν [

$\left\{\begin{array}{l}\text{O}^3\\\text{O}^8\end{array}\right.$ ε . ψυχοc α[. .]ρωc ζηc ο . υνηρ[. .] . . . εν . [
$\phantom{\left\{\right.}$]c οδυνηρωc α[

$\left\{\begin{array}{l}\text{O}^3\\\text{O}^8\end{array}\right.$ ον[.]ιδοc\ᴴ/αυτη τητουτο . . . λε[.] . ειν[]ε . . ι
$\phantom{\left\{\right.}$] καταλιπειν cε[

$\left\{\begin{array}{l}\text{O}^3\\\text{O}^8\end{array}\right.$ αθανατ . ν ευ παθουc᾽ ετιμ . . . . ατο
$\phantom{\left\{\right.}$] . cαc τιμω[

$\left\{\begin{array}{l}\text{O}^3\\\text{O}^8\end{array}\right.$ τον ταγαθ᾽ αυτη δοντα· πωc [. .] . ε[.] . . μοι
$\phantom{\left\{\right.}$]τη δοντα πωc ο[

O^8 contains traces of the next fifteen lines.

Lines 959-974

$\left\{\begin{array}{l}\text{O}^2\\\text{O}^3\end{array}\right.$ απο τη . [
$\phantom{\left\{\right.}$ [. . . . . . .] . . . . αν . . [

$\left\{\begin{array}{l}\text{O}^2\\\text{O}^3\end{array}\right.$]φαινε[
$\phantom{\left\{\right.}$ [. . . .] . . γαρ αγαθ . ν νυ . [960

$\left\{\begin{array}{l}\text{O}^2\\\text{O}^3\end{array}\right.$ διδοαcιν[
$\phantom{\left\{\right.}$ διδ[.]αcι coι γυναικα . . [

$\left\{\begin{array}{l}\text{O}^2\\\text{O}^3\end{array}\right.$ προcευξ[
$\phantom{\left\{\right.}$ προcευξαμην . . αυ . . . [

$\left\{\begin{array}{l}\text{O}^2\\\text{O}^3\end{array}\right.$ ουτωc αγ[
$\phantom{\left\{\right.}$ ουτωc αγαθο[.] γε[

$\left\{\begin{array}{l}\text{O}^2\\\text{O}^3\end{array}\right.$ ουκ εξα[
$\phantom{\left\{\right.}$ . . . . ατασδε[

88 CHAPTER 3. COMPOSITE READINGS

$\left\{\begin{array}{l} O^2 \quad \underline{\pi\omega\varsigma\ \varepsilon\iota\pi} \\ O^3 \quad [\ldots]\ \varepsilon\iota\pi\varepsilon\nu\text{:}\eta\rho[\end{array}\right.$ 965

$\left\{\begin{array}{l} O^2 \quad \tau\alpha\ \rho\eta\mu\ .\ [\\ O^3 \quad [\ .\ .\ ]\ .\ .\ \mu[\ .\ ]\tau'\alpha\upsilon\tau\alpha\ \mu\upsilon\iota \end{array}\right.$

$\left\{\begin{array}{l} O^2 \quad \underline{\lambda\varepsilon\gamma\omega\nu\ \tau}[\\ O^3 \quad \lambda\acute{\varepsilon}\gamma\omega\nu\ \tau\ .\ \chi\alpha\ \tau\rho\varepsilon\chi\varepsilon\iota[\end{array}\right.$

$\left\{\begin{array}{l} O^2 \quad \underline{\varepsilon\lambda\varepsilon\gamma\varepsilon\nu}\ .\ [\\ O^3 \quad \varepsilon\lambda\varepsilon\gamma\varepsilon\nu\ \theta\upsilon\gamma\alpha\tau\rho\iota o\ .\ [\end{array}\right.$

$\left\{\begin{array}{l} O^2 \quad \underline{\nu\alpha\iota\ \varphi\eta\varsigma\iota}[\\ O^3 \quad \nu\alpha\iota\ \varphi\eta\varsigma\iota\ \pi\alpha\pi\alpha\ \beta\upsilon\upsilon\lambda[\end{array}\right.$

$\left\{\begin{array}{l} O^2 \quad \underline{\eta\kappa\upsilon\upsilon\varsigma\alpha}[\\ O^3 \quad \eta\kappa\upsilon\upsilon\ .\ .\ .\ \eta\kappa\upsilon\upsilon\varsigma\alpha\ .\ \varepsilon[\end{array}\right.$ 970

$\left\{\begin{array}{l} O^2 \quad \underline{\varepsilon\kappa\pi\lambda\varepsilon\iota}\ .\ [\\ O^3 \quad \underline{\varepsilon\kappa\pi\lambda\varepsilon}[\ .\ ]\gamma\varepsilon\lambda\ .\ .\ .\ \gamma\eta\pi\ .\ [\end{array}\right.$

$\left\{\begin{array}{l} O^2 \quad .\ ]\gamma\alpha\theta\alpha\ \lambda[\\ O^3 \quad \alpha\gamma\alpha\theta\alpha\ \lambda\varepsilon\gamma\varepsilon\iota\varsigma\text{:}\ \varepsilon\varphi\ .\ \delta\ .\ .\ .\ [\end{array}\right.$

$\left\{\begin{array}{l} O^2 \quad .\ .\ \varphi\varepsilon\iota\ \tau\iota[\\ O^3 \quad \underline{\psi}\ .\ .\ \varepsilon\iota\ \tau\iota\varsigma\ \alpha\upsilon\tau\omega\nu\text{:}\ \overset{\Delta H}{\overline{\pi\rho}} \end{array}\right.$

$\left\{\begin{array}{l} O^2 \quad .\ .\ \lambda\omega\varsigma[\\ O^3 \quad \kappa\alpha\lambda\omega\varsigma\ \pi\upsilon\iota\omega\nu\text{:}\ \pi\alpha\iota\delta[\end{array}\right.$

O^3 is our only source from here until the end of the play.

Chapter 4

Translation

Act One

	[*enter Thrasonides*]	
	O Night, who has the largest share of Aphrodite	
	among the gods, in whom most words about this	
	subject are spoken, and cares of the heart–	
	did you ever see a more unfortunate man?	
	A lover more bedevilled by fate?	5
	I stand now outside my own front door	
	pacing up and down in the narrow street,	
	wavering until you are near half over,	
	while I could sleep and hold my beloved one.	
	She is *there* inside, I could do that,	10
	I want that as much as any who is crazily	
	in love, yet I don't do it. I choose	
	to stand here outside in this thunder storm,	
	shivering while I talk with you.	
	[*enter Getas, Thrasonides' batman*]	
Get.	You know the saying, a dog–by god!–	15
	shouldn't be out tonight. But my master's out	
	walking as if it was summer, muttering to himself	
	endlessly. He'll kill me. Tough as oak. No chance	
	of sleep with his endless cries and [lamentations].	
Thr.	[Who's coming out] my door?	
Get.	Wretch,	20

	why aren't you asleep? You're exhausting me	
	with your walking. [Unless you *are*] asleep. Stop	
	if you're awake and see me.	
Thr.	Getas, you out too?	
	What for? Were you told to do so by [someone	
	indoors]? Or did you come out of your own accord?	25
Get	No one sleeping gave the order!	
Thr.	Getas,	
	[you came], it seems, as my protector!	
Get	[*cajolingly*] Come inside now, old sport! [Weren't you]	
	the lucky one in all things?	
Thr.	Me? I'm terribly unhappy, Getas!	
	[I've suffered] most terribly. There was no [time]	30
	to see you yet. Just yesterday you arrived	
	back at my house after some considerable time.	
Get	Yes, because when I left you back in camp	
	[you were] understandably happy. But since I was put	
	in charge of the transport of our spoils, I [arrived]	35
	back last. [But what's] troubling you?	
Thr.	I've been terribly wronged.	
Get	[Who by?]	
Thr.	By the captive girl! I bought her	
	[as a slave], gave her her freedom, declared	
	her [mistress] of the house, gave her servants,	
	jewelry, [dresses], thought her my wife.	
Get.	Then what?	40
	[Your girl's] offending you?	
Thr.	I'm ashamed to say,	
	[by Ath]ena!	
Get.	Tell me nevertheless.	
Thr	[An unholy] hate for me–	
Get.	Are you a lodestone?	
	[She hates you? Strang]e thought!	
Thr.	Well, is this human	
	[or appropriate] behaviour?	
Get.	Nor [is she] mi[str]ess	45
	[*4 broken lines*] … a long time since … for to be … we try [*Thrasonides*	
	explains to Getas why he is outside in the rain]	
Thr.	] I'm keeping an eye	50
	on the pouring rain, it's night, flashes of lightning,	

Act One   91

                    thunder rumbling, and I'm lying down with her.
Get.   Then what?
Thr.   I cry «Girl, I must go out now
                    and meet someone», adding some name or other.
                    Any other wife would surely say: «In such rain?   55
                    You poor dear! [Which someone] or other?
                    It's dark … »

There follow a number of fragmentary lines

78 saying on[ly … the wall … 80 will say … not likely … (Get.) O sir … a way …
(?Thr.) over-indulgent …

                    she is. Give me [your attention], darling!   85
                    If you ignore me you'll [stir in me]
                    strife, worry and craziness [
Get.   What, poor man?
Thr.   But if I'm called «dearest»
                    just once, I'll sacrifice to all the gods.
Get.   What can be the problem? You're not so very   90
                    awfully unpleasant, so to speak. Perhaps
                    it's the low soldier's pay's the problem?
                    You *look* quite charming. But when it [comes
                    to your age, of course…
Thr.   Go to hell! We must root out the reason   95
                    whatever it is, lay the underlying cause
                    bare.
Get.   Women are a bothersome lot, master.
Thr.   Stop!
Get.   But from what you say, master,
                    [she's playing up], putting you to the test
                    on purpose. A woman's not always a rational   100
                    being…

A few lines missing, then probably the delayed prologue, to which two fragments
have been assigned:

Fr. 2 (7)

Σ in Hom. *Od.* 17.442. That Cyprus always had numerous kings is attested by Menander
also in the *Misoumenos* in a kind of aside:

Faring in Cyprus very brilliantly.
For there he served under one of the kings.

Fragmentum dubium: P.Strasb. WG 307 verso col. i.30-col. ii.3 = fr. com. a-desp. *1036 K-A

Look favourably, all, on this man, who unites
the virtues in himself. He's good, noble, straight,
a royalist, brave, very trustworthy,
sensible, a philhellene, mild-mannered, courteous,
shunning wickedness, honouring truth,   5
knowing how to …
honour ?gods …
control himself…

There follows a small fragment of O^5 which, because of the mention of the 'thieves' (line 6) and 'fleeing' (line 7), reminds one of a typical Menandrean ending of a first act, when the riotous chorus first appears.

Thr.	… going down… […
	…] of her not… being, Getas, […
	…] …; but going away […
(Get.)	How manly], by Apollo!, and very military […
	…]… you look now. I'm going inside [… 5
	…] thieves me wandering round […
	…] flee from these and hast[en …
	…] O wretch […

[Chorus]

Act Two

All we have of act two comes from the very fragmentary O^4. First line endings survive (in a very rudimentary hand), then line beginnings of the next column.

[*Thrasonides is conversing with Getas*]
                                                ]…
                     ].[   ]…

Act Two 93

      ]

]...

] (he/she) reckons   405

] happened

  ] you suspect

Get.   ] master

Thr.   ] going inside, Getas. [*exit*]

               ]...   410

               ] freeing ...

               ] opened

               ] opened this for me

               th]ink [

               ]... but if one   415

               ]...   [*exit Getas(?)*]

        [*enter Demeas*]

Demeas   ] letters [about her]

               he]re I bring

               ] what does it mean?

               t]hat door   420

               ] the house

        [*enter Syra*]

Syra   ] who might if you knock

Dem.   ]... I stand

               ]...

Syr.   this man, stranger.

Dem.   ] letter [from] him   425

Syr.   ] give it.

Dem.   take it.

Syr.   ... did you com]plete, stranger?

Dem.   ] . . eight days

               ] increasing the sufferings

               ] I cannot say.   430

               ] shout.

Syr.   Where are you from, stranger?

Dem.   Me? From [Cyprus.]

Syr.   Do you come ransoming [people]?

having heard [some news]?

Dem.   [By] Apollo, that's not true,

but because of the [misfortune] that befell me

they are seeking me... be accomplished   435

	But she…	
Syr.	] you say.	
Dem.	Me this…	
	do this together.	
Syr.	]… this, old man,	
	others … […]	
Dem.	[… t]racking back	
	but if [	
Syr.	--	
Dem.	]…	
	[you will be called] saviour [	440
Syr.	What is [her] name?	
Dem.	Krateia [	
Syr.	There is [at the neighbors']	
Dem.	–	
Syr.	For he … [	
Dem.	O Zeus of Victory!	445
	unexpected …	
	for us what's [necessary]	
	If … [	
	S]peak … [	
	]… [	450
	] for individuals there is [	
	…	
	… [	
Syr.	…]to pray, old man,	
	wind …	
	…	455
	and then of the gods what is necessary	
	…	
	how …	
	Krateia …	
	…	460
	the …	
	…	
	… back not [	
	and there you are!	
Dem.	…	
Syr.	By Zeus, as far as this [	465
Dem.	Two turnings in either direction …	

Act Three 95

Syr.	And this is fearsome [
Dem.	Come now, if you take the lead [
	on the way. Laughable if [
	if he takes inside [
Syr.	But straightaway to him the [
	wherever it is, and do not... him [
	Do your job first [
	well; and I will [assist you] brie[fly].
Dem.	... but how?
Syr.	[...[3]] deception [
	the woman herself [running to
	and you will do [
	... [...] you delivered [
Dem.	By the gods ... [
Syr.	Turning well[
Dem.	to see ... [
	taking it terribly [
Syr.	Of a bad man [
	... to do it [
	] of all [
	] finding [
	] woman [
	th]e thanks [
	if] we say [
	]...

Line numbers: 470, 475, 480, 485, 490

(gap of approximately 8 lines including *entr'acte*)

[Chorus]

Act Three

] ...
l]ittle
]...
]...
a]gain expect [505
] ...
] so became

```
                              ] dots
                              ]....
?Get.                    Sw[ords
                         ] ...                                        510
                         ] ...
                            ] ...
                                   ] ...
?Get.                         ] ...
        ... [                      ]... ·                             515
        ...
        ... ] and someone ... [
        ]... .
?Syr.        This man going in[
        When you've said who ... [ ... ] time [
Chr.    I could not [              ]... [                             520
        me to be [
        a suppliant branch [
        ... ].[
        ... [                 ]
Get.                     bec[ome
               ] ... [            of] the stran[ger                   525
        ]... [
(??)                   [           ]... [
        ... [              ] straightway [ ...
        ...        ] he has [sur]passed [          ] these words [
        ... [              ]... very much her [
        ... [         about[    ]... straightway                      530
        ...                 s]acrifice for the friends [
        a suppliant branch.
Syr.                    Saying what?
Chr.                               «Oh no, you'll fight me?»
        «God no, him» he says. «It's a terrible life
        he's living and a miserable one. No? *Hers*
        is happy and enviable, as far as one can see.»                535
        Well, she understands her own affairs much better.
        [*Getas, carrying a load*]
?Get.   Is it possible this neck of mine
        can carry [all this] piled on top of it?
        [*aside*]
Chr.    What's that? What can it be? It must be
```

Act Three   97

	from someone this whispering sound, I know that.	540
	[*to Syra*]	
	You get away from here. I'll see what's up.	
Syr.	I'll be at the ready, my dear.	
Get.	[*enumerating*] A grey cloak	
	he has.	
Chr.	Clearly when he says that he means	
	the fringe of the gar[ment.]	
Get.	[*continuing*] And among them one	
	... ...] ring [and] gold jewelry	545
	and metal rods ... [	
	of friends	
Chr.	[*aside*] What does he want,	
	this character?	
?Get.	[*to helpers*] First carry [them] in,	
	these garments. Then these drinking cups(?).	
	Then [I'll be] off to the party, beating	550
	a hot retreat. ... [	
	they'll pour libations until they turn to the meal.	
Syr.	[*aside*]	
	There are such beasts, and one may trick us	
	smuggling stuff inside our house, but not any more	
	if the gods are so inclined.	
Chr.	Let's be off, Syra.	555
	But I'm very annoyed too, by Artemis.	
	we ... [ ].	
Get.	[*alone now*] In what company actually is	
	master drinking? There I'd believe anything!	
	...] beginning somehow	
	I left behind. A man was singing who was [pretty] large	560
	in appearance, a pig of a man ... [	
	the girls, to judge from outer appearances.	
	Is he a Mysian? Then, [holding] a lyre	
	one of them, the stronger one, started singing	
	– he was a sight to see! O gods in heaven! –	565
	«to grow rich fairly» you know, the common ditty,	
	singing the drinking song for honest men. But *you*	
	came over as a pleasant sound to us. So why	
	do you twist like that and turn away despite	
	paying your dues, if you don't mean us harm?	570

	Poppycock! Should I invite him back to dinner	
	after he's invited master? It's clear he's	
	[wicked.] I'll go inside and try by [hiding]	
	myself to see what's going on inside	
	and what all the talk's about. [exit]	575

Syr. By god, a [strang]er guest than this man
I've [never] seen. Dear me, what is he about?
For [in the] house the swords of the neighbours
                                    ... [   ] them in the middle
                                    ]... [   ] a long time   580
                                    ]... [   ] ... to mean these
                                    ]... if he wishes
                                    ] but [
Dem.   ] show.
Syr.   He will place these
                                      ] half of them.
Dem.   well;   585
                              ] ... [   ]
Syr.   I
                              ] saw.
Dem.   Well it could [
                                      ] knocking at the door for me.
Syr. [You knock yourself.] Why are you bothering me?
Dem.] ... [
Syr.   [Ta]ke! I'm off. I've shown you.   590
                                      ] call out and speak!
                              ]... [
?Dem.   Of the [swords]
I come across is this really mine I'm looking at?
Syr. [Why don't] you knock at the door?
Dem.   Still having knocked
[?I thought] ... truly [...].   595
Syr.   ] ... oh dear ...   ; fine.
Dem. Tru[ly] do [I [th]ought
... [   ]... once
... [
Dem.   ] wanting ... [
                              ]... [   ] forward   600
... [

Act Three 99

	] ... [ ] free.	

Syr.   ]... [   ] by the goddesses.

       ... [

       this troubled thought has just occurred to me   605

            ] [...] (?)so that [...] not even one.

       [*Demeas knocks on Thrasonides' door*]

Dem.   I'll draw near. Hey, servants! I'll step back. There's a noise

       from someone coming out through the door.

Krateia [*entering*]

       I couldn't stand [the man. He was so aggressive]

       to [me] then. What's this you say? I don't understand.   610

Dem.   O God, what is this unexpected sight

       before my eyes?

Kra.   What is it, nurse? What's this you say?

       My father? Where?

Dem.   Krateia – my child!

Kra.   [Who]

       is calling me? Father! Fondest welcome to you!

Dem.   I embrace you, child.

Kra.   Fondly missed, you've come!   615

       I see you, whom I never thought to see again!

       [*Enter Getas who interrupts them*]

Get.   She's gone outside. What's going on? What's

       she to you? What are you doing? Didn't I say?

       I've caught the person *in flagranti*

       we were looking for. True, he's a grey old man   620

       of about sixty. But still he'll regret it!

       [*to Demeas*]

       Who [do you think] you're embracing and kissing?

Kra.   This is my father, Getas, here.

Get.   What rubbish

       is this? I don't [

       Who are you? Where are you from [?   625

Dem.   I came myself [?and have stumbled now]

       on her.

Get.   Is this really [your father, Krateia,]

       this old man here?

Kra. [*indicating Simiche*]

              Let her be my witness.

Get.   What's this? You too old maid, is this

	your story? Good sir, where have you come from now?	630
	From home?	
Dem.	I wish it were so.	
Get.	But do you happen	
	to be a stranger from abroad?	
Dem.	Travelling from Cyprus	
	I see *her* first of my family members here.	
	Clearly the common enemy – war – has scattered	
	my family members all over the place.	635
Get.	Yes, that's so. As a prisoner of war	
	she came into our hands in exactly this manner.	
	I'll run and call my master for you.	
	…	
Dem.	Please do so.	

[*a series of hopelessly damaged lines*]

	… [	640
	[ ] … [	
	] suppliant branch [	
	[ ] … [	
	[ ] … [	
(?Kra.)	] appears [	645
	we were […] from home.	
?Dem.	When from far [	
	[H]e's no longer living.	
?Kra.	Who has told you this?	
?Dem.	[I know it well.] He is dead.	
Kra.	What misfortune! [I'm] devastated	
	by this blow. Dearest father, it is a lamentable thing,	
	we've suffered. He's really dead?	
Dem.	By the hand of someone close.	650
Kra.	You know this person?	
Dem.	Yes, and [you share the knowledge]	
	as you were taken and are a trophy [of the captor].	
	Why, Krateia –?	
Kra. [*interrupting*]	Wait, [what did you just say?]	
	The man who did this [took me?]	
Dem.	[Exactly.]	
Kra.	But father […	655
	everything [	
	we must now consider. And how I should live	

Act Four   101

	in a proper way needs thought after that.	
Dem.	Oh the vicissitudes and trouble of this [life!] [*exeunt*]	
	[*enter Thrasonides with Getas*]	
Thr.	Krateia's father's just arrived, you say?	660
	Now I'll prove to be the happiest or most	
	miserable being of all living people.	
	For if *he* doesn't approve me, and give me	
	her hand in marriage, Thrasonides is no more.	
	God forbid! Let's go in. No longer	665
	should we guess the outcome of this matter,	
	but be certain. On shaking, hesitant foot I go.	
	There are bad forebodings in my heart, Getas.	
	I am afraid. But everything's better than	
	speculation.	
Get. [*a parte*]	How so? I'd be surprised.	670
	[*enter Kleinias with a cook*]	
Kleinias		
	There's one guest, caterer, me, and third	
	a girl of mine, if she's arrived, by god.	
	I'm on tenterhooks myself. If not, only	
	the guest. I'm going to run round [town]	
	looking for her all over. But, caterer,	675
	get on with it and look smart!	

Chorus

Act Four

Kle.	What's that? Having recognized the sword	
	lying in our house, he rushed off to the neighbours	
	having heard it was theirs? When was it	
	they put it here and whatever for did they	680
	give it us, old woman? Why of all the spoils	
	this one exactly? Obviously [you know].	
	Well, somebody seems to be coming out	
	from next door, so I'll hear all clearly.	
	[*enter Getas*]	
Get.	O reverend Zeus, the incredible cruelty	685

	of them both, quite inhumane, by Helios!	
Kle.	Did a stranger just stop by, Getas,	
	at your house?	
Get.	By Herakles, such pigheadedness!	
	To snatch a woman from a lover, and a worthy one	
	at that!	
Kle.	He's not hearing anything I say.	690
Kle.	] Demeas	
	…	
Get.	] he [cares] not a whit.	
	…] «Demeas, you know	
	I love Krateia, as you see, I do,	
	and [you're her fat]her and guardian.» Such words,	695
	pitifully imploring, pleading, fall on deaf ears!	
	[*Kleinias falls into step with Getas*]	
Kle.	I'll walk with him myself, seems best.	
Get.	All he can say is: «I demand her freedom,	
	having come here, as my paternal right.» «But I	
	ask for her hand, as I stand before you, Demeas.»	700
	[*exit Getas*]	
Kle.	The man has gone inside for a moment.	
	He mentioned the name of Demeas as he spoke.	
	[*Getas re-enters*]	
Get.	By Herakles! Couldn't he take the matter	
	like a gentleman? Argumentative swine!	
	If that weren't bad enough, *she* looks	705
	askance while he cries, «I beseech you, Krateia,	
	don't abandon me! I received you as a virgin;	
	I was your first lover, I loved you then,	
	I love you now, adore you, dear Krateia. What	
	do you hold against me? If you leave me	710
	it'll be my death, you'll see.» No response.	
Kle.	Whatever's wrong?	
Get.	A barbarian, a lioness	
	of a [woman!]	
Kle.	Have[n't] you seen me, wretch, all this time?	
Get.	Incredible!	
Kle.	He's not in his right mind.	
	[*Getas touches the stage statue of Apollo*]	

Act Four   103

Get.   By Apollo here, I wouldn't have   715
            set her free! We know the common Greek custom,
            valid everywhere: it is right to show pity
            if one receives it! If you don't show me any
            don't expect me to show you any concern!
            «You're not able?» So what? Nothing unusual there,   720
            I think.
[*changing subject*]
                      No doubt he'll shout and threaten
            to kill himself. Standing, with bloodshot eyes,
            he cannot sleep, he tears at his hair.
Kle.   Man, you're wearing me out!
Get.   [*suddenly noticing Kleinias*]   Hello, Kleinias.
            [*aside*] Where's *he* come from?
Kle.   Our guest is causing   725
            some commotion inside your house [
            ... [
??   ... [
                             ]..[
                             ]... second [730
                        ] ... [
            ... [
                      ] I for my part.
Get.   ...   Kle]inias
Kle.   not ...   ] by the gods
??   good work [   ] Demeas.
Kle.   ...   735
            ... [   ] go out [   ], Getas [
?Get.   ... [
            ... [
            ... [
?Kle.   I [   ] for he freed her   740
??   ] it is thought
Kle.   I'll go in [   ] very much indeed
Get.   On the one hand [   ] best[
            ...
            he denies ... [745
            ... [
            ... [
            ... [   ] according to [

Kle.	Do that [before falling] victim to experience.	
?Get.	… [wandering [.	750

[*enter Thrasonides*]

Thr.	… [ ] slave? [	
??	… [ ] bring out [Kra]teia [	
	… [c]rying, Demeas	
	… [all] but a little, Kleinias	
Kra	… [ ] himself. O dear! [	755
Dem.	… [ ] here, daughter.	

[*Thrasonides pacing up and down*]

Perhaps someone called me pusillanimous
seeing me make such heavy weather of these things.
But if you consider impartially [and take thought,]
why would this for others […   ? Still]   760
I must endure and [make] a stone of my heart
and keep my ailment hidden from companions.
Will I be able [to hold out,] Getas? In what way
will I hold this in and bear it more lightly?
Drink will eventually strip this plaster off me   765
although I wish to avoid attention…
I'll let myself go when [
    ] I am destroyed [

…

but I exhibit [770
    ] bad [

…

[… *gap of at least one verse*]
…]

…

…   775

…

I would still never [
loved by me [
did we not pledge this [?
to bear pains and well [780
would say approaching [
it is possible, Krateia, for you to sit [
painful chains [
and I [   ] this [

Act Four 105

having said I mourned [785
but tie [   ] the noose [
still better [
for all [
but as [   ] but what?
... [   ] has   790
... [   ] I sank
... [   ] to [
...
... [   ] if ever [I] spoke [
...   ] for if you will judge the reason [795
...   ] for to mention [
she entered [
you in anger, poor thing! Simiche's come [out.]
What? «She's suffered in all respects?» You speak for her?
I'm only interested in her for my own sake? Don't say that!   800
It's [all] just bad luck? [Don't] I blame *him*?
Isn't that your one and only chance, to stop
him taking her away? [But every]where
this holds true: one's past destroys one's life.
You'll let her go? She'll say: «Touching! You want   805
to [swing] my hatred round to your side by pity?»
And what life's left? Where's that emblem
of victory? If one could only charge against emotions!
Is it asking too much? If [only!] Looking to plunder
you're brave enough then. Well now, take thought,   810
be brave. Your life's a misery, painful, abject–
it's up to you to leave this eternal reproach
against her: *Although well treated, she avenged*
the man who was her benefactor. What's to stop me
from [merely] pretending [that I've kill]ed my[self]   815
then sending this [servant] to [the house... ?]
...   ] to send him [
...
...   ] for [... it] is thus [
...   820
...   ] you might happen [
...
...   ] most ungodly [
...

106   CHAPTER 4. TRANSLATION

...   ] and most miserab[le   825

                                  Chorus

Act Five

Gap of over one hundred verses including the scene depicted in the Mytilene mosaic.
Our manuscripts give us only single words or expressions:

817 him   **818** painful   **819** the remedy (or: 'the poison')

single words of a small unplaced fragment of O^8 including:

4 two   **5** sword   **6** I think

Single words from col. 1 of O^2 including:

926 bad   **931** was present

From line **948** onwards O^2 joins with the last page of O^3 first to produce line beginnings, then, in places, continuous text:

	[*??Krateia's brother*]	
	No longer [	
	Thrasonides [	
	what [?	950
	well [	
	not the (?)girl [	
	jealous[y]	
	what (he/she/they) now say [	
	on the matter [	955
	two hundred [	
	by Zeus [	
Get.	Come on [	
??	You, [get away] from the door!	
Thr.	[What's this, boy?]	
	You seem about [to tell me some] good [news].	960
Get.	They are giving you [your beloved] to wife.	
Thr.	I was praying for that [	
Get.	Bless you [	
Thr.	You're not deceiving [?	
	What did he say?	

Act Five   107

Get. [*impatiently*]   Give me strength!   965
Thr.   Tell me the exact words [her father Demeas] spoke
                  then run home quickly to [my house.]
Get.   He said: «Daughter, [do you want to marry this man]?»
                  «Yes,» she says, «Daddy, I do. Before I heard
                  [bad things]. What I heard [appears now null and] void»   970
                  She bursts into gen[tle] laughter [
Thr.   Good, what you say!
Get.   I'm glad. [Listen, the door:]
                  someone's coming!
Dem.   [Now I'm coming out to you.]
Thr.   Quite right!
Dem.   [For the birth of legitimate] children
                  I give you my daughter [in marriage]   975
                  and two talents dowry [to go with her].
Thr.   [I accept.]
                  Just hand the girl over to me, Demeas!
                  All the opposit[ion she put up in words]
                  [events] spontaneously [have turned to nothing.]
                  Feasting, guest friendship [and ...   980
                  But [let's] go inside [

                  ...

                  ...

                  until tomo[rrow

                  ...   985
                  is inside [
Dem.   Bring [them] out now [
                  Well, well. She regretted [it
                  Slave boy, light tor[ches and hand them round,
                  and garlands [990
                  and don't [?] the meal [
                  Stay for [
                  you [... youths and beautiful boys,]
                  grown men all, [applaud in seemly fashion.]
                  [Virginal] Victory, noble daughter, fond of laughter,   995
                  may she always favour us [with her support.]

Thrasoni[des or *The Hated Man]*

---

974 I give the words in brackets, but this is the marriage formula, so almost certainly right.
994 Again, the last three lines are formulaic so may be confidently supplied.

CHAPTER 4. TRANSLATION

by MENANDER
Favour to the Reader
And the Writer

Miscellaneous unplaced book fragments

1. Epictetus *Dissertationes ab Arriano digestae* 4.1.19
But if you are ashamed to admit your position, look at what Thrasonides says and does, who, although he had served so often, more than you even, first he comes out at night, which not even Getas ventures to do without being pressured by the other, shouts loudly and laments his bitter servitude. Then, what does he say?

> A cheap little girl has subjugated me [he says]
> which not one of the enemy ever managed.

You wretch, who are the slave of a little girl, and a cheap one at that. How can you still call yourself free? Why do you boast about your campaigning? Then he calls for a sword and lambasts the person who withholds it out of good will. He sends gifts to the girl who hates him and entreats her and wails, then on scoring a small success recovers somewhat.

2. (7). Schol. in Hom. *Od.* 17.442
That Cyprus always had many kings Menander says in the same play, *Misoumenos*, in a sort of *parabasis*:

> [arrives] from Cyprus wonderfully
> well off; he served there under one of the kings

3. (12) Pollux 10.145.5-146.2
That they have called a sword *spathē* one finds in Menander's *Misoumenos*, too, when he says:

> the swords (*spathai*) have vanished

4. (4) Ps.-Justin Martyr. *De mon.* 5.107CD p. 142 Otto
Or again in the *Misoumenos* when he talks about those forming their opinions with reference to the gods, or rather, disproving their very existence, this same Menander (says):

Unplaced book fragments 109

> If I could only witness that, I might
> take courage again – but where might one
> find such righteous gods, Getas?

5. (10) Schol. in Aristoph. *Thesm.* 423 (= Sud. λ 64)
Menander in *Misoumenos* (*Misoumenai* Suda):

> It seems I must carry around with me
> a Spartan padlock.

They say that it (sc. the Spartan lock) is closed from the outside by means of a bolt which is drawn, or some such contrivance, such that it may not be opened by those inside.

6 (13) Orus fr. 35
Text corrected by Dobree:

> They may hate
> Thrasonides, father, but they have not slain him

7 (14) Phot. σ 429
spathān: Menander in *Misoumenos*: to boast, to brag

8 Phot. ε 893
enerochrōs: 'deathly pale' Menander in *Misoumenos*

9 Photius α 2519: 'pluck off'.

Fragmentum dubium

> Have you never loved, Getas?
> (Getas) I've never had a full belly!

Chapter 5

Commentary

Act One

Scene One: Thrasonides and Getas

Menander launches the play *in medias res* with Thrasonides pacing up and down on stage before his own front door at the dramatic time of darkest night (day, of course, for the spectators). He speaks his woes to the audience in a monologue addressed to Night, explaining that his beloved girl is inside but he dare not go inside. The entire opening monologue is addressed to Nyx, which is the first word, and closes with σοι, the same addressee. Although the first scene with Thrasonides and Getas goes on for at least one hundred lines, we should assume that a delayed prologue, spoken by someone 'in the know', came next in the gap before our text picks up again at line 241; nothing survives of this prologue, except perhaps for one ancient quote and one uncertain papyrus fragment. It must have stood contrapuntally to the opening scene, explaining what the audience needs to know to understand the irony of Thrasonides' predicament. This is in the manner of *Aspis*, for example, in which the opening scene with Daos sets the scene from the point of view of the characters – Kleostratos has fallen in battle; now the relatives must divide his estate – whilst Tyche, Lady Luck, appears in the second scene to construct the ironical background: Kleostratos is not in fact dead, he will reappear later safe and sound. Similarly here in the missing prologue of *Mis.* a person or divinity with privileged knowledge will have explained why Krateia's grievance against Thrasonides is in fact a chimaera. Sisti (1985a, 83) observes that the structure of opening dialogue followed by divine prologue allows Menander to depict the problems and character traits of his characters first, leaving for the divine prologue only those details of the plot necessary for the audience's understanding. See further Sisti (1973-74), Dworacki (1973), Jacques (1974).

111

For the opening scene with Thrasonides pacing up and down outside his home in the middle of the night cf. the opening scene of Eur. *IA* in which Agamemnon frets outside his tent, accompanied by an old servant. There, too, Agamemnon is in two minds whether to send the fateful letter to Argos, as Thrasonides here is in two minds whether to go in to Krateia. An anonymous fragment of comedy (P.Ant. 1.15 = *PCG* VIII 1084) shows a man complaining about his marriage and appealing to Nyx as witness (line 4), in a manner which is strongly reminiscent of Thrasonides here. Handley (2006) suggests that the author is indeed Menander himself, this opening of a play being so similar to *Mis.*; this question is reconsidered by Cartlidge (2016a). For other similar nocturnal scenes cf. McC.Brown (1981, 25); apart from P.Ant. 1.15 (just mentioned) he discusses Afranius *Ep.* fr. 1. Plautus may have had the beginning of *Mis.* in mind when he wrote (*Mer.* 3) *non ego item facio ut alios in comoediis / <vi> vidi amoris facere, qui aut Nocti aut Dii / aut Soli aut Lunae miserias narrant suas*, 'I won't repeat what I've seen others do in comedies who through the power of love tell their woes to Night, or Day or Sun or Moon'.

One could also see the opening scene as a variation on the *paraklausithyron* motif; that is, Thrasonides as a kind of *exclusus amator*: see Zagagi (1986), and Goldberg (1980, 52). However, Thrasonides is not 'locked out' here; on the contrary, he is reluctant to step inside his own home as Krateia rejects him (as we learn when Getas joins Thrasonides). He is only locked out of Krateia's favour. Zagagi (1994, 39-40) writes:

> The conclusion to which one is led by all these changes (sc. to the stock theme) is that Menander deliberately takes liberties with an accepted literary genre, and also with a familiar aspect of the situation of lovers in Greece, in this way indicating to his audience at the very outset of his play how great is the new departure from the accepted romantic story that he is about to show them. The irony of this unusual situation, the result of Menander's unconventional handling of the genre, in itself creates a focus of special interest for the spectator, from the very first lines of the play, in both the protagonist and the girl who is in his power.

Note how the entire opening mini-*rhesis* is composed, basically, of three long sentences (1-5, 6-9, 10-14), using *symplokē* to tie the syntax together over multiple lines. It is one of Menander's favourite techniques for making a string of iambic trimeters into plausibly spontaneous speech.

The title of the play as given in O^3 is 'Thrasonides [or Misoumenos]'. The alternative title has to be supplemented, mainly from secondary sources, which quote from the play as 'in Misoumenos' (or a close variant thereof). Thrasonides is certainly the main character and focus of interest in the play, as discussed in the introduction (1.2).

Act One 113

Alkiphron has another Thrasonides in *Letters* 2.13, in which a mother warns her son of the dangers of the career on which he is embarking, that of mercenary soldier. Papyrus O[7b] (Turner) may also give part of the title: ΜΕΙΣΟΥ[/ ΜΕΝΑ[.

The play was usually cited in antiquity (as noted above) by the name *Misoumenos* (or a variant of that), as we see from the book fragments. Moreover an epigram of Phronto (*AP* 12.233.3) cites 'Misoumenos' among other play titles (*Georgos* and *Perikeiromenē*; note, not *Polemōn*).

Μισούμενος, the 'hated man', is usually taken to mean 'hated by Krateia' (cf. line 43) but an expression in Chariton (*De Chaerea et Callirhoe* 2.6.1) gives one pause for thought. Kallirhoe, daughter of the Syracusan commander Hermokrates, in the story has been brought by pirates to Miletos, where the regent Dionysios is promptly enamoured of her beauty, but discovers that she is not available to marry:

> Διονύσιος λυπούμενος ἧκεν εἰς οἶκον τὸν ἴδιον καὶ μόνον καλέσας
> Λεωνᾶν «κατὰ πάντα» φησὶν «ἐγὼ δυστυχής εἰμι καὶ μισούμενος
> ὑπὸ τοῦ Ἔρωτος.»
> Despondent, Dionysios returned to his own home and, calling Leōnas alone, said "In all respects I am unfortunate and hated by Love".

That Chariton knew *Mis.* is shown by his citing of line 9 at *Kall.* 4.7.7. Since Aphrodite plays such a conspicuous part in Thrasonides' opening words addressed to Night, whilst Krateia's dislike of him is not even mentioned (yet), one wonders whether this might not be the sense, or *a* sense, of *misoumenos* in our play: the man unlucky in love.

1 ὦ Νύξ, 'O Night!' The address to Night (*apostrophē*) is otherwise only found in comedy in Aristoph. *Thesm.* 1065 Ὦ Νὺξ ἱερά. σὺ γὰρ δή, as an opening formula cf. Eur. *Sciron* (Austin, 1968, Hypoth. 18 p. 94). Similarly the invocation to the Sun (Men. fr. 678 K-Th) opens: Ἥλιε, σὲ γὰρ δεῖ προσκυνεῖν πρῶτον. Ἀφροδίτης Aphrodite, the love goddess, sets the theme of the play in the first line. She and φροντίδες ἐρωτικαί (3), troubles in love, indeed constitute the substance of the play.

1-2 μέρος μετέχεις. For the construction of μετέχω here, where the part or share is given in the accusative, cf. Hdt. 1.204 τοῦ πεδίου οὐκ ἐλαχίστην μοῖραν μ., Xen. *Kyr.* 7.5.54 πλεῖστόν σου μέρος μεθέξομεν. We can call such usages 'internal accusatives', where the part is the internal object of μετέχω 'to have a part'. So here 'you have the largest share of Aphrodite'.

2-3 Night is also the time for talk of love and its concomitant problems. The theme of unhappy love is a distinctly Hellenistic one; one thinks of Theocritus' lament of the Cyclops (*Id.* 11), and the anonymous poem known as *The Maiden's Complaint*

114   CHAPTER 5. COMMENTARY

(*Germ. Des Mädchens Klage*, see Powell (1925, 1.775)). In Menander, Thrasonides is in the company of Polemon *and* Moschion in *Perik.*, both unhappily in love with Glykera, and Chaireas in *Asp.* 286-7. For unhappy lovers in Menander cf. Cusset in Sommerstein (2014a, 167-79).   φροντίδες ἐρωτικαί, 'troubled love', or, in Germ. 'Beziehungsprobleme'. These cannot literally be 'spoken' (λέγονται) in the night, but rather belong to the night. Probably we should take λόγοι and φροντίδες by hendiadys as 'unhappy words of love'.

4-5 For a rhetorical question opening, or near the beginning of, an opening *rhesis* see Eur. *Her.* 1-8 with Bond's note. Bond notes that Aristophanes commonly uses a colloquial question to open a play, once (*Thesm.*) a rhetorical question.

4 ἆρ' ἄλλον. With the exception of ΣC2 (which has τίνα ἄλλον) the manuscripts of Plutarch, who quotes this line of *Mis.* at *Cupid. divit.* 4 (525a), have Ἄπολλον here, which was emended already to ἆρ' ἄλλον by E.W. Handley, even before the discovery of O^5. Although the lettering here of O^5 is anything but clear, the reading can only have been ἄρα ἄλλον rather than Ἄπολλον. But an appeal to Apollo here when the whole passage is addressed in *epistrophe* to Night would surely be out of place, even if the expression Ἄπολλον has become a general 'by god!' rather than a real invocation of Apollo (so G-S). It is interesting that the change from ἆρ' ἄλλον to Ἄπολλον is facilitated when the line is taken *out of context* (i.e. Night goes missing), illustrating the general danger of slippage in the so-called 'book fragments' (Handley, 1990). Fantuzzi (1982) aptly quotes a fragment of Theodoridas (fr. 10.1-4 Snell) which also backs up Handley's emendation (line 3 εἶδές τιν' ἄλλον κτλ.).

ἀνθρώπων All ancient sources (with the possible exception of O^5, where the reading is doubtful) have gen. pl., whilst editors have almost universally preferred acc. sg. ἄνθρωπον, which, agreed, is probably more 'normal'. But the partitive genitive ἄλλον ἀνθρώπων τινά, is reasonable enough.

4-5 ἀθλιώτερον, δυσποτμώτερον. ἄθλιος and δύσποτμος are both tragic words. Thrasonides phrases his troubled love in tragic terms. Comic audiences will not buy this, but rather sense the disparity between such high-faluting words and Thrasonides' ridiculous position of not going inside to his warm bed and girl despite the horrible weather and time of night. I+K has the variant reading (ἄλλον τινὰ) ἀθλιώτατο[ν] and δυσποτμώτατο[ν], forms which almost make sense but not quite: 'have you seen another most miserable person [as I]?'. The same (superlative for comparative) has apparently happened in the manuscript at *Dys.* 128 (Kraus, 1971b, 286).

τινά, which is written in I+K above a correction, must have fallen in the gap of O^5.

4-5 The cliché 'was there ever an unhappier man?' is mitigated by the fact that each unhappy person *feels themselves* to be unhappier than anyone has ever been. Moschion complains similarly in *Perik.* 533-37 (with my note). Davis (1978) has

Act One   115

seen 'reception' of Menander in Ovid's description of the desperate Narcissus' appeal to Nature: *ecquis, io silvae, crudelius, inquit, amavit?*, 'has anyone, O Woods, suffered in love more cruelly?' (*Met.* 3.442-3). Fantuzzi (1982) compares Theodoridas fr. 10.1-4 Snell: ὦ καλλιφεγγῆ λαμπάδ᾽ εἱλίσσων φλογὸς / Ἥλιε, ποθεινὸν πᾶσιν ἀνθρώποις σέλας, / εἶδές τιν᾽ ἄλλον πώποτ᾽ εἰς οὕτω μέγαν / ἐλθόντ᾽ ἀγῶνα; 'O Sun, brandishing your beautiful torch of light, light desired by all men, have you ever witnessed another going into such a momentous contest?' And the (mock-)tragic turn of speech emerges from a comparison with Eur. *Her.* 1015 οὐκ οἶδα θνητῶν ὅστις ἀθλιώτερος, said by the messenger after Herakles has murdered his family.   ἆρ᾽ ἐρῶντα. The active participle immediately establishes Thrasonides' part in whatever relationship it is he is involved with: the active male lover, whilst the partner according to Greek convention is the ἐρώμενος or, in this case, ἐρωμένη (line 9). Diggle (2007) suggested, following a comparison with Catullus 45.25f., that ἔρωτα (Venerem in Catullus) might be preferable as a reading to ἐρῶντα, but I think not: in the previous line we had ἀνθρώπων τινά, and it's not exactly the love between Thrasonides and Krateia which is ill-fated, but Thrasonides personally in his role of rejected lover.   δυσποτμώτερον. δύσποτμος, lit. 'ill-fated' is paratragic, cf. Aristoph. *Ach.* 419 (Euripides speaking) μῶν ἐν οἷς Οἰνεὺς ὁδὶ / ὁ δύσποτμος γεραιὸς ἠγωνίζετο; 'did not the ill-fated old man Oineus contest among these?'

5-14 Thrasonides wants desperately to go inside to Krateia but something (as yet unstated) holds him back; this is the situation summed up by Diog. Laert. *Vit. Philosophorum* 7.130 τὸν γοῦν Θρασωνίδην καίπερ ἐν ἐξουσίαι ἔχοντα τὴν ἐρωμένην διὰ τὸ μισεῖσθαι ἀπέχεσθαι αὐτῆς, 'that although Thrasonides, for example, has his beloved one in his power, he keeps away from her because of her hatred' – a reference which goes back to the Stoic philosopher Chrysippos (*On Love*: see intro. p. 6). The irony of the situation is that he really does have her in his power because he has bought her as prisoner of war. In a way it reflects well on Thrasonides that he pays such heed to her feelings and does not simply force her.

7 ἐν τῶι στενωπῶι, 'in the narrow town street', depicted here by the stage showing two house doors (those of Thrasonides and Kleinias) and – probably centre stage – an inn (see intro. Staging). Sandbach compares Hegesipp. fr. 1.23, Plautus *Pseud.* 961, 971 *angiportum*. Further instances are Philippides fr. 22.2, Pherekrates fr. 113.4 K-A. This *stenōpon* is, in fact, essential to comedy, as it is the place where *all* action except reported action takes place.   περιπατῶ τ᾽ ἄνω κάτω, 'and I walk up and down' or 'back and forth', cf. Alexis fr. 147.2 Arnott: ἄνω κάτω τε περιπατοῦσ᾽. The paratactic τε is quite delayed in the sentence, and perhaps encouraged the scribe of O⁵ to write περιπατῶν τε, which however cannot be right.

8 ἀμφοτερ‹ίσ›ας, 'dithering', 'dilly-dallying', or 'wavering', lit. 'being in two minds',

116   *CHAPTER 5. COMMENTARY*

cf. Simplicius, *Comm. in Aristotelem Graeca* 7.708.11 Diels: ἐπάγει περὶ τῶν μέσων, ὅτι ταῦτα οὕτως ἐστὶ βαρέα καὶ κοῦφα ὡς ἑκατέρωι αὐτῶν ἀμφοῖν ὑπαρχόντων καὶ διὰ τοῦτο ἀμφοτεριζόντων, 'he expounds on those in the middle, that these are (both) heavy and light such that in each case both (qualities) are present and are therefore ambiguous'. In a fragment of a novel, *Erotika Adespota*, P. Michael. 4. col. i.21 (Stephens & Winkler, 1995), we hear of an Egyptian peninsula which faces toward the Nile and the Sea (νῦν δ' ἐστὶν ἀκρωτήριον ἀμφοτερίζον Ποσειδῶνι καὶ Νείλῳ). A scholion on Aristoph. *Plut.* 1098 (*Jo. Tzetzae commentarii in Aristophanem*, Ed. L. Massa Positano, Groningen 1960) comments somewhat similarly: ταῦτα δὲ καὶ μακρὰ καὶ βραχέα εἰσὶ καὶ ἀμφοτερίζοντα, 'such things are both long and short and ambiguous'. Although we encounter ἀμφοτερίζω in the sense 'be undecided' (between two options) regularly in late antiquity, the more common word with this meaning in the classical period is undoubtedly ἐπαμφοτερίζω, 'halt between two opinions' (LSJ s.v.), Plato *Phaidr.* 257b; 'play a double game' e.g. Thuc. 8.85. For further discussion of the conjecture cf. Furley (2015). Otherwise one might accept Sandbach's suggestion of ἐπ' ἀμφοτέρας, 'in both ways', although ἐπ' ἀμφότερα is the usual expression for this (LSJ; three instances in Menander). O^5 has merely ἀμφοτερας here, which is unmetrical and non-sensical. Other conjectures: ἀφ' ἑσπέρας Austin, ἀμφότερ' ἀεὶ M.L. West, ἀμφότερ' ἐ‹μοὶ› Sisti, ἀμφοτεράκις Arnott (a very rare word; he translates with a question mark: '? both ways'). For discussion of these and others cf. Sisti (1985a, 86-88).

Thrasonides means that he is 'in two minds' what to do: although it is possible to go in to Krateia (9 ἐξὸν) he does not do so (12 οὐ ποῶ δ'). He desperately *wants* to join Krateia inside (11-12 καὶ βούλομαι τοῦθ' ὡς ἂν ἐμμανέστατα / ἐρῶν τις) but refrains from doing so. For another undecided person wondering whether to knock on a door see *Geo.* 17 (Chaireas); and, indeed, in our play the scene in act three where Demeas and Syra endlessly ponder knocking on Thrasonides' door to see whether Krateia is there, is also comparable (588ff.).

μέχρι νῦν Turner preferred to write μέχρις μεσούσης σοῦ σχέδον, but μέχρι is well documented in Menander, e.g. *Sam.* 666, *Sik.* 270.   **μεσούσης σου σχεδόν** 'in about the middle of you' (i.e. Night). This is the standard way of expressing beginnings, middles and ends of seasons in Greek: genitive of the period of time + participle for beginning/approaching the middle/ending' e.g. Thuc. 5.57.1 τοῦ δ' ἐπιγιγνομένου θέρους μεσοῦντος. After Thrasonides' quarrel with Krateia earlier that evening (perhaps at their evening repast), and her turning a cold shoulder to him in bed that night (lines 50-56), Thrasonides has now been pacing around outside for several hours and it is about the middle of the night. It is interesting how Thrasonides has only to *tell* the audience that it is around midnight, and stormy, for the audience immediately to visualize the conditions, although in real life it may have been a lovely spring day. The point about *mimēsis* is that it does not *copy* reality but imitates it in

Act One 117

the sense of conjuring up a visualization of reality (Grethlein, 2020). For Sandbach's idea that the bad weather points to a performance at the (wintry) Lenaia, see intro. p. 25.

9 τήν τ' ἐρωμένην ἔχειν. The papyri and the quotation in Chariton 4.7.7 (ἐξὸν καθεύδειν τήν τ' ἐρωμένην ἔχειν) point toward an infinitive here (after ἐξόν), but a couple of scholia (see *app. cr.*) quote the expression τὴν ἐρωμένην ἔχων as an example of a 'familiar inconcinnity' (Turner; the participle would have to be in the dative or accusative to be grammatically 'correct'): Σ Eur. *Phoen.* 478, Σ Ar. *Ach.* 1164b p. 144 Wilson. Turner (1978) accepts this, omitting τ' accordingly, but I do not think the evidence is compelling. The passages in Euripides and Aristophanes need not parallel Menander's line here. Moreover, 'to sleep holding one's lover' is less attractive than 'to sleep and embrace' (= to sleep with, make love to) one's partner.

In Chariton's novel, the line is quoted in the context of Dionysios' regrets about his present predicament. Worried by the possibility that Mithridates may be trying to steal his pretty wife Kallirhoe, he denounces him to Pharnakes, who promptly writes to the King of Persia, Artaxerxes; the latter summons both Dionysios (with Kallirhoe) and Mithridates to his court for adjudication. Dionysios sees 'rivals in love' everywhere round him and thinks to himself: 'I could be lying in bed with my girl', i.e. peacefully, without all this fuss. Whether the plot of Chariton's novel has *anything* to do with *Mis.* is unclear; see introduction p. 6 for traces of jealousy as a motif in the play. **ἔχειν**, 'hold', 'embrace' (as in 615), not just 'have', i.e. be in possession of, as in line 52.

10-12 These lines (to ἐρῶν τις) are quoted by Plutarch *De cup. divit.* 524F to illustrate something which had become proverbial: ἐν τοῖς Θρασωνίδου κακοῖς (εἶναι), 'to be in Thrasonides' shoes', a saying which applied to when one has something but draws back from enjoying or employing it (as Thrasonides did Krateia). As pointed out above, the point is Thrasonides *could* (ἔξεστίν τέ μοι) go in to Krateia, indeed that is what he *wants* to do (βούλομαι τοῦθ') but he *does not* (οὐ ποῶ δ'). Why? We are not told yet, but the answer is she dislikes him, which is sufficient deterrent to lock Thrasonides out.

11 ὡς ἂν ἐμμανέστατα, 'totally crazily', a phrase picked up by Lukian *Philops.* 14 περιβάλλει τὸν Γλαυκίαν ὡς ἂν ἐμμανέστατα ἐρῶσα, 'she embraces Glaukias like a crazily passionate lover'. Cf. Pseudo-Lukian *Amores* 8.14.8 τοῦ Χαρικλέους ἐμμανέστερον ἀνεβόησεν, also in an erotic context.

12 ὑπαιθρίωι, 'in the open air', is a predicative adjective agreeing with μοι like a description of time e.g. τριταῖος, [I arrived] on the third (= second) day. 'It is preferable to me to stand *in the open air* in this storm'. The word seems again to be paratragic: Aesch. *PV* 113 ὑπαίθριος δεσμοῖς πεπασσαλευμένος, 'nailed by chains in the open';

118   *CHAPTER 5. COMMENTARY*

Ag. 335 τῶν ὑπαιθρίων πάγων δρόσων τ' ἀπαλλαχθέντες, 'freed from the frosts and dews of open air'; Eur. *Androm.* 227 ῥανίδ' ὑπαιθρίας δρόσου, 'drop of dew from the sky'.

13 χειμ[ῶνος ὄν]τος, 'in a storm'. There is barely room in O^5 for nine letters which are missing there (ωνοσοντος), but ὄντος is secured by I+K and O^6. As argued below this is the same stormy night as saw the quarrel between Thrasonides and Krateia (50-57). It must have been an autumnal storm or perhaps early winter, as Thrasonides has just returned from military campaign. See note on line 8 for the suggestive power of language here.   αἱρετώτερον, 'more desirable'. The comparative (and superlative) of what is actually a verbal adjective αἱρετός, choosable, to be chosen, occurs elsewhere, e.g. Aristoph. *Knights* 84 ὁ Θεμιστοκλέους γὰρ θάνατος αἱρετώτερος, 'for the death of Themistokles is preferable'.

14 σοι. Night, that is, not Krateia in his mind. Thus the speech returns to the beginning ὦ Νύξ. There is pathos in the fact that Thrasonides is forced to converse with Night rather than Krateia inside in his warm bed: it emphasizes his isolation from her. The choice of λαλοῦντι here, 'chatting to', connects perhaps with the thought at the beginning: most talk of love takes place by night (ἐν σοί).   τρέμοντι, 'shivering', from the cold, that is, not fear. The audience is asked to imagine a cold stormy night in which, in Getas' words, not even a dog should have to go out. This is definitely not a warm, moonlit night, conducive to romance; the season and the time of night underline, or reflect, Thrasonides' inner emotional state.

By the end of this opening monologue we can look back on it as a miniature masterpiece of theatrical rhetoric. It has conveyed so much in so short a space. We have been told what the time and meteorological conditions are; we have heard of Thrasonides' unhappiness in love and the tricky situation now obtaining: she is there inside and there is nothing stopping him from entering except—here Menander keeps back the reason for Thrasonides' reluctance to enter (it will emerge soon enough in the conversation between Thrasonides and Getas). The situation – darkness and rain – reflects, or symbolizes, Thrasonides' mental state. The alternating course of the speech (I want, but I can't) reflects perhaps Thrasonides' walking to and fro on stage. Thrasonides' opening speech is like a Euripidean prologue, but its main purpose is setting the scene rather than containing a synopsis of key points in the plot, as a Menandrean (delayed) prologue usually does. It is, in fact, an 'entrance monologue', ('Zutrittsmonolog'), cf. Blundell (1980).

Enter Getas.

Colantonio (1976) discusses P.Oxy. 2826, whose Menandrean content is analagous in structure to this entrance scene in *Mis.* First a young man (the *trophimos*) laments his misfortune in love to the night, then a slave Syros joins him and commiserates with him. Syros is considerably more sympathetic to the plight of his master than Getas

Act One   119

appears to be in the following scene. It seems to be a cloudless night as Syros says he is not 'star-gazing', unlike the storm in our play. The fragment is not assigned to a particular play.

15 τὸ δ[ὴ λεγόμ]ενον, 'as they say'. Speakers in Menander usually flag a proverb they are about to use quite clearly. Many of these popular sayings or proverbs concern domestic animals, like the dog here. They are frequently used by people of slave status; perhaps there was some identification between their role and that of domestic animals, to be pushed around by their owners. Clearly here Getas identifies himself with the dog which is reluctant to do its job of guarding the premises in very bad weather.   **μὰ τοὺς θε[ούς]**. O[5] has]τω θεω[which would be a recognizable oath (μὰ τὼ θεώ) but only in the mouth of a woman, hence the letters need correcting.

16 [ἐξι]τητέον. West's correction of O[5]'s -τέον is certainly attractive, given the expression in Alkiphron 2.27.1 Πολὺς ὁ χειμὼν τὸ τῆτες καὶ οὐδενὶ ἐξιτητόν, 'much stormy weather this year, not fit for anyone to go out', which certainly looks like a reminiscence. But a dog is usually *sent* out (as opposed to going out of its own free will), just as Getas has been called out now against his will, and the 'gerundive' form in -τέον, 'one should do s'th.', should be retained from O[5], in my opinion. Note ἀπολεῖ μ', 'he'll be the ruin of me' and [οὐκ] ἐᾶι μ' 'he doesn't let me [sc. rest inside]' (18) for the (perceived) pressure put on Getas by Thrasonides. Epictetus (*Diss.* 4.1.19 = book fr. 1) clearly says that Getas only went outside because he was 'forced to by him' (ἀλλ' εἰ προσηναγκάζετο ὑπ' αὐτοῦ sc. Thrasonides). Getas means here: one doesn't ask even a dog to go out on such an evening (but lets him shelter in the kennel), so why should he now have to go out to attend to his master? For the slight metrical difficulty of the 'split anapaest' involved in ἐξιτητέον, cf. Sisti (1985a, 89), who also retains the -έον form. In fact ἐστίν is closely joined to the previous word metrically as an enclitic. Moreover, we could take -έον as a monosyllable, like θεόν in poetry.

17 φιλοσο[φῶν. Thrasonides is not exactly 'philosophizing' but rather 'brooding' (like a philosopher). One can't help suspecting a joke in combination with περιπατ-ῶν in 21: like a Peripatetic philosopher! Evidence for Menander's connection with the Peripatos is genuine enough and the literature seeking to identify Peripatetic beliefs in his plays is quite extensive. See Barigazzi (1965), Gaiser (1967), Angelo Casanova, 'Menander and the Peripatos: new insights into an old question', in Sommerstein (2014a, 137-151) and in the same volume Christophe Cusset, 'Melancholic lovers in Menander', 167-179; Cinaglia (2014). If Menander is poking fun here at the school where he received an education it seems to be of the form: Thrasonides' pacing up and down outside (regardless of the weather) and obvious obsession with a problem in his mind might remind one of a Peripatetic philosopher mulling over an intractable

120   CHAPTER 5. COMMENTARY

problem; cf. Arnott (1996a, **446**). One might also think of depictions of Sokrates sunk in thought while others go about their normal business: *Symp.* 220c3 ff., and his imperviousness to extreme conditions (*ibid.* 220a6). But Thrasonides' troubles are of a much more personal nature than some abstract philosophical conundrum. Smikrines' disgruntled rumblings also earn him the description 'philosopher' in *Epitr.* 144 (supplemented). A work such as *Hermotimos* (Ἑρμότιμος ἢ περὶ αἱρέσεων) by Lukian in later antiquity shows how philosophers had generally fallen into disrepute as miserable old souls. On the image of philosophers in the early Hellenistic period see Korhonen (1997), which I have not been able to see in the pandemic.

18 **ἀπολεῖ μ'**, 'he'll be the death of me'. Austin (ap. G-S) draws attention to Aristoph. *Thesm.* 2, where the old man, tired by Euripides' walking up and down, complains ἀπολεῖ μ' ἀλοῶν ἄνθρωπος ἐξ ἑωθινοῦ, 'the man will finish me, driving round and round from dawn'.   **τοσαῦτ'** (Barigazzi) is preferable to τοσοῦτ' for 'such a lot'. **δρύϊνος**, 'oaken', but metaphorical, i.e. 'tough as oak'. This was not a common figure of speech, and is not recorded at all in our lexica. But a comic fragment recorded by Pausanias Atticistes (ed. H. Erbse, Berlin 1950) records that the Acharnians had the reputation for being tough and unbending as oak: <Δρυαχαρνεῦ> (= com. fr. adesp. **498** K-A)· δρύϊνε Ἀχαρνεῦ, ἀναίσθητε. ἐκωμῳδοῦντο γὰρ οἱ Ἀχαρνεῖς ὡς ἄγριοι καὶ σκληροί, 'oaken Acharnian, insensitive; for the Acharnians were lampooned as being rustic and tough'. This is probably not an indication, however, that Thrasonides was an Acharnian. Much later we find the word used like this by Philo *De congressu eruditionis gratia*, vol. 3, ed. P. Wendland, Berlin 1898, 61.4, who records that Esau was called 'poem' or 'oak' in a metaphorical sense: ... Ἠσαῦ, ὃς τοτὲ μὲν ποίημα, τοτὲ δὲ δρῦς ἑρμηνεύεται, δρῦς μέν, παρόσον ἀκαμπὴς καὶ ἀνένδοτος ἀπειθής τε καὶ σκληραύχην φύσει, συμβούλωι χρώμενος ἀνοίαι, δρύϊνος ὄντως, 'Esau, who is now called "poem", now "oak", "oak" inasmuch as he is unbending and unsurrendering, stubborn and stiff-necked in nature, taking lack of knowledge as his guide, "oaken" in truth', cf. id. *De fuga et inventione* 39.2. So the metaphorical usage of 'oaken' applying to a person's character is rare but not unheard of in Greek. In English 'hearts of oak' has entered the language, though with a positive connotation of brave, enduring. Hesiodic ἀλλὰ τίη μοι ταῦτα περὶ δρῦν ἢ περὶ πέτρην; (*Theog.* 35) 'what are these things to me by oak or by stone?', remains elusive, whether proverbial or something else.   **οὐκ** K has traces of what is probably οὐκ here. Omikron and upsilon are relatively clear.   For **ὕπνον** with **λαμβάνω**, 'going to sleep', cf. Soph. *Phil.* 767, Plato *Symp.* 223b.

19 An extremely difficult line of which the first half **λαβεῖν δ]ιατρίβων** has been satisfactorily repaired by Austin. My reconstruction of the second half is highly tentative, but recommends itself with the asyndetic tricolon of δ]ιατρίβων γ' ἐγκραγ[ὼν] πεσ[ὼν χαμαί], 'spends his time shouting and falling to the floor', a picture of a

Act One 121

man in distress, as Thrasonides is. For other examples of these breathless tricola cf. lines 87, 811. In my reconstruction I take διατρίβων ἐγκραγών (and πεσών) as 'spend (or 'waste') time shouting' with διατρίβω + participle as in Xen. *Kyr.* 1.2.12 αἱ δὲ … διατρίβουσι μελετῶσαι. In Epictetus' paraphrase of this passage, Thrasonides 'yells and laments his bitter enslavement (sc. by Krateia)': πόλλ' ἂν ἐπικραυγάσας καὶ τὴν πικρὰν δουλείαν ἀπολοφυράμενος (*Diss.* 4.1.19). The supplement ἐγκραγών, 'wailing', 'yelling', is close in meaning to Epictetus' two participles and suits the traces well enough (which are, unfortunately, unclear). ἐγκράζω has a strong aorist of this type (LSJ s.v.) and is attested as a *v.l.* in Aristoph. *Plut.* 428 (ἐνέκραγες). π-ε-ς are relatively clear in the papyrus, everything else a guess: πεσ[ὼν χαμαί]. Rival guesses such as the combination in Blanchard ἐγκατέλιπ' ἐσπουδακώς, which goes back to Austin, seem to me flawed in meaning – surely we need a description of Thrasonides' despair here – and the supplement will not fit in the space available but will considerably overrun the right margin. When one compares (I+)K 96v here the visible traces at first sight appear to be]οιεν.[but this may represent]ων ενκ[which would be situated at the right point in the line to correspond to διατρίβων ἐνκραγών with an unassimilated nu before kappa (I leave the gamma in the text undotted on the strength of this nu). It has to be said that all this is tentative, and must be treated with caution. It is strange that other editions do not seem even to consider (I+)K 96v.

Getas' meaning can be paraphrased thus: 'He doesn't even let me catch some sleep with his goings on, crying and falling to the ground'; cf. Archilochus fr. 128 W, line 5 μὴ … καταπεσὼν ὀδύρεο (thanks to H.-D. Blume for ref.) In later ages Getas might have called his master a 'drama queen'. I comment below on the semi-mocking tone of Getas' treatment of his master's despair.

20 τίς νῦν ἀνακρο]ύσει τὴν θύραν; I read]υ ει at line beginning of O[6]; upsilon is faint, but discernible; Turner records] ει. With θύραν (Handley) following, this is clearly an announcement of a stage entry (Getas has just made his appearance) but the usual verb ψοφεῖ cannot be made to fit. I therefore suggest a future tense of ἀνακρούω, another verb which can mean '[strike] open [sc. the bolt of a door from inside]'. Cf. Aen. Tact. 18.6. Eustath. *Comm. ad Hom. Od.* 2.249.9 ὡς ἀνακρούειν τὰς βαλάνους (cf. ibid. line 46); *Anth. Graec.* 5.242.3 Τοῦ σοῦ ἀνακροῦσαι δύναμαι πυλεῶνος ὀχῆας, 'I am able to knock open the bolts of your gate' (Eratosthenes Scholastikos). The use of ἀνακρούω here (if correct) might point to the fact that the door was bolted from the inside (Krateia wanted to lock Thrasonides out) and Getas would have to 'throw' the bolt (βαλάνους) before opening the door. In fact he has already opened the door and spoken his first lines before Thrasonides reacts and says 'now who's coming?'. **τὴν θύραν.** Editors seem not to have noticed that Handley's conjecture here is validated by I+K at the relevant spot.

ὦ δυστυχής must be spoken by Getas, as it is an awkward distraction from Thrasonides' misery if *he* addresses his batman in these terms. Getas has come out to see what is wrong with his insomniac master; it must be him addressing these words to Thrasonides. Although this is an address calling for vocative case, one might think, the convention in such addresses is for the nominative form. Choeroboscus *in Theodos. can.* p. 176.40-177.3 Hilgard, says that the vocative is (here) the same as the nominative through εὐηθείαι, 'simplicity', 'naiveté'; cf. *Heros* fr. 8, *Dys.* 574, 919. Or one can see the expression as a mini-sentence, 'oh, poor [you]!'

21 ἀποκναίεις, 'you're wearing me out'. ἀποκναίω has a literal meaning 'scrape, rub [off]' in e.g. Antiphanes fr. 245.2 Kock, but metaphorical 'wear out', 'exhaust', is more common, e.g. *Asp.* 425 (Smikrines to Daos, who is tiring him out with his endless quotations). Aristoph. *Wasps* 681, *Knights* 1087, Theoph. *Char.* 7.4, Demosth. 21.153, Plato *Rep.* 406b. διακναίω in similar sense at Eur. *IA* 25. *Lex. Seg.* α p. 125.19-22 Bachmann defines as διαφθείρει, ἀποκόπτει, ἀπολλύει. ἢ λυπεῖ, ὀδυνᾶι, ἐνοχλεῖ, παρεκτείνει and then quotes Menander τί — περιπατῶν. These two areas of definition do not accord with the literal and the figurative meanings we recognize now.

22 εἰ μὴ καθε]ύδεις. 'Unless you *are* sleeping'. The suggestion I think gives reasonable point. First Getas asks (conventionally): 'why aren't you asleep?' Then, on second thoughts he wonders whether Thrasonides might not after all be asleep: 'If you're *not* asleep'. The third clause then follows from that: 'stop, if you're awake and can see me'. The epsilon-iota could also be taken as eta, suggesting ἂν μὴ καθεύδηις, but there is no need for a prospective subjunctive here. Sandbach's ἢ καὶ καθεύδεις; gives similar sense 'or *are* you asleep?' We should imagine Getas somewhat wearily trying to come abreast of his master who is walking swiftly to and fro in his distress. He tells him now to wait if he's awake and can register his presence. There may be irony here in that later Kleinias has exactly the same difficulty keeping up with *Getas*, when he excitedly reports on the goings on in Thrasonides' house and fails to notice Kleinias (in act four). There is a somewhat similar exchange about sleeping and waking in *Kōneazousai* line 2 Blanchard, where one speaker says [ἆρ' ἐστὶ τοῦτ' ἐνύπν]ιον; to which the second speaker says εἰ καθεύδομεν, 'Is this a dream?' – 'If we're asleep'. περίμεν' εἴ μ', 'wait if [you can see me]!' This articulation of O[6] makes an imperative of the verb; Parson's version περιμένει μ' ἐγρηγορὼς / [ἔνδον τις;] makes the verb indicative and the whole a question. Thrasonides is asking eagerly 'is someone awaiting me inside?', perhaps in the hope that that person is Krateia. The masculine form of the participle does not necessarily tell against Krateia being the imagined τις.

23 σὺ δ'. Handley interpreted ms. ϲυδιαυτος as ϲυ δ' αὐτός, comparing the Bodmer scribe's διεμοι at *Asp.* 73 for apostrophe sliding into the text as iota. This is indeed

Act One   123

possible but the sign after delta might be gamma, not iota, and there is ink under the delta which may be a mark of deletion: σύ γ' might be also a possibility. Thrasonides expresses surprise at Getas' appearance. The next four lines turn on who called him.

24-25 τί βουλό]μενος; 'what wanting?' is fairly standard for 'what for?', e.g. Aristoph. *Frogs* 71, *Lys.* 480, Machon fr. 18.406 Gow.   ὑπό τ[ινος, '[were you called] by somebody?' Blanchard prefers a reconstruction with Austin's supplement at line end: πότ[ε]ρα κελευσθε[ί]ς; οὔποτε / [ὑπ' ἐμοῦ γάρ,] 'were you commanded (to come out)? Not by *me*, at any rate!' οὔποτε is said by Cartlidge (2016a, 22) to be otherwise unattested in Menander, and altogether very rare in comedy.   τῶν ἔνδον (Barrett) '[somebody] inside'. The point of this line as reconstructed with Barrett's supplement is surely that Thrasonides momentarily raises his hopes that someone – Krateia – has told Getas to summon him inside.

26 Getas' sarcastic reply, 'well, the sleeping weren't going to command me!' establishes his somewhat insubordinate character vis-à-vis Thrasonides; cf. Arnott (1996d, 31 n. 5). This comes out strongly later when Getas wonders what it might be about Thrasonides which Krateia dislikes (90-94). Thrasonides, on the other hand, leans on him as a trusted supporter (27 κηδεμών), without taking offence at the servant's supercilious stance. If Getas is right that everyone is sleeping inside, it shows that Krateia is not particularly worried by Thrasonides' plight. Parmenon in *Sam.* displays a somewhat similar attitude to his young *trophimos* Moschion (e.g. 65-76). For slaves in Menander in general see Krieter-Spiro (1997) and for a short summary of Getas' character, language and attitude to Thrasonides see *ibid.* p. 247.

27 παρῆσθας, 'you attended', 'you came to my side'. Blanchard ignores the tense – 'tu m' assistes' – and curiously renders κηδεμών (see below) as 'parent'. Menander sometimes uses this rarer second person singular ending for metrical convenience, e.g. at *Epitr.* 373, *Perik.* 290, *Sik.* 129. Sisti comments that Sandbach's παρῆσθας is a trifle long for the space; ἐπῆλθες (or ἐξῆλθες) might be an alternative, one letter shorter.   κηδεμών is a guardian or protector, one who κήδεται, 'takes care of', e.g. *Georg.* 56 (Kleainetos needs a *kēdemōn*); *Dys.* 737 (Gorgias is *kēdemōn* of his sister); fr. 663 κηδεμόν' ἀληθῶς, οὐκ ἔφεδρον ἕξεις βίου ('you'll have a true protector, not a … etc.'); Aristoph. *Wasps* 242. In conjunction with πάρειμί τινι, 'stand by the side of s'one', 'support', cf. Xen. *An.* 3.1.17 κηδεμὼν οὐδεὶς πάρεστιν. Similarly Dionysios says to his bailiff Phokas in Chariton's novel *Kallirhoe* 3.11 σὺ κηδεμὼν ἀληθής; there, too, Phokas has helped Dionysios in the – apparently – lost cause of his love for Kallirhoe.

28 κἂν νῦν. This is the reading of the scholion on Demosthenes and Σ Isokr. 3.41; O[6] has [κ]αὶ νῦν, i.e. καί instead of κἂν. Turner (and most editors in his train) gives his seal of approval to κἂν. Cf. Schwyzer/Debrunner *Griech. Grammatik* (1950) 352. The sense, with either reading, is 'now at least'. The variant readings seem to

124   *CHAPTER 5. COMMENTARY*

have been ancient.   ὦ μακάρι', 'my good man'. For the – relatively common – address, see Dickey (1995, 140 and word-list 278).

29 ἦσθας μακ]άρι[ο]ς, '[in everything] you were blessed [with luck]'. Getas gives his own somewhat tongue-in-cheek explanation for using the word ὦ μακάριε in the previous line. The thought is similar to fr. 1, that the brave soldier Thrasonides should not be defeated by a mere girl prisoner. At first (see *app.*) Turner thought]αρχος should be read after the bracket, leading to suggestions such as ὕπ]αρχος (Handley) and χιλί]αρχος (Thomas, 1982). Rea's reading of μακ]άρι[ο]ς, however (ap. Turner (1981)) is closest palaeographically. For another's fall from *makarios* to abject misery, see Chaireas in *Asp.* 294-5.   τίς; [ἀ]τυχῶ (Gronewald). There is dicolon after τις in O⁶ but this might be equivalent to punctuation, i.e. a break in Thrasonides' words (thus Gronewald). As for ἀτυχῶ, there can be little doubt about the reading in O⁶ as I+K (P.Köln) has at the appropriate point indisputable]τυχ . [. In O⁶ the chi is written like a cross, and was taken by previous editors as tau, but can be supported by the similar chi in ἐχθές, for example, in line 31.   Γ[έτα. After δεινῶς Turner saw τ[, others π[. I suggest Γέτα, where the gamma may be thought to be compatible with the trace.

30 τὰ μέγιστ' ‹ἔγωγ'›· If another word stood after οὐδέπω (Turner states '*vacat*'), it can hardly have been longer than one iambus. But then ἀλλ' οὐδέπω becomes unmetrical (−−∪−). Assuming a gap before τὰ μέγιστα of c. 9 letters, and line end at οὐδέπω, the line as it stands seems metrically too short. The best remedy I can find is to assume a kind of haplography in line middle, whereby ἔγωγ' fell out after μεγ-. (I+)K clearly has the ending]\c/τα\:/α[, pointing to μέγιστα: ἀλλὰ (*scriptio plena*). An objection to Turner's putative ἔα με σημῆναι at line beginning would be that Getas hasn't asked anything yet (he does in 36).   The construction from ἀλλ' οὐδέπω … σε is theoretically ambiguous: either 'for [me] to see you' or 'for you to see [me]'. Probably the former is meant as Thrasonides is the one looking for help.

31 καθο]ρᾶν. As emerges at *Perik.* 159 with my note, 'see' can also mean 'talk to', so Thrasonides means here 'explain' what is going on. On the other hand, at *Georg.* 42 the verb means simply 'spot', 'lay eyes on'.   ἐχθὲς γάρ, 'just yesterday'. We learn in the next lines (if the distribution of speakers there is correct) that Getas was in charge of conveying the haul of war spoils home and for that reason arrived later than Thrasonides. A reconstruction in the past has run along the following lines. If among these trophies was the notorious 'sword of the brother' of Krateia, she might have seen this tell-tale object on the eve of the play. The stormy night, then, was the one following Getas' arrival, during which, it seems, Thrasonides and Krateia quarrelled. The description of the storm in lines 50-52 is strictly speaking redundant, as Getas experienced it as well, but it is useful for the audience, in order to set the scene, and

Act One   125

is meant thus. For discussion of the 'brother's sword' hypothesis see introduction p. 7ff. There I expressed scepticism that this was what sparked off Krateia's dislike of Thrasonides.

32 ἐλήλυθας. The manuscripts jumble the position of this word: O⁶ must have had it before τὴν ἡμετέραν (if at all), whilst O⁷ has it *after* those words, still preserving the metre.   **διὰ χρόνου**, 'after some (considerable) time'. That Getas arrived home a good while after Thrasonides is some slight handhold on where the play is set. Since the journey home started in Cyprus we must assume a journey long enough to allow for this disparity in the arrival time of the officer and his servant. Some have suggested that the play was set in Rhodes (Webster, 1973): is this far enough from Cyprus to allow for this time factor? It is certainly a good deal closer than Athens.

33-35 Turner (1968) gave these lines to Thrasonides and he has been followed by most recent editors (Sisti), where some had thought Getas was the speaker: Brown (1980), Arnott (1996c), and now Blanchard (2016)). What is more likely: that the master or the slave supervised the transport of spoils? In *Aspis* it is very clearly Daos who has this job (prologue), but here one could argue that Kleostratos was no longer around to do the job. However, in lines **36-39** of the same play, it is Daos who is charged by Kleostratos with escorting the prisoners and spoils from Lykia to Rhodes. One also needs to ask what is meant by λάφυρα: presumably private gains, not common pickings belonging to an army. It seems to me, therefore, that it is more likely that Getas was responsible for the transport of Thrasonides' private haul, rather than vice-versa; for both points cf. Brown (1990). This is independent of the question of whether we follow the reading of O⁶ in line **34** or that of O⁷ (see note *ad loc.*). Of course, everything depends on whether we restore first or second person singular (Gronewald) as the subject of the verb to which εὔψυχος is complement in **34**, but our choice is decided by the former question: who supervised the transport of spoils? I think second person is better (Getas addressing Thrasonides) as this gives point to Thrasonides' misery now: Getas observes that Thrasonides was happy enough when he last saw him, so why is he plunged in misery now? Reconstructed like this, the lines give Getas' answer (explanation to the audience, note γάρ) to Thrasonides' previous statement that he had not yet had a chance to see (= talk to) Getas since the latter's (late) arrival.

33 ἐν στρατο]πέδωι. O⁷ clearly has]ωι γαρ at the left edge, pointing to the dative reading (Gronewald). This is a possibility as words such as στρατόπεδον, πόλις, can stand without the definite article. The dative goes well with καταλιπών (sc. 'you') 'in the camp'. O⁶ on the other hand shows]πεδου pointing to the genitive τοῦ στρατοπέδου (Turner), which goes well with ὡς ἀπῆρα, 'when I left' (+ genitive). In both manuscripts an object of καταλιπών seems to be missing: it is quite easy to insert ‹σ› after ὡς, which may have dropped out by haplography.   [ὡ]ς ‹σ›

126   *CHAPTER 5. COMMENTARY*

ἀπῆρα, 'when I departed (leaving) you'. Such an omission of σ' in the manuscript is paralleled by the famous case in the transmission of Sappho 31 ὡς γὰρ ἐς ‹σ'› ἴδω, 'whenever I look at *you*'. Getas' point is, that is the last time he saw Thrasonides and *then* he was in a pretty good mood. So why is he *now* so despondent?   **γὰρ** We need to consider the context. Thrasonides is telling Getas that he is terribly upset; his servant has had no time to take this in as yet, because he only arrived the day before. **γὰρ** does not give the explanation why Getas arrived days (weeks?) after Thrasonides, but why Getas is surprised to see Thrasonides miserable now when he was in a good mood when he had last seen him in camp. Cf. McC.Brown (1981, 26). **ἀπῆρα** (Cockle), cf. Eur. *El.* 774 ἐπεὶ μελάθρων τῶνδ' ἀπήραμεν πόδα; Men. *Asp.* 41. Turner remarks 'ἀπαίρω belongs to the technical military vocabulary, frequent in Diodorus etc.' This is borne out by e.g. Thuc. 4.46.1, 7.19.5; Dem. *De falsa leg.* 163.8 etc. In prose it is usually construed with ἀπό + gen.

34-36 The logic of Getas' point from ὅτι δὲ τάττομαι ... ἥκω is elliptical. He means 'because of the time taken transporting the spoils he was last to arrive' *and therefore* had as yet not had time to see Thrasonides properly (cf. 30-31 Thrasonides' remark).

34 Gronewald's **ἦσθ'** gives good sense. Of course, if Thrasonides is the speaker, then ἦν is required, but see note on 33-35 why it is more likely that Getas was responsible for the transport of the spoils.   **εἰκό]τως εὔψυχος**, 'understandably happy'. Again the tone borders on the cheeky when one realizes that the slave is addressing the master (and proud warrior). In two of the manuscripts (O^5 and O^6) the traces before psi look like anything but upsilon (mu perhaps? ἔμψυχος? cf. Arist. fr. 129 Bonitz, ἔμψυχοι λέξεις, 'animated speech') but O^7 certainly has upsilon. O^6 is in fact rubbed at the crucial point, so does not bear reliable witness. Why was Thrasonides merry? Perhaps because of his haul of wealth, or perhaps because of Krateia.

[ὅτ]ι δὲ τάττομ[αι]. The traces in O^6 have been well supplemented by Turner. With the next line we get the sense (with historic present) 'but because I was encharged with the transport of the war spoils ... ' τάττω and τάττομαι, 'appoint/be appointed *to* (sc. some – typically military – duty)' are found with ἐπί and accusative, dative, and (quite rarely) genitive case (LSJ s.v. II); e.g. [Dem.] 10.47.1-2 (ἐφ' ἧς [sc. τάξεως] ὑμῖν τετάχθαι προσῆκεν ...); Plut. *Kleomenes* 59.11.4: τὸν ἐπὶ τῆς σφαγῆς τεταγμένον (cf. *ibid.* 49.4.2). According to this reading Getas explains that he arrived considerably later than Thrasonides and Krateia back home as he was in charge of the slower goods transport.

But what to make of the reading in O^7? I read ˌΔΗΥˌΡˌˌˌΟΜΑˌ[where Turner read δηχˌρ[ˌˌ]τομαˌ[, commenting 'restoration is baffling'. Where he read χ, he says 'υ possible'. Indeed: what I think we have is ὡ]ς δ' ὑ̣δρ[εύ]ˌομα̣[ι, with a rough breathing in the old capital form Η, over the upsilon in the exemplar, which has slipped down before υδρ-. A rough breathing of this form is rare in papyri (but

Act One 127

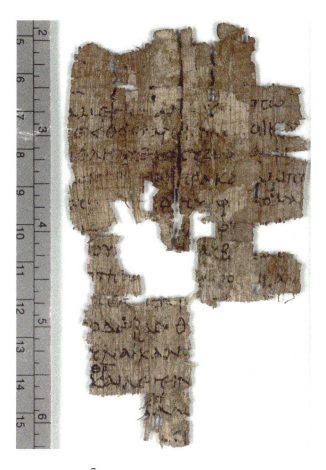

Figure 5.1: P.Oxy. 3370 = O⁷, lines 30-43. Courtesy of the Egypt Exploration Society and the U. Oxford Imaging Papyri Project

common in inscriptions, of course), but see line 812 in the hand of O³, where we see what must be a rough breathing in the form of eta written above αυτηι (i.e. αὐτῆι). For the old form of the breathing cf. Cartlidge (2017a). A less adventurous explanation of the eta would be that δή was written erroneously for δέ. The trace before ομα̣[ι might be taken as the top right stroke of sigma (ὑδρεύσομαι). Syntactically we would have a rare form of a final clause ὡς + future indicative instead of subjunctive (Smyth *GG* §2203).
Getas would mean in this version that because he needed to water his men and animals while transporting the spoils, he was delayed. However, the construction – ὡς with future indicative to express purpose – is unusual, and the authority of O⁶ is not to be discounted lightly (Turner). On the whole I prefer to adhere to O⁶ here, al-

128   *CHAPTER 5. COMMENTARY*

though O[7]'s variant reading, if correctly reconstructed, very nearly gives acceptable sense.

35 λαφύρων, 'spoils' of war, formed presumably from the same root as εἴληφα (< λαμβάνω); cf. Frisk, *GEW* ii 91, s.v. In line 682 we have λήψεις (τῶν λήμψεων Π), 'takings', presumably with the same meaning (and related etymologically). For the question of whether λάφυρα means 'common booty' (of the whole army) or 'private booty' (of Thrasonides) see Brown (1990). He disputes the claim of Belardinelli (1989, 32), that λάφυρα technically meant the former. On war booty generally see Pritchett (1974, 54-58); for the distribution of booty: *ibid.* 82-84. We note in passing from this line that the military campaign on which Thrasonides and Getas had been serving must have been tolerably successful. In the introduction (p. 25) I suggested that Demetrios Poliorketes' conquest of Cyprus in 306 BC might provide a good backdrop. That, of course, points up the contrast: Thrasonides is successful in war, but unsuccessful in love. Fr. 2 (probably a citation from the prologue) says about Thrasonides that he fared wonderfully well in the campaign in Cyprus (ἐκ Κύπρου λαμπρῶς πάνυ πράττων), and fr. 1 shows him boasting that a girl has enslaved him, which no enemy ever managed. This remark by Getas explaining (what Thrasonides must already know) why he arrived late must contain information which Menander wanted his audience to have. As will appear probable, these λάφυρα will turn out to be central to the play, if among them was Demeas' son's sword.

35-36 ἔ[σχ]ατος / [ἥκω] (or [ἥκον]) 'I arrive(d) last'. With O[7]'s reading as reconstructed (see note on 34), one could read ἦγον, 'I came last'; cf. Soph. *El.* 734, ἤλαυνε δ' ἔσχατος, 'he was riding last'. The reading ἔσχατος (as opposed to e.g. ὕστατος) hangs on a tiny trace in O[6]. But the trace is undeniable: it looks more like part of epsilon than of upsilon. Turner guessed that ἔσχατος was part of the proverb ἔσχατος Μυσῶν (Germ. 'als hinterletzte') here; apparently Menander *did* use the expression in *Androgynos* (see note on line 563 and discussion in Sisti (1985a, 92)). Apart from anything else, this would leave the sentence here without a main verb.

36 τί δὲ τὸ λ]υποῦν σε; 'so what's bothering you?' For the expression cf. *Kith.* 42 τί δὴ τὸ λυποῦν σ' ἐστί;

37-40 Thrasonides has offered his bride-to-be the world only to have it thrown back in his face. His words give an interesting little snapshot of the things thought desirable for a wife: freedom, being mistress of a household, servants, gold, (expensive) clothes, marital status. Similarly in *Perik.* Polemon ruefully shows Pataikos all the nice clothes and jewelry he had given Glykera before she left him (516ff.).

37 ὑπὸ τῆς αἰχμαλώτου. The first mention of Krateia, a captive of war. But was she captured on this latest campaign of Thrasonides in Cyprus or on a previous occasion? Getas' description of the way in which Thrasonides acquired Krateia does little to

Act One   129

clarify the matter. Following Demeas' remark that war has scattered his family in all directions, Getas says 'yes, that's right. This girl came to us in this fashion, when she became a prisoner of war' (636-37). The remark leaves it quite open whether Thrasonides acquired Krateia on his last campaign (in Cyprus) or on a previous one. In lines 651-52 Demeas seems to say to Krateia that she was captured on the same occasion as her brother met his fate. Conceivably both these things happened some time in the past, but it seems more likely that her brother went missing in the recent campaign (or he would have had more time in the meantime to reappear!). On the whole I agree with Brown (1990) who concludes: 'The most economical hypothesis is that Krateia formed part of the booty captured in Cyprus by the army with which Thrasonides was serving, and that Thrasonides bought her either during or at the end of the campaign.'

37-40 All five participles in this catalogue of philanthropic actions are to be taken with ἑλείν' ὑβρίζομαι in the previous sentence: '(and that) after I'd given her her freedom etc.' Thrasonides is typical of Menander's lovers: the man is abject, at the mercy of the young woman, whilst she wields power over him by offering or refusing him her favours. The contrast is pointed up by the fact that the man is often a valiant soldier (Polemon and Thrasonides) on the battlefield.

38 δούλην, '(having bought her) as a slave'. This supplement gives more point to περιθεὶς ἐλευθερίαν than αὐτήν (Austin), but is not necessarily right. [π]εριθεὶς ἐλευθερίαν, 'having given her freedom', but not in an official, juridical sense cf. Blanchard (2016, 253 n. 1): 'L'expression n'indique pas un affranchissement en bonne et due forme … Cratéia est libre dans la mesure où elle accepte de rester avec Thrasonidès comme *pallakè*. S'il veut la reprendre, son père devra la racheter'. Demeas would not need to ransom her in the altercation of act four (698-9) if Krateia were legally free.

38-39 τῆς οἰκίας / [δέσποιν]αν ἀποδείξας, 'having declared her mistress of the house'. The phrase recurs more or less *verbatim* in Chariton *Kall.* 3.7: καὶ δέσποιναν αὐτὴν ἀπέδειξε τῆς οἰκίας. There, too, Dionysios has, technically bought Kallirhoe as a slave, but now wishes to make her his wife.   ἀποδείξας is quasi-official. 'After I'd appointed her mistress of the house'.

40 ἱμάτια. Austin cites fr. 951 K-Th ἱμάτια καὶ χρυσία in support of this supplement.   γυναῖκα νομ[ί]σας, 'after I'd considered her my wife', i.e. treated her like a legally married wife. That, of course, Krateia could never be, unless she discovered her citizen father – which she does in the course of the play. Like Polemon in *Perik.* 489, Thrasonides claims he had accorded Krateia the honour due a 'proper wife'. On this question see Traill (2008, 40-41). For the expression cf. *Georg.* 58-59 οἰονεὶ / νομίσας ἑαυτοῦ πατέρα, 'as if it were his own father'; *Asp.* 334-5 ὃν νενόμικας / υἱὸν σεαυτοῦ, 'who you thought of as your own son' (Chaireas is in fact

130   *CHAPTER 5. COMMENTARY*

the step-son of Chairestratos).   εἶτα τί; Getas interrupts Thrasonides' long chain of participles with an impatient 'Then what?' leaving Thrasonides' sentence without a main verb. But Getas' suggestion 'the woman's hurting you?' is very much what Thrasonides would probably have said: 'after I gave her everything, she treats me like this!'

40-41 Punctuated like this Getas first asks 'then what?', before going on with his second question 'the woman's hurting you?' but one could let Getas' question run on to the next line: 'So what has the woman done to offend you?' Now the girl has become, in a fashion, Thrasonides' wife (γυναῖκα νομίσας), Getas can refer to her without the article. The reconstruction with γυνή goes back to Turner (1982), who points out that Apollonius Dyscolus *De constructione* I 41.10 (p. 37.7 Uhlig) contains a *testimonium*, if not a (free) quotation, of this passage: πῶς ἡ γυνή σε ὕβρισε; Austin's supplement ([ἑλεῖν' ὑβ]ρίζει;) would necessitate a quasi-ironical use of ἑλεῖν' in Getas' mouth: 'are you being abjectly abused?' ('you poor thing!' – not meant seriously): not impossible, but I prefer Turner's version.

42 μὰ τὴν Ἀθ]ηνᾶν. Turner (1968) tends finally toward reading]ηναν as opposed to]αιναν, which might also be possible. He thought in the direction of ἀπηυξάμ]ην ἄν or ἀπεκρυπτόμ]ην ἄν; Sisti suggests impf. or aor. of ἀπέχομαι, but the sense is not clear. I would prefer (with Lamagna) ἀπηγχόμην ἄν, 'I'll be hanged', if we are looking for a verb. Even more suitable seems to me the emphatic oath μὰ τὴν Ἀθηνᾶν, 'I hesitate to say it, by Athena!' The choice of goddess might reflect precisely Krateia's reluctance to have sex with him, as Athena ran from Hephaistos, and as the goddess shunned men generally (see *HHymn to Aphrodite* 8). If the supplement is right, it is (not conclusive) evidence that Thrasonides was an Athenian. In *Sik.* 144 the parasite Theron appeals to the goddess Athena, adding 'make him (sc. Stratophanes) one of yours', i.e. make it turn out that he is an Athenian: ὦ δέσποιν' Ἀθηνᾶ, τουτονὶ σαυτῆς πόει. For the oath cf. *Asp.* 319 νὴ τὴν Ἀθηνᾶν (Chairestratos), also at line beginning. Demeas swears by Athena in *Sam.* 213, also in a situation where he believes he has been let down by his sweetheart. There Sommerstein (2013) maintains that the oath by Athena in Middle and New Comedy has largely replaced the oath by Poseidon, common in Old Comedy. For another example in Menander cf. fr. 420.1-2 K-A = 656.1-2 K-Th.

43 [ἐξαίσιόν] με μῖσος–, 'an unholy hatred'. I suggest this combination in view of Aristainetos 1.22.13-14 σὲ δέ, εἰ καὶ παράδοξον ἐρῶ, μισεῖ μῖσος ἐξαίσιον, a letter which has very Menandrean overtones (a story of love and hate), and was thought by Katsouris (1985, 228f.) to be based on *Mis.* The expression εἰ καὶ παράδοξον ἐρῶ in Aristainetos also chimes with Menander's [ἄτοπ]α γὰρ ὑπονοεῖς (44), if correctly supplemented. In Aristainetos, then, we would have a sentence of the shape 'even if it sounds paradoxical, she hates *you* with an unholy hatred'. In Menander: '(Thras.)

Act One   131

[sc. She hates] me with an unholy hatred. (Get.) Difficult to believe!'
If the suggestion can stand, we must assume that Getas interrupts Thrasonides immediately after these words with his exclamation 'O you lodestone!' and that the
missing verb is then supplied by Getas: εἰ μισεῖ σε. Such *antilabe* in mid-line when
Getas interrupts Thrasonides occurs also in lines **40**, **45**, and **52**. Previously, and
quite plausibly, editors have adopted Austin's suggestion μισεῖ νέον] με μῖσος, 'she
hates me with a new (or terrible) hatred!' Clearly the supplement νέον, 'new', ties
in well with the brother's sword theory which proposes that Krateia went off Thrasonides when she recognized this weapon. Before she might have liked Thrasonides
but now she hates him. In fact, we might say that the supplement is tailored to the
brother's sword theory. However, I have argued in the introduction that the brother's
sword cannot have been the initial reason for Krateia's antipathy (that comes later).
We do not need to assume any time up to now in which Thrasonides and Krateia
harmonized.

ὦ, Μα[γ]νῆτις εἶ;, 'Are you a lodestone?'. There seem to be two letter traces after the
sigma in O[6], and Turner (1978) marked them as such. They seem to me to match
epsilon-iota very well, as, for example earlier in the line μεισος (one can see a low
dot marking the end of iota's long descender). This could represent εἶ, 'you are …
', or, possibly, εἰ, 'if', connecting with the next line. Turner, on Parson's suggestion,
preferred an acc. + infin. construction σὲ / [μισεῖν· ἄτοπ]α γάρ, with 'exclamatory'
infinitive: 'that she hates *you*!' However, this fails to account for the dot of ink after
(probable) epsilon and gives a rather awkward construction.
Details aside, we naturally assume Getas' jibe is intended to compare Thrasonides
with a magnetic stone which can repel as well as attract: he may have attracted
Krateia initially, but now he is repellent to her. On the other hand, he *may* only
be referring to the lodestone's ability to *repel* (not a common thing in nature, after
all). How we take the jibe depends on our interpretation of the plot: if Krateia has
recognized her brother's sword, then a sudden swing from favour to hate would be
understandable. If, on the other hand, and as I have argued in the introduction, she
disliked his bragging manners from the start, then the jibe depends on *one* power of
the magnet, to repel.
Μαγνῆτις is a feminine form with ἡ λίθος understood, and means 'Magnesian', i.e.
stone from Magnesia in Thessaly (or Lydia). Eur. fr. 567 (from *Oineus*) refers to
the Μαγνῆτις λίθος in comparison with someone who 'examines the minds of men
and both draws opinion and repels' (τὴν δόξαν ἕλκει καὶ μεθίησιν πάλιν), a clear
reference to the power of a magnet both to attract or to repel. Magnets also featured
in love magic, as they were attributed magical powers to attract; note in particular
the 'magnetic heart' in *PGM* IV.3141-2 καρδίαν μαγνητίνην in a magical spell. Cf.
PGM III.187-262, ibid. 494-611, IV.1724-25 (thanks to Adria Haluszka for refer-

132   CHAPTER 5. COMMENTARY

ences); cf. Faraone (2019) 'a stone that was used as an amulet by the Greeks to seduce and charm both mortals and gods, if worn on the body'; see *Orphic Lithika* 319-33 and *Kerygma* 10 (Halleux & Schamp, 1985).

We note the servant's cheeky tone in the face of his master's woe. But it is a common tone to adopt in the face of another's infatuation. In *Her.* we may compare the slave Getas' cheek in talking to fellow slave Daos, who is in love with Plangon (opening scene). Menander sometimes uses expressions of the pattern 'that man is a —'; in *Sam.* 555-6 Demeas says of Nikeratos στρόβιλος ἢ / σκηπτὸς ἄνθρωπός τίς ἐστι, 'the man is a whirlwind or a twister!' Or *Dys.* 88-9 κακοδαιμ⟨ον⟩ῶν τις ἢ / μελαγχολῶν ἄνθρωπος 'the man's possessed by an evil spirit, or he's a madman!' Getas takes the pattern 'so-and-so is a —' a step further with his direct address 'But you're a magnet, if ... !'

44 ἄτοπ]α γὰρ ὑπονοεῖς, 'Strange thought!' Getas continues in a tone of mock incredulity, as if every woman *must* fall for the master. ἄτοπος is a prominent term in Menander, not by chance probably: it denotes what is 'out of place', 'bizarre', 'peculiar'. Menander's comedy might be said to centre on the ἄτοπον, that is, on the peculiar circumstance which leads to the comic mix-up. Examples: *Asp.* 160, 436; *Dys.* 288, 417, 609; *Epitr.* 436, 819 (new reading), 1099. Here it is exactly what Getas calls ἄτοπον – that Krateia has conceived a hatred for Thrasonides – that lies at the heart of the play. On the semantic nuances of ἄτοπος in Menander, see the detailed remarks of Arnott (1964, 119-22). ὑπονοεῖς, 'you suspect'. With ὑπόνοια, double-figure occurrences in Menander. The word is important for the psychology of Menander's characters; they *suspect* thoughts and motives in their fellows. As Onesimos says in *Epitr.* 457, without knowledge, νυνὶ δ' ὑπόνοιαν καὶ ταραχὴν ἔχει, 'now there is (only) suspicion and disturbance'. In this case Getas suggests that Thrasonides must be reading Krateia's mind wrongly.

44 ἢ 'νθρώπινον The point of this exchange is that Getas has protested that it is an uncanny thing (ἄτοπα γὰρ ὑπονοεῖς) if Krateia hates Thrasonides, to which Thrasonides now replies: 'well, do you think it normal ... ?'

45 ἢ κατὰ τρόπο]ν {τ' εἶναι} τόδ' ἐστίν; 'or is this appropriate?' O[6] has both εινα. and εςτιν, and, with Turner, the reduplication of forms of 'to be' is difficult to include in one construction. Morever, the line appears too long by two metrical positions, given that the missing letters at the beginning are about ten. Most editors' solution has been to dispense with ἐστίν and retain εἶναι, acc. + inf. construction following a supplied verb δοκεῖ (Turner), οἴει (Arnott). I prefer the other option, to dispense with εἶναι and to fill the gap at the beginning of the line with a conjectural ἢ κατὰ τρόπον. The expression is common in Menander e.g. *Dys.* 134, 215, 424, *Perik.* 492 οὐ κατὰ τρόπον σου χρωμένου / αὐτῆι, 'because you didn't treat her properly'. This is the nuance I suspect here in *Mis.*, too: Thrasonides feels Krateia is

Act One   133

not treating him properly. Arnott's supplement is ten letters long; mine, too (Turner's nine).   οὐδὲ κ[υ]ρία, 'nor is she [sc. her own] mistress … ' Getas presumably went on to say that Krateia is not her own mistress (as Glykera is in *Perik.* 497), so she has no right to behave like this. In [Demosthenes] **59.46** *Against Neaera*, the arbitrators decided that Neaera *was* her own *kyria*, 'mistress', i.e. free in theory to take her own decisions (who she 'went' with).

48 πειρώμ[εθα, 'let us try'. If the supplement is correct, we might imagine Getas saying something like 'let us try to reconstruct what happened'. I assume the form is subjunctive, but it may be indicative. This word presumably triggered Turner's theory that the following narrative was a 'test' of Krateia's affections.

50-57 These lines (and possibly more) describe an event which proved to Thrasonides that Krateia felt no sympathy for him. They concern a stormy night in winter when Krateia did *not* try to dissuade him from going out to meet someone. It seems likely then, by the rule of economy, that this stormy night is the same one as that with which the play begins, when we find Thrasonides pacing up and down outside his house: cf. Sisti (1985a, 86), Katsouris (1985, 210). The account comes immediately after Thrasonides has confided in Getas about Krateia's antipathy; it is likely, therefore, that they explain how Thrasonides became convinced of her hatred. This interpretation is supported by the tenses Thrasonides uses in the narrative: vivid present, largely, suiting something fresh in his memory. The 'present perfect' κέκραγα, 'I shout' (53), is also in line with this (so also Handley *ap.* Turner: 'vivid narration of past actions'). So it seems that we are hearing the immediate background to the initial scene of the play, Thrasonides' lament to Night. He has quarrelled with Krateia; she has *not* tried to dissuade him from going out in this miserable night, so he has gone out and stayed out, lamenting his misfortune in love. If that is all there is to it, one might say Thrasonides is a bit of a wimp (Germ. 'Sensibelchen'); a rougher lover might not have taken any notice of such a minor perceived slight. But of course there is text missing after line **56** so Krateia may have become more explicit.

50-51 τηρῶ τὸν Δία ὕοντα πολλῶι, 'I'm keeping a wary eye on Zeus who's raining cats and dogs'. The reading is now clear from O^5, but an earlier and incomplete version had been preserved in Nonius Marcellus 387.33 Mercier (= IV 619-620 Lindsay = fr. 721 K-Th); for an interesting history of the philology attached to this quotation, with Porson's correction which brilliantly anticipated the papyrus find, see Sisti (1985b).

But what is the sense of τηρῶ? τηρέω (and ἐπιτηρέω) followed by accusative and participle *can* have the meaning 'wait *for* something to happen', not 'watch out *while* something is happening'. Cf. [Dem.] *Against Neaera* **59.103** οἱ δὲ τηρήσαντες νύκτα καὶ ὕδωρ καὶ ἄνεμον πολύν, 'they waited for a rainy, windy night'. Assuming this sense here, Turner reconstructs a kind of plan in Thrasonides' mind: he was waiting *for* an inclement night in order to test Krateia's love. He had it planned that on such a night he would announce he had to go out to a friend somewhere; Krateia would object, saying the weather was too bad, and – there he would be, in bed beside her (52 ἔχων αὐτὴν δὲ κατάκειμαι). Instead, she had not objected, thus showing she did not care for him (and Thrasonides had gone out into the terrible night).

I am not sure this is right. Certainly the clause ἔχων αὐτὴν δὲ κατάκειμαι cannot be taken in this way. Rather it is a further point in Thrasonides' description to Getas of how he had been lying in bed beside Krateia that night following the progress of the storm. So, does τηρῶ mean waiting *for* in the sense Turner envisaged? I think the details Thrasonides gives – the heavy rain, the thunder and lightning – better suit a description of what *was* happening that night rather than what Thrasonides awaited theoretically in the future. He tells the sequence to Getas: 'there I was in bed beside Krateia with a wary eye on Zeus hurling down rain, thunder, lightning. I mentioned I had to go out to see someone. Now any normal caring wife would have objected … ' This is surely narrative (with vivid present tenses) rather than a plan of action. In that case what does τηρῶ mean? I think 'watch' suits better, in the sense of watching for a *lull* in the storm. Thrasonides was not so much testing Krateia as discovering circumstantially that she cared not a whit for his well-being. On a foul night he was waiting for the rain to ease off, perhaps; he announced he had to meet someone and had to go out, and Krateia *failed* to restrain him. Thrasonides deduced that she disliked him, because 'any normal woman' would have tried to stop him. As Sisti points out in the above-mentioned article, Nonius' quotation from these lines makes *servare* in Vergil *Georg.* 1.335 equivalent to Menander's τηρέω: '*quod superest, coeli menses et sidera serva.' quod est Menandri* τηρῶ *… πολλῶι*. But here *servare* surely means 'observe' rather than 'await' suitable weather for planting etc.; cf. Mynors (1990) *ad loc.* The meaning 'pay strict attention to' of τηρέω is common in Menander, e.g. *Asp.* 361 (supplement), and 384, *Dys.* 910; esp. *Epitr.* 345-7: ὄντ' ἐπισφαλῆ φύσει / τὸν βίον ἁπάντων τῆι προνοίαι δεῖ, πάτερ, / τηρεῖν, 'since life's tricky by nature, one must pay it strict attention with foresight'. Cf. Antiphon, *First Tetralogy* 2.8: τὴν ἀσφάλειαν τῆς ἐπιβουλῆς τηροῦντα φυλάξασθαι, 'to guard against (sc. danger) by paying attention to the safety of the attack'. There is no reason why we should not assume a similar construction and sense in the *Mis.* passage here. Thrasonides says he was keeping a wary eye on Zeus who was creating a storm.

For what it is worth, Thrasonides would probably have returned from campaign in Cyprus in autumn, so the weather described here suits an autumn or early winter storm in Greece.

There is a further problem with Turner's view, in my opinion. On the 'brother's sword' hypothesis, to which Turner subscribes, Thrasonides cannot have been waiting *for* bad weather to test Krateia's affections, as this was the first night following Getas' arrival, bringing the spoils of war (and, putatively, the brother's sword).

Act One 135

51 The text of O⁵ is faulty here as βροντάς, as it stands at line end, is unmetrical. O⁶ gives us an ending -ης before ἀστρα[πάς which Handley supplemented as νυκτὸς [οὔσ]ης, and moved βροντάς to the following line, thus mending things. Such an error, one might think, points to an error of copying by dictation (see p. 219 on O³) rather than by eye from an exemplar (originally). There is a further fault in O⁵ in line 52 in the position of δέ which needs to be moved to a position *after* αὐτήν.

52 ἔχων αὐτήν, 'holding her'. An example of Menander's understatement, a phenomenon I made much of in the *Perik.* commentary (Introduction pp. 32ff.). The point here is that Thrasonides is holding Krateia in his arms, a situation suited to sex. When he suddenly breaks off, announcing he must be off to meet 'somebody', any normal woman, as he says, might protest and say 'why now?' But not one who spurned his advances; she would be happy that he broke off in this way.   κατά-κειμαι, 'I'm lying'. Handley *ap.* Turner points out that κατάκειμαι might mean 'lie at table' as well (as in line 723?); cf. Eur. *Her.* 956 κλιθεὶς ἐς οὖδας. Then the scene would not be a 'bedroom' scene, but the moment during the evening repast when Thrasonides announced that he should meet someone. For all we know, he may have left Krateia following this scene at the *deipnon*, gone off to see whoever it was, and then, returning, had qualms about going inside to the unwelcoming Krateia.

53 κέκραγα. The point of the loud shout is that the noise of the storm would drown out words spoken at normal volume (Traill, 2008, 28). The perfect of κράζω is used more frequently than the present, as an intensifying 'present perfect' (*CGCG*, 33.37).   βαδίσαι. Turner read βιδισαι here in O⁵, but in fact I think what we have is a compressed and indistinct alpha after all. Some of the ink is quite rubbed.

54 Thrasonides announces that he 'already should' (δεῖ ἤδη) be off to see someone, 'adding some name or other'. Possibly this 'someone' is significant to the plot and links up with the dubious characters Thrasonides is involved with in lines 560ff. Unfortunately too much text is lost to know the truth here.   ἤδη, not gratuitous, but significant: 'I must already be on my way' says Thrasonides, while the storm is still raging.   ‹ἐπ›είπας, 'adding'. O⁵ has merely ειπας, but that will not do metrically and prosodically. Although Arnott (1996d, 31) argues that ὑπειπ- is more idiomatic than ἐπειπ- for 'adding', I think the form ὑπείπας is too 'precious' for its context; moreover ἐπείπας would lend itself rather better to the haplography which seems to have happened in O⁵ (ἐπειπ-→εἰπ-). Arnott also discusses the question of weak aorist forms of εἰπ- in Menander generally.   φημί, δεῖ. O⁵ has φημϊδει where the diaeresis would normally mark the beginning of a word (i.e. ἰδεῖ[ν]?). But that is clearly not the case here, so the dots seem to mark the *end* of φημί.

55-57 Here Thrasonides imagines what the 'normal woman' would say in such a situation. Whether the actor put on a woman's voice for the imagined speech is open to question. Would Thrasonides at this (for him) emotional juncture be interested in putting on a funny woman's voice? Possibly but not certainly. ὦ τάλαν, at least, is a distinctly feminine expression and might sound funny if spoken 'normally' by a man. On female speech in Menander see Bain (1984), and on speech within speech see Nünlist (2002) and Handley (2002, 178-86).

55 δήπ̣[ο]υ [τόδ'], '[would] doubtless [say] this'. The trace after δη- matches pi rather than previous editors' tau; and τόδ' avoids the usual stopgap γ'.

56 [πρὸς ἄνθρω]πόν τινα; 'to some person or other?' I think after much consideration that this supplement (Austin) which involves incredulous repetition of Thrasonides' words is the best solution to date. The point is: any normal woman would be horrified if her lover, when about to make love to her, announced he was off to meet 'somebody or other'; she would feel slighted. Handley's suggestion ([μέθες τρό]πον τινά, 'change your style!' with 'idiomatic' τινά) is ingenious but I think a little pretentious for the girl's style. Instead of his μέθες one could equally imagine ἄνες, 'let go', 'take it easy!'

57 σκότ[ους]. These letters, which look like part of σκότος, in combination with the paragraphos under them, show this line is probably a continuation of the 'normal' woman's comment on the atrocious weather (which begins in 55). The beginning of the next line (after paragraphos) is then probably spoken by Getas, and began with ἥδε, 'she … ' Not much to choose between σκότου or -ους, but *Dys.* 57 has the sigma-stem.

57-83 Here lines are missing or hopelessly truncated. Presumably Thrasonides gives more details about the night in which he quarrelled with Krateia. By 84ff. he seems to have moved on to a general lament of his condition: if Krateia spurns him he will be the most miserable man. If she shows some affection for him (85) he would give a thank-offering to all the gods. Here Thrasonides depicts himself as the classic *exclusus amator*, desperately hoping for a positive sign from his beloved, which will grant him entry to—his own house! Menander consistently twists conventional scenes and here the additional twist lies in the fact that Thrasonides is excluded from his own house; cf. Sisti (1985a, 88) and above p. 112. For the figure of *exclusus amator* cf. Copley (1956).

79 ὁ τοῖχος, is the wall of a house. Or could Thrasonides be using the word metaphorically, to mean the 'wall' which has come between himself and Krateia? Elsewhere he uses similarly bold metaphoric speech (e.g. lines 761, 765).

80 ερειϲεαυτ. This could be variously divided either with a future of λέγω or, conceivably, after the mention of τοῖχος in the previous line, with an aorist of ἐρείδω (ἔρεισ' ἑαυτ[ήν]). As a guess, perhaps ἐρεῖ «σεαυτ[ὸν] … » 'she'll say: "— yourself" '. Lamagna in Bastianini & Casanova (2004, 200) thinks in this direction, pointing out that any other division (ἐρεῖ σεαυτ[or ἐρεῖς ἑαυτ[) is difficult syntactically.

Act One   137

82 ὦ τᾶν, a quite common address in drama (tragedy and comedy, not Aristophanes), 'my good friend', e.g. Men. *Sam.* 202, *Com. Adesp.* 21.11 D.

84 ὑπερεντρ[υφ-. The surviving letters point inevitably to a form of the rare verb ὑπερεντρυφάω, 'to be exceedingly haughty', elsewhere used by Alkiphron 4.10.2 (Myrrhine to Nikippe) with ἡμῖν, 'to us', and in Σ Soph. *Trach.* 281. The simple verb ἐντρυφῶν occurs in Menander fr. 718.8 K-Th (fr. 508 K-A). In context Thrasonides must be saying that Krateia is treating him 'exceedingly haughtily'. It is not surprising that Alkiphron then picks up this word – also in a context of soured relations – as he was fond of Menander; cf. Vox (2014), Funke (2016).

86 παρορωμένωι δέ, 'if you scorn me, however'. Thrasonides is telling Krateia (in dialogue with Getas) that she should not 'treat him thus discourteously' (to use the phrase in *Greensleeves*) but should pay attention to him: if he is 'shunned', he lists in asyndetic series the uncontrolled behaviour he will exhibit: 'striving for attention, exertion, madness'. The facets of behaviour remind one particularly of the mad fervour caused by love according to Plato in the *Symp.* and *Phaidros*: *erōs* as *mania*, but with the capacity to precipitate stupendous acts of valour and self-sacrifice. For madness as a motif in the play see lines 11-12 already.

87 πόνον The pi in O⁵ is very badly formed, and doubt surrounds it; an alternative does not suggest itself.

88 «φί[λτατε»] 'dearest', or, with Lloyd-Jones, φιλοφρόνως (perhaps a little formal?). The repetition of a form of φίλτατος after 85 (Turner) does not seem to me grave. Also at line end in *Dys.* 632 (Simiche to Sikon). Cf. Eur. *Her.* 490 ὦ φίλτατ' (Megara to Herakles).

89 θύσαιμι πᾶσι τοῖς θε[ο]ῖ̣[ς. 'I would sacrifice to all the gods!' as an expression of his delighted gratitude. Cf. *Sam.* 386 νὴ καὶ τοῖς θεοῖς θύσει, 'Yes, and she'll sacrifice to the gods' (sc. from gratitude). In *Her.* 50-51 we may have a similar situation when Daos (?), who is unhappily in love, avers ἐγὼ γὰρ κλη[...] / θύσαιμ' ἀνονητο.[, particularly if the last visible trace in line 50 is eta (a form of καλέω?), and not iota, as the OCT prints: 'For I, if (?)called [...] would sacrifice selflessly' (reading ἀνόνητος with Jensen). What Daos might be called is unclear, as in our passage, but something involving betrothal to the girl, no doubt. At this point Thrasonides is not asking for much: merely to be called by an endearment by Krateia.

90-94 Getas engages with Thrasonides in light-hearted banter, running through his possible handicaps as a lover. We have already noted that Getas is anything but intimidated by his master. The sequence consists of a number of twists in direction, like a hare running: 'you're not overly unattractive, but of course the military pay … actually quite urbane in appearance, but then there's your age … ' Thrasonides can only snort in indignation at the end 'to hell with you!'

138   *CHAPTER 5. COMMENTARY*

90 **[ο]ὖν.** This suits the space a little better, I think, than Sisti's τί νέον, 'what's new that … ?' Morover it does not beg the question what that new development is (see note on line 43). What Sisti seems to have taken for omikron (before nu) is, in fact, the right side of upsilon. The combination τί οὖν is very common in Menander e.g. *Asp.* 39, 171 etc.

90-91 **σφόδρ' … ἄκρως ἀηδής**, 'very exceptionally unattractive', lit. 'very highly'. The double adverb is paralleled in Men. fr. 176.3 K-A, *Kol.* 9, *Epitr.* 932 (πάνυ κακῶς ἔχω σφόδρα).   **ἀηδής.** στρατιωτικὴ ἀηδία, 'a military unpleasantness', is the quality which, according to Choricius, put Krateia off Thrasonides (42.1.1 see introduction p. 5). So this remark of Getas' actually tells *against* Choricius' view. Turner (1979, 110) comments: 'Choricius, on present showing, does not appear to have read the play with any attention'.   **ὥστε γ' εἰπεῖν**, 'so to speak', a variant of ὡς εἰπεῖν, the so-called limitative infinitive; perhaps paralleled in the *monostichoi* (Jaekel, 1964, 5.8): ὥστε … λέγειν (see now: Pernigotti (2008)).

91 Hard to see how the paragraphos can be correct here. σο[ι at line end cannot be μοι, and the sentence definitely runs on.

92 **ἀμέλει**, a colloquialism, 'naturally', 'doubtless'. The remark is probably ironical, meaning that Thrasonides in fact has considerable wealth and Krateia could not fail to be impressed by that. For the ironical use of ἀμέλει cf. Aristoph. *Frogs* 532. If this explanation of the line is correct, Choricius did not get the point, see note on ἀηδής (above).   **τοῦ στρατιωτικοῦ** (sc. ἀργυρίου), soldier's pay, e.g. Dem. 13.4.   **[νοσεῖ]**, 'is a problem', 'won't help'. The conjecture is supported by Choricius 42.1.1, p. 509 Förster-Richtsteig (see intro. p. 5), commenting on Thrasonides in *Mis.*: στρατιωτικὴν γάρ φησιν (sc. Menander, or Getas?) ἀηδίαν **νοσοῦντα** τὸν ἄνθρωπον κτλ., whereby this author mentions Thrasonides' 'military unpleasantness' generally rather than anything to do with his pay specifically. Nevertheless, the reference to this passage of the play seems clear. For νοσέω in the general sense of 'suffer', 'be in a bad condition' (Germ. 'krankt') see LSJ s.v. 3. Eur. *IA* 1403 τὸ τῆς τύχης δὲ καὶ τὸ τῆς θεοῦ νοσεῖ, 'chance and the divinity are unpropitious', fr. 497.1 ἐντεῦθεν νοσεῖ τὰ τῶν γυναικῶν, 'hence women's condition suffers', id. *Med.* 16 νῦν δ' ἐχθρὰ πάντα καὶ νοσεῖ τὰ φίλτατα, 'now everything is hostile and closest kin are at loggerheads', id. *Tro.* 27 νοσεῖ τὰ τῶν θεῶν, 'the gods are hostile'.

93 **ὑπεράστειος**, 'exceedingly polished', or 'witty'. Elsewhere only in a fragment of the 2nd c. BC historian Hegesander. Like Ἑλληνικόν, civilized Greek (compared to barbarian), ἀστεῖος is something of a keynote in Menander: behaviour 'fitting to the ἄστυ', or civic community, 'urbane' (Lat. *urbanus*). Of the many instances e.g.: *Asp.* 375, *Her.* fr. 4.2 Sandbach, *Dys.* 569, 658, *Kith.* fr. 4.2, *Sam.* 17, 364, 657, *Fab. inc.* 49. ἀστικός, on the other hand, is found at *Dys.* 41, *Her.* fr. 9 Sandbach. For Menander's use of ἀστεῖος and ἀστικός cf. the Byzantine lexicographer Ōros

Act One   139

fr. B50 (Alpers, 1981). D.M. Bain, *Liverpool Classical Monthly*, vol. 8, 1983, 94
cites the word ΑΣΤΕ(Ι)ΟΠΡΟΣ(Ω)ΠΟΣ, 'of urbane appearance', perhaps, from a
Thasian inscription (mid-4th. c. BC) in connection with this line (not seen).
The combination with ὑπέρ here, applied to external appearance (τὴν ὄψιν) indicates that something like 'very well turned out' is meant. One thinks of the anecdote
told by Phaedrus V 1 (test. 9 Körte; Fortenbaugh & Schütrümpf (2000, no. 44)) how
the leaders and mob of Athens saluted Demetrios of Phaleron after his assumption of
power in 317. Last came the *resides et sequentes otium*, the ἡσυχάζοντες, among
them Menander, oiled, dressed in a magnificent robe and mincing along with delicate
step. Demetrios did not know the man but admired his works. When Demetrios saw
him he said 'Who is this poof (*cinaedus*) who dares to come into my vision?' The
answer came: 'This is Menander, the writer'. Immediately he changed his tune: 'A
man,' he said, 'cannot be more comely'. There is no guarantee that the anecdote has
any historical basis (Arnott, 1964, 114), but I think an air of urbane polish emanates
from Menander's works. The reader can form their own opinion from the Menander
portraits surviving either in the original or in Roman copies; see Studniczka (1918).
Getas is here complimenting Thrasonides (ironically) as embodying this quality (*ur-
banitas*) to the highest degree. Menander himself, of course, was well known to
have had a squint (Sud. s.v. Μένανδρος· στραβὸς τὰς ὄψεις = Test. 1 K-Th; cf.
Studniczka (1918, 31)). Could it be that ὄψιν ὑπεράστειος, 'very cultivated in appearance', is a metapoetic joke against the poet himself?

93-4 ἄγ[εις. Arnott (1996d, 32) suggested reading ἄγεις here with ἐφ' ἡλικίας in the
following line, understanding something along the lines of 'but you are bringing (?
an attractive young girl) at her prime'. I would suspect rather a jibe such as: 'well,
you're getting on a bit', i.e. ἡλικίας would apply to Thrasonides' age – with ἄγεις
or perhaps ἄγαν in the previous line. The lack of certainty at line end 93 makes
supplementing 94 particularly difficult. If ἔτη is right before ποθέν, we might expect
some numeral in the gap – either much too few for Thrasonides' real age, or far too
many, but the word(s) elude me. I assume the line had roughly the shape of 'And of
course you're in (reading ἄγεις) the absolute prime of life!' That 93-94 contain some
sort of jibe is clear from Thrasonides' irritated expletive in 95. In Ovid *Met.* 3.455-6,
(a passage Davis (1978) suggested shows affinities with the beginning of *Mis.*), the
age of Narcissus is mentioned as a possible reason why the mysterious boy might not
love him – and promptly rejected.

95-97. Although O[5] clearly has paragraphos below line 95 it is probably better, with
most editors, to ignore this and have Thrasonides continue on to the beginning of line
97. After Getas has jokingly pointed to a number of faults in the soldier's appearance
or lifestyle, Thrasonides says now 'To hell with you! We must find the real reason
… ' (sc. for Krateia's disliking).   αἰτίαν ἀναγκ[α[]αν, 'a compelling reason',

140   CHAPTER 5. COMMENTARY

a phrase found commonly used in imperial age scientific literature including Philo,
Damascius Phil., Dionysius Hal., Galen, Flavius Justinianus, Joannes Chrys. Particularly in the Peripatetic School ἀνάγκη is often set in parallel to αἰτία. It seems that
Menander is jokingly alluding to Thrasonides' troubles in terms of a knotty philosophical problem to be analysed and explained by its root cause.   [δεῖ]ξαι Nothing of
the xi is visible except a high dot.

97 μιαρ[ὸ]ν τὸ φῦλόν [ἐσ]τι. 'They're a poisonous bunch, master' (sc. women).
Getas responds to his master's plan with a pithy *gnōmē*, which was, in fact, something
of a stock expression: examples in Lukian *Fug.* 12.3, Plut. *De liberis educandis* p. 13
B8, Dion. Hal. *Ant. Rom.* 4.24.8 (none referring to women). μιαρός is a favourite
word of Aristophanes as a derogatory term: e.g. *Ach.* 285 μ. κεφαλή; μιαρώτατος
ib. 182; μ. φωνή coarse, brutal voice, *Knights* 218; μιαρώτατος περὶ τὸν δῆμον
ib. 831. Alkaios once uses the word to mean 'licentious' (39). Here, too, Getas may
be insinuating that 'there's no trusting women, master', as they may take a fancy to
someone else. In this play, that is clearly a suspicion surrounding Krateia, as Getas
thinks he has found the rival lover when he first encounters Demeas (her father) embracing her (618-22).   φῦλον, 'tribe'. Already Hesiod and Homer talk of the
'tribe (or 'tribes') of women' (*Theog.* 1021; *Il.* 9.130 φῦλα γυναικῶν), but one feels
here the word is somewhat derogatory (the examples of the phrase μιαρὸν φῦλον
above are all derogatory), hence my gloss 'bunch' above. Getas' point of course is
that women collectively are 'a bad lot', so Thrasonides should not be surprised by
Krateia's hurtful behaviour. One may wonder at the servant giving his master advice on women, particularly as he belonged to the reputedly brutal tribe of Getai
(see *Asp.* 243-4, *Sam.* 519-20), but this is the charming classlessness of Menander's
artificial world.

98 ἂν μ]ὴ παρῆι[ς], 'if you don't give over … !' (sc. I'll beat you). Sommerstein is
probably right that οὐ παρήσεις in *Sam.* 520 means 'won't you let me past?', i.e. 'get
out of my way!' (Nikeratos to Moschion), but it seems to be different here. For an
elliptical threat Turner compares *Dys.* 112 ἀλλά σ' ὁ Ποσειδῶν.   σὺ δέ γ' ἃ
διηγεῖ, δέσπ[οτα. If correct, this must mean 'But as to what you're saying, master',
where σύ is the subject of the relative clause, and the main clause is what follows (how
Krateia's behaviour is to be interpreted).

99 οὔτε γ'] ὁμοθυμεῖ. ὁμοθυμέω occurs as *var. lect.* for ὁμονοέω at Xen. *Kyr.*
4.2.7. I take Getas to be saying 'she's not of one mind with you … ' and πρὸς [σὲ] as
equivalent to σοί. Here we would have οὔτε … τε, 'not A, and B'. Turner's ὀμόσαι,
adopted by Blanchard, does not fit the traces well, nor is it easy to see how an infinitive
fits.   συκάζει, lit. 'pick figs', seems in comedy to have carried sexual innuendo;
Photius glosses it by συκοφαντεῖν, which, we are told, can have the sense κνίζω
ἐρωτικῶς, 'tease (or perhaps 'pet') erotically', as in Plato Com. 255, and Menan-

Act One 141

der fr. 464 K-A. Turner (1968) cites Hsch. συκάζειν· κνίζειν ἐν ἐρωτικαῖς ὁμιλίαις, 'tease in erotic converse'. σῦκον/συκῆ, fig, seems itself to have the innuendo of female genitalia in comedy (Aristoph. *Peace* 1350); cf. McClure (2003, 269). We might take συκάζω here, in an erotic context, to mean 'talk lasciviously to', 'flirt with'. Arnott (1996c) seems to be thinking along these lines when he translates 'she's enticing [you]'. One instance in Strattis *Atalanta* fr. 3 K-A, may go further in its innuendo. There (in a quote in Athenaios 13.62.24 Kaibel) a certain 'I' claims 'to have seen Lagiska, the *pallakē* of Isokrates, συκάζουσαν while still in bed, and the flute-borer himself'. What Lagiska was doing is glossed in our lexika only with *sensu obsceno*; I suppose *fellatio* is meant (by analogy with the plain meaning of eating figs). For commentary on the fragment see Orth (2009, 62-68). Perhaps this is also the joke in Aristophanes *Birds* 1699 (γλώτταισι συκάζουσί τε). But that is hardly what Menander's Getas means here, even by innuendo. A passage in Aristainetos' *Letters* will probably help us most. There the context is a rift in the relationship between Charisios and his girlfriend Glykera. He seeks advice from one Doris, asking 'shouldn't I entreat her on my knees?' to which Doris answers: 'Probably, my friend. There's nothing preventing you from testing the attitude of your loved one, [to see] how she stands with regard to making up with you' (1.22.21 Mazal «εἰκός γε, ὦ φίλτατε· οὐδέν, οἶμαι, κωλύει συκάζειν τῆς ἐρωμένης τὸν τρόπον, ὅπως ἔχει συμβάσεως περὶ σέ»). This sense of συκάζω, 'test' (from testing a fig to see if it's ripe) is found in ancient lexika: Σ Aristoph. *Knights* 259c.4: οἱ δὲ δοκιμάζειν. ἀποσυκάζειν γὰρ τὸ τὰ πέπειρα σῦκα διαλέγειν, 'some say "test". For ἀποσυκάζειν means to sort the ripe figs'; cf. Hsch. s.v. συκάζει· δοκιμάζει. Now we are closer to what Getas is probably telling Thrasonides: Krateia is testing him in some way, perhaps with her stand-offish behaviour. This part of the sentence, then, will be 'and she's testing you on her own initiative'.

100 αὐτό]νομο[ς, 'as an independent agent', i.e. 'wilfully', 'on purpose'; cf. Soph. *Ant.* 821; in comedy the word is only found elsewhere in Cratinus fr. 419 K-A, but there probably with the meaning (politically) 'independent'.   ε]ὔλογος, 'rational'. Presumably Getas means women are unpredictable, unreliable, so γυνή or θῆλυς (θήλεια) must have stood somewhere in the following line (in the next column, as line 100 is the bottom line of the second column). The irrationality here consists, in Getas' eyes, in Krateia's apparent dislike of Thrasonides as a way of testing his mettle as a lover. This is not the truth: Krateia has taken a dislike to Thrasonides for other reasons.

142   *CHAPTER 5. COMMENTARY*

Scene Two: Delayed prologue

We have absolutely no evidence who spoke the delayed prologue in this play, nor what he/she said. Turner (1979, 126) suggests it was personified Polemos, War (already in Aristoph. *Peace*), which would resonate with Demeas' remark in 634-35 that war is the 'common enemy' which 'has scattered my family' to the winds. One might hazard another guess: Erōs, as Maximus of Tyre, *Dialexeis* 20.5.c2 Hobein, mentions Erōs as the cause of desperate love and refers to ὁ ἐν μύθοις μισούμενος, which sounds like Thrasonides. In previous editions, a sole fragment (fr. 2, below) has commonly been attributed to the lost prologue. Since the omniscient 'play-goer's notes' style of prologue is a feature of Menander's art which (so far) is universal (*Sam.* is something of an exception), we can safely assume there was one such and that it came after the opening dialogue between Thrasonides and Getas, which has already told us quite a lot about what is happening. But the audience still needs to be filled in on vital points. Above all, we need to know why Krateia has an aversion to Thrasonides; if it is really because at this stage she thinks he has killed her brother, then we need to know why this belief is mistaken, in other words, what misconception lies behind this play, for there is usually a basic misunderstanding triggering events and tensions in Menander. In *Asp.*, for example, the human actors think Kleostratos has died in action and hence his estate needs an heir, but Tyche in the prologue informs us that in fact he escaped death and will return. Most commentators have assumed that something similar underlies *Mis.*: Krateia's brother will turn up alive and well and cut the Gordian knot. And we need to know from the prologue who Demeas is and why he has come to (?)Athens. Finally, Menander's audience probably learned something about the subplot of which we only have indistinct smoke signals in the extant fragments: the peculiar incident related by Getas in the third act, and (probably) showing that someone was plotting against Thrasonides. Another thread which is only glimpsed once in the fragments is Kleinias' girlfriend (cf. 671-2): this seems to have been a secondary 'love interest' of the play, but who or what was involved is lost. Was it, perhaps, Chrysis? So, unless more papyrus turns up, we are left groping in the dark as to much of the plot and must content ourselves with what survives, which consists of the main story line involving Thrasonides and Krateia, and the recognition of Krateia as Demeas' daughter.

Fr. 2 is probably from the prologue of the play. It has the right kind of expository tone. The scholiast's expression that it is spoken ὡς ἐν παρεκβάσει seems to point in the same direction: the divine (or otherwise) prologue in a Menandrean play is spoken, rather like the Aristophanean *parabasis*, out of context of the dramatic action: the prologue figure steps forward and out from the play's action (παρεκβαίνω) to address the audience directly. παρεκβάσει is Heath's correction of mss. παραβάσει. In this fragment we learn that Thrasonides has enjoyed a successful campaign in Cyprus, fighting under 'one of the kings'. In other words he was a *xenos*, a mercenary sol-

Act One   143

dier, like Polemon in *Perik.* Mercenary service became a feature of Hellenistic life, following the demise of the *polis* as the community requiring military duty from its free citizens (Trundle, 2004). Hellenistic rulers became the focus of power, a power which was maintained and, if possible, increased, by campaigns fought by mercenary armies. This meant, in broad terms, that patriotism as a motive for fighting gave way to that of personal enrichment and advancement. In this play the situation is reflected by the *laphyra*, spoils of war, which feature so prominently. At the same time the overseas service which came to typify the soldier's life led to a certain 'globalization' (within the Mediterranean world), with nationalities and citizenship becoming mixed up. Demeas is given a line which encapsulates this tendency: 'war, the common enemy, has scattered members of my family in all directions' (634-5). The expression 'under one of the kings' is not a very good handhold for determining what is meant historically. I suggest in the introduction (section 'Dating' p. 25f.) that Demetrios' defeat of Ptolemy at the sea-battle of Salamis in 306 BC might provide a suitable backdrop. The expression is, of course, deliberately vague.

Fragmentum dubium

Gelzer (1996) has argued that a fragmentary Strasburg papyrus (P.Strasb. WG 307 verso col. i 30 - ii 3) may contain a fragment of this prologue. Parsons (1996) had already argued that the verses belong to New Comedy, and suggested Thrasonides (p. 115) as possible subject. In the legible verses a plurality of people (1 ἀγαπᾶτε πάντες) is encouraged to take a favourable view of a man, who is said to 'unite the virtues in himself'. A list of his virtues then follows (*enumeratio*), including courage, loyalty to kings (φιλοβασιλεύς), simplicity of character, courteousness etc. Gelzer argues that the plural address to the audience is in place in a Menandrean prologue (or at the end of the play), and that the prologue-speaker's praise of Thrasonides would stand in appropriate contrast to Thrasonides' current problem: he is hated by Krateia. The prologue-speaker would be filling the audience in on Thrasonides' true character: a good man. Gelzer argues that all the positive attributes of the man can be attributed to Thrasonides (for some points, see below). Certainly the description of a brave, loyal, stout-hearted man suits Thrasonides *generally* well enough. Gelzer (p. 66) cleverly observes that the lines would suit the end of the prologue speech, where it serves as *recapitulatio* of what the speaker had said before. Similarly we find at the end of the prologue in *Perik.* (162-71), spoken by Agnoia, advice to the audience not to take Polemon's apparent brutality too much to heart, as she has caused it as a way of getting things moving. For equally persuasive arguments that the fragment does not belong to *Mis.* (or even comedy as a genre) see Austin & Stigka (2007). Their main points are that the enumeration of virtues is not typical of Menander's prologue speakers, that there is nothing comic in the lines, and that such open praise

144 CHAPTER 5. COMMENTARY

of Thrasonides by the authoritative figure of the prologue speaker hardly accords with
the nuanced picture of the soldier the play otherwise gives us. The jury is definitely
still out on this one.

1 ἀγαπᾶτε πάντες, 'all of you, look favourably'. Gelzer correctly argues that such
an exhortation is likely to be addressed to the audience, as Menander regularly does
either in the prologue or in a closing request for favour.

3 φιλοβασιλεύς, 'king-friendly'. Parsons (1996): 'Thus the word generally indicates
loyalty to the monarchic principle.' Clearly only applicable to a situation where the
monarchy stood in good repute, as was the case in Athens following the 'liberation'
of Athens by Demetrios Poliorketes in 307 BC, who acquired the honorific title of
βασιλεύς, see p. 25. As was suggested in the introduction, it is quite possible that
Thrasonides served (fictionally) in Demetrios' army which took Cyprus in 306 BC
from Ptolemy.

4 φιλέλλην. Getas says that Thrasonides' generosity in releasing Krateia to her father
and *kyrios* Demeas was Ἑλληνικόν, truly Greek (line 716). πραΰς. Said to be the
older form by Parsons (1996), πρᾶος being usual in Attic drama. However a papyrus
of the *Monostichoi* (VII 4 Jäkel) has -υ-.

εὐπροσήγορος, 'with the social graces' (Germ. 'umgänglich'). In lines 90-93 Getas
teasingly calls his master 'not very terribly unpleasant', and 'very urbane in appearance'. These virtues might be said to tally, to a degree.

7 Parsons (1996) would supplement τιμᾶν θεού[ς.

8 αὑτὸγ κυβε[ρνᾶν, '[how] to control himself'. This may be one of the strongest
pointers toward Thrasonides. Not only did he control himself on the stormy night,
when he wanted, above all else, to go in to Krateia, but also the passage in lines 761-70
are a long rumination by Thrasonides on how he will find it difficult not to show his
misery to the outside world, if Krateia continues rejecting him. In this passage he turns
and turns in his mind the torture of keeping his misery to himself and concludes that
it will be of no avail, as 'drink will one day strip bare the plaster' (sc. over the wound
to his heart). We recall the Chrysippos passage (above p. 6) which attested restraint in
Thrasonides. κυβερνάω ('steer') used metaphorically in Menander: fr. 372.4 K-A,
said of *tychē* which governs, steers and saves all (from *Hypobolimaios*).

Scene Three: Thrasonides and Getas?

This fragment of O[5] seems to come from dialogue between Thrasonides and Getas.
Turner considered placing it in col. ii of O[5], where it would have to fit between lines
57 and 85, but this is uncertain. The mention of 'thieves' and Getas' wish to evade
them (6-7) remind one of the formulaic lines before the first choral interlude when

Act One   145

the threatening proximity of drunken young men is announced, cf. Blanchard (2016, 257 n. 5) and Zagagi (1994, 73). If that were the case, it would seem that we have the sequence: initial dialogue between Thrasonides and Geta – delayed prologue – continuation of their dialogue until the first *entr'acte*. But this is quite uncertain. Approximately one hundred and fifty lines are missing before we begin to pick up the thread again in act two: no wonder it is difficult to make sense of many things after this gap.

1 καταβήσ[ομαι, 'I'll go down', is only one possibility, of course.

4 μάλα στρατιωτ[ικῶς …] ὁρᾶις. Quite probably we have here the sense of ὁρᾶν, like βλέπειν, either with adverb (e.g. Eur. *IA* 1122) or with internal accusative. 'You are looking very military', probably said by Getas and chiming with other fragments which point toward Thrasonides' military bravado (book frr. 1-3). It seems that Thrasonides is on his way 'down' somewhere (καταβήσ[ομαι in line 1 of this fragment) and has dressed in a military fashion, perhaps to impress someone. If this is truly the end of act one (see below) it would be Menander's habit to begin the next act with Thrasonides appearing in his military costume, continuing where he left off at the end of the previous act (Zagagi, 1994). Perhaps this is where he displayed boorish and threatening behaviour toward Krateia, which put her off him (still further?). In lines 95-97 he had stated the necessity of finding out what was behind Krateia's dislike of him; perhaps he tried in act two to discover what the αἰτίαν ἀναγκαίαν (96) was by adopting a threatening or aggressive stance toward the girl. We recall that Polemon, with Sosias, in *Perik.* laid siege to Myrrhine's house to force Glykera out of hiding. On the other hand, Krateia was *already* at loggerheads with him, so this cannot have been the first time he had displayed such behaviour, or there is some other cause (the brother's sword, after all?).

5 εἰσέρχομα[ι. This appears to mark Getas' exit, near the end of this first act.

6 λωποδύτας μοι περιπ[ατ-. The idea seems to be that Thrasonides, or Getas, may attract muggers (λωποδύται) by wandering around the streets (περιπατ-) at night. The syllable following περιπ[ατ-] must be long, unless we have the infinitive περιπατεῖν, so ⏑— might still follow in this line. There are several indicators here that Getas' words announce the arrival of the dancers of the *entr'actes*. 'I'm going in', 'thieves', 'fleeing them', 'hurry', are all pointers to precipitate exit pursued as it were by the chorus members. In other plays by Menander we hear of drunken revellers making up the intimidating street band (*Epitrep.*) or dancers in Pan's cult (*Dys.*). The thieves may play an equivalent role here. On the role of the chorus in Menander see Lape (2006). Her main, and interesting, point is that in Menander the comic chorus has become a *kōmos*, a group of drunken young individuals cavorting in the street. Traditionally the *kōmos* was associated with symposia, victory

celebrations, marriages. Lape argues that the *kōmos* is well suited to ushering in the marriage ceremony or celebration which typically closes a play. There are accounts of robberies and muggings by *kōmoi* by night in Athenian streets; Antiphon's first *Tetralogy* concerns a case of a man and his servant being mugged and robbed by night; in Demosthenes' speech *Against Conon* (54.8-9), Ariston describes the way Conon and his drunken cohorts fell upon him one night when he was out for an evening walk in the agora' (Lape p. 104). This anarchic, unruly behaviour of the *kōmos* well suits the introductory descriptions which typically preface the chorus' first performance in a Menandrean play. Hughes (2012, 221) points out that the new (round) orchestra was 20 metres in diameter, probably intended for a much larger company of choreuts (50?) than previously. He suggests that the dancing was probably dithyrambic in style. περιπ[ατ-. περιπατέω occurs quite frequently in the plays and fragments of Menander though with no clear connection to the philosophical school. See *Phasma* 10 with Cusset's note and above line 7 of our play, with note.

7 σπεῦδ[ε, 'hasten'. This seems preferable to Turner's ἐκλύτ[ως, although several letters are half occluded by a hole in the papyrus. ἐκλύτ[ως is not a good match of the traces, and the sense of this rare word is also suspect. I guess the sense to have been 'run away from these [men] and hasten … ' Getas is addressing Thrasonides and seems to be telling him to watch out for the drunken *kōmos* rapidly approaching.

8]τερος. Perhaps something like μαλακώ]τερος, 'gentler', ἐλαφρό]τερος, 'lighter'; the form seems to be a predicative adjective agreeing with the subject Thrasonides.

Act Two

Scene One: ??

Now we face a gap of approximately one hundred and fifty lines. Blanchard suggests that in the missing sequence Kleinias appeared, on his way to hire a cook for the meal which is mentioned again in 671-76. That cannot have been everything, and we are left in the dark by the surviving fragments. We left Thrasonides at the end of act one in military dress about to embark on some action. Somewhere, if ancient reports of the play have any substance, Thrasonides must have offended Krateia with his soldierly *braggadocio*. Perhaps there was a scene with the two of them in this gap, or report of such a scene. I suspect Krateia did not appear in the play until she enters in line 609 and is recognized by her father. I have argued (below) that her first words on appearing for the recognition scene probably refer to unpleasant behaviour on Thrasonides' part, which Krateia 'cannot stand any more' (609 οὐκ ἂν [δυ]ναίμην κ[α]ρτερ[εῖ]ν).

Act Two 147

Scene Two: Thrasonides and Getas

Where O⁴ begins to open a window on the second act we seem to be nearing the end of another conversation between Thrasonides (408 [δ]έσποτα) and Getas (409 Γέτα). Thrasonides leaves the stage quite soon (409 εἰσιών). The next scene is played out by Demeas and Syra, Kleinias' elderly servant. The two have never met. It seems that Demeas is bearing a letter, perhaps an invitation from Kleinias (425). In 433 he denies he has come to ransom someone. In 438 we find the words 'following tracks back' (ἰχνεύων πάλιν), which *might* mean he is trying to trace his scattered family members. In 442 he mentions the name of his daughter, Krateia, and learns – to his astonishment – that a Krateia lives next door (443 πα[ρὰ γείτοσι], my supplement). Syra agrees to show him the way, which she accordingly does later in the play (576ff.)

O⁴ is a wretched piece of copying, made worse by wear: readings are more than usually 'divinatory', to use Turner's expression. As Arnott (1996d, 32) says: 'The 92 mutilated lines of O.11 (P. Oxyrhynchus 2657) pose an infuriating set of problems to which there are no certain answers'. Nevertheless the scanty sense it yields gives us important clues as to the development of the plot.

406 γ]εγεν{ν}ημένον. Turner's correction to a form of γίγνομαι (τὸ γεγενημένον) is probably right, but strictly speaking τὸ γεγεννημένον from γεννάω is metrically possible. It might mean 'baby'. However there is not to our knowledge a conspicuous baby in this play.

407 ὑπονοεῖς. Quite uncertain.

409 εἰ]σιών, Γέτα. Blanchard supposes that Getas should go into Thrasonides' home to retrieve valuables with which to charm Krateia.

410 ικακ[..].ονους. The alpha of κακ- is clear enough, against Turner, who read epsilon. Unfortunately the trace before -ονους is so badly rubbed that one cannot decide between e.g. pi or mu. The ending is definitely not -μενους, i.e. a participle with κακόω.

413 ἀν]οικτον τοῦτ' ἐμοί. A probable restoration of the first word as ἄνοικτον gives the sense 'pitiless this to me', a sense which chimes with a leitmotif of the play that Krateia shows Thrasonides no pity. Less likely would be a verbal adjective οἰκτός or ἀνοικτός, 'which can be opened'. On the other hand we have just had a form of ἀνοίγνυμι, 'open', in the previous line, lending some support to the latter guess.

Scene Three: Demeas and Syra

Blanchard assumes at this point that Demeas arrives from Piraeus, having sailed there from Cyprus ('Crète' is presumably a misprint). O⁴ is dreadfully mutilated and allows us only to peep through a tiny keyhole at what is going on in the following scene.

148   CHAPTER 5. COMMENTARY

The scene is played out between Demeas and Syra, an old serving woman in Kleinias'
home. The scene prepares the ground for the later recognition scene, in which Syra
leads Demeas to Thrasonides' house, Krateia emerges, and Demeas recognizes his
daughter. If we could read more of the lines we would no doubt learn more about
Demeas, his relations with Kleinias, and the contents of the letter he is carrying (417,
425). The stranger arriving with a letter is a motif as old as Bellerophon in the *Iliad*
(6.168-170) and was employed by dramatists for introductions or recognitions. The
letter which Stratophanes' (foster-)mother sends to him on her deathbed in *Sik.*, in-
forming him of his true parentage, is a case in point. And the letter which Orestes
was to take back to Argos in Eur. *IT* (727ff.), and which permits the recognition of
brother and sister, is a good example. Lines 466-7 here are probably enough to see
that Menander indulged in paratragedy in this scene, marking up the affinity of the
scene with similar tragic scenes. We seem to start with a small 'entry monologue'
of Demeas, in which he enters and announces his purpose. There is mention of a
'door' (420) and a 'house' (421), and presumably Demeas has arrived in front of
Kleinias' house, bearing an invitation of some sort. It is certainly not a missive telling
him about Krateia, as the whole point of the Simplicius passage (intro. p. 3 and below, note on 432-2) is that Demeas arrives *by accident* but then (finds and) frees his
daughter Krateia.

417 γράμμα[τ]α, 'letter(s)'. Presumably these are operative in the plot, as in *Sik.*
136ff., *Thras.* 9, bringing important new information by an 'artificial' means. Who
is meant by ἐκεί]νης is not clear. Handley supplemented περὶ ἐκεί]νης which might
point in the direction of Krateia: 'a letter about her', but that is probably wrong, as
mentioned in the previous note. Presumably this is the same letter as in line 425, when
Demeas brandishes it in front of Syra's eyes. In 425 one might interpret ἐκεί]νου as
'from Kleinias'.

418 δε]ῦρ' ἄγω, '[which] I'm bringing here (sc. with me)', i.e. the letter.

419 τί βούλεται; Not necessarily 'what he/she wants', but possibly 'what it means'
referring to the letter.

420 Movement at a door. This is the beginning of an encounter between Demeas and
Syra. Syra is Kleinias' elderly maidservant, as first recognized by Arnott (1996d), so
presumably Demeas has knocked at the door of Kleinias, whose *xenos*, guest-friend,
he is. As mentioned above, there are paratragic elements in the conversation which
follows (e.g. Demeas' vocabulary in 428-31, 445-47, Demeas' part in the conversation 468ff.). It is probably fair to say that Demeas speaks in paratragic mode, but not
Syra. The playwright likes to remind his audience that his play is like a tragedy but
different: i.e. played out by everyday characters against a background which is only
pseudo-tragic.

Act Two 149

420 ἐ]κ[εί]νην τὴν θύραν He arrives at Kleinias' front door and either asks, or says to, himself 'this is the door'.

422].ος γὰρ ἂν κόψαντί σοι. Something like: '[I'll see] who [might answer] your knock'. It seems that Demeas has now knocked on (Kleinias') door and Syra has shown herself.

423 Demeas: 'as I'm standing here'. Before ἕστηκ(α) ἐγώ we have either]η γ' or, more probably I think,]ης.

424 οὑτοσί, ξένε. Turner's correction of the papyrus' itacism ουτοσει gives the sense 'it's him (indeed), stranger'. This might answer an inquiry by Demeas 'is this where Kleinias' lives?'

425 παρ' ἐκεί]νου. Some preposition before putative ἐκείνου is necessary, and the close conjunction of preposition and pronoun mitigates the 'split anapaest' in the second foot. If correct, probably 'from him' = Kleinias.

426 δὸ[ς] ταυτί. The letter, γράμματα, which Demeas then hands over: λαβέ. The position before δός must be short. In passing one might note that the words preserved seem to imply that Syra can read, although she may simply want to show the letter to Kleinias.

427 ἐπε]ράνω (‿ – –). I imagine Syra to be saying something like '[how] did you complete, stranger?' (2nd p. s. aor. med.) to which Demeas answers 'I sailed … ' but περανῶ; (shall I continue?) is also possible. Cf. Pindar *P* 10.28 for 'completing a voyage', ὁδόν Aristoph. *Frogs* 403. Other words are also possible, e.g. ὑπ' οὐρανῶι, or future of εὐφραίνω.

428-30 If these words are spoken by Demeas, I guess that he is saying something about his journey here. He may mention how many days it took (ὀκτώ γ' ἡμέρας), then the troubles he encountered (πιαῖνον πάθας, 'increasing [my] sufferings') and then some admission of ignorance (οὐκ ἔχω λέγειν). For what it is worth, eight days sounds about right for the journey Cyprus to Athens and tallies with what I said above (n. on 32, p. 125) on Thrasonides' and Getas' journeys home. The reading ὀκτώ γ' is conjectural.

429] πιαῖνον πάθας. The last word is something of a *cause célèbre* in the edition of this play. For the variant readings see *app.* Turner (followed by Blanchard) added a sigma and read σπάθας, swords, as he saw swords everywhere in this play. True, they play a role, but not necessarily here. For the use of the word σπάθη = 'sword' in this play, cf. line 677 and fr. 3. Why should Demeas be talking about swords here? πάθας means 'sufferings' and may suit Demeas' sufferings either through the war in Cyprus, or his sea journey here. The pi is an odd shape but may be compared to the pi in line 433 (πυθόμενος). If the first word can stand in this form it is a neuter participle from πιαίνω, 'increase', 'enlarge'. For metaphorical meanings of this word see LSJ

CHAPTER 5. COMMENTARY

s.v. II. In Porph. *Abst.* 1.34 we find exactly τὰ πάθη πιαίνει. It is very hard to guess what might be subject of the verb, but for example θαλάττης κῦμα might match the sense. Otherwise Austin's σέβας with αἰνὸν before it (]πι αἰνὸν σέβας ?), perhaps, is worth considering, although the first iota would be elided.

431]β.α. This might be [μὴ] βόα *vel sim.* but there seems no reason for either one to shout at this point. Then Syra asks Demeas where he has come from. Cf. *Asp.* 241 (note orthography ποταπός, with Beroutsos (2005, *ad loc.*)); Alexis fr. 177 , 232 K-A; Aesch. fr. 61 R. (thanks to H.-D. Blume for refs.).

432-3 παρὰ [Κύπρου κτλ.. Simplicius seems to be referring to these lines when he says (*In Aristotelis physicorum libros commentaria* 9.384.15, see intro. p. 3): 'when we say that the stranger came by chance and, having freed the prisoner, as in Menander Demeas did Krateia, departed'. This is difficult in a number of ways. (1) In Simplicius the stranger is said to arrive 'by chance' (ἀπὸ τύχης), whilst Demeas appears to arrive with some kind of letter of invitation, not completely by chance. The chance element must be that he happened upon Krateia, his daughter, living next door to his host. (2) Simplicius says that the stranger 'ransomed' (λυτρωσάμενος ... ἀπῆλθεν) the prisoner of war (= Krateia) and went away. In the play we see a kind of impasse in act four with Demeas demanding of Thrasonides that he free (= ransom) his daughter, and Thrasonides counter-demanding that he marry Krateia. However, by the play's end we can assume that Thrasonides *has* freed Krateia, as he proceeds to marry her. In line 805 (ἀφήσεις) Thrasonides seems still to be considering the question whether he should free Krateia (likewise, lines 802-3). (3) It is not clear in the extant remnants of the play that Demeas sails off again (ἀπῆλθεν). He might have intended to do so, but in fact stayed, when the marriage was agreed upon. And, indeed, ἀπῆλθεν is *var. lect.* in the Simplicius passage; alternatively, ἀφῆκε. Generally, we might say that Simplicius' comparison served as an example of chance circumstances arising from non-purposive action. We note that Simplicius does not mention Cyprus – but Demeas himself does in line 632, so the supplement is justified here.

432 λυτρούμενος. λυτρόομαι (middle) means 'release by payment of a ransom' (the λύτρον, from λύω, release). Syra assumes Demeas has come on a mission to ransom missing persons (see previous note). He denies this vehemently; at this point he has no idea he is going to find Krateia in servitude. Syra may know about the recent campaign in Cyprus and hence assumes the nature of Demeas' mission. I have supplemented what remains on the assumption that the letter has somehow 'called' Demeas on some family business: 'because of the disaster which befell me, they are seeking me ... and chance herself has played a role'. Demeas enjoys a relationship of guest-friendship with Kleinias.

433 ἥκεις πυ[θόμενος, 'have you come having heard?' (sc. about the people be-

Act Two   151

ing ransomed). pi and upsilon are clearly legible, ruling out the previous reading (Turner) σὺ [δεῦρο; For the construction with 'delayed' participle cf. *Sam.* 458-9 τί τ]οὺς φίλους / προσδοκᾶις ἐρεῖν πυθομένους; 'what do you think your friends will say when they hear about it?' and *ibid.* 491 χαλεπανεῖ γὰρ πυθόμενος, 'he'll be annoyed when he hears about it'; Aristoph. *Birds* 263.   μὰ τὸν Ἀ]πόλλω, 'γὼ μὲν οὔ. For the form of denial with oath cf. Aristoph. *Birds* 263.

434 [τῆς ἐμοὶ κακότη]τος γενομένης. Perhaps a word like [κακό]τητος, 'because of the disaster which befell me'. Demeas would be referring to the warfare in Cyprus which broke up his family.

435 μ[ε. After ζητοῦσι one expects an accusative, although με causes a split anapaest. Perhaps it was elided before a vowel.

437 seems to be divided between the speakers although no paragraphos is marked. At the beginning Demeas seems to be asking Syra to help him, whilst she addresses him in the second half of the line. Perhaps [ἐγῶι]μαι, 'I think'.

438 ἰ]χνεύων πάλιν, 'tracing back', another tragic word. This looks as if it refers to Demeas trying to trace the whereabouts, or fate, of his family members.

439 ἀμ[. Perhaps something like ἄμιλλα, or ἀμέλει, or just ἄμα. If the paragraphos is true, there is one, or two, changes of speaker in mid-line.

440 σωτὴρ κ[εκλήσει, 'you will be called saviour'. If Turner's guess is right, the words express Demeas' joyful anticipation of hearing news of Krateia.

441 τί τοὔνομ' [ἐστί;] Syra inquires what the daughter's name is. Demeas tells her in the next line (Κράτ‹ε›ιαν), to which Syra may say in 443 that a person of that name lives next door (with Thrasonides).

443 If we are to honour the paragraphos under this line, some remark of Demeas must have stood in the second half.

444 οὗτος γὰρ. At a guess this will be Thrasonides: 'For he took her to wife … '

445 Ζεῦ τρ[ο]π[αῖε, 'Zeus of the victorious turning point!'. The tau of τροπαῖε looks more like an upsilon, making me wonder about an alternative epithet ὕπατε here, but the hiatus is probably intolerable, and ὦ Ζεῦ τροπαῖε is certainly the more common oath; Eur. *Hcld* 867; Soph. *Trach.* 303; the Σ on the latter passage glosses the word as ἀποτρεπτικέ, ἀλεξίκακε, which would make the word equivalent to ἀποτρόπαιε, an epithet found with Apollo in Aristophanes *Wasps* 161; *Birds* 61; *Plut.* 854. In any event Demeas seems to be exclaiming in joyful, rather than dismayed, surprise. The next line with ἀπροσδόκητον shows his surprise at finding Krateia here. All these expressions are paratragic, i.e. reminiscent of a recognition scene in tragedy; in *Perik.*, the recognition scene between Pataikos and Glykera in the fourth act is heavily paratragic. There the effect is laid on heavily; here it is much more moderate (also we

150 CHAPTER 5. COMMENTARY

do not have the complete text!). For more detailed discussion of the effect cf. Furley (2009, Intro. 1.2), with further literature and Zagagi (1994, 51-57).

449ff. The second column of O⁴ begins here with some badly damaged second halves of lines. From 453 the papyrus shows *first* halves of lines with paragraphoi.

453-4 εὔξας[θαι, γέρ[ον] / ἀνεμ[. Perhaps Syra is saying something like, 'You owe a debt of gratitude to the wind for bringing you here … ' Something about sailing πλε- or πλο- might be in the next line. The whole is uncertain but receives some support from line 456 where Syra seems to say that he should offer worship to the gods. The tone continues paratragic.

459 Κρά[τεια]. A doubtful supplement.

463 παι...... This might be the conventional formula of knocking on a door παῖ παιδίον: *Dys.* 911, 912, 921, but then one might expect some 'door action' to follow.

464 καὶ πάξ: Although only the xi can be clearly read, καὶ is present in a ghostly way, and πάξ, 'and there's an end to it!' is about the only word which can plausibly stand before xi and fill the gap. Dicolon follows. There is a *nota personae* above ἀλλ which can plausibly be interpreted as ΔΗ[.

465 μὰ Δ[ία, τ]ὰ τουπι . . ωι· ἀλ. After Δία there seems to be space for at least one letter before alpha. Then τουπι appears legible, which might constitute the expression τοὐπὶ, which is quite a common crasis, as in Eur. *Alk.* 666 τέθνηκα γὰρ δὴ τοὐπὶ σ᾽, 'I'd be dead as far as you're concerned', and *IA* 1557 καὶ τοὐπ᾽ ἔμ᾽ εὐτυχοῖτε, 'and as far as I'm concerned, fare well'; Soph. *Ant.* 889 τοὐπὶ τήνδε τὴν κόρην 'as regards … ' or Aristoph. *Lys.* 1026 τοὐπὶ τὠφθαλμῶι. But the following letters defy decipherment. If the expletive is correctly attributed to Syra reacting to something Demeas has said, her follow-up remark in 467 seems to correspond in 'that *too* is worrying … '

466-67 τρο[παὶ] δύ᾽ ἑκατέρωθε. τροπαί or Turner's τρόποι. τροπή is a 'turning'. The expression seems to mean 'two ways to turn in either direction'. Still in paratragic mode Demeas may be saying that he faces a quandary, to which Syra replies in the next line that it (the choice) or something is **φοβερ[ό]ν**.

468 εἰς τὸ πρόσθεν Cf. Eur. *IA* 619 αἱ δ᾽ ἐς τὸ πρόσθεν στῆτε 'you (sc. young women) stand before (sc. the horses)'. In effect 'lead on!' Demeas says to Syra, meaning that she should lead him to the neighbours' house in which Krateia may reside. Arnott (1996d, 32) correctly dismisses Turner's suggestion that 'the two speakers are contriving to bring Krateia out into the street'.

470 Perhaps Demeas means it will be embarrassing if he encounters Thrasonides: therefore Syra should take the lead.

471-2 Perhaps: 'ask him (Thrasonides) where we may find her (τήν)'.

Act Two 153

473-4 Perhaps something like 'Set your business right first and I will (?act) together
... ' σύν is very unlikely to be the preposition with a dative (? σὺν βραχέσι), as μετά
+ Gen. is far more common in comedy. A composite verb suited to Syra does not
readily suggest itself (? συμβραβεύσομαι), so σύν is likely to be adverbial, but how
βρα- continued is not clear. As a guess: σὺν βραχέως ποήσομαι (= συμποιήσομαι).
Demeas then asks 'how?' but the following lines are fragmentary. If ἀπάτην in 475
is right, some slight intrigue seems to be indicated.

475 ἀπάτην. Turner read here ἐρώτα τὴν, but the rho in ἐρώτα is definitely not
right; although the papyrus is torn in the middle here, the reading is much more likely
pi, and before that a vowel: alpha, giving a word like ἀπάτη, or perhaps upsilon
(ὑπάτην ?). Perhaps we have something like δι' ἀπάτην at the beginning of this
sentence.

476 εὑρεῖ[ν] μὲν Others have been content with a form such as εὕροιμεν (Turner)
but there is room for three letters between ευρ- and -μεν.

478-89 In these lines there are several mentions of a wife (e.g. 478 γυναῖκα). Is Syra
already considering the possibility of Krateia being given to Thrasonides as his wife?
Krateia was already designated a γυνή by Thrasonides in line 40, a word picked up
by Getas (probably) in the next line. She's certainly not his 'married wife'; perhaps
'woman' rather than 'girl' in the sense of no longer being a virgin. She must have been
pretty young at this juncture, one feels. In 477 and 490 there is talk of 'gratitude'
(τὴν χάριν): does she mean the gratitude Demeas should feel on rediscovering his
daughter?

479 καὶ [γ]ὰρ πο[ή]σεις, 'and you *will* manage it ... ', constructed out of ghosts of
letters, but *what* is unfortunately gone.

484 δειν[ὸν] λαβών. The first four letters are plausible (although Turner read δαν)
and in the next word beta is difficult to recognize, but similar to another weird beta
in line 470 (λαβόντα).

487]μι παντὸ[ς. Probably an aorist form in -οιμι such as τύχοιμι, 'may I encounter'
or 'gain'.

At the end of this scene Demeas probably exits into Kleinias' house where (in the
next act) he will have a chance to recognize the brother's sword brought in among
others by Getas. Although Syra seems to have mentioned a Krateia living next door
to Kleinias, Demeas must enter the house of his host (in Athens?) before he can visit
Thrasonides. There is a gap in the text here of approximately eight lines, including
XOPOY. Just conceivably, but without any positive handholds, one might fit in here
the fragment of P. Montserrat inv. 127 discussed by García (1987), who suggests,
without any reasons which are clear to me, that the fragment may come from *Mis*.

Act Three

Scene One: Getas' secret mission

Here begins the major source for this play P.Oxy. 2656, O[3], painstakingly reassembled from bits and pieces by Eric Turner, with the help of others. It is amazing what he (they) managed to squeeze from these tattered remnants. Then quite soon the new find P.Oxy. 5198, O[11], chimes in, which, in turn, is supplemented in places by the deceptive and recalcitrant P.Berlin, B[1] and B[2]. The first scene of this act is desperately lacunose. If my guess is right, following an appearance of Getas with attendants, Syra and Chrysis engage in conversation about the situation in Thrasonides' household. Syra is Kleinias' serving woman; Chrysis, as pointed out in the intro. (1.3.5), is probably an hetaira, rather than, as had previously been thought, Krateia's *trophos*. Then, unnoticed by them at first, Getas enters, weighed down, it would seem, by a burden (537). While Chrysis watches on, Getas seems to enumerate the goods he is carrying, mentioning among other things a grey coat, a ring and other jewelry. At one point he orders someone to 'take these inside' (548) and then announces his departure (550). Syra and Chrysis exchange disparaging words about this person who has been sneaking into Kleinias' house (553-55). We know that Getas carried the swords in Thrasonides' ownership into the neighbours' house, thus preventing him from committing suicide by sword, but there is no mention of swords in this scene, unless we can retain a very uncertain occurrence of ξί[φος] or ξί[φη] in 509 for this scene. Rather, the things listed by Getas seem more like the finery Thrasonides might have given Krateia in order to bring her round (see note on 532ff.). A great deal of this reconstruction of the text is based on extremely flimsy evidence, and could be swept away by new discoveries of text.

509 ξί[φ-, ξίφος, 'sword' (Austin) or, of course, ξίφη. Above the line Austin (*ap.* Turner) made out two letters of a *nota pers.*]ρα[which he took to be (K)ra(teia) or (Th)ra(sonides), but the marks are difficult to read and could be made to say almost anything. I believe I can make out γε. here, which is easy to identify as Getas, but should be treated with the utmost caution. But the marks almost certainly represent a *nota personae*, so ξι[is the beginning of his/her speech, and we should not combine it with the previous letters to form ἀναξι[. We know swords played (at least) two roles in this play: one identified by Demeas at the beginning of act four, and one demanded by Thrasonides to commit suicide (Arrian *Diss. Epict.* 4.1.19 = fr. 1 p. 63).

518 The *antilabē* in this verse indicated by paragr. and dicolon make it unlikely that this is the entry verse of (?)Syra. As we have seen, she seems to be attributed with lines from 509. Getas can be read (barely) as *n.p.* in 521, 524 and 557 making it highly likely that he is one of the speakers in this scene. That he whispers (540), however,

Act Three   155

makes it likely that he is *not* engaged in dialogue with Syra or Chrysis but rather is either talking to himself, or secretly to servants accompanying him (the version I prefer). After the women exit (557) he speaks loudly to himself, that is, to the audience.

519 σ]ὺ δ' ἥτις εἴπασ'[, It is not certain whether one or two letters are missing at the left edge before the upsilon. One might envisage σύ as here (or οὐδ'), but ποῦ e.g. would not be impossible. Likewise the articulation of ειπα- is anything but secure. I believe I can discern σ' at the end, which would point toward εἴπασ', a feminine participle aorist, but e.g. εἶ πας- would still be possible. The previous line seems to have made explicit that Getas has gone inside (into Thrasonides' house?), now Syra may be asking Chrysis a question. Since Syra (of Kleinias' household) must know Chrysis (wherever she lived), the question can hardly be 'who are you?' The answer certainly comes in the next line.

520 οὐκ ἂν δυναί[μην. If correctly supplemented, the words chime with Krateia's entry speech in line 609. With ̣νον[one might consider e.g. οὐκ ἂν δυναί[μην ἔνδον ἔτι χρό]νον μένειν. On the other hand, if it is Chrysis speaking, then δύναιο is equally possible, or the words are quoted.

521 εἶναι. There might be room at line beginning for another letter such as θ, e.g. θεῖναι, 'lay' or 'place', which might go well with ἱκετηρίαν in the next line, 'lay a suppliant bough'. But the uncertainty is great.

522 ἱ]κετηρίαν, is an olive branch, wrapped in woollen thread, of supplication, used by an ἱκέτης (or -ις) to ask for clemency; for more information cf. Gould (1973), Pötscher (1994,1995), Naiden (2006, 56-58). Blanchard (2016, 226 and 263) takes the suppliant to be Krateia, who intends to flee Thrasonides' house and seek sanctuary at an altar of the city. In 532 the olive branch is mentioned again, and the following exchange seems to point toward a reported altercation between Krateia and Getas, who says he is not opposing Chrysis but rather Thrasonides, who is living a wretched life. See note on 532ff. Kraus (1971a, 4) suggests that it was Chrysis who carried the suppliant branch for Krateia to some altar; Krateia would not have been allowed to leave the house (but Glykera does in *Perik.*). This would not have been the case if Chrysis is *not* her old nurse. Anyway, Krateia is at home when Demeas calls.

524 The *n.p.* in O[11] begins with a gamma and the next traces are unclear. Henry *et al.* (2014a) argue that alpha or lamda are most likely and suggest that perhaps an otherwise unknown female character, a Glykera for example, may make an appearance here. However, this lady is not identified by any other legible *n.p.* nor is she mentioned in the text. On the whole I concur with Blanchard that we can read Getas here as γε^τ.

528 ὁδ' [ὑπερ]πέπαικ[ε, 'he has surpassed'. A guess based on the legible letters]πεπαικ[, metre, and ὑπερπέπαικεν in *Asp.* 117, from ὑπερπαίω, 'surpass', 'outdo'.

156   *CHAPTER 5. COMMENTARY*

The *Asp.* passage runs πονηρίαι δὲ πάντας ἀνθρώπους ὅλως ὑπερπέπαικεν, 'altogether he has surpassed all men in wickedness'. I agree with Arnott, and Turner (1965, 24), that alpha is preferable to epsilon (πέπεικ[). But of course a form of παίζω, 'joke', or the simple verb παίω, 'strike', is quite possible. It seems that an accusative expression followed at some point – λόγους τούτους perhaps – 'he has surpassed these words'.

531-2 θ]ήϲει τοῖς φίλ[οις / ἱκετηρίαν; Henry *et al.* (2014a, in comm.) suggest θ]ήσει, someone (Krateia?) 'will place', with object, it would seem, the suppliant branch, ἱκετηρία (see note on 522). But the form could be 2nd p.s. future middle: 'you will lay?' and the words might be addressed to Krateia. Blanchard (263) pursues the idea that Krateia will lay a suppliant branch on an altar of the city, supplicating for her release from bondage.

532ff. Arnott (1996d, 33) is probably on the right lines, although less text was available to him: 'It is tempting to guess that immediately before line 532 the nurse (Chrysis) mentioned a conversation held recently with Getas, who may have tried to stop her leaving Thrasonides' house on her mission of supplication.' However, as we have seen in the introduction (p. 18), there is considerable doubt whether Chrysis is Krateia's nurse. Blanchard leaves the speaker of 533ff. unidentified.

In the following scene I *think* it is clear that the women (Chrysis and Syra) are having their chat, whilst Getas speaks *sotto voce* to himself or to others while despatching his clandestine business. It would be nice to think this is the moment when he smuggles all the swords from Thrasonides' house into the neighboring house of Kleinias (Arnott, 1998), but a distinct irritation is that the objects he mentions from **542-49** have nothing to do with swords or indeed weapons of any sort. Rather they look like finery which Thrasonides might be giving Krateia to bring her round; cf. book fr. 1 (p. 63) καὶ δῶρα τῆι μισούσηι πέμπει. In line **553** it seems to be Syra who complains that Getas is smuggling goods into her house, which is Kleinias', not Thrasonides'.

532 τί λέγου[ϲ]α; I assume this is Syra asking Chrysis what Krateia said to Getas. I follow the editorial convention of giving *scriptio plena*, without elision, when there is change of speaker in mid-line.

533 [μ]ὰ Δί' ἀλλ' ἐκεί[νωι] To use the modern idiom: 'and he's like, "God no, with *him!*" '. According to the interpretation above Getas is the subject of φησί.

533-34 δεινὸν γὰρ βίον / ζῆι κ[α]ὶ ταλαίπωρόν τιν'. For the wording cf. Plutarch *Nik.* 5 ἐπίπονόν τινα καὶ ταλαίπωρον ... ζῶντος αὐτοῦ βίον. **ταλαίπωρον**, 'miserable, wretched'. Thrasonides says of his own life at 811 ἀ[πό]ρως ζῆις, ὀδυνηρῶς, ἀϲθενῶ[ς. ταλαίπωρος is a favoured adjective of Menander's, occurring over ten times in the extant passages. Like e.g. ἄτοπος (see p. 132), it is perhaps one of the 'tonal' adjectives in Menander: life is no joke! – and yet it is precisely the stuff

Act Three 157

of Menander's comedy.

534-36. On balance I should think Getas continues to speak (as quoted by Chrysis) down to τιν' in 534, where there is clear dicolon in B². The γάρ in 533 indicates that this is Getas' justification for his position. If, as indicated in the introduction (p. 18), Chrysis is an hetaira, then her remark about Krateia's lifestyle (not bad!) might make sense as coming from a kind of rival. But 536 is then a kind of shrugging of the shoulders: 'well, she knows her own mind far better'.

534 οὐ γάρ; 'well, isn't it true?' or French 'n'est-ce pas?' Chrysis corroborates Getas' remark.

534-5 μακάριον / αὕτη (sc. Krateia). An ellipse carried over from the previous sentence δεινὸν βίον ζῆι (sc. Thrasonides). Krateia is living it up, according to Chrysis, at Thrasonides' expense, whilst keeping him at arm's length. The suppliant branch hypothesis, however, tells against Krateia's sense of well-being.

535 ὅσα γ' οὕτως ἰδεῖν·, 'as far as one can see', in the sense 'to judge from outward appearances'; cf. *Kith.* 108 ὅσα γ' οὕτως [ἰδεῖν] (suppl. Nünlist), see Austin (2012, 55); Aristoph. *Peace* 856-8 ὅσα γ' ὧδ' ἰδεῖν. The Berlin parchment has οὕτω γ' ἰδεῖν here, which does not change the sense. This is the so called 'limiting' infinitive, like ὡς ἔπος εἰπεῖν. There is dicolon in B² after ἰ . . ιν:

536 'But she knows her own mind much better herself', meaning, perhaps: she knows best where her interests lie, like the hetaira Daphnis in Aristainetos 1.17.12-14 οἰκείῳ μόνῳ δουλεύει σκοπῷ, καὶ πάντα δεύτερα ποιεῖται τοῦ δοκοῦντος αὐτῇ, 'she serves solely her own purpose, and considers everything secondary to what she wants'. Similarly Glykera in *Perik.* 749 says ἐγὦιδα τἄμ' ἄριστα, 'I know my own business best'.   αὐ]τὴ δ'. Chrysis speaking (above). This way of taking the traces (αὐτή Henry) at least avoids word-for-word repetition of the preceding line. One might consider reading ἀλλ' ἡδ' here, but the trace in O³ suits tau marginally better than lamda (and there is no apostrophe).   πολύ. Henry (Henry *et al.*, 2014a) reads here ἐγώ in the Berlin parchment, which is adopted by Blanchard and runs on to the next line ἐγώ / τοῦτ' κτλ. Nobody can say that a reading of the Berlin parchment is secure as there is so much bleed-through, nevertheless I think I can make out πολύ here, which can be kept in the sentence spoken by Chrysis here: 'she knows her own mind much better'.

537-8 τουτ' [?εἰκός ἐστιν] τὸν τράχηλον τουτονί ... τὸν ὑποκαθήμενον; Much conjecture here, but something like this is likely to have been the sense: '(sc. Is it reasonable to expect) this neck beneath might support this [burden]?' Or '... the person underneath (it, sc. the neck)'. Henry *et al.* (2014a) suggest that this is Getas' neck, with a heavy burden (of swords?) on it and that he is 'the person underneath it'. Blanchard refers to Aristoph. *Frogs* 19-20: τρισκακοδαίμων ἄρ' ὁ τράχηλος οὑτοσί, ὅτι θλίβεται μέν κτλ. 'this neck here (= of mine) is triple-unfortunate because it's weighed down ... ' Getas' namesake in *Dys.* complains similarly of the donkey's burden he's shouldering (402-4). ἀ[νενε]γκεῖν, from ἀναφέρω, of burdens, loads etc. see LSJ I 3. The supplement is little more than e.g.

540 ψιθυρισμός, 'whispering'. The two women overhear a voice whispering. Note the predominance of sibilants in the poorly preserved lines 527-32: perhaps they came over precisely for that reason as a kind of background whispering. This seems to be the first known instance of the 'stage whisper' in European theatre. Getas is carrying a load on his neck/back but the objects he enumerates from 542 sound like women's finery rather than swords. As he walks or tiptoes on stage he whispers to himself, or more likely to non-speaking attendants, about the objects his master has acquired and the drinking party which he has temporarily left. The word is found elsewhere in comic texts only at [Lukian] (49) *Amores* 15.

541 ἀναλή[ψο]μαι. The papyrus here has the late erroneous spelling -λημ[ψ- as in line 682 λήμψεων for λήψεων. Cf. Mayser (1906, i.194-5). The sense seems to be 'I'll take up the matter' or 'I'll take him (the new entrant) on', 'I'll receive him'. The stage action seems to be the following: Chrysis sends Syra somewhere out of sight. She herself remains close to the action (so as to follow it) but presumably out of sight of Getas, or he would notice her. The audience can see all parties. Somewhat similarly in *Georg.* the two women Myrrhine and Philinna draw back when Daos appears, to see what he will say (32-33).

απαλλαγηθ'ἐ[in O³ seems to have rough breathing over epsilon, which is wrong for ἐνθένδε, but which the scribe may have thought was called for after theta of -ηθι (with iota elided): wrong, but perhaps understandably so. ἐγὼ ‹δ'› in O¹¹ seems to have had kappa before αναλημ[ψομαι] but ἐγὼ κάναλήψομαι is not metrical. Henry's δ' is almost certainly right, though hardly legible in B².

542 ἴσθι δέ μ' ἔτ[οιμον]. The first letters are difficult to distinguish because there is a lot of extraneous ink where the scribe seems to have corrected himself. Initial iota is obscured; sigma-theta are then legible, then a gap, then τε with δε written above it, then mu followed by epsilon with a small rough breathing after it; finally what must be the cross-bar of tau: a form of ἔτοιμος – either -ην or -ον – fits, giving the sense 'but know that I'm ready to help, my dear' or '... at the ready, dear', said by Syra, as she withdraws from the scene. In a somewhat comparable situation in *Asp.* 328-9, Chairestratos assures Daos that he's ready to help him with any ruse he plans to deceive Smikrines: ἐγὼ γὰρ ὅ τι βούλει ποεῖν / ἔτοιμός εἰμι. For the ellipse of a form of εἶναι after ἔτοιμος see Kühner-Gerth i 40 (c); examples in Eur. *Her.* 453 with Bond's note, *El.* 796 with Denniston's note; cf. J.E. Harry, *Cincinnati Studies* II i 3 (1905). For the thought cf. Gorgias' reassurance to Sostratos ἅμα γὰρ μεταπείθεις ταῦτα καὶ φίλον μ' ἔχεις (*Dys.* 317), 'you persuade me of these things *and* have

Act Three 159

me as your friend'. Above ἴσθι are faint superscript letters which Turner took to be the traces of αλλ but which I believe are a *nota personae*: either Chrysis or Syra; according to this reconstruction it is Syra.

543 ἐφεστρίδιον Parsons (Green & Edwards, 2015, 27-29) notes on his suggestion: 'ἐφεστρίς occurs fairly commonly as a kind of cloak, worn over the chiton (Xen. *Symp.* 4.38); the diminutive is otherwise attested only in Luk. *Merc. cond.* 37. Wearers include soldiers (Luk. *Dial. mer.* 9.1, περιπόρφυρον; Plu. *Luk.* 28.1, κροσσωτήν, tasselled, fringed) and philosophers (Ath. 3.98A), Charikleia (Heliod. 3.6.1) and a statue of Aphrodite (Agathias, *AP* 9.153.3); mourners wear μέλαινα ἐφεστρίς in Hdn. *Hist.* 4.2.3. As a term, it overlaps χλαμύς (Ath. 5.215C), and the military context may be relevant here, if the item formed part of Thrasonides' booty.' A fragment of Duris notes that Demetrios Poliorketes had, among other expensive items of apparel, 'military cloaks [sc. of] a lustrous sheen of brownish grey' (*FGrH* 76 F 14 = Athen. XII 50 p. 535E-536A, trs. F. Pownall: αἱ δὲ χλαμύδες αὐτοῦ ἦσαν ὄρφνινον ἔχουσαι τὸ φέγγος τῆς χρόας). We should, perhaps, assume that the rather bald description 'grey' here means something more like Demetrios' expensive and embroidered cloak, rather than a cheap or dirty grey. Cf. *Sik.* fr. 9 Sandbach.

Blanchard gives this sentence to the speaker of μακαρία (Syra) as there is no visible dicolon after this; but this hardly makes sense with **543 λέγηι** (3rd p.s.) as Chrysis is not likely to refer to Syra's words in the third person ('it's obvious when *she* says that ... '). Assuming Getas is the speaker, I suggest that he is referring to an item in Thrasonides' treasures, a valuable piece of clothing (see above). Parsons points to the Mytilene mosaic of act five of this play showing Krateia with a conspicuous black fringe on both garments she is wearing (cloak and tunic). This is interesting, but an *ephestridion* is more likely from the instances above to have been a man's military overcoat, or cloak, rather than a woman's dress; however, one notes that Charikleia in Heliodorus (*loc. cit.*) had an *ephestris*. One might posit here a woman's cloak with a dark grey border which by the end of the play Thrasonides has given to Krateia.

544 ὑφα]σμά[τω]ν τὰ κράσπεδ', '[clearly these are] the fringes of the garment', with ἐστίν understood. ὑφασμάτων is not much more than an e.g. supplement, but the mu-alpha was read by Austin in the Berlin papyrus and O³ gives the tops of something like σ-μ. The main objection palaeographically is that ὑφα- at the beginning does not fill the space, unless we have a very wide phi. The sense of these lines is surely something along the lines of 'it's obvious that when he says this he's talking about the fringes (or 'borders')', meaning that the fringes of the *ephestridion* are grey or black, the actual garment some other colour (see previous note). This sentence is an example of how Chrysis is 'taking up' (ἀναλήψομαι) Getas' words and explaining them either to herself or to Syra, who is somewhere behind her.   **τὰ κράσπεδ'**, 'the fringes' or 'borders' of a garment (cf. Aristoph. *Wasps* 475). O³ clearly has **τὰ κρ[**, whilst O¹¹

160   CHAPTER 5. COMMENTARY

seems to have τοκρασπεδ; since the singular article with elided κράσπεδ' does not make sense, one might guess that the omikron is, in fact, a mistake. The new fragment O^{11} shows that the right hand fragment of Turner's Page A (horizontal fibres) of O^3 has slipped down a line. All line endings from τακ.[should be shifted up one.   ἐν δ' αὐτῶι μό[νον 'he has only one (sc. ring, δακτύλιον). ἐν, 'in' (but what?) is also possible, but ἓν μόνον, 'only one', go well together.

545 δα]κτύλιον [καὶ χ]ρυσίᾳ, 'ring and golden trinkets'. Here we seem to have moved on to the jewelry amassed by Thrasonides on his campaign. If this *daktylion* happened to be the ring of Krateia's brother we would have an alternative means by which she recognized her brother's slayer (he was in possession of his signet-ring) as opposed to the sword. A ring is, of course, a common *gnōrisma*, as in *Epitr.*   546 ἐ[ν] δ' ἄξου[ες, 'and some bridle-bits among them'. My supplement continues the list of valuables got by Thrasonides. Austin preferred δεῖξον [, 'show!', but I do not see who would be showing to whom. ἄξονες, 'axles', can be of valuable silver (*Il.* 5.723), or 'bridle-bits' Xen. *Eq.* 10.9, and could, presumably be gold or silver.

547 ε .[.]ειθε might give τ(ε) ἔπειθε, with *scriptio plena*, 'he was persuading … of friends', meaning Thrasonides wanted to win over Krateia's heart with these gifts. τί] βούλετ[αι; 'What's he up to?' Chrysis observes Getas' moves, I think, and wonders out loud what his plan is.

548 εἰσενέγ[κατε (or -ετε), 'carry [these garments] inside'. An aorist form of εἰσφέρω suits the traces of O^{11} very well here. Metrically this imperative plural is nearly the only form which will fit. I imagine that Getas is speaking to helpers who are sharing the load. They *might* be carrying the valuables into Thrasonides' house (sc. as a bribe to Krateia) but Syra's indignant remark in lines 553-4 makes it more likely that the men are intruding into Kleinias' house. Moreover, *somehow* the swords (etc.?) have to arrive in Kleinias' house for Demeas to browse through them and recognize one of them. And when Kleinias comes to question Syra on Demeas' recognition of the sword he indicates that it was only one of many items of war spoils (681-2). So, on the whole, I suggest that this is indeed the scene in which the spoils of war from Cyprus arrive in Kleinias' house. *Why* Getas should have to move *all* the booty like this is, I am afraid, a puzzle to me.

549 [λαβρ]ώνια, 'wide (or 'Persian') cups'. The conjecture in Henry *et al.* (2014a) looks plausible but not inevitable as a valuable item which might belong to spoils of war. In *Asp.* 35 we learn that drinking cups formed a good part of Kleostratos' war spoils from the campaign in Lykia (ποτήρι' ἐπιεικῶς συχνά). Fr. 26 K-A (from *Halieus*) lists objects owned by a rich man: gold, Persian gowns, purple blankets, drinking cups, Indian reliefs, animal-cups (*tragelafoi*), wide cups (*labrōnia*). We see the same mix as here of valuable banqueting services and fine textiles. The vessel *labrōnion* is mentioned again in fr. 395 K-A (from *Philadelphoi*) along with other

Act Three   161

other fancy ware. Athenaios XI 484c-d cites the fragment, explaining that the *labrōnion* is a 'kind of Persian cup, wide and broad, with large handles'. The word can also be masculine. Of course, other supplements are conceivable such as ὀψώνια, 'salary', i.e. money.

550 πρὸς κ[ο]τύλας, 'to the cups', meaning 'to the drinking party in the inn'. **ἄπ[ειμι.** The left part of pi is usually indistinguishable from gamma; here that is the case. Previous scholars have thought in the direction of ἄγει here, or ἄγων, but απ[is perfectly possible. I supplement a first person ἄπειμι, 'I will be on my way'. In my opinion Getas is saying he will return to the drinking party having secreted all the spoils in Kleinias' house.

550-1 κ]αταλιπ[ὼν / τὴν γῆν κροτοῦσαν, 'leaving the ground ringing'. There are no parallels for intransitive κροτέω, 'resound', 'rattle', instead of the transitive sense 'make to rattle', but that is what I suggest here. κροτέω in the sense 'applaud' can be used absolutely, so one could squeeze the sense out here 'leaving the ground applauding' (i.e. my hasty retreat). The expression would be a lively image for 'beating a hasty retreat'. Previous scholarship has thought in the direction of somebody making the ground ring with dance steps, but there is no feminine antecedent anywhere in sight except γῆν itself, unless the speaking subject is feminine (Henry: ἄγει με καταλιπών), which is as good as ruled out: there are enough traces of Getas in this passage (521, 524, 537, 557), and none of another lady, to make it as good as certain that he is the speaker. A corrupted passage in Eur. *Her.* 1303f. (cf. Bond *ad loc.*) gives further food for thought. There Herakles laments that his disastrous fall from grace will leave Hera triumphant: χορευέτω δὴ Ζηνὸς ἡ κλεινὴ δάμαρ / †κρόουσ' Ὀλυμπίου Ζηνὸς ἀρβύληι πόδα†, which seems to mean something like: 'let the famous wife of Zeus dance (in triumph), beating †Olympian Zeus (= Mt Olympus?) with her foot in her shoe'†. Murray suggested κροτοῦσ' here, Triklinios κρούουσ', both giving the meaning 'beating'. Here the expression 'striking the ground' (sc. in dance steps) seems to connote 'triumph'. But I cannot see how this helps with the present passage. Which woman could be triumphing?

552 σ]πείσονθ' ἕ[ως] If Turner's supplement is correct, the meaning should be 'they will pour libations together' by way of making up some quarrel or disagreement. Could Getas be referring to the quarrel between Thrasonides and certain people intent on doing him harm which emerges in Getas' monologue (568ff.)? We do not know enough of the context. I wondered about an alternative reading ἃ] πέπονθ', 1st or 3rd p.s. of πάσχω. Palaeographically there is not much to choose between these alternatives, as the letters which Turner read as iota-sigma may in fact be pi. However it is hard to see how the relative clause would fit syntactically. A third alternative would be to read σπείσονθ' as an active future participle, either acc. or dat., but for neither case is there a clear referent. Following σπείσονθ' Austin suggested

162   *CHAPTER 5. COMMENTARY*

ἐπιτρέπωσι after that but acknowledged that one would expect σπείσοντ' in that case. I might add that the construction with the subjunctive remains unexplained. Instead, I propose ἕως with τρέπωσι, 'until they turn to (sc. feasting)'. ἕως + subj. without ἄν occurs in tragedy and is common in later Greek (LSJ). Perhaps we have an instance here in comedy.   ε[ἰς] ἔρανον, 'to the shared meal' or 'party', in the inn. Note line 570 with note, in which it is said that one man has paid his contribution (τὰς συμβολάς). This was, then, a δεῖπνον ἀπὸ συμβολῶν, a 'bring-your-own' party, but unlike nowadays when people bring food, then one brought money. Thrasonides is drinking (and eating) with his club of friends. Otherwise unattested in Menander (except in a metaphorical sense fr. 282 K-A), ἔρανος occurs in Alexis fr. 280.1; *Mandragorizomene* fr. 1.5; *Tarantinoi* fr. 3.16; Aristoph. *Lys.* 653; Philemon fr. 213.14; Antiphanes fr. 124.9 Kock. For the sense 'loan' (sc. from the club of friends) cf. Antiphon *First Tetr.* 2.9.6 ἔρανον παρὰ τῶν φίλων συλλέξας.

After 552 Getas exits briefly into Kleinias' house with his load of spoils, and returns to stage again in 557. In the meantime Syra and Chrysis make their comment about unsavoury characters coming and going in Kleinias' household (553-57).

553 A very tricky line to reassemble from three papyri, O^3, O^{10}, and O^{11}. At line beginning Turner's ἐστὶν τοιαῦτα looks a reasonable interpretation of the traces in O^3. Then Gonis' publication of O^{10} showed that Turner's explanation of ηριων in O^3 as ἱκετηριῶν could not be right, as O^{10} has]αθ....[.]ν at the relevant point. Gonis suggested θηρίων between theta and nu, but admitted that the supplement looks a little short for the gap. I suggest a slight change: O^{10} may have had θηριαων here (one letter longer) which we can take as *scriptio plena* for θηρί' ὤν, i.e. the beginning of a relative clause. In O^3 we clearly read]ηριων, i.e. no *scriptio plena*. In O^{11} we have]ηρια with the alpha, it seems, crossed out, and an omega written (more or less) above that. So there is some palaeographic support for θηρί' ὤν written in some papyri as θηριαων. Then O^{10} has παρεισφ . . . ν. Previous suggestions have involved some composite participle with παρεισ-: Gonis (in comm.) considered παρεισφέρων, 'carrying past inside'; on the strength of the new readings of O^{11}, Henry *et al.* (2014a) suggested παρεισφρέων, 'smuggling in', or 'secretly bringing in past'. It seems to me that neither participle quite suits the traces in O^{10} perfectly. παρεισφρέων certainly did not stand in O^{10} as the two traces after the phi are simply not compatible with -ρε-. I think Gonis' supplement παρεισφέρων is acceptable, or perhaps παρεισφορῶν, where omikron suits the trace marginally better in O^{10}, I think, than epsilon. παρεισφορέω is attested only once: J. Tzetzes, *Versus de poem. generibus. Proleg. de comoedia* line 77 Koster. The sense links up with εἰσενέγκατε in 548: there Getas tells someone 'carry in!', and now Syra comments that 'one of these beasts' is 'secretly carrying in' to Kleinias' house. The ending -ων is clear in O^{11}. It is masculine, as is τις in the next line, by 'natural gender' after the neuter

Act Three   163

plural θηρία, who, after all, are men; cf. *Dys.* 481 (ἀνδροφόνα θηρί᾽), *Perik.* 366 (ἱερόσυλα θηρία). So, putting all this together, we get:

ἐσ]τὶν τ[ο]ιαῦτα θηρί᾽ ὧν παρεισφορῶν

'There are such beasts (of people) and one of them (sc. may elude us) carrying (sc. things) inside … ' According to this reconstruction Syra is calling Getas a beast, which, considering he was a fighting man *and* a rough Thracian (cf. *Asp.* 243-4), may not be far off the mark. The reconstruction as a whole fits with the interpretation of the context, in which Getas indeed seems to be doing just that: secretly conveying booty, including all the swords (??), from Thrasonides' Cypriot campaign.

555 ἂν οἱ θεοὶ θέλωσιν, 'God willing'. For the conventional form of prayer cf. *Georg.* 44-45, also spoken by a woman character.   **Σύρα**, correctly guessed by Arnott (1996d, 34), before the appearance of O[10]. It is the only known occurrence of this slave name in Menander; but known from other *komōdoi*; Syros is common enough (e.g. *Dys., Georg., Dis Ex.*), see MacCary (1969, 292).

556 [συν]άχθομαι. Although συν- is given in square brackets, O[3] has something like cυη[written immediately after ε]γω, but it seems to have been erased, and was probably written again more clearly (where there is now a gap in the papyrus). So there can be little doubt about the supplement. Otherwise one might consider unattested συνεπάχθομαι. Anyway Chrysis is expressing solidarity with Syra, who is annoyed that Getas has been smuggling wares into Kleinias' house.   **νὴ τὴν Ἄρτεμιν**, 'by Artemis!' Probably exclusively a women's oath, cf. *Dys.* 874 (Simiche), *Geo.* 112 (?Philinna). It is not just that Artemis is female herself, but she was very much the goddess of women's rites and the community of girls and women. The oath gives vent to Chrysis' indignation (ἐγὼ συνάχθομαι).

557 The women exit here but where to? After Getas' monologue describing events in the inn, Syra (or is it another woman?) enters from Kleinias' house with Demeas. She must have exited in 557 thereto. So Arnott is probably right (p. 297) that the two women go their separate ways, Syra home, and Chrysis to – we do not know. Blanchard reads the smudged *nota personae* in O[10] as KPA[T] but this is very uncertain (only the tau is anything like clear). I cannot imagine that Krateia suddenly breaks in here; surely this is Getas describing a scene he has witnessed at the drinking party in the inn. If a woman were speaking she would have to say ἐμαυτήν in 574, not ἐμαυτόν. If δεσπότης is right in 558, this suits Getas as speaker much better than Krateia. And it is unlikely that Krateia would announce in 574-5 that she was going to spy on the goings-on inside. I think it is conceivable that the scribe wrote ΓΕΤ over original KPAT, realizing his mistake (Krateia *does* appear shortly).

At this point Getas returns on stage, probably from the inn, and continues his description of the drinking party in the inn. He starts with a rhetorical question 'who *are* these

164   *CHAPTER 5. COMMENTARY*

people with whom my master is drinking?' Since Greek theatre never shows interiors except (extremely rarely) via the wheeled trolley (Philippides, 2019, 322-24), we get descriptions of interior scenes through a narrator. *What* Getas narrates here is clear enough, but its context not. We seem to have some plot against Thrasonides. Could this be some assassination plot we hear about here, initiated by Krateia? One notes the garbled book fragment **6** (Orus fr. 35) which, when corrected, reads μισοῦσι μὲν / Θρασωνίδην, ὦ πάτερ, ἀπεκτάγκασι δ' οὔ, 'they hate Thrasonides, father, but they have not killed him.' This would seem to be Krateia speaking to her father, and revealing knowledge of some plot against Thrasonides. The lines must come after the recognition scene between Krateia and Demeas, in act four or five, as there is no overlap with lines of Krateia before that. If πάτερ was used in the colloquial sense 'old man', it would lack the formal ὦ (as in e.g. *Epitr.* 231, Syriskos to Smikrines). The scene Getas describes is colourful. There seems to be a fat, effeminate man singer who strikes up a melody. There seems also to be another person involved (**564** θάτερος) who sings 'more strongly'. What he sings is (conjecturally) the traditional *skolion* 'wealth honestly gained' (**566**) and Getas acknowledges that it is a pretty tune (**568** ἀγαθὸν ἄκουσμα). But his behaviour is suspicious and Getas suspects that he wishes his master, Thrasonides, harm. In its main lines this account seems reasonably coherent, but it is heavily restored and where there is restoration, there is doubt.

557-8 μετὰ τίνων πίν[ε]ι ποτὲ / ὁ δε[σπότ]ης: Getas is talking to himself in a rhetorical question: 'who *are* those people my master is drinking with?' where ποτέ changes a simple question looking for information to a rhetorical one expressing consternation. This is Getas' opening remark with which he begins his monologue describing the goings-on in the inn.   There is not much of **δε[σπότ]ης** to read, but beginning and end are enough to secure the supplement.

558 ἐντ[αῦ]θ' ἄπιστον οὐδ[ὲ ἕν, 'anything's possible there!', lit. 'not one thing is inconceivable there!' **ἄπιστον** is a favourite word of Menander's (word count at least 8), probably because that is a key-note of his comedy: the incredible or strange in human behaviour. Elsewhere I have pointed out the same thing for **ἄτοπον** (p. 132), and indeed the terms are similar in shape and semantics. Here Getas means that the scene which he has witnessed in the inn defies belief, or is at least very strange. Cf. *Asp.* ἄπιστον, ἄλογον, δεινόν, *Sam.* 545 ἄπιστον πρᾶγμά μοι δοκεῖς λέγειν, fr. 685.1 K-A οὐκ ἔστ' ἄπιστον οὐδὲν ἐν θνητῷι βίωι ('anything's possible in human life').

559 ἄρχοντά [πως A complete guess, adapted to context. The only letters which are at all secure are rho and ?chi. I imagine Getas to be saying something like 'I left when someone was just beginning to sing' (sc. at the party in the inn).

560 κατέλειπον, 'I (or 'they') left' someone or something, but unfortunately the previous line is lost in gaps of O³ and O¹⁰. Austin's supplement at the end of line 559 ἔρχεται πάλιν is unlikely as it does not match the traces after -ρχ- (the chi itself is

Act Three   165

uncertain).   ἦισ' ἄν[θ]ρω[πος]. There now follows a description of a singer at the party, a fat man described as 'a pig of a man' (561) with effeminate features, 'as far as one could judge from the outside'.

560-61 [ἐπιεικῶς] παχ[ὺς / τὴν ὄψιν 'with a pretty fat face', i.e. very fat (by understatement), with ἐπιεικῶς – which has the status of an e.g. guess; cf. *Asp.* 24 ἐπιεικῶς μάχαις / πολλαῖς, 'in a fair many battles'. For ὄψις = face, cf. [Demosthenes], *Against Neaera* 105.10. For the type of expression cf. *Sik.* 215 ὄ]ψει τις ἀνδρικός πάνυ, 'very manly in appearance'.

561 ὖς ἄνθρωπ[ος, 'a pig of a man', lit. 'the man was a pig', seems to be the meaning, not necessarily in terms of fatness, but possibly bodily bulk, like a boar. Direct comparisons of people with animals are relatively rare in Menander, although proverbial comparisons are common enough. In this play a proverbial pig features in a comparison with Demeas, who Getas says is behaving like ὖς ὄρει, τὸ τοῦ λόγου (704). A little earlier he had compared him to a proverbial donkey: ὄνος λύρας (696). But the expression here does not seem to be proverbial, rather direct and blatant. In *Asp.* 372-3 the greedy Smikrines is compared to a hungry wolf who goes away empty-handed, or rather empty-mouthed (by Chairestratos, or Daos [Austin]): τὸ γὰρ λεγόμενον ταῖς ἀληθείαις "λύκος χανὼν ἄπεισι διὰ κενῆς". In *Sam.* Nikeratos shouts at Moschion that he is a 'barbarian, a Thracian!' (519-20). As a matter of interest proverbial pigs feature elsewhere in the sayings 'a pig among roses' (Krates fr. 6 K-A), a 'fat pig sat on his mouth' (Men. fr. 25 K-A). For an animal metaphor cf. Solon fr. 11.5 εἷς μὲν ἕκαστος ἀλώπεκος ἴχνεσι βαίνει 'each one of you walks in the steps of a fox'.

562 τὰ γύναι' might be an adjectival epithet following a noun, 'his effeminate—', or a noun following e.g. ὡς, 'like little women'; for γύναιον as noun cf. *Epitr.* 557; γύναια *Dys.* 568 (used by slave Getas); Aristoph. *Wasps* 610, *Thesm.* 792 = 'gossipy woman' in a mildly derogatory sense, Andok. 1.130.6.   ἵν' ἔξωθεν κτλ., 'as far as one was able to see from the outside'. What Getas is describing sounds almost like a 'drag queen' as a performer in variété.   ἐδέδοτο. For δίδωμι + infinitive 'grant' see LSJ s.v. 4.

563 Μυσό[ς], a man from Mysia, proverbially feeble and effeminate (LSJ s.v.). There is, in fact, little doubt about the reading. O³ has μυς [quite clearly, whilst B² seems to have].ου.ος, most plausibly read as δοῦλος (Turner, Austin). If that is right, it would seem to be a gloss on Μυσός (a certain nationality of slave) which has entered the text. The joke seems to be that Getas suggests cheekily that the man is a Mysian, to judge from his effeminate outward appearance. A Σ on Plato's *Theaet.* 209b quotes from Menander's play *Androgynos* ('The Effeminate Man') the saying Μυσῶν ἔσχατος / πολέμιος (= fr. 54 K-A, cf. 153, 658 K-A), which possibly supports the idea that Mysians were proverbially effeminate (not warlike). Cicero *Pro Flacco* 65 says that the proverb was used for despicable people: *si quis despi-*

catui ducitur, ut *Mysorum ultimus esse dicatur*, 'last of the Mysians'. In Aristoph. *Clouds* 922 the Mysian Telephos is said to be a poor beggar. Note the denunciation of a certain Apollonides in Xen. *An.* 3.1.31 who allegedly has 'pierced ears like a Lydian' (ὥσπερ Λυδὸν ἀμφότερα τὰ ὦτα τετρυπημένον), with Huitink-Rood's note. The denunciation is enough to exclude him from the parley. The traces in the latter part of the line in O³ (Turner:]ε̣ι̣[ ) are not distinct enough to prove or disprove my conjectural supplement.

εἶτα σχὼν Arnott printed †καὶ λύω, but the kappa breaks the metre. Since λυρ- can be read in the Berlin parchment B² we seem to have some mention of a lyre. My supplement is pure e.g. Cartlidge (2017b) suggests ⟨ὃς⟩ κελεύεται, 'Is that a slave who's receiving orders?' The main difficulty with that is the connection in sense with the following line.

564 θάτερος. For the 'barbaric form' cf. Men. fr. 491 K-A.   σθε̣ν̣[αρώ]τε[ρον, 'more strongly (sc. than the other)', has the (slight) advantage over Turner's σαφέσ- τερον that the letter in second position in O³ is more likely a theta than an alpha, and the extra letters between σθ . . . . . . τε suit the space available much better. If one could tolerate the split anapaest, ἀσθενέστερον would also be a possibility, but perhaps it does not suit the exclamatory following line, which seems to stress the man's large stature.

565 τὸν ἄνδρ' ὁρᾶν πάρ', 'it was possible to see the man', i.e. 'there was no overlooking *him*', a way of emphasizing the bulky stature of the singer, followed by an expletive for emphasis. For πάρα used verbally (for πάρεστι LSJ s.v. F) cf. in comedy: Arist. *Ach.* 862 ὑμὲς δ', ὅσοι Θείβαθεν αὐλειταὶ πάρα, 'and all you flautists who are here from Thebes'; for the type of expression cf. Aeschylus *Cho.* 961 πάρα τὸ φῶς ἰδεῖν; Eur. *IA* 456 ἅ μοι πάρα; [Eur.] *Rh.* 284 εἰκάσαι γε μὴν πάρα. The problem with Austin's ὁρᾷς γάρ is that the listener *cannot* see the man at present; he exists only in Getas' narrative.   ὦ πολυτίμητ[οι θε]ο[ί, 'O much honoured gods!' or 'great gods!'. The oath is quite common e.g. *Asp.* 408 (supplemented), *Dys.* 202, 381, 479; Aristoph. *Wasps* 1001,

566 πλουτεῖν ἀμ̣[έμπ]τως, 'wealth honestly acquired'. This guess is supported by some legible letters in O³ and B² and by the fact that it was proverbial: Plato *Gorg.* 451e1-5: οἴομαι γάρ σε ἀκηκοέναι ἐν τοῖς συμποσίοις ἀδόντων ἀνθρώπων τοῦ- το τὸ σκολιόν, ἐν ᾧ καταριθμοῦνται ᾄδοντες ὅτι ὑγιαίνειν μὲν ἄριστόν ἐστιν, τὸ δὲ δεύτερον καλὸν γενέσθαι, τρίτον δέ , ὥς φησιν ὁ ποιητὴς τοῦ σκολιοῦ, τὸ πλουτεῖν ἀδόλως 'I expect you've heard people singing that *skolion* at symposia, in which they enumerate in their song that to be healthy is best, in second place comes good looks, and third, as the poet of the *skolion* says, to gain riches fairly'; cf. *Carmina convivialia* (PMG) fr. 7 line 3 Page τὸ τρίτον δὲ πλουτεῖν ἀδόλως. ἀδόλως πλουτεῖν is regularly listed by the paroemiographers as the third blessing of a happy

Act Three 167

life. ἀμέμπτως here might well be substituted for ἀδόλως (which does not scan in this position). As Solon says (fr. 13.7-10 with comm. Mülke (2002, 251ff.)):

> χρήματα δ᾽ ἱμείρω μὲν ἔχειν, ἀδίκως δὲ πεπᾶσθαι
>   οὐκ ἐθέλω· πάντως ὕστερον ἦλθε δίκη.
> πλοῦτον δ᾽ ὃν μὲν δῶσι θεοί, παραγίγνεται ἀνδρὶ
>   ἔμπεδος ἐκ νεάτου πυθμένος ἐς κορυφήν·

> I desire to possess wealth, but not to obtain it unlawfully. Justice always catches up (with one) later. But the wealth which gods dispense, is a lasting possession for man, from the very bottom (of the barrel) to the top.

Handley's ἐπὶ πᾶσιν ἀγαθοῖς mistakes the sigma in πᾶσιν, in my opinion, for epsilon, and ignores the three clearly legible letters in the reliable O[3]]τωϲ.
One might speculate about the significance of this song; the singer seems in some way to have threatened Thrasonides. He sang well, but offended the man by his behaviour. Could the choice of song indicate that Thrasonides had not acquired his wealth honestly? The plot, we think, involved a fateful sword which Thrasonides had won through his prowess in battle, but which stood for the misfortune of Demeas' family. Was someone plotting revenge against Thrasonides? Perhaps future finds of text will reveal the secret.

567 πίνων ᾖσεν, 'sang while he drank', perhaps approaching προπίνων, 'sang a toast to':– [I give you:] 'unblemished wealth for just men' – takes the form of song, or more precisely, a *skolion*.

568 ἀγαθὸν ἄκουσμ᾽ ἥκεις, 'you come as a pleasing sound', or perhaps 'you come across as a pleasing sound', referring to the *skolion* sung by the stronger man. Cf. οἷον πατάγημ᾽ ἥκεις fr. 563 K-A, 'what a rattle you come as!': without context difficult to place. Somewhat similar, too, is Eur. *Or.* 951-2: ἔρχεται δέ σοι πικρὸν θέαμα καὶ πρόσοψις ἀθλία, 'he (Orestes) is coming to you (Elektra) as a miserable and sorry sight'. In *Kith.* fr. 5 Blanchard, ἀκούσματα seem to be 'melodies', or 'songs', said to be much liked by the *philomousos* man. Perhaps ἥκεις is like our 'you come across' as something. Clearly there is a contrast between appearance and reality (*Schein und Sein*). For discussion of the appellative use of verbal nouns in -μα, cf. Barrett (2007, ch. 16, 351-364): 'A Detail of Tragic Usage: The Application to Persons of Verbal Nouns in -μα'. ἄκουσμα is not on Barrett's list on p. 363.

569-70 τοιαῦτα κάμπτεις καὶ πάλιν στέλλει, '[why] do you turn in such a manner and retreat?' στέλλομαι (στέλλει is 2nd p.s. med.) comes from seafaring, to 'shorten' or 'furl' one's sail so as to lose way, stop. Applied to speech it can mean 'hold

168   CHAPTER 5. COMMENTARY

back', 'withhold', e.g. Eur. *Ba* 660. Both B[1] and B[2] seem to have had [ἔ]καμπτες (impf.) but the more reliable O[3] has]πτεις and στέλλει is certainly present, so it seems best to keep the present form κάμπτεις.   **τὰς συμβολάς** are the 'contributions' paid or given for a common meal, such as that which is taking place in the inn (cf. 552 ἔραν[ον]): LSJ s.v. IV with references. Blanchard: 'après avoir payé ton écot'. *Sam.* 603 has ἀσύμβολον, 'without the payment of contributions'; cf. *Epitr.* 504; fr. 437 K-A (μικρὰς - μακράς v.l. - συμβολάς). Taken together Getas means that the man's behaviour is odd: on the one hand he pays his dues for the shared meal, but on the other he seems to take a step back from the proceedings. The meal is presumably that to which Getas refers in 571: 'should I invite him to dinner *again*?' Perhaps here he means that the man actually departs, having made his contribution. στέλλομαι can mean simply 'depart'.

571 **λῆρος**, 'rubbish!' cf. Aristoph. *Plut.* 23.

571-2 **κελεύσω … καλέσαντα;** We learn that this dubious character has invited Thrasonides to the ceilidh (καλέσαντα). As suggested above, this may have been to assault him. For some reason the person held off (569). Now Getas thinks to himself that the person does not deserve a return invitation. καλέω is 'invite'; κελεύω sounds stronger, but 'bid', 'request', is in the range of attested meanings (LSJ s.v. 1).

573 **μιαρός**, 'wicked' (Arnott, Blanchard) looks a likely guess. We need some pejorative adjective here.

573 **β]αδιοῦμ' εἴσω**, inside, but where? Into the inn where the men are drinking, or into Thrasonides' house, where Krateia still is? When Demeas and Krateia meet face to face in the next scene, Getas interrupts their reunion, beginning with the remark (617) 'she has gone (or 'come') outside'. So at that point Getas enters, but from the *same* house as Krateia, or from a different one? My reconstruction would prefer Getas to exit in 575 into the inn; in that case he would have to notice the fact that Krateia has appeared from inside that inn (door ajar? loud exclamatory noises from outside?). His announced intent – 'to pay attention to what's being done and said' (575) probably suits the inn better than Krateia's house, as he has just been describing the antics of two dubious characters in the inn.

574 **κρύπτω]ν ἐμαυτόν**, 'concealing myself'. Wilamowitz' supplement has generally found favour. But how easily could Getas 'hide himself' in an inn (if I am right that that is meant by εἴσω)? I wondered about κύπτων, 'bending' or 'keeping my head down', but the reflexive pronoun is not normally needed with this verb. Fr. 741 K-Th., however, has κύψας καθ' αὑτόν. One would think that Getas would best hear secrets if he stood close to those discussing them, seeming not to listen.

Act Three 169

Scene Two: Syra and Demeas

576 Although O³ has ΓΡΑ̣ (= presumably, Γραῦς) in line 584, this must be Syra to judge from her knowledge of the goings on in Kleinias' house. Thus, too, Blanchard. She appears now from Kleinias' house and comments on the odd behaviour of their guest, Demeas (ξένον 576), on seeing the spoils of war which Getas has just secreted in this house (previous scene). It seems that Demeas gazed at them for some time (580), after they had attracted his attention. In our reconstruction we can guess that he recognized the sword of his son. Lines 578-9 refer explicitly to swords. We should not forget that he already knows about the presence of one Krateia living next door (441-2), but he has yet to see her (that recognition scene is imminent). [ἀτοπώ]τερον, 'odder'. For ἄτοπος as a key Menandrean word see p. 132.

578 τὰς σπάθας. This word ἡ σπάθη, for 'sword', is commented on in book fragment 3. Perhaps this is the occurrence Pollux is referring to.

582 After the break Mette thought he could see τῶν σπ]α̣[θ]ῶ̣ν but this is overoptimistic in my opinion, unless something has broken off the papyrus since then. Apart from the nu there are minimal traces before it.

584 δειξ.[.]. Editors commonly supplement δεῖξον but there is nothing to go on. Some other form (ἔδειξα, -ας etc.) is equally possibly.   τ]αύτας θήσεται. Arnott (1996d, 35) is right that a dicolon in O³ is unlikely to have stood before αὐτάς. But O³ also has a *nota pers.* (ΓΡΑ̣?) above the dicolon, and, moreover, there is space before αυτας for a rubbed off tau. Therefore I stick with the division of parts indicated in the manuscript. On the whole the traces do not support the supplement commonly adopted by editors θήσομαι; θήσεται has the edge, in my opinion.

588 τὴ]ν̣ θύραν κόψασά μοι. This is the first mention of knocking on a door. We know that Demeas had procured Syra's help in act two in finding Krateia. It looks, then, as if they have now moved from Kleinias' doorway across to Thrasonides' and that the next scene plays out here. This door is the next-but-one to *chez* Kleinias, so the idea of Syra *leading* Demeas there is stage convention. The next line shows a Syra reluctant to knock herself, for whatever reason.

590 [λά]β'. ἀ̣π̣οτρέχω. δέδειχά σοι· What Demeas should 'take' is not clear: perhaps the sword with which he wants to confront Thrasonides? Then Syra says she will go (ἀποτρέχω), because she has now shown the house to Demeas (δέδειχά σοι). But in 594 Syra is still there and the pair of them continue to dilly-dally in front of the door. Turner (1965, 12) suggested Menander was building suspense before the *dénouement* of the recognition.

592-3 ὧν τ̣[υγ]χάνω. The letters χανω in O³ are written above θανω which are crossed out. ὧν is then genitive plural of the relative pronoun, not ὤν, participle

(Blanchard). The next sentence is repaired from scanty remains, but stands a chance of representing the original train of thought. ἐναργῶς, 'truly', is repaired from relatively clear εν[α]ργ ̣ ̣c and one can actually read the second half of the line τὴν ἐμὴν ταύτην ὁ[ρ]ῶ. As soon as one realizes Demeas is talking about a sword and not his daughter, the meaning becomes clear: 'Of those I hold, am I looking at one which truly belongs to me?' The talk has been of swords, and Syra has been showing (590 δέδειχά σοι) Demeas the swords which Getas has lugged from Thrasonides' house to Kleinias. I say that categorically, but all is surmise. This is a mini-recognition scene, in which Demeas recognizes his own sword. If there is a son, Krateia's brother, in the play, then we could surmise that Demeas has passed down a family heirloom to his son and this has passed into Thrasonides' hands as a war trophy. Webster (1973, 292) compares Theseus' recognition of Hippolytos' sword in Eur. *First Hippolytos*. Fans of all things metatheatrical might see an ironic touch in ἐναργῶς here from Menander: for what can be 'real' in the theatre?　ὁρῶ; It is not completely clear whether there is another letter after ὁρῶ (Blanchard marks one, Turner not). Although there is a smudged trace, I follow Turner here.

594 This barely decipherable line has been added afterwards in O³. The writing is somewhat thicker, but looks like the same hand. Syra and Demeas seem still to be vaccillating as to who should knock. Demeas' response seems to require a question from Syra along the lines of 'why don't you knock?' which I have constructed accordingly.

595 μ[̣ ̣ ̣ ̣ ̣]σαμην. If the second mu is correct, probably a first person aorist ending e.g. ἡγησάμην, ἐνοησάμην. Since this word or words formed the first metron of the line, there is quite a lot of room for whatever stood here.　νονθ' ὅλως. A very doubtful reading, but if the theta (inserted by way of correction) is right, it is difficult to see what else might have stood at the end. For a similar nearly-redundant ὅλως at line end see *Asp.* 116, a line similarly describing the ethical character of a person (bad): πονηρίαι δὲ πάντας ἀνθρώπους ὅλως / ὑπερπέπαικεν. Also *Dys.* 613, 865.

597 ὀντ[ως] ποησ[　...　ἡγ]ησάμην. If the supplements hit the mark we may have Demeas saying here 'I'm *really* going to do what I envisaged', like Smikrines at *Epitr.* 658-9. E.g. ὄντως ποήσομ' ὅτι τότ' οὖν ἡγησάμην.

601 τισε. If nothing followed the epsilon, we might articulate]τι σέ, but we might also have a form like ἐφρόντισε.

605 Cf. *Lexicon Symeonis* (Vat. 1362 f. 83v) s.v. ἐνθύμημα· οὐχ οὕτω (sc. = προστρόπαιον) Μένανδρος· ἀλλ' ἐπὶ διαλογισμοῦ τινος καὶ ἐνθυμήματος· ... καὶ ἐν Μισουμένωι «ἐνθύμιόν μοι τοιοῦτον (sic) γέγονεν ἀρτίως». O³ has] τουτο γεγονεν [, of which the last two letters are twisted downwards. The overlap is probably sufficient to justify the placing of this book fragment here.　ἐνθύμιος is 'that

Act Three   171

which weighs upon the mind', so the line seems to mean: 'this cause for concern has just entered my mind' or 'this has just become a cause of concern to me'. It seems that Syra pretends (?) that something has just occurred to her which makes it pressingly urgent for her to be elsewhere. In Eur. *Her.* Amphitryon is said to feel an *enthymion* about fetching Megara and the children out of the house to their death (722: ἐπειδὴ σοὶ τόδ' ἔστ' ἐνθύμιον). Clearly this means something like 'scruples' (Bond), 're-luctance' (Germ. 'Bedenken'); Cf. Antiphon, *First Tetr.* 3.10.6 and 4.9. Since here too Syra seems reluctant to enter Thrasonides' house we might envisage a similar sit-uation here: for some reason she feels 'scruples' or a 'reluctance' about doing that. Understandable, perhaps, if she has referred to Thrasonides as a 'beast' (θηρίον) in line 553. What the reason might be we cannot (yet) know.

606]τοϲωϲτ[. Probably not τόϲωι from τόϲοϲ, as this does not occur in Menan-der. Perhaps e.g. οὖ]τοϲ ὥϲτ[ε. If ουθ[εν] is correctly read, then the (relatively common) line ending οὐδὲ ἕν, 'not a whit', is plausible.

607 Syra announces her departure from the scene, leaving Demeas finally to act. He calls out to a servant inside (παῖ, παῖδεϲ), then draws back (ἐπανάξω) when he hears someone coming out. It is Krateia herself, with her 'nurse', Simiche (Bonollo, 2019), behind her. In the following scene Simiche has a non-speaking part (she just nods or gesticulates in lines 612 and 629-30), as Getas enters with the third speaking part in line 617; cf. Sandbach in G-S 449.   ἐ[π]ανάξω, 'I will draw back'. Intransitive use of ἐπανάγω, like other compounds of ἄγω in comedy (e.g. παράγω, ὑπάγω). The point of this is that Demeas and Krateia do not come face to face with each other immediately. Sandbach says it is also necessary stagecraft: 'The ensuing scene, involving four persons, would be intolerably cramped if they were all clustered in the doorway' (the difficulty is lessened if Getas appears from the inn, as I believe).

Scene Three: Recognition (1)

609ff. Enter Krateia, speaking backwards to Simiche inside (see next note). Her initial remark is presumably addressed to her nurse rather than the audience, as this is not an *apostrophē*, in which a player turns away from the scene and addresses the audience. We note that Krateia goes outside now through an inner necessity, not because Demeas knocked. So it seems she had decided that she had to get out rather than staying in Thrasonides' house any longer. Had the *hiketēria* been successful? Had someone offered her asylum? Anyway, she acts like Glykera now in *Perik.* who goes next door to Myrrhine when life with Polemon becomes intolerable. She will be quite absorbed in her own thoughts, so it takes a while before she realizes that her *father* is there at the door. For the recognition of father and daughter cf. the tragic precedent in Sophocles *OC* 324ff. There Ismene turns up at Colonos and embraces

172 CHAPTER 5. COMMENTARY

her father and sister Antigone in happy reunion. The chief Menandrean parallel is the recognition scene between father and daughter (Pataikos and Glykera) in *Perik*. But there the two must recognize each other by tokens as Pataikos had parted with his daughter when she was a baby.

Alexis wrote a play called *Krateia* or *Pharmakopôlês* (Athen. III 48.2, XV 22.26), which Arnott (1996a) says 'was a conventional new comedy (its characters include a soldier and a *pharmakopōlēs*, together …), with Krateia as name of a maiden'. So Alexis' play (there was a second production of it in 306 BC) may have borne some similarity to Menander's play.

609 οὐκ ἂν [δυ]ναίμην κ[α]ρτερ[εῖ]ν, 'I couldn't stand it!' But what? Remaining indoors with all the talk going on outside her door? In a bad marriage (or partnership) one might guess Krateia is saying she can't stand it any more with Thrasonides, and has come out. But he, surely, is at the drinking party in the inn (Krateia and Demeas enter Thrasonides' house in line 658; Getas runs off to fetch Thrasonides to meet them in line 638 and returns with Thrasonides, from the inn presumably, in line 660ff.) Since, as I noted, Krateia is addressing Simiche with this remark, she may be saying to her old nurse that she cannot stand the unpleasant life with Thrasonides. For Krateia 'talking back' to Simiche as she enters from Thrasonides' house; cf. Zagagi (2004), Frost (1988, 83-4). Kraus (1971a, 8) compares Alcumena's words in Plautus' *Amphitruo* 882: *Durare nequeo in aedibus.* **κ[α]ρτερ[εῖ]ν**, 'stand', 'put up with', with an accusative object (LSJ s.v. II). One example: at the beginning of Iphigeneia's 'change of heart speech' in *IA* 1370 she says **τὰ δ' ἀδύναθ' ἡμῖν καρτερεῖν οὐ ῥάιδιον**, 'It is not easy for us to endure the intolerable', meaning she must bow to the inevitable. **[τὸν γενόμενον]**. Only a guess but the idea is that Krateia is talking about *him* being brash to her in the past.

610 τ[ό]τ' ἔ[ντο]νον, 'violent then', 'vehement' (LSJ s.v. 2). Used in comedy by Aristophanes (*Ach.* 666). I assume Krateia is referring to Thrasonides' braggadocio earlier in the play (see intro. p. 5f.). Other supplements – ἐλεινόν, ἐκεῖνον (Austin) – do not scan with τί following. **τί ταῦτ[α] φ[ήις; οὐ μανθάνω]**, 'what's that you're saying? I don't understand'. Of this purely e.g. guess there is only a first trace, compatible with phi. Whilst Krateia had been addressing Simiche, probably about her decision to leave him (that was the point of the suppliant branch), now she picks up on what Simiche has apparently said to her ('your father's at the door').

611-12 Whilst Demeas recognizes Krateia immediately, she at first seems not to see him but to ask her nurse what she's on about. Still, perhaps, inside, Simiche obviously says to Krateia that her *father*'s there, as Krateia repeats her words: 'my father? Where?' and only in 614 seems to recognize him. Menander has added a particular twist to this recognition scene: Krateia's mind is elsewhere (on her troubles with Thrasonides) and it only dawns on her slowly who the person is in front of her. Also note

Act Three 173

the clever way Menander has orchestrated the actual meeting. Demeas goes to knock on the door (607) but at that moment Krateia bursts out engaged in an altercation with Simiche. So much more effective than if Demeas had simply knocked, Krateia had answered and the two had recognized each other. Frost (1988, 84) finds elements of this scene 'illogical' but surely that is the point: the usual routine of knocking and answering is turned on its head here.

611-12 ὦ Ζεῦ, τίν' ὄψιν [...] ὁρῶ;, 'Zeus, what a sight I see!', cf. *Dys.* 656 (Sikon speaking: τὴν ὄψιν αὐτοῦ τιν[[probably τίνα as here]). The tone is probably paratragic: cf. Eur. *Her.* 1132 οἴμοι· τίν' ὄψιν τήνδε δέρκομαι τάλας; *Hel.* 557 τίς εἶ; τίν' ὄψιν σήν, γύναι, προσδέρκομαι; paratragic likewise in Aristoph. *Thesm.* 905 ὦ θεοί, τίν' ὄψιν εἰσορῶ. Cf. Kraus (1971a, 8). I have discussed elsewhere the mixed aesthetic effect such touches must have had for the audience (*Epitr.*, intro. 1.2). The paratragedy certainly does not make Demeas appear ridiculous, but on the other hand the audience were aware they were watching a comedy involving people 'just like you and me' so the tragic colouring must have involved a twin response: on the one hand sympathy for the *pathos* of the scene, on the other awareness that this is a take-off of tragedy. Zagagi (1994, 51) subsumes the effect under the label 'polyphony', that is, more than one 'voice' playing at the same time. On the paratragic diction of this scene see Zanetto (2014, 91-2).

612 τηθία, said by Aristophanes of Byzantium (ap. Eustath. 971, 45, p. 140N) to mean μαῖα καὶ ἡ ἁπλῶς πρεσβυτέρα γυνὴ ἐλέγετο, ἡ δ' αὐτὴ καὶ τήθη καὶ τηθία, 'the older woman generally was called *maia* too, and the same was called *tēthē* and *tēthia*'. Cf. Sandbach in Turner (1970, 179). Chantraine *DELG* 1115 explains: «terme de la *nursery*, redoublé». Bonollo (2019, 99) identifies this old nurse as Simiche, and not Chrysis, as editors have previously thought (introduction p. 18).

615 ἔχω σε, 'I embrace you', with tragic colouring, cf. Soph. *El.* 1285, Eur. *El.* 579, *Alk.* 1134, *Ion* 1440, *IT* 829.　τέκνον. In this paratragic section τέκνον unusually has long first syllable (cf. Maas *Griech. Metrik* §124).　ὦ ποθούμενος φαν[είς, 'O you who, much longed for, have appeared'. G-S point to the Euripidean precedent, *El.* 578 ὦ χρόνωι φανείς, ἔχω σε.

616 ὁρῶ σ', 'I see you (before me)' cf. *Sik.* 286 (in a similar recognition scene) ἐμβλέπω σε, παῖ.　ὃν οὐκ ἂν ὠιόμην ἰδεῖν ἔτι, 'whom I no longer would have thought to see': either because Krateia had long since given up hope of ever seeing her father again through being taken into captivity, or because she thought her father dead in the troubles in Cyprus.

617ff. Getas appears, but from where? According to my view he had returned to the inn in 575 to keep an eye on things there. If that is correct, he must have noticed that Krateia had come out by the sound of her voice. There are many instances

174   *CHAPTER 5. COMMENTARY*

in Menander of people lurking in doorways, or on the inside of doors which are ajar, and following developments outside (e.g. Moschion in the recognition scene in *Perik.*). G-S say that he now appears from Thrasonides' house.   ἐξῆλθεν does not decide matters, as it can mean '*go* or *come* out'. In line 790 ἐξελήλυθεν definitely means 'has *come* out'. Similarly εἰσέρχομαι means 'come in' (from interior perspective) in 672 and 'go in' (exterior perspective) in 687.

617-18 The multiple staccato questions express Getas' confusion and consternation. They show a kind of 'double take' as Getas tries to take in what he sees before him.

617 παῖ, τί τοῦθ'; Getas can hardly be saying that to Krateia or to Simiche, so G-S are probably right to call the expression a 'fossilized exclamation of surprise' (cf. *Dys.* 500, *Sam.* 360, 678), similar to American 'O boy!' Cf. Dickey (1995, 69): 'A completely separate use of παῖ is found only in Menander, where the term can be used as an exclamation not really connected to the addressee.'   αὕτη τί σ[οι], 'what is she to you?' Editors usually punctuate like this, which gives reasonable sense, although B[1] has clear punctuation (high dot) after αυτη, which might lead us to think αὕτη was an address: 'you!' Then we could supplement τις[as τίς εῖ, going with ἄνθρωπε in the next line: 'who are *you*, fellow?' That, too, would give reasonable sense, the only difficulty being the *non sequitur* of αὕτη· τίς [εῖ]; Getas knows who *Krateia* is.

617 τί ποεῖς οὗτος; 'You! What are you up to?' G-S call this use of the nominative of the demonstrative pronoun οὗτος 'familiar', but it is a touch vulgar, too: examples from Menander: *Dys.* 880; *Epitr.* 436-7 Syriskos: ποῦ 'στ[ιν, ὃν ζη]τῶν ἐγὼ περιέρχομ' ἔνδον; οὗτος [ἀπόδος], ὦγαθέ, 'Where is he, the man I've been running round looking for inside? Hey, you! Give it back, there's a good chap!' *Sam.* 675 οὗτος, οὐ φέρεις;

618-19 Getas acts as if he had suspected all along that there was 'another man' in Krateia's life. Now – comically – he takes Demeas for this dark horse lover, although he concedes soon enough that the man is a white-haired sixty-year old. Clearly Getas thinks that the only plausible reason for Krateia's aversion to Thrasonides is a rival lover whom she prefers. Whether there really was a rival lover in the play – as Chairestratos is Charisios' rival for Habrotonon's affections in *Epitr.*, or Moschion Polemon's rival in *Perik.* – there is, at present, no way of knowing. Zagagi (1994, 19-22) comments on Menander's use of this conventional scene – false suspicion of a person as lover – in this and other plays.

619 ἐπ' αὐτοφώρωι, 'red-handed', 'in the act'. Getas means Demeas and Krateia are embracing. A similar embrace is the cause of all the trouble in *Perik.*, and, there too, it is a false alarm, as it turns out. Here it is established very soon that Demeas is the father, not a lover.

Act Three   175

620-1 The description shows very approximately what kind of mask 'Demeas' was wearing: Pollux *Onom.* 4.143f. lists eight masks of old men in New Comedy, of which some can clearly be eliminated for Demeas. Most likely is perhaps either of the first two listed: the πρῶτος πάππος, said however to be 'very old', or the ἡγεμὼν πρεσβύτης, who has a 'binding of hair' (στεφάνη τριχῶν) round his head, a hooked nose, broad face with raised right eyebrow.

622 περιβάλλειν. It is interesting that both papyri here have περιβαλειν with second lamda added later as a (necessary) correction in O³.

627 σο[ί], Κ[ράτεια, γὰρ πατὴρ]. The traces of the first word suit σοί better than Sandbach's original γάρ (which I have positioned later).

628 λάμ[βαν' αὐτὴν μάρτυρα.] If the supplement (Arnott) is correct, Krateia suggests Getas checks her statement about her father's identity with her old nurse Simiche (who would obviously know him).

629-30 [τοιαῦτά γε] / [λα]λεῖς;, 'do you speak such things?' or 'is this your story?' Getas is taking up Krateia's suggestion to check with Simiche. As noted above, Simiche must be a silent witness here as Demeas, Getas and Krateia have the speaking parts. She nods, presumably, in confirmation. See Kumaniecki (1965, 57) for another reconstruction (called 'not plausible' by G-S).

631 οἴκοθεν; Demeas cannot answer 'I wish I was' to a question 'where have you come from?' (630). So I punctuate at the end of 630 and make οἴκοθεν a question by itself: 'from home?', to which Demeas *can* answer 'I wish it were so'. G-S 451: 'Demeas wishes he had come from home, because he no longer *has* a home, his family in Cyprus having been scattered.' Sandbach's view seems to be confirmed by Getas' follow-up question: 'but you are overseas from that place?' In other words, even if he cannot be said (any more) to be away from *home*, he is away from the place that was home: if not οἴκοθεν, then at least ἀπόδημος ἐκεῖθεν.   ἀλλὰ [τ]υγχάνε[ις. I do not see the advantage of changing the tense to imperfect (Kassel in Austin (1973), Blanchard, who translates in the present!).

632 ἐκ Κύπρου παρ[ὼν. Support for the conjecture in line 432. That Thrasonides was campaigning (successfully) in Cyprus is told in fr. 2.

634 Austin *CGF* aptly quotes Thuc. 2.27 οἱ δὲ ἐσπάρησαν κατὰ τὴν ἄλλην Ἑλλάδα, 'and they were scattered over the rest of Greece'. ἔσπαρκε, 'has strewn'. The meaning is originally metaphorical from 'sow' of seeds. But there is presumably no irony intended in war 'strewing' people like seed over the land. σκεδάννυμι might be considered the 'standard' verb for 'scatter, strew', but a perfect is lacking.

635 ὁ κοινὸς ἐχθρὸς πόλεμος. This expression in the mouth of Demeas surely speaks volumes about Menander's world view. The normal use of 'common enemy' is to depict someone or some country as the enemy of others in order to stir them to unite

176   *CHAPTER 5. COMMENTARY*

against this perceived common enemy, e.g. Demosth. *De fals. leg.* 302.7, where Philip of Macedon is depicted as the κοινὸς ἐχθρός of the other Greek states. In *Contra Aristog.* 81.1 it is Aristogeiton who is said to be the common enemy of all. But Menander turns the expression round to mean that war itself is the common enemy (sc. of the warring parties); in a way, no one wins, all suffer. I would not be surprised if Menander was deliberately recalling Demosthenes' use of the expression (three instances), and given it a pan-Hellenic, humane, twist. Cf. Katsouris (1980).

636-7. Getas' reply – that Krateia had indeed come their way 'by this means' – confirms Demeas' observation that war had scattered his family members. Krateia had become a prisoner of war and been acquired by Thrasonides and taken home by him. The prologue of *Sik.* shows us how this might have happened. There Philoumenē's family were captured by pirates and she, along with a slave, was sold on the market-place at Mylasa in Asia Minor. A military commander (like Thrasonides here) bought her while still a child and brought her up (2-10). The words **αἰχμάλωτος γενομένη** pick up and confirm what Thrasonides had said about Krateia in lines 37-40. Although there were, no doubt, plenty of real-life prisoners-of-war-cum-mistresses in Menander's day, the role also had famous epic and tragic precedents: Briseis, Achilles' concubine in the *Il.* was a trophy; Kassandra in Aesch. *Ag.*; or Andromache in Eur. *Andr.* Lape (2003, 192) suggests that Tekmessa's position in Sophokles' *Ajax* is closest to Krateia's: 'Tecmessa, like Krateia, has become the wifelike concubine to the very man responsible for killing her natal family (Ajax 490–91)', but she points out that the two women figures behave very differently. One might say that Krateia acquired grandeur from these literary forebears. She was no cringing, pathetic victim. For Lycurgus' law against Athenians buying prisoners-of-war who had been free, see p. 11.

638 Here Getas runs off (to the inn) to tell Thrasonides of the new development. He will return with his master, who approaches the new situation in his own house with trepidation, in line **660**. This leaves Demeas and Krateia alone (with Simiche?) to discuss private family matters.   **σοι** must be Demeas: either 'I will run for you' or 'I will call for you'. Getas' eagerness shows that he at least has no idea about the sword and its previous owner. Even as a servant, he would understand that relations between Demeas and his master were likely to be strained if the latter had killed the former's son. Demeas has certainly recognized a sword, which had been among the *laphyra* of Thrasonides, as his own (578 and 592-3). Nowhere was it said –yet– that it was his *son's* sword.

642 ἱ]κετη[ρ]ίαν. If the ghostly traces are correctly restored, we seem to have mention here of the suppliant branch which Krateia seems to have wished to place (cf. 532). If the traces which follow: …[..]φο. happened to stand for ἀδελφοῦ, we would have a suppliant branch for a brother, but it's a long shot.

Act Three   177

646 ἡμ]εῖς πάτρ[ας] ἦμεν, ' … we were […] from home'. Conjecturally, the thought may be 'we were living (as exiles? as *klērouchoi*?) in Cyprus far from home'. The idea behind this supplement is to link up with Demeas' response which seems to involve the notion of (geographically) 'far away'. There is dicolon after ἦμεν.

τηλ.[The point of Handley's thoughts along the lines of τηλ[ο]υρος or τηλ[ο]υ, 'far', seems to be that Krateia's brother fell 'far afield'. We cannot make much of this geographically but if Krateia is now speaking in Athens, then Cyprus is far enough afield indeed; on the other hand if she is speaking from a mental vantage point of Cyprus, then presumably her brother 'fell' there, where Krateia was, rather than far afield.

647 O³ clearly has dicolon after ἐστί, indicating change of speaker.

648 ἀπόλωλε The final epsilon, which will be elided in speech, is relatively clear in the papyrus, giving the meaning 'he is dead', not ἀπόλωλα, 'I am lost'.

650 O³ has no dicolon after (putative) πεπόνθαμεν but O¹ does. O³ in fact seems to have erased something after final nu, following on with τέθνηκε: Then Demeas is marked clearly as speaker of the following remark ὑφ' οὗ κτλ. Merkelbach (1966) and Kraus (1971a, 11) thought this must be wrong and transposed the *nota personae* to τέθνηκε before, making it into a question spoken by Demeas. According to my reconstruction, Demeas has recognized the sword as belonging to his family and has hence worked out that Krateia's brother must have been killed by Thrasonides. *He* knows this nexus of events, not Krateia. Hence my distribution of parts here; likewise Zagagi (1994, 26).   ὑφ' οὗ γ' ἥκιστ' ἐχρ[ῆν. O³ has ὑφ' οὗ τ' and Austin's correction to γ' is probable: 'is he dead?' 'Yes, by the hand of the person you'd least expect it from'. Cf. *Asp.* 92 ἀπαγγελοῦντες τοῦτον (sc. λόγον) οἷς ἥκιστα χρῆν. It seems that variants of the phrase οἷς, οὗ etc. ἥκιστ' ἐχρῆν are a kind of euphemism for 'close family', or 'someone very close'; i.e. you wouldn't expect close family to do such a terrible thing. Note the similarity in expression and *sedes* of Eur. *IA* 487 ἀλλ' ἀπολέσας ἀδελφόν, ὅν μ' ἥκιστ' ἐχρῆν, 'But having destroyed my brother, whom least I should … ?' Menelaos is talking here, considering whether he should cause the misfortune of his brother Agamemnon by demanding the sacrifice of his daughter. This is hardly an argument that Demeas and Krateia are here discussing the loss of Krateia's brother but neither does it tell against that! Medea in Euripides' play laments that she has injured precisely those people she should not have: οὓς δέ μ' οὐκ ἐχρῆν κακῶς / δρᾶν, σοὶ χάριν φέρουσα πολεμίους ἔχω (*Med.* 507-8). That we have here something of a set phrase is indicated by its recurrence in Antiphon 1.4-5: ἀναγκαίως ἔχει οἷς ἥκιστα ἐχρῆν ἐν διαφορᾷ καταστῆναι ' … that it becomes obligatory to antagonize precisely those whom I should not'; and again in 1.21.7 ὑφ' ὧν ἥκιστα ἐχρῆν. The formulation in id. 1.22.6 ὑφ' ὧν ἥκιστα αὐτοὺς ἐχρῆν ἀποθνήσκειν, is very similar to Menander's verse here. The indication is strong that

178   CHAPTER 5. COMMENTARY

the phrase denotes close relatives who (or to whom) one would not normally expect to behave in such a way. The parallels give support to the assumption that Demeas is referring to someone very close to Krateia at this point, perhaps most likely her brother.

651-54 My supplements have the status e.g. as no traces survive to support or refute them. These are a case of supplements *ad sensum*. I have observed the paragraphoi given in O^1 and O^3 (or both), although these may not be correct.

651 σύν[οισθά γε, 'and *you* share that knowledge (sc. with me)' (LSJ s.v. II). Demeas means that he is aware who killed the (putative) brother and that Krateia shares that knowledge through the circumstances of her capture.

652 ἀλοῦσ' ἅμιλλά [τ'] οὖσα τοῦ[δ' εἰ]λη[μμ]έ[νου., 'when you were taken captive, and because you are a trophy of the captor'. I can make out very little on the photograph of O^1 which P. Parsons kindly lent me. Hunt in the *ed. pr.* read ελοῦσαμιμο..[here, remarking (on μιμ) 'or κικ, but not μικρ. The first letter of the line may be α'. ἀλοῦσα has been generally accepted; then Turner's ἅμιλλά τ' οὖσα, 'and being a trophy' (cf. G-S 453). This sense of ἅμιλλα is unattested, as it usually refers to a 'contest', or 'competition', not to the prize of that contest. However, at Eur. *IA* 963 Achilles refers to himself in perhaps a comparable way as θήραμα παιδός, 'prize of his daughter'. The case of ἆθλον/ἆθλος is slightly different, as the neuter is usually 'prize' (except in the plural) whilst the masculine denotes the competition itself. Nevertheless one might imagine a comparable extension of meaning of ἅμιλλα to include 'prize of a competition'. Alternatively, one might suggest that ἅμιλλα here is 'source of contention' rather than 'contention' alone: Krateia is certainly a source of contention now between father Demeas and suitor Thrasonides. Austin seems to have been thinking of the dative singular when he suggested ἀμίλλαι, 'in battle', but the form should be ἀμίλληι.   τοῦ[δ' εἰ]λη[μμ]έ[νου (or τοῦ γ'), 'of the man who has laid hands on (sc. you)'. A very uncertain supplement.

653. Here I guess that Demeas begins to ask Krateia about the suppliant branch she is carrying, as a diversion from the dreadful truth about the death of the brother at Thrasonides' hands, but Krateia interrupts him to ask him what he meant precisely. As mentioned above, this arrangement respects the paragraphoi in B^2 and O^3.

655-58 Krateia invites her father in, saying they must consult about how she should live in the future (sc. with the man she now thinks is her brother's killer). Webster's conjecture ε[ἰσίωμεν] (655) is reasonable in context but by no means necessary. ἔνδον e.g. would be equally possible.

657 ἀλλ' ἦι. O^3 has the letter combination αλλη with no diacritics. Various combinations for the end of the line are possible and have been proposed: ἀλλ' ἦ, ἦι, ἤ, and, I suppose, ἄλληι, 'differently'. For ἀλλ' ἦ introducing a question cf. Aesch. *Ag.* 276,

Act Three   179

Cho. 774 (LSJ s.v. II 1 b). It is clear, at any rate, that Krateia is here contemplating the stance which befits her in future.   κὰ[μ]ὲ, 'I as well'. In this reconstruction, this will mean 'how I too' (should live), where the 'too' references the fact that the pair have just been discussing the (putative) death of Krateia's brother. Sandbach's κἄμ' ἔδει is also possible. Krateia seems to mean 'How am I to live decently?' now that her brother is dead and her captor and lover has been found to be the killer.

658 ζῆν εὐπρε[π]ῶς. Hunt read ζην ευ in O[1] although I can make nothing of the second word on the photograph. There seems to be room for two or three letters between ζην and πρε. If the reading is correct, it is hard to decide whether ευ (as adverb εὖ) should go better with ζῆν ('and how I should live well') or with πρεπ- either as adverb εὖ ('it well suits') or as prefix εὐπρεπ- which I prefer here. The letters after πρεπ- in O[3] are hard to make out but the last could well be sigma, hence my εὐπρεπῶς. Kraus (1971a, 12) suggests the following– divergent–reconstruction: [sc. βουλευτέον νῦν ἐστιν] ἀλλ' ἢ κἀμὲ δεῖ / ζῆν εἰ πρέπει μετὰ τοῦτο τὸν ἐμὸν δεσπότην; 'should I consider whether my lord should live after *this*?' But this seems grammatically faulty as we cannot have δεῖ βουλευτέον or πρέπει δεῖ together. Much uncertainty in Krateia's train of thought here, which is unfortunate as her words may be a matter of life and death! My hypothetical reconstruction makes her consider how best to live now she has discovered the awkward plight she is in: she is the property and deflowered (old word!) mistress of a soldier responsible (she thinks) for killing her brother.

659 Although O[1] gives this line unequivocally to Θρ(ασωνίδης), we also have paragraphos after **659**, indicating another change of speaker. I agree with Sandbach (G-S 454) and del Corno (1970, 258), that the words of this line are better given to Demeas, as they are in keeping with the sentiment he expressed at **634-5**. Moreover, **660** is a suitable entry line for Thrasonides inquiring about Demeas. Like this, **659** becomes the final gnomic flourish to the exchange between father and daughter. It is indeed paradoxical and problematic that, the minute Demeas discovers his daughter, he also discovers that her captor and lover is the brother's killer (in the opposite order, in fact). Menander has constructed this paradoxical situation, of course, and this line reminds one of Aristophanes of Byzantium's remark about Menander's art and life mirroring each other.

660-70 Thrasonides enters from the inn, where Getas has gone to fetch him. For the audience's benefit he repeats what Getas must have told him inside. Thrasonides' speech now is an entry monologue ushering in a new scene. One notes how the suspense Menander builds here carries us over the *entr'acte* to the next act. Similarly Habrotonon in *Epitr.* 555-6 prays to Peitho before embarking on her deceit of Charisios. Such speeches go some way to compensating for the fact that Greek theatre does not show interiors. The speaker anticipates what might happen when they embark on

180   CHAPTER 5. COMMENTARY

their chosen course. Thrasonides now goes to discover his fate (665 εἰσίωμεν). Afterwards, we will hear the result – negative for Thrasonides – from Getas who conveys the gist. Powerful literary models of such speeches are found in tragedy: e.g. those of Kassandra as she goes inside to her death in Aeschylus' *Ag.* (1072ff.); Medea's speech in Euripides (*Med.* 364-409), where she announces her plan to take decisive action. Thrasonides' speech now is heavily paratragic. Apart from the regular trimeters we have words such as οἴχεται (664), 661 in its entirety, likewise 667-69, the trembling approach to imminent disaster.

660 φή‹ι›ς, 'you say?' Thrasonides asks Getas, who had announced he was off to call Thrasonides in 638 and this is the result. Getas accompanies Thrasonides in this short monologue (668). In my version he has one short remark in 670, whilst others (see below on note 670) believe he has a non-speaking part.

661 τρισαθλιώτατον, 'thrice-most-miserable'. A ridiculous exaggeration, conveying Thrasonides' extreme consternation at the thought of being rejected by Krateia now, contrasting with μακάριον, 'blessedly happy', as its antonym. τρισάθλιος, 'wretched', itself is a favourite of Menander, with double figure occurrences. The motif of the rejected lover being (feeling) the most miserable of men is a mainstay of Menander (e.g. Moschion *and* Polemon in *Perik.*), one that Thrasonides had already started in lines 4-5.

662 τῶν ζώντων ἀπάντων, 'of all living beings'. Another crass exaggeration, but one felt by the lover, whether he is jilted, as here, or accepted. Similarly Moschion in *Perik.* 532-37.

663 δοκιμάσει, 'approve'. Thrasonides means whether Demeas will approve his marriage to Krateia. At this point Thrasonides has no reason to think Krateia has suddenly taken to him after her shrewish behaviour; now that Demeas has appeared, he sees him as the key to his fate, the one who can decide for or against his daughter's marriage. Thrasonides seems totally unaware of the intelligence the other two think they have against him. And, indeed, Thrasonides himself is presumably in no position to enlighten them, otherwise he would do so in the dialogue reported by Getas in the next act. Only the audience know the truth through the omniscient prologue speaker whoever he or she was. The tense here, future (δοκιμάσει, δώσει), in the protasis of the conditional is an example of this tendency of Menander no longer to use the classical construction of the 'prospective' subjunctive: ἂν μὴ δοκιμάσηι, δῶι.

661-2 κυρίως δώσει, 'give [her to me in marriage] as her *kyrios*'. This is the decisive act of the marriage rite: the legal guardian of a girl (usually father or brother) gives her over to her new master, the groom. Cf. Dem. 36.32 κυρίως δόντος τοῦ πατρὸς τοῦ σοῦ κατὰ τοὺς νόμους αὐτὴν γεγαμῆσθαι.

664 οἴχεται Θρασωνίδης, 'Thrasonides is done for'. Thrasonides speaks about him-

Act Three 181

self in the distancing third person, as if he were already standing above his own corpse. Cf. Eur. *Med.* 402, where Medea refers to herself by name; id. *Her.* 3 πατέρα τόνδ' Ἡρακλέους (Amphitryon speaking about himself); Seneca *Med.* 164-66 *Medea superest.*

665-7 The word order is almost the reverse of what is 'natural': οὐκέτι δεῖ ἡμᾶς κτλ.

666 τ]ὸ τοιοῦτον, 'such a thing', refers to the matter in hand: whether Krateia will have him or not. ο[ὐ]κέτι / ... εἰκάζειν, εἰδέναι δέ, δεῖ. Thrasonides wishes to acquire certainty about his fate. On a metatheatrical level this is what the spectator wants, too: by watching the outcome of the play, to replace surmise (εἰκάζειν) with knowledge (εἰδέναι). The audience's anticipation is similar to that of Thrasonides himself; the use of such words shows, I think, that Menander was aware of what theatre 'did' in the minds of viewers.

667 ὀκνηρῶς καὶ τρέμων, 'hesitantly and trembling'. These were obviously ways an actor could show trepidation visibly. We hear of a number of 'hesitant' entries in Menander: for example when Daos fears punishment in *Perik.* 317 with my note; *Epitr.* 636. How the actor in fact played Thrasonides here would reflect how ridiculous he was meant to appear: a ludicrously trembling Thrasonides would hardly command the audience's respect.

668 μαντεύεθ', 'feels foreboding' (Germ. 'ahnt'), a metaphorical sense of the verb which usually means 'consult an oracle', or 'prophesy'. Here Thrasonides' soul is, so to speak, the seat of the oracle. The great precedent for the inner oracle was Sokrates' *daimonion* which he himself, and others, consulted when they wanted advice. Cf. *Dys.* 571, Sostratos anticipating a happy outcome.

669 ἀπαξάπ[αντα (Turner) or ἀπαξάπαν γε (Arnott)? In Turner's version we would have a neuter plural subject 'everything' and a neuter singular complement βέλτιον, which appears possible, although βελτίω would be metrically possible, too. Arnott's suggestion (followed by Blanchard) would be more literally correct. In meaning the plural 'all possible things' seems to me to have the edge over Arnott's singular, and the neuter singular complement not agreeing with the subject is a well known phenomenon, e.g. Xen. *An.* 2.5.9 φοβερώτατον δ' ἐρημία.

670 οἰήσεως. There seem to be letters in the right margin of O[3] which Turner reads as .γνο.[and supplements as ἄγνοια (or ἀγνοίας). This, then, could be a gloss on οἰήσεως at line beginning. ΓΕ[Τ]. There is paragraphos under this line and a clear *nota personae* above πῶς; indicating that, at least in the opinion of this scribe, Getas spoke the following words. This makes sense: the servant comments sceptically on his master's words: 'How so? I'd be surprised!', meaning that he doubts that 'everything is better than uncertainty' (certainty for Thrasonides will be much worse). Others (Sandbach) object that Getas would then be a fourth speaking part in this

182 CHAPTER 5. COMMENTARY

scene (Demeas, Krateia, then Thrasonides, then Getas). But an actor playing Demeas or Krateia had the duration of Thrasonides' entry monologue to change costume, probably enough. The words hardly make sense in Thrasonides' mouth. Blanchard, too, observes the *n. p.* After this line both men exit into Thrasonides' house.

671 There is an illegible *nota personae* in the left margin of O^3 which Turner interprets as compatible with K]ΛΕ[Ι]^N. Kleinias enters here (from the agora?) with the cook he has hired. He announces that one guest will be present at the evening meal, himself, and a third, a woman friend, who has not appeared yet.

673 ἀγωνιῶ, from ἀγωνιάω, 'be distressed or anxious' (not from ἀγωνίζομαι). Kleinias seems to be referring to some crucial matter from his point of view involving the girl concerned. This is the only reference we have to such a secondary love interest in the play; no doubt there was more elsewhere. It seems to me unlikely that Kleinias was a rival suitor to Thrasonides for Krateia, *pace* Zagagi (1994, 63). Apart from anything else, Krateia was not *free* to raise the hopes of anybody that she might transfer her favours to them: she was a prisoner-of-war *belonging* to Thrasonides. I suppose a rival admirer might *buy* her from Thrasonides but he would have to be amenable to the sale, which he certainly was not. **καὐτός**, 'I too'. Who else? Thrasonides, presumably. So Kleinias is aware of his neighbour's troubles. The remark seems to indicate that both male householders were on tenterhooks in this play in their love life. I assume Kleinias' relatively mild symptoms of love's distress were meant to contrast with Thrasonides whose life was endangered by his depression.

674-5 περιδ[ρα]μοῦμαι τὴν [πόλιν] ... πᾶσαν, 'I'll run round the whole city'. A remarkable feat and hardly possible just before dinner. The exaggeration clearly expresses Kleinias' keen desire to find the lady in question. Blanchard cites Theophylactus *ep.* 24.4-5 Zanetto ἐγὼ τὴν πόλιν ἐσκινδαλάμιζον ἅπασαν, which seems to mean 'I splintered the whole city' (σκινδαλαμίζω/ σχινδ- not in LSJ). In Plato's *Symp.* Agathon says he looked for Aristodemos in order to invite him to his dinner-party, but could not find him (174e7-8 ζητῶν σε ἵνα καλέσαιμι, οὐχ οἷός τ' ἢ ἰδεῖν, 'although I looked for you in order to invite you, I couldn't find you').

678 τοῦ ταχέως ... φρόντισον, 'keep speed in mind', 'concentrate on speed', 'look sharp'. A slightly unusual turn of phrase, not exactly paralleled in comedy; Turner cites fr. 558 τοῦ καλῶς πεφρόντικεν, fr. 648 ἐν τῶι καλῶς, *Dys.* ἐν τῶι ταχέως, for the adverb with τό.

Act Four

Act Four 183

Scene One: Drama indoors

The act opens with Kleinias in conversation with Syra who has told him how Demeas went over to the neighbours' house on seeing a sword among the spoils brought from Thrasonides' to their house. That means his main guest for dinner has disappeared, as well as the girl. He has been deserted from all sides. The previous act closed with Kleinias going inside preparatory to dinner, now the next act shows him coming out again very soon afterwards, having discovered that his guest of honour has disappeared. The choral *entr'acte* bridges only a short time interval here. Cf. Zagagi (1994, 76-79) on 'linking devices' from the end of one act to the beginning of the next.

677 Luckily for us Kleinias fills us in on the important recent development in the plot. Demeas has recognized a sword among the spoils taken by Thrasonides, which have been deposited (for whatever reason) in Kleinias' house. If my reconstruction is right, that was the scene in act three in which Getas was apparently smuggling items into Kleinias' house (532ff.). Demeas then immediately made off to the neighbours' house (that was the fragmentary scene in act three – 576ff.– in which Demeas and Syra dithered at the doorway before Krateia herself came out). As explained in act three Demeas has recognized a sword as belonging to *him* (578ff. and 592-3); since he is too old to fight, we may infer that he has bequeathed his sword to his son; finding it now among the spoils of a mercenary (Thrasonides), he concludes that this man has killed his son.

679 πηνίκα, 'when?' I think the answer is in the third act when Getas brought them across (see reconstruction there). οὗτοι are the neighbours, in fact Getas, if I am right.

681-2 Lines which unfortunately elude certain restoration, although a number of letters are visible. Line 682 has been corrected *in toto supra lineam* after initial μον-. The latter half of both lines is unfortunately rubbed. π[λ]είστων, if correct, should go with λήψεων in the next line, and mean 'very many', but the reading is anything but secure, as the first two letters are non-existent.   κε[ι]μ[ένων]. More or less nothing of this can be read, so it is e.g. With λήψεων in the next line we get the meaning 'Why, when there are so many items of gain ... ?'

682 λήψεων. O³ has λημψεων here, influenced, as Sandbach says, by λαμβάνω. And for this play we now have the form ἀναλήμψομαι in line 541 (in O¹¹; see note there). λῆψις, from λαμβάνω, normally means 'taking hold', 'seizure'. Thuc. 4.114 has ἡ λῆψις τῆς πόλεως, 'the seizure of the city'. But here we seem to have the meaning 'what is seized', i.e. the booty from capturing and plundering a city. In the

184 CHAPTER 5. COMMENTARY

plural the meaning 'receipts' is documented (LSJ 2a), i.e. what is 'taken in'. These λήψεις are surely the same as the λάφυρα, spoils taken by Thrasonides on his service in Cyprus, a word also formed from the root λαβ-. If this is right, the sentence must have meant something like 'Why is this (sc. the sword) the only thing (μόνη 'οτί) [of importance?] when there are many items of plunder (πλείστων κειμένων λήψεων)?'

682 [γνοῦσα γὰρ]. An e.g. supplement with εὔδηλος εἶ in the next line. 'Obviously you know'. I assume Kleinias is trying to squeeze the truth from Syra about Demeas and the sword, but she, for some reason (see next note), is not 'coming clean'. When someone then emerges from Thrasonides' house Kleinias thinks he will hear the truth.

683 Sandbach's reconstruction is the more correct, in my opinion (see *app.*).   εὔδηλος εἶ, 'obviously you ... ', probably 'know all about it' or some such. Kleinias suspects that Syra knows all too well what's going on, as regards both the spoils in the house and Demeas' surprising behaviour. If my reconstruction of act three is anywhere near the mark, Syra was privy to Getas' secret mission to remove the spoils from under Krateia's nose.   On the ψοφεῖν of a door (of Thrasonides' house) when it is opened from the inside, see my note on *Epitr.* 875 and Bader (1971). Cf. *Perik.* 126, *Sam.* 324, fr. 883 K-A: ἀλλ᾽ ἐψόφηκε τὴν θύραν τις ἐξιών, fr. com. adesp. 1071.4. This is a stage convention: a character comments on the noise of a door as a way of alerting the audience to an entry. It is equivalent to 'all eyes on this door!'

685ff. It is Getas, emerging from the scene in which Thrasonides met Demeas and asked for his daughter's hand, unsuccessfully as we shall hear from Getas. In this scene we have one of those 'not noticing' scenes in which one person is so engrossed in their thoughts and mutterings (Getas) that they fail to notice another person present on stage (Kleinias). An example comes in act one of this play, in fact, when Getas vainly follows in Thrasonides' footsteps, trying to attract his attention. So now the tables are turned: Getas fails to notice another. Another example is *Epitr.* 908ff., where Charisios talks to himself impassionedly and fails to notice the presence of Onesimos. On the technique of this scene see Handley in Turner (1970, 153ff.); Frost (1988, 87). Another feature of this scene is Getas' rapid entries and exits; in effect he is giving a running commentary on the argument going on inside in Thrasonides' house. We might compare this technique to that in act four of *Sam.* (532ff.) in which Nikeratos rapidly goes in and out of his own house, reporting what has happened inside and becoming more and more agitated. One might see this as a functional weakness of Greek theatre – that interior developments cannot be shown – but it has its own comic potential, here with Kleinias trying to make himself noticed to the distracted Getas; see Mitch Brown's Cincinnati dissertation on this theatrical technique (Brown, 2016). As usual Menander has tempered the gravity of the situation – the couple's future hangs

Act Four 185

in the balance – with an extraneous distraction (Zagagi, 1994, 25); Cusset & Lhostis (2014, 166): 'Le monologue commenté et mis à distance par les apartés de Clinias permet en quelque sorte une conciliation du pathétique (de la situation) et du comique (celle de la scène) au sein de la même scène.' Here Kleinias is more concerned about what has happened to his dinner guest. He keeps on interrupting Getas as he tells us about the difficult discussion indoors. This scene is, in fact, a *tour de force* with the passion of Thrasonides reported at two removes: first by the reporting of Getas, who here is sympathetic to his master, and secondly by Kleinias' nearly complete lack of sympathy. Such is life.

685-6 Getas enters with two lines of flabbergasted consternation. It is not clear what has motivated Getas' entry: Kleinias has not knocked as we see in lines 683-4. Two oaths frame a noun and two epithets, all in the so-called genitive of exclamation. We have already commented on Menander's predilection for the word ἄτοπος (p. 5); here we have a variant, **ἔκτοπος**, literally 'out of place', or 'out of line' perhaps, together with another significant epithet for Menander's psychology, **ἀπάνθρωπος**, 'inhuman' or 'inhumane', see below p. 188. The pair of epithets for the behaviour shown by both Demeas and his daughter (686 ἀμφοῖν) shows, in the eyes of Getas, a kind of deviance from all acceptable norms. Zeus oaths are very common among Menander's speakers, the oath **νὴ τὸν Ἥλιον**, 'by the Sungod!', has a count of eight in existing fragments elsewhere. These are well-worn oaths, in fact, and one wonders whether the effect is not a little tired, designed to temper the effect of shock in Getas' words. Note the alliteration of dentals in line 685. Again, perhaps the effect is a little clichéed; one thinks of music-hall exaggeration. It has been remarked upon by others that Getas imitates others' voices in this scene (Thrasonides 693-95; Demeas 698-9; Thrasonides again 699-700; a whole impassioned speech by Thrasonides in 706-711); the actor will have needed to be gifted to convey these other voices convincingly but comically; cf. Blanchard 274, who refers to the long narrative in the fourth act of *Sik.*, in which Eleusinios relates the exchanges in the public assembly.

687 In a matter-of-fact way Kleinias puts his question to Getas who is, however, quite oblivious.

688 αὐθαδίας, another exclamatory genitive, 'such wilfulness!', combined with yet another oath, by Herakles. The word seems to be derived from αὐτ- ἥδ, pleasing (only) oneself (Germ. 'eigensinnig'). Theophrastus defines αὐθάδεια (*Char.* 15) as ἀπήνεια ὁμιλίας ἐν λόγοις, 'rudeness in converse with words' (or just 'conversation'). Cf. Aristoph. *Thesm.* 704, *Frogs* 1020 Αἰσχύλε, λέξον, μηδ' αὐθάδως σεμνυνόμενος χαλέπαινε. Antiphanes fr. 300.4 Kock; Euboulos fr. 25.1 K-A (αὐθαδέστερος).

689-90 The supplements should give the sense. **λαβεῖν** is an 'explanatory' infinitive after αὐθαδίας. It is a bit of an exaggeration to say that Demeas is taking a wife away from a worthy man, but Krateia might be described loosely as 'his woman'; cf. lines 802-3 where Thrasonides wonders how to prevent Demeas from taking Krateia from him. Her status at this moment is actually that of bought prisoner-of-war, hence slave. Blanchard imagines a different sense: that a man has the right to take (λαβεῖν) a woman (γυναῖκ[α]) in marriage.　**ὅ]τι λαλῶ.** O^3 clearly has λαλω whilst O^1 has λ . . ω; there is therefore little justification for Arnott's λάβω here (followed by Blanchard).

692 μ[η]δὲ γρῦ. Probably better to keep the reading of O^3 (μ[.] . ε) over O^1 (ουδε) here, as O^3 is usually the more reliable. The expression οὐδὲ γρῦ 'not one whit', recurs at *Sam.* 655. Explained by the scholiast on Aristoph. *Plut.* 17 as 'not even a grunt' (from γρύζω), but the *Suda* gives a definition as a 'small coin', which make more sense. If ἐκεῖνος is right Getas is probably saying that Demeas is paying no heed to Thrasonides' pleadings.

693 [κ]αὶ γ[ά]ρ, Δημέα. The accepted supplement here (Handley) rests on scant traces in O^1, but suits the vocative Δημέα, which can be clearly read, and the sense of the next line.

695 πατ]ὴρ ‹καὶ›. One has to choose here between O^3's [πατ]ὴρ κύριος and O^1's]τηϲ κ[which is probably to be supplemented as αὐτῆς κύριος *vel sim.* I have preferred, with Turner and Sandbach, the reading of O^3, although ‹καὶ› has to be added. The sense must be that Thrasonides is appealing to Demeas in his role of *kyrios* of the girl, hence entitled to give her away.

696 ἐλειν]ὰ κλάων, 'crying piteously'. ἐλεινά (used adverbially) looks a reasonable description of Thrasonides' behaviour, on the model of line 36. Blanchard prints ἅ[παν]τα (Sudhaus) but there is no trace of tau.　**ὄνος λύρας,** 'the donkey (heard, or rather, did not hear) the lyre'. Machon 140 Gow gives the full expression ἡ δ' ὅλη παροιμία «ὄνος λύρας ἤκουε καὶ σάλπιγγος ὗς». Λέγεται δὲ ἐπὶ τῶν μὴ συγκατατιθεμένων μηδὲ ἐπαινούντων, i.e. about those who 'neither agree nor approve', but remain deaf to another's pleas. Cf. Photius and *Suda* s.v. Μένανδρος Ψοφοδεεῖ (= fr. 418 K-A); Aristainetos *Ep.* 1.17.18 ἀλλ' οὐδὲν αὐτῆι τῶν ἐμῶν ἐμέλησε λόγων· ὄνος λύρας, 'but she wasn't at all concerned about my words: donkey [and] lyre'. The fact that the proverb is attested for the play *Psophodeēs* should not lead us to imagine that this was another name for *Mis.* (J. Rea's suggestion *ap.* Turner (1965) 5). I suppose the expression comes from the dumb indifference of these animals to music. For what it is worth, not all animals were thought to exhibit such insensitivity to music: the dolphin in the Arion legend, for example, comes swimming to his kitharody (Hdt. 1.23-24), and Dorkon's cattle in *Daphnis and Chloe* respond to his lyre playing (1.29-30). There is another donkey saying in Menander's *Plokion*, fr. 296 K-A = 333 K-Th: ὄνος ἐν πιθήκοις, 'a donkey among monkeys', which seems to mean a donkey's (sc. ugliness) rivals, or exceeds, that of monkeys. In

Act Four 187

context it's 'she's a donkey among monkeys'.

697 συμπεριπατήσω, 'I'll wander round with him'. There are some thirty instances of περιπατέω and cognate words (two of συμπεριπατέω) in extant Menander. Although the meaning is always unloaded (simply 'walk around') I cannot believe that the frequency is coincidental (see above n. on 17). Menander's affiliations with the Peripatos have been much discussed and are reasonably well documented. It is not that Menander's plays are overtly philosophical – far from it. Rather, the characters and the assumptions they make are unthinkable without a Peripatetic background. A recent discussion is Angelo Casanova 'Menander and the Peripatos: New insights into an old question' in Sommerstein (2014a, 137-151). Book length treatments of the whole complex: Barigazzi (1965), Cinaglia (2014). From Kleinias' words here we can deduce how Getas acted out his indignation here – walking agitatedly back and forth, with Kleinias on his trail. As pointed out above, the scene reverses Getas' role in the first scene of the play (see esp. line 21). This underlines, perhaps, the fact that Getas' attitude to his master's plight now seems to be diametrically opposite to that in the former scene. Already in lines 533-34 Getas seems to be expressing sympathy with Thrasonides' situation.

698 ἓν τοῦτο δ' εἴρει, 'he strings this one thing' (as of someone stringing beads repeatedly on a string). LSJ s.v. II say of the post-Homeric active of εἴρω: 'esp. in speech, string together', ὁ εἴρας καὶ συνυφάνας ἕκαστα [λόγος] Philo 1.499; ε. θρῆνον Josephus, *BJ* 6.5.3; Philostratos, *Vita Apollonii* 1.20 πολλὰ ὀνόματα, cf. 6.17; Sextus Empiricus, *Adv. Mathematicos* 1.98 οἱ μηδὲ δύο σχεδὸν ῥήματα δεξιῶς εἴρειν δυνάμενοι; Dio 36.12.1 τῶν μακράν τινα καὶ συνεχῆ ποίησιν εἰρόντων, '[poets] who compose long and continuous poetry'. Getas had said before Kleinias' aside that Demeas had ignored Thrasonides' pleas like a 'donkey (sc. deaf to) a lyre'. Now he continues by saying: 'all *he* came out with was (sc. free my daughter).' Turner originally printed ειρει in O³ with a *crux*, but subsequent editors have endorsed it happily enough. Ariana Traill (2007, 44) defends the sense of εἴρει, 'insert', with reference to an instance in Zaleukos *ap.* Stob. 4.2.19, of someone 'inserting (εἴρει) their neck into a noose'. She writes: 'Thus Demeas "inserts" (sc. into the flood of Thrasonides' pleas) this one comment'.

Palaeographically the situation seems to be this: O³ has ειρει; in O¹ (photograph) one reads the following: εἴρη . ε where the eta is unlikely to be epsilon-iota. The letter after eta looks most like mu, but it *might* be kappa, giving εἴρηκε, he has said, or possibly a miscopied version of that. It looks then, that we have to choose between εἴρει and εἴρηκε, of which the latter is clearly *lectio facilior* (but unmetrical).

In the past I have considered ἔρρει, (the talk) 'flowed', or εἴρ<γ>ει, 'prevents, stands in the way', but on the whole I do not think we should deviate from what is a relatively clear reading in O³. The reading ἔρρει would be defensible as one sees in second

188   CHAPTER 5. COMMENTARY

position only traces of a descender, which *could* belong to rho if the top loop had become erased. However the descender is a little long for rho and more typical of this scribe's iota, giving ειρει. It might be said that the reading of O¹, if correctly read, εἴρηκε, could have originated as a gloss on εἴρει. This would amount to support for O³. Arnott, *ZPE* 111, 1996, 23, wondered whether an archaic form εἴρει (LSJ s.v. B) 'he says, speaks', was resurfacing here, but I think that is very unlikely. Archaisms are not a feature of Menander's style.

698-700 ἀξιῶ ἥκων ... αἰτῶ ἐντετυχηκώς. The parallel structure emphasizes that the men are at loggerheads. Demeas 'demands having come', Thrasonides 'demands having met'. Arnott comments that 'the absence here in Menander's text of names or other indications to identify the quoted speakers implies the actor playing Getas would be required to imitate their different voices and gestures if he wished their identities to be readily understood by the audience' (see discussion above). The sentence describes in a nutshell 'women's position' in this society: the men argue about the daughter's fate. One has rights over her as her father; the other as her (prospective) husband. In fact the situation is a little different here as Thrasonides in fact 'owns' Krateia: but he *treats* her like a wife. Cf. Traill (2008). However, one should not forget that Krateia has discussed her position with her father prior to this altercation (655-58). In this private discussion she will have been able to express her viewpoint freely.

699 ἥκω[ν] ἀπολυτροῦν. We recall that Demeas in line 433 specifically denies having come here to ransom 'bodies' and Simplicius says that Demeas arrived by chance and *then* had the opportunity to ransom his daughter; see discussion on p. 3. In other words, Demeas' formulation here is somewhat disingenuous. **ἀπολυτροῦν** is the active infinitive, so here Demeas is demanding that 'you (Thrasonides) release my daughter on receipt of ransom money'. We never hear how much Demeas is prepared to pay, but that is not the point: Thrasonides is not interested in money, but in the hand of Krateia in marriage.   It seems that O¹ had something like ἥκω τ' ἀπολυτροῦν ἄγων πατήρ. The late manuscript has little regard for metre, or grammar for that matter!

700 αἰτῶ γυναῖκά σ', 'I demand of you [Krateia] as wife'. This is **αἰτέω** with double accusative, to demand something from someone. **ἐντετυχηκώς** must stand alone, 'having met (sc. with *you*)'.

701-2 Kleinias comments on Getas' disappearance again inside. He has not yet succeeded in attracting Getas' attention. He comments in **702** that Getas *did* mention Demeas' name, thus half answering the question which Kleinias wants to put to him. In **703** Getas pops out again with the next instalment of commentary.

703 ἀνθρωπίνως, an important concept in Menander. In *Asp.* 165-6 Daos comments that one must bear fortune as befits a mortal: ἐκ τῶν δ' ἐνόντων ὡς μάλιστα

Act Four   189

δεῖ φέρειν ἀνθρωπίνως τὸ συμβεβηκός. And *ibid.* 260-1 Chairestratos exhorts Smikrines similarly: ἀνθρωπίνως τὸ πρᾶγμ' ἔνεγκε, Σμικρίνη, πρὸς τῶν θεῶν, 'by heaven, Smikrines, take this like a (sc. decent) human being!' Fr. 874 K-A ἀνθρωπίνως χρὴ τὰς τύχας φέρειν, ξένε. It seems then that the word or concept is particularly applicable to τύχη or τὸ συμβεβηκός, that which eventuates (usually in a disastrous sense). A man should bear such misfortune with equanimity, as far as possible, as it belongs to the human condition to face disaster. Here Getas laments that Demeas refuses to take a worldly, or perhaps, philosophical view of his children's fate. That is life, Getas intimates, war causes such upheavals and losses. It would be better for Demeas to accept that and simply let Krateia stay with Thrasonides (she cannot, after all, marry anyone else now, having lost her virginity). It would be wrong to read any real philosophy into the line: Menander always incorporates an escape clause, in this case, the speaker Getas, who can hardly be taken seriously.

704 τὸ συμβεβηκός, 'happenstance', with implications of 'disaster' (see previous note). Getas means what has happened to Krateia (and perhaps her brother).   ὗς ὄρει, 'pig on the mountain'. In view of this unintelligible proverb, not otherwise known in Greek, J. Kells suggested that one should read ὗς ὀρεῖ, meaning 'pig to a mule', ὀρεύς being a non-Attic word for Attic ἡμίονος, as in Aristoph. *Frogs* 290. We might then understand 'one stubborn creature to another', but again there is no Greek parallel. Austin (1966, 296) was not impressed and commented: 'we can do without Kells's mule'. Lelli (2007), however, has tracked down a proverb in Calabria, which he says is known to preserve old figures of speech. The Calabrian proverb runs «A quadràra vulli e lu puorcu è alla muntagna», in (proper) Italian: «il calderone bolle e il porco è in montagna», 'the cauldron boils and the pig is on the mountain', said, apparently, of 'those who rarely agree'. That seems to tally well with Demeas and Thrasonides who are at loggerheads, so the explanation seems to suit, even if obscure.

Another pig proverb is preserved: ὗς ὀρίνει, 'the pig stirs' (or a variant πάλιν ἡ ὗς παρορίνει in *Mantissa Proverbiorum*), which is said by several paroemiographers (Diogenianus and Michael Apostolius) to be applied ἐπὶ τῶν βιαίων λέγεται καὶ ἐριστικῶν, 'to aggressive and contentious people'. The sentiment only partly suits Demeas here, who is perhaps more stubborn than aggressive. We cannot suppose that the text is corrupt, as the version ὗς ὀρ‹ίν›ει would not scan as the line stands. Yet another possibility might be to see in ὀρεῖ a future of ὄρνυμι, cf. fut. med. ὀρεῖται *Il.* 20.140, which might give the sense 'the pig will stir' (sc. something). This seems a bit far-fetched, but at least it would place the saying in parallel with known pig-proverbs. Otherwise various sayings with ὗς are said to apply to unfeeling people: e.g. Βοιωτία ὗς: ἐπὶ τῶν ἀναισθήτων καὶ ἀπαιδεύτων (Macarius Chrysocephalus); for others see p. 165.

190   CHAPTER 5. COMMENTARY

705 πάλιν, in the sense of 'in her turn' (LSJ s.v. III). Getas has dealt with Demeas' behaviour, now he turns to Krateia.

706 ὑ[φο]ρᾶι βοῶντος, 'she looks askance while he cries'. Austin's suggestion ἀφορᾶι, 'she looks away' (Austin, 1966, 296), although initially rejected by Turner (in *Oxy. Papyri*) on the grounds that one might expect to see some trace of the phi, has subsequently found the general approval of editors. Some problems remain with it, however. First, the first letter trace suits upsilon, in my opinion, better than alpha. If it is an alpha, it is very low on the line (Austin (1966, 296) avers that initial ọ is 'certain', but it is anything but). The absence of a trace of phi is less important, in my opinion, as I can see no trace of a second letter at all. Second, the sense required of ἀφοράω here, 'look away', is not the normal sense of the verb, which is to 'look directly at' something (i.e. *away* from all else). True, a passage of Xen. (*Kyr.* 7.1.36) seems to attest the sense 'with backs turned' (of people being struck), although I am not sure that Krateia would literally turn her back on Thrasonides here. Austin (1966, 296) cites as parallel for the dramatic situation Soph. *Phil.* 934f. οὐδὲ προσφωνεῖ μ' ἔτι / ἀλλ' ... ὧδ' ὁρᾶι πάλιν, where one notes that Neoptolemos does not 'turn away' from Philoktetes but 'looks back at me (sc. stubbornly)', which suits my ὑφορᾶι better. A slight problem remains (with my suggestion, too) that the iota adscript is rarely given in O³. But ὑφοράω, in the sense 'look suspiciously at' (LSJ s.v.) suits well and is amply attested. In particular note Luk. *Dial. Deorum* 23.1.15 (Erōs speaking) Ἀλλὰ ἐκεῖνος ἑκὼν προσίεταί με καὶ προσκαλεῖται, ἡ Ἀθηνᾶ δὲ ὑφορᾶται ἀεί, 'He (Ares) sends for me of his own accord and calls me to him, whilst Athena always looks askance at me' (= rejects me); cf. Xen. *An.* 2.4.10, οἱ δὲ Ἕλληνες ὑφορῶντες τούτους, 'the Greeks, however, suspecting these ... ' ὑποψία, 'suspicion', comes from this verb. παρορωμένωι in the sense of 'neglect', 'take no notice of', is used by Thrasonides himself in line 86, but does not suit the space or the traces here.   βοῶντος. The traces are pretty minimal up to -τος but the first letter does not look like lamda to me (Austin's λέγοντος). 'Cry' is more vivid than 'say', and suits Thrasonides' impassioned appeal better. Since this cannot be an indirect object of ὑφορᾶι, we need to assume a 'truncated' gen. abs. 'while he cries'. The sense is clearly that Krateia looks on unsympathetically whilst Thrasonides pleads. We may even have the precise sense of 'look suspiciously at', as Krateia strongly suspects by now that Thrasonides is not the man he seemed (a bragging soldier), but is the murderer of her brother.

706-11 Thrasonides' desperate plea is quoted *verbatim* by Getas. Similarly Onesimos reports on his master's desperation inside the house (*Ep.* 878-900). Perhaps it is not irrelevant to note that Getas would be lost if Thrasonides *did* commit suicide.

707 ἐγκαταλίπηις, 'abandon', 'leave in the lurch', a strong word typifying Menander's jilted lovers: cf. *Epitr.* 934 (where Onesimos uses the word in imitation of Chari-

Act Four   191

sios); in this play again a few lines later (711) for emphasis. When a form is repeated in this manner, it is frequently with different emphasis (or perhaps better,
sedes in the line), which means that the repetition is not identical. Similar repetition of καταλείπω in *Perik.* 506-7, but here with chiastic effect: 506-7 Γλυκέρα
με καταλέλοιπε, καταλέλοιπέ / με Γλυκέρα, Πάταικ'. O³ clearly had the form
ἐγκαταλείπῃς (pres.) which would also scan, but a negative command in Greek is
usually μή with aorist subjunctive.

707-8 παρθένον ... [ἀ]νήρ. Unequivocal evidence that Krateia and Thrasonides
are married in the sense of having had sex. This compromises Krateia for all future
relationships and rules out marriage (to anyone else) even if Demeas does 'free' her
from Thrasonides. The sentence and those following also go some way to showing
that Thrasonides and Krateia did share some kind of love (though how one-sided this
was, we cannot tell) before Krateia's feelings turned to hatred. ἀνήρ in the unofficial
sense of 'partner in a sexual relationship' (as in 'he was her man' in *Frankie and
Johnny* by Louis Armstrong); cf. Chariton *Kall.* 2.11.1 τρεῖς γεγόναμεν, ἀνὴρ καὶ
γυνὴ καὶ τέκνον, 'we have become three: man (= father), woman (= wife) and child'.
Sandbach takes this sentence differently: 'It shows that Thrasonides and Krateia were
believed to be living as man and wife, although that was not in fact the case' (he
takes ἐκλήθην in the sense 'people said [but I wasn't]'). I think, on the contrary, that
παρθένον and ἀνήρ are intended to show the change in her status in Thrasonides'
hands, from virgin to mistress or quasi-wife.

708-9 ἠγάπησά σε, / [ἀγ]απῶ, φιλῶ, Κράτεια φιλτάτη. Fourfold emphasis by
repetition with variation. Although Sandbach is right that ἀγαπάω need have no
sexual component, that is not true of φιλῶ and φιλτάτη. Moreover Thrasonides
would never have said ἐρῶ σου in the company of her father. That would not have
persuaded him to give him his daughter in marriage. One hears (LSJ s.v. III) that
ἀγαπάω commonly means in Attic 'to be well contented with'. The meaning 'love'
begins it seems in the fourth century with Plato, Demosthenes and Menander himself
(LSJ s.v. I): fr. 659, *Sam.* 32. The occurrences in Aristophanes and Alexis (fr. 125-
6.7) still predominantly have the meaning 'be content with', whilst the meaning 'love',
indeed 'passionately love', occurs in Menander *Dys.* 824 (ἀγαπῶ ἐκτόπως), and
Machon fr. 16.265 (ἐκτενῶς ἀγαπώμενος, 'earnestly loved'). It sometimes does
have connotations of sexual love: Arist. fr. 76, Lukian *Juppiter tragoedus* 10.2. Thrasonides has expressed his love as strongly as he could.

709-10. Thrasonides has not yet discovered the reason for Krateia's hatred. This
means that if there was a scene of bitter contention between the couple, it did not dis-
close any specific reason for Krateia's dislike of Thrasonides, certainly not the sword
of the brother. Krateia's expression in line 609 οὐκ ἂν [δυ]ναίμην κ[α]ρτερ[εῖ]ν,
'I couldn't bear it (any longer?)' does not sound as if she has *discovered* something,

192 CHAPTER 5. COMMENTARY

rather that she finds her situation intolerable. As so often *agnoia*, ignorance or misconception, lies at the heart of the knot Menander creates for his characters.

710-11 A completely unveiled threat to commit suicide if Krateia leaves him. Up until the fifth act it seems that suicide, or feigned suicide, is on the cards, if we are to interpret the Mytilene mosaic in this way.

711 οὐδ᾽ ἀπόκρισις, 'no answer', as we say.

712 βάρβαρος, λ[έ]αινά τις, 'a barbarian, a lioness!', in contrast to the proper Greek mode described in 716-17. Leaina was also the name of a famous hetaira favoured by Demetrios Poliorkētēs (Machon fr. 12.168-73; Athen. VI 253a), cf. Elderkin (1934, 30); the word also denoted, by innuendo, a sexual position of an hetaira (crouching, like a lion ready to pounce), cf. McClure (2003, 278). Menander's audience might have seen an allusion here, but the chief reference in combination with βάρβαρος is of course the savage leonine character displayed by Krateia when Thrasonides implores her, and any literary allusion is likely to be to Euripides *Med.* 1358, where Medea says to the crushed Jason 'you may call me a lioness, too, if you wish!' (πρὸς ταῦτα καὶ λέαιναν, εἰ βούληι, κάλει). The recalcitrant hetaira Daphnis in Aristainetos 1.17 is also repeatedly branded 'barbaric'. For the 'barbaric' nature of ignoring the ethical norms of Greek civilization cf. Lape (2003, 195 n. 66), who adduces parallels in *Epitr.* 898–99, 924; *Sam.* 519.

713 ἄν[θρωπος], feminine (= ἡ ἄνθρωπος) as at *Sam.* 348. Not exactly derogatory, the expression is not polite, either. To refer to a person as 'the woman', 'the man', instead of using his/her name dehumanizes to a degree. **κακόδαιμον**, 'wretch!' Kleinias is beginning to lose his patience.

715 μὰ τὸν Ἀπόλλω τουτονί. Getas can appeal to 'this Apollo here' because of the statue, or altar (or both) of Apollo Agyieus which stood on the Athenian stage, reflecting common Athenian household practice of honouring this god in front of houses, see e.g. Aristoph. *Wasps* 875 and esp. Philippides (2019, 314-15). See *Dys.* 659 with Sandbach's note (G-S 235) with plentiful references, and *Phasma* 74, here addressed Ἄπολλον ὦ π]άροικ᾽ ἄναξ, with Cusset's note (Cusset & Lukinovich, 2019). The difference between a normal stage oath and one to Apollo lay precisely in the fact that this god was felt to be present at the performance. It might seem odd that this god rather than Dionysos was personally present in the theatre, but it presumably reflected the reality of Athenian street 'furniture'.

716 οὐκ ἂν ἀπ[έ]λυσ᾽, 'I wouldn't have released her'. Traill (2008, 27) takes this as 'I wouldn't ransom her', but the aorist with ἄν should normally indicate past unreal. From this we see that Thrasonides *had* just released Krateia from the bondage he had acquired over her, or at least made the offer. On the other hand in line 805 (ἀφήσεις;) he is still considering whether to 'let her go'. Getas is commenting on the next devel-

Act Four 193

opment indoors. In this and the following lines consider the extraordinary fact that Getas, a slave (and rough Thracian at that), is commenting on the morality of accepted conduct among free Greeks. This shows the almost privileged position slaves have in Menander of being apart from their master's troubles and able to comment on them in an almost superior manner. See E. Bathrellou 'Relationships Among Slaves in Menander', in Sommerstein (2014a, 40-57). Whilst slaves may have had their private thoughts in Athenian reality, they hardly enjoyed such a privileged position. This observation is supported by the educated language used by slaves (note ἐπιστροφή in 719). Menander never makes them talk like yokels, but often in sophisticated language (as here). The prime example is Onesimos running (metaphorical) rings round Smikrines at the end of *Epitr.*, using quasi-philosophical language. Daos in *Asp.* is also the clever slave ('servus callidus'), e.g. lines 189-93, where he permits himself an educated comment on the Delphic slogan 'know yourself': Σμικρίνη, πάνυ μοι δοκεῖ / τὸ ῥῆμα τοῦτ' εἶναί τι μεμεριμνημένον / τὸ «γνῶθι σαυτόν», 'Smikrines, the saying "know yourself" seems to me something extremely well thought-out'.

716 Ἑλληνικὸν καὶ πανταχ[ῆ / γιν[όμε]νον, '[we know] that this is the Greek custom, practised everywhere'. The *Hellenikon* here contrasts with Krateia's reluctance to pity Thrasonides which is said in 712 to be βάρβαρος, barbaric. I.e. Greek ethics are thought to be way superior to barbarian, that is, foreign (particularly Oriental) customs. In *Perik.* 1010 Pataikos comments that it was 'according to Greek custom' (τοῦτ' ἐστὶν Ἕλληνος τρόπου) for Glykera to take pity on Polemon just at the moment when her luck had changed for the better. See my note there (on lines 1007-8) for further references, and add Xen. *An.* 3.1.30, where Apollonides is denounced by Xenophon for not living up to 'Greek' ideals. Fr. 762 K-Th runs Ἕλληνές εἰσιν ἄνδρες οὐκ ἀγνώμονες, / καὶ μετὰ λογισμοῦ πάντα πράττουσίν τινος, 'The Greeks are not unthinking people, and they conduct all their affairs with a certain rationale'. It is exactly this 'rationale' or 'reckoning up' to which Getas alludes here (note [λό]γον 719): Thrasonides has 'pitied' Krateia in freeing her from bondage, now Demeas should show pity to him. Webster (1960, 21-25) sees as background to such 'boasting' about Greek moral superiority the ideal of Greek *paideia* and the *pepaideumenos* ('gentleman') which spread through the Mediterranean in the Hellenistic age: that level of cultivation through education which led to higher ethical norms in society.

717-18 ἐλεεῖν ὀρθῶς ἔχει / τὸν ἀ[ν]τελεοῦνθ'. 'It's right to show pity to the person showing pity back'. Getas' point shows that Thrasonides had given Krateia her freedom without in return getting anything back from her; i.e. she and Demeas had not shown pity to him by agreeing to the marriage. He goes on to say 'If you show no consideration for me, nor do I for you.' Sandbach comments that, although unparalleled, ἀντελεοῦνθ' should not be doubted as a form. One could, however, imagine alternatives e.g. τὸν ᾳ[ὖ] σ' ἐλεοῦντα.

718-19 ὅταν ... ἔχω. 'If you don't [sc. pity] me, I care not a whit for you'. The sentence is further explanation of the *Hellenikon*, Greek custom, mentioned before, that pity is reciprocal. For (a politicized view of) reciprocity in Menander see von Reden (1998). For the sentence structure, one may compare Eur. *Alk.* 690, a passage in which Pheres is angrily retorting to Admetos that he is not obliged to die in his stead: μὴ θνῇσχ' ὑπὲρ τοῦδ' ἀνδρός, οὐδ' ἐγὼ πρὸ σοῦ, 'don't *you* die for this man (i.e. me), and I won't for you'.   **ἐπιστροφὴν**, 'regard for', 'consideration', literally a 'turning toward', LSJ s.v. II 3 e.g. Eur. *IT* 671; Xen. *HG* 5.2.9. Not in comedy itself, only as an adverb ἐπιστροφῶς, 'diligently, exactly', in Ephippos 3.10, Memn. 7.3. This is a very high-faluting word for Getas, a slave, to use; see note on line **716**.

720-1 ' "It's not possible for you?" So what? I don't consider that anything peculiar'. Getas imagines the reaction of the person opposite him when he says he feels no compassion or consideration; the other person is first quoted, then Getas gives his imaginary answer. The train of thought depends originally on line **716** 'I wouldn't have freed her!' Getas means that since Demeas and Krateia show Thrasonides no pity, why should he? He should have kept the girl in bondage in the first place. Blanchard: 'Tu ne *peux* faire cela!' Cf. Blundell (1980, 77): '(you say) you can't (return pity)' (addressed to Demeas).   Sandbach's remark that **δοκῶ** (Mette) in 721 is a little long for the space available is not right, in my opinion.   **ἄτοπον**, 'unusual', 'strange'. ἄτοπος is one of Menander's theme words for behaviour which contravenes the civic norm (see above p. 132). Literally it means 'out of place', quite similar to Germ. 'fehl am Platz', which has a similar meaning of abnormal. I count eighteen instances in the extant plays and fragments. A line from *Epitr.* (704) became proverbial (464 Jäkel; see now Pernigotti (2008)): μί' ἐστὶν ἀρετὴ τὸν ἄτοπον φεύγειν ἀεί, 'one virtue is always to shun an abnormal person'. Since ἄτοπον is unvaryingly a bad thing, its frequency seems to mirror the characters' desire *not* to behave in a socially unacceptable way. For a sociologist this would be evidence of a strong tendency toward conformity in Menander's Athenian society.

721-3 The brief description of Thrasonides' despair is comparable to the desperation of Charisios as described by his slave, too, Onesimos in *Epitr.* 878-900. Cf. Bonollo (2019, 90-91) for detailed analysis, and Christophe Cusset 'Melancholic lovers in Menander', in Sommerstein (2014a, 167-79).

721 βοήσεται δὲ καὶ βουλεύσεται. This is a new train of thought, going back to Thrasonides' despair after the remark that pity should be reciprocal. The jingle here reduces the seriousness of Thrasonides' ranting, at least in Getas' portrayal of it. It has a teasing ring to it. As if we should say: 'he'll rant and cant and plan his plans'.

722 κ[τα]νεῖν. Arnott (1996d, 37) points out that the strong aorist infinitive κτανεῖν

Act Four 195

(Webster) would be unique in later Greek comedy. However, it may recur in line 815 of this very play. We probably should not question the simple verb κτείνω here when ἀποκτείνω 'prevails' in comedy (LSJ, Sandbach, Austin (1966)). It seems that *Mis.* contained a truly remarkable form of the perfect of ἀποκτείνω, ἀπεκτάγκασι (fr. 6). Aristoph. *Birds* 1063 has κτείνω (of killing an animal; in a lyrical passage). There is also καίνω, kill, but it is not a comic word.   βλέπει δὲ πῦρ, 'he's fiery-eyed', cf. *Ep.* 900 βλέπει θ' ὕφαιμον ἠρεθισμένος, 'he's looking with bloodshot eyes in his consternation'; Aristoph. *Knights* 631 ἔβλεψε νᾶπυ 'looked sour (like mustard)'.

723 οὐ[δὲ] κατάκει[τ]αι, 'and doesn't find rest', going with στάς before ('he stands there, nor does he … '). κατάκειμαι does not necessarily mean lie down to sleep, but rather to lie down in the pleasant company of an hetaira, e.g. Aristoph. *Ach.* 985, *Lys.* 920, 925, Alexis *Philok.* fr. 1., Bato fr. 3.1, or indeed to lie down at the dinner table (see note on l. 52 above). Not being able to relax lying down as a symptom of agitation, seems a fair guess here, and it suits the traces well. Note the sleeplessness of the love-sick Pheidias in *Phasma* 9 ὅταν δ' ἀγρυπνεῖν εἴπηις.   δράττεταί ⟨τε⟩ τῶν τριχῶν, 'he tears at his hair', cf. *Epitr.* 893 τιλμός, a 'tearing of the hair'.

Scene Two: Kleinias and Getas

724 κατακόψεις, 'you'll wear me out'. Cf. *Sam.* 285 with Sommerstein's note, and Austin (1966, 297). Here, too, the joke is that someone wears another out by talking too much, or in too wearisome a manner. Literally κατακόπτω means 'chop up' (or 'down'), which leads to the *double entendre* in the *Samia* passage. Getas finally registers Kleinias' presence here, when he says this. Perhaps the actor shouted it. χαῖρε, Κλεινία. Finally Getas notices Kleinias and greets him as if the previous tirade hadn't happened.

725 π[όθεν πάρ]εσθ'; 'where did he come from?', if correct, seems to be a kind of aside.

725-6 'My guest seems to have caused quite a stir inside when he […] came to you'. Kleinias comments in ironical manner on the scene which Getas has been describing. ἐν]δὸ[ν παρε]λθών (Austin) looks more or less inevitable once one has placed -λθών. Between -]λθών and ὡς ὁ ξένος there follow traces which have not been deciphered yet. The missing word must be of metrical shape —∪— and ending with an elision -ει.'. I detect a phi after θων. Before ὁ ξένος either ὢν or ὤ[ς] (Blanchard), perhaps ὡς in postposition.

From 727 O³ (start of a new column) descends again into a miserably lacunose state.

736 ἐξ[έρ]χ[ετα]ι. If correct, Thrasonides, presumably, who speaks at 751.

743 εἰσέρχο[μαι. Presumably Kleinias exits into his own house here, leaving Getas alone on stage to deliver a brief 'transition' monologue ('Überbrückungsmonolog').

749 πρ[ὶν π]ες[εῖν] ἐμπειρίαι., 'before falling (victim) to experience'. If close to the mark this reconstruction of scanty traces would show Kleinias telling Getas to do something before experience teaches them a lesson. Perhaps a contrast is made with πλάνης, 'wandering' (of mind), in the next line. For πίπτω with dative alone see LSJ s.v. A, e.g. Eur. *Or.* 88 π. δεμνίοις, Soph. *Aj.* 759 π. δυσπραξίαις, id. *Tr.* 597 αἰσχύνηι.

750 If καὶ πλάνης is right, the sense of this line must be something like 'yes, for otherwise everything becomes random and unpredictable' (sc. without *empeiria*). Kleinias and Getas seem to be philosophizing together before Thrasonides appears. I could read fewer of the letters which Turner apparently read in this line.

Figure 5.2: P. Oxy. 4025 = O^9, lines 751-57(?). Courtesy of the Egypt Exploration Society and the U. Oxford Imaging Papyri Project

751-757 For the lines 752-56 O^9 offers a small fragment of text which bears a limited degree of correspondence with line endings in O^3 for the lines 755-56, as Austin saw. Specifically, the words τάλαν and θυγάτριον in 755 and 756 respectively match up with traces in O^3 to an extent which, I think, cannot be overlooked. In particular, in line 756, O^3 has δε[..]ο[..]γατρ, which, in combination, matches δεῦρο θυγ- in O^9. Others have doubted the match. Arnott, for example, writes 'If O.26 (our O^9)

Act Four 197

did contain portions of 752-756, however, the text of O.10 (O^3) in lines 752-754 was either misread by its first and subsequent editors, or differed from that offered by O.26'. I think that is unduly negative. The truth is that nothing can be clearly read at the critical points of O^3 (in particular line 752 where early editors of O^3 read]περι[close to the line ending). Although editors, including Turner, tried to identify the ghosts of some letters at these points, nothing can be said with confidence, whereas the legible letters of 755-56 match up well. Blanchard is obviously in two minds as he cites O^9 as a source for these lines but mainly omits its readings in the text. Recently in an interesting paper Roberta Carlesimo (2018) has argued that O^9 stems from the same column of writing as O^{12}, a collocation which she argues on the basis of letter forms as well as fibres. The latter, she maintains, place the legible letters of O^9 in the second *metron* of text rather than the third, as Austin would have it. She says, however, that the precise distance between the bottom of O^9 and the top of O^{12} cannot be established as no definite overlap with O^3 presents itself. It seems to me, however, that the observable overlap between O^9 and O^3 (above) is strong enough to cast doubt on her argument from the alignment of fibres between O^9 and O^{12}. Her paper is useful evidence for the fundamental placement of O^9 (somewhere just above O^{12}) but I doubt the cogency of her argument from the alignment of fibres. Without any certainty, then, I include the readings of O^9 at this point. Its inclusion is by no means trivial: as we shall see it necessitates an important change in dramaturgy at this point.

Scene Three: Thrasonides' monologue

751 Enter Thrasonides, who greets Getas with a conventionally derogatory saluta-tion (if Turner's supplement ἄπληστε παῖ is right): 'greedy servant boy!' Cf. *Perik.* 545-7, where Daos is said to care more about his belly than his master's predicament. ἄπληστος recurs at *Sik.* 43. τὴν [ἀργ]ίαν, 'your indolence', or μωρίαν, 'foolish-ness', might be a reasonable guess as part of this rude greeting, implying that Getas is lazy.

752 Κρά]τειαν ἔξαγε[. If the placement of O^9 is right, someone calls Krateia out (from Kleinias' house, see note on line 797). Getas is the most likely speaker. ἔξαγε[might be imperative, indicative, infinitive even. Early editors' reading of O^3 here]περι[clearly does not fit here, but the traces are very indistinct. One of Carlesimo's suggested placings of O^9 here – line 736 – can be eliminated on the basis of letter traces, I think. Although one can clearly read -εξ- in line 736 of O^3, the traces fol-lowing that are not compatible with any word formed with εξαγε-.

753 δ]ακρύει, Δημέα. Carlesimo suggests that it must be Thrasonides who is crying from distress; but Demeas might be lamenting the loss of his son.

198   CHAPTER 5. COMMENTARY

755 The speaker of this line seems to be female because of the **τάλαν**. Krateia is the most likely speaker, or perhaps Simiche whose job it is to call Krateia out.   The **ἑαυτόν** might point to 'kill himself', i.e. Thrasonides (thus Carlesimo).

756 δεῦρο, θυγάτριο[ν. I suggest that Demeas calls Krateia to one side so as to listen to Thrasonides' long speech unseen. It would be the same situation as in *Epitr.* (act four), in which Charisios overhears Pamphile's speech to her father, and Onesimos eavesdrops on Charisios' great 'confession' speech. In *Perik.* Moschion overhears the emotional reunion scene between Pataikos and Glykera. The advantage of this arrangement is that one character can gain insight into others' private thoughts or words without them knowing. But the point is conjectural, depending on the correct placing of O^9. See note above on 751-57 on the coincidence of letters in this line between O^9 and O^3. Blanchard prints [θυ]γάτριο[ν], too, a reading which depends on this placing of O^9. Demeas is the only character who can, accurately, address Krateia as 'little daughter', as he does in line **968**.

757 ὅλ]ως suits the small traces of two letters quite well, and the space, but is uncertain. Thrasonides seems to be responding to the criticism of Kleinias and Getas in the previous conversation.   **μικρόψ[υ]χον** is defined as 'littleness of soul', 'meanness of spirit' in LSJ, but a fragment (3) of *Georg.* shows us perhaps more clearly what may be meant here: οὗτος κράτιστός ἐστ' ἀνήρ, ὦ Γοργία,/ ὅστις ἀδικεῖσθαι πλεῖστ' ἐπίστατ' ἐγκρατῶς·/ τὸ δ' ὀξύθυμον τοῦτο καὶ λίαν πικρὸν / δεῖγμ' ἐστιν εὐθὺς πᾶσι μικροψυχίας, 'But he, Gorgias, is the greatest man, who understands how to suffer the greatest injustice with restraint. But being short-tempered and overly sharp, is the surest sign to all of *mikropsychia*.' In other words the meaning seems to be less 'pusillanimous' here, but rather 'petty-minded' in the sense of 'short-tempered', 'easily offended', 'quick to fly off the handle'. Instances in prose: Isokr. *Archidamos* (or. 6) 84.4, *Philippos* (or. 5) 79.1. In Demosthenes the sense 'petty-minded' dominates, the opposite of 'magnanimous'. Webster (1973, 291) says of Thrasonides' use of μικρόψυχος here: 'evidently in the Aristotelian sense of being excessively grieved by misfortunes'. Now if the *Georg.* passage is instructive here, it seems that Thrasonides is accusing himself of being too 'petty-minded' in the sense 'easily offended', and, presumably, too ready to react sharply when offended (presumably by Krateia). All this may link up with what I suggested on lines **609-10**, and in the introduction, that it was mainly Thrasonides' quick-temper (σοβαρός, a quality of the *miles gloriosus*) and rough talk which upset Krateia at first. Cf. Giacomoni (1998, 96 n. 16): 'incapace cioè di controllare l'ira e la disperazione sorte in seguito a un'offesa subita.'

758 ἀ[λ]ύονθ' ὧ[δε] πολλὰ πρ[άγ]ματα, '(sc. seeing me) making such heavy weather of everything'. ἀλύοντα must be accusative singular masculine with με in previous line, πράγματα an internal accusative. Henry *et al.* (2014b, 113) take it as a transitive form with πράγματα as object, but that seems unlikely. **ἀλύω** ranges in

Act Four   199

meaning from 'to be distraught, beside oneself' to milder 'to be vexed, perplexed'. In later authors it sometimes = 'wander, roam about'. It is one of the 'psychological' words favoured by Menander as giving insight into someone's state of mind; cf. *Epitr.* 559 with my note. Perhaps no coincidence that this is the word used of Achilles' distraught and wandering mindset after the death of Patroklos: *Il.* 24.12 δινεύεσκ' ἀλύων παρὰ θῖν' ἁλός, 'distraught in his mind he paced up and down on the strand of the sea'.

759 εἰ δ' ἐς μέσον. Expressions with ἐς μέσον in Menander seem to mean 'into the middle' in the sense of 'making a point explicit' in a dispute between two sides. In *Perik.* 522 τί φέρω νῦν εἰς μέσον / τὸ μέγεθος; Polemon asks himself why he has just mentioned Glykera's size as a kind of debating point in his dialogue with Pataikos. In *Asp.* μηκέτι / Δᾶον ἄγετ' εἰς μέσον, Daos means 'keep Daos out of it' (sc. your dispute). Like a card played on the table, or perhaps a roll of the dice, between two players, a speaker advances an opinion 'in the middle', sc. of the discussion. Here, then, I believe Thrasonides is *relativizing* the opinion he is considering (that he's *mikropsychos*) by making a counter-point.   **μ[εθε]ὶ[ς π[ερ]ιφέρ[ε]ι[ς καὶ νοεῖς.** The second half of this is palaeographically quite insecure and merely an e.g. supplement. The intended sense may be something like: 'But if you turn it round and look at it the other way', meaning that his behaviour, whilst it might look petty-minded, also offers a different aspect. For this meaning of περιφέρω LSJ s.v. 1.7.

760 Something like 'What would be bad about this for others to choose?' might be the sense of this line. One might supplement e.g. ἂν αὖ κακὸν ἑλομένοις. ὅμως. I assume *what* Thrasonides means he has chosen is suicide, which might be perceived as a cowardly way out.   **[ὅμως] ἔστω** concedes the rhetorical point in order to show the consequences of *that*: 'Nevertheless, granted I endure ... ' (*synchōrēsis*).

761 στέγειν, 'endure' in an absolute sense, cf. *Lyr. Alex. Adesp.* 1.30, or perhaps 'keep secret', 'conceal' (LSJ III 2), cf. Eur. *IA* 872 στέγεις λόγους, 888 νάματ' οὐκέτι στέγω, *Phoin.* 1214, Soph. *OT* 341. The basic idea is that of a vessel *containing* contents such as to protect them, not let them out. Thrasonides imagines himself trying to 'cover over' his inner feelings, keep them from the outside world. The thought is emphasized and clarified in the following two clauses: 'and let me have a stone for a heart' 'let me manage to hide my malady from my fellow men'. Sandbach's reconstruction seems preferable to both that of Turner and of Handley (ἔστ' ὥστ' ἔχειν).   **λίθον ψυχὴν φ[ορε]ῖ[ν,** 'carry a stone as heart'. The irony is presumably not intentional with line 43, where Getas jokingly accused Thrasonides of being a lodestone, by repelling Krateia. Twice, then, we hear of Thrasonides' hard heart. Getas had called him δρύϊνος (18) because he was walking around outside in a thunderstorm, and now when he wishes he could harden his heart. In fact, his heart is an open wound and he keeps his despair from nobody.

200   CHAPTER 5. COMMENTARY

762 τὴν νόσ[ον. In fact this whole passage contains medical imagery. The patient should endure, steel himself, suffer inwardly without showing it on the outside. His fortitude will be like a 'plaster', covering up his wound. But then Thrasonides reasons that alcohol will one day weaken his resolve and strip the plaster from the wound.

ποιεῖ‹ν› τ' ἄδηλον. The theme of repressed emotion is well paralleled in *Sam*. 447-8, but there Demeas prays that his *anger* will not reveal itself to people around him. Here it is Thrasonides' *despair* that he imagines himself hiding.

763 δυνήσ[ομα]ι … Γέτα; This line may be construed as a question 'will I be able, Getas?' (one of a series of desperate rhetorical questions) but the central portion is missing.

763-4 τίνα / τρόπον καθέξω, 'how will I restrain?' (sc. his inner turmoil and despair). Thrasonides soul-searching questions here remind one of Eliot's *Prufrock* (e.g. 'Then how should I begin / To spit out all the butt-ends of my days and ways? / And how should I presume?)

765-6 Henry *et al.* (2014b, 114): 'These two lines are quoted to illustrate ἀπαμφιεῖ meaning ἀποκαλύψει by *Synagoge* cod. B α 1600 Cunningham = *Suda* α 2891 = Phot. α 2245; cf. Hsch. α 5768 ἀπαμφιεῖ· ἀπογυμνώσει'.　　ἀπαμφιεῖ is 'Attic' contracted future of a putative verb ἀπαμφίζω (thus LSJ), or a rare contracted future of ἀπαμφιέννυμι, whose future is normally -έσω. Indeed, in O^{12} the form ἀπαμφιέσει is given; for the contracted form, however, cf. Aristoph. *Knights* 891 προσαμφιῶ, cf. H.W. Hauri, *Kontrahiertes und sigmatisches Futur* Göttingen 1975, 56. Henry *et al.* (2014a) discuss the new reading of O^{12}, deciding that the scribe has gone for the more current form, although ' "Attic" futures maintain a sporadic presence in the Roman period, whether by tradition or through atticist zeal, … but they are on the decline'. In all events, it is a remarkable metaphor 'drink will strip the plaster from my wounds' (see note on 762). The interest of the metaphor lies in the application of medical treatments (a plaster) to psychological problems, although the ancient grammarians were more interested in the rare future form. Fr. 298.3-4 K-A has μήτ' ἂν ἀτυχήσας εἰς τὰ κοινὰ τοῦ βίου / ἐπαμφιέσαι δύναιτο τοῦτο χρήμασιν, 'nor when afflicted with misfortune in public life can he (man) dress the wound with money'.

Plasters and sutures in all possible varieties were one of the chief remedies of antiquity and in hand-to-hand warfare, where cuts and lacerations were the most common injury, they must have been particularly common (Lat. *vulnerarium emplastrum*). Thrasonides' choice of metaphor may reflect his profession as a mercenary soldier, perhaps. A number of treatises *On Plasters* are known from antiquity, see W. Furley, 'A medical treatise On Remedies. P. Zereteli no. 318a+b', in Andorlini (2009, 35-48).

As these lines are transmitted in the indirect tradition βουλόμενον is, strictly speaking,

Act Four   201

ungrammatical as, if anything, it should be genitive agreeing with μου in the previous line. The sense is not in any doubt: 'Drink will one day strip this plaster from me, although I want to pass unnoticed'. Book fragments easily suffer some corruption through being excised from their context and through being copied out of context, as Handley (1970) has shown. The easiest change would be to insert a με in the second line and omit the article with μέθη. Nevertheless the tendency of Greek syntax to fall back on an accusative (βουλόμενον) + infinitive (λανθάνειν) construction is well known and με can easily be supplied. There is no trace of line 766 in O^3. This is because the top of Turner's page D (horizontal fibres) is missing.

767 ἀσχημονήσω, 'I will behave badly', 'disgrace myself'. Thrasonides imagines how his distress will lead him to unseemly behaviour and perhaps appearance. Cf. fr. 744.2 K-A ἀσχημονοῦντος, and perhaps *Georg.* fr. 2f Blanchard, where the paraphraser of Menander's views on poverty has used the word ἀσχημοσύνης ('poverty causes *aschēmosynē*'), which may or may not represent an original reading in Menander. Only one instance in tragedy, in Eur. fr. 259.1 N ὀργῇ δὲ φαύλη πόλλ' ἔνεστ' ἀσχήμονα, 'there is much that is unseemly in base anger', but several in comedy of ἀσχήμων and ἀσχημονέω. It is interesting in this whole passage to see what store Thrasonides sets by maintaining a decent or controlled appearance. He seems to champion the values of the stiff upper lip, perhaps, too, because he is a soldier. What followed is unfortunately lost.

767-72 Since these lines are very definitely attested (though largely illegible) in O^{12} they must be included in the new line count. From here until line 919, then, my line numbering diverges from Blanchard because of the insertion of these verses. Equivalents in Blanchard are given beside the main line numbering.

768 [ἔ]φθαρμαι, 'I'm ruined'. Although the traces are faint, the reading is plausible. Perhaps the verb was a compound, e.g. διέφθαρμαι. Anyway the sense suits, as Thrasonides contemplates the psychological abyss before him.

770 ἐμφανίζω[, 'I reveal', 'manifest'. Henry *et al.* (2014a) say omikron rather than omega after zeta at the end, but I do not agree. The new reading of O^{12} shows Thrasonides still considering how he won't be able to keep his pain to himself, but will reveal it.

771 κακὸν. The traces are very indistinct.

772]υτον ο. There is room for e.g. ἐμαυτόν. Since the drift of the speech is toward suicide one wonders here whether the thought may be intimated.

Here there is a gap in our text (see Text) whose exact length is not known. Note the departure from Blanchard's line numbering here (above on 767-72). When O^3 picks up again in line 774 (768 Blanchard) we are still in Thrasonides' monologue. He is passing thoughts through his mind about his relationship with Krateia. Her

202 *CHAPTER 5. COMMENTARY*

rejection of him has made him pensive, introverted (Greek σύννους). At first we only hear snippets of his ramblings, but by 798ff., when he imagines the old maid Simiche talking to him, the text becomes visible. Probably the next few remarks are imagined conversation between himself and Simiche, before he falls once again into introverted monologue.

779 ἡρμόσαμεν. ἁρμόττω can mean 'betroth' (LSJ s.v. 2) and this is quite likely here. The next word is difficult to decipher, but looks like αὐτό, perhaps of the relationship, or perhaps agreeing with a word like παιδάριον. 'Did we not join our relationship in marriage?' says Thrasonides.

780 ὀδύν[ας ἐ]νέγκα[ς] (vel [ἐ]νέγκα[σ']) εὖ θ'. The sentiment seems to presage the modern marriage formula 'in good times and in bad, in sickness and in health'. The first part means 'to endure affliction' but what followed εὖ θ', we do not know except that the word began with an aspirate.

784 and **790** are later insertions in the text of O³. They were omitted initially.

782-3 The combination of an offer to Krateia, 'it is possible for you, Krateia, to settle … ' with the mention in the following line of 'painful ties' might indicate that Krateia can throw off her 'painful ties' of bondage in order to 'settle down' as his wife. One might envisage an e.g. reconstruction along the following lines:

ἔστιν, Κράτειά, σοι καθίζεσθ[αί τε καὶ
λυπρὰ κατ[αδ]έςματ' ἀ[ποβαλεῖν ἐλευθέρως

783 λυπρὰ κατ[αδ]έςματ' ἀ[-. First word could be λυπρά, λυγρά, λύτρα, agreeing with plural καταδέσματα (probably elided καταδέσματ' ἀ-) following. The split double-short (-πρα/κα-) is tolerated in the first metron. In the previous note I suggested that Thrasonides is talking about the painful bondage of slavery which Krateia is technically enduring at present.

786-7 ἄψατ', 'affix', is clear and with a little imagination we could see a form of **βρόχ-** 'noose' at the end. We know of course that Thrasonides was suicidal, and the Mytilene mosaic is thought to allude to a possible suicide by hanging or throttling. The combination of words might point to the sense 'fasten the noose'. Cf. Maximus Soph., *Dialexeis* 20.5.c2 Hobein: Οὗτός ἐστιν ὁ ἔρως … ὁ ξίφος λαμβάνων, ὁ ἄπτων βρόχον, 'this is the love which snatches up a sword, which fastens the noose … ' The reference might be to two features of our play: Thrasonides demanding a sword, and fastening a noose round his neck (note later in the same passage ὁ ἐν μύθοις μισούμενος, 'the hated man in stories'). Chaireas, the unhappy lover in Chariton's novel, at one point attempts suicide by the noose (*Kall.* 5.10.6). One might observe that the modern 'crime of passion' (killing the partner who has betrayed one) does

Act Four   203

not occur in extant Menander: the unhappy lover contemplates killing himself, not
his partner (Polemon, Thrasonides).

In the next line ἔτι βέλ[τιον, 'still better', might point to another form of doing away
with himself, perhaps by the sword.

795 (787 Bl) κρίνη is certain in O³, γάρ more or less so, and then O⁸ chimes in
with the remaining letters. κρινῆι (or κρίνηι) is either subjunctive or, more probably,
2nd p.s. future middle (more commonly in comedy κρινεῖ). It might belong to the εἰ
clause, or not. The sense is not certain, but I assume 'if you discern the reason … '.

797 (789 Bl) ἐ]ξῆλθεν ἐκ. I would prefer this division over Turner's ἐξ]ῆλθ' with
Blanchard's ἔνεχ' to follow as that involves a split anapaest in the second foot. There
is no diastole after theta in O³. O⁸ is unfortunately rubbed bare after εν. There
is certainly not sufficient room in O⁸ for ἐκ τῆς οἰκίας (e.g.). I measure the gap as
6-7 letters. Blanchard is probably right to surmise that Krateia is the subject and
she has 'departed' the house of Thrasonides with her father Demeas for Kleinias'
house.   συν. Probably not preposition with dative ('with [s'one]') but perhaps
part of a compound verb or an expression such as σὺν θεῶι.

798-end of act (790ff. Bl). In this longer monologue ('Selbstgespräch') Thrasonides
changes between first, second and third person in this 'stream of consciousness' speech.
We may compare Demeas' speech of self-exhortation in *Sam.* 349ff. (Maehler, 1992,
60). Maehler also points out (p. 62) that his monologue contains echoes of the passage which prepares the ground for it, Getas' monologue in 715-24. This parallels
the construction in *Epitr.* (act four) in which first Onesimos describes his master's self-
destructive misery, then Charisios' own speech bears that out. Menander's plays are
built round these revelatory monologues in which the main character lays bare his
heart: Charisios in *Ep.*, Knemon in *Dys.*, Demeas in *Sam.*: they all reach a point of
emotional pressure at which they can no longer keep their feelings in but give vent to
them in an impassioned outburst. It is this crescendo of expression, confession almost,
which leads eventually to a reversal for the good. In this structure of emotional tan-
gle (δέσις) – 'confession of sins' – reconciliation (λύσις), the influence of Aristotle's
theory of *katharsis* can surely be seen; see, among much else, Gaiser (1967). In their
purged state these central characters (all men) are ready for a new understanding of
themselves and their relationships. In fact the reconciliation between Thrasonides
and Krateia in this play is brought about by an external factor: they discover that the
brother is not dead (we think). In this confession speech Thrasonides seems to decide
on the course of suicide (or possibly feigned suicide, see below). Nevertheless, the
speech can be seen as Thrasonides reaching 'rock bottom' in self-esteem, a necessary
step on the path back to recovery. Although it is not complete, we can see Menander
here pulling out all the stops to show Thrasonides' state of mind. The speech is characterized by many swift changes of direction as his distraught mind rushes first in one

204   *CHAPTER 5. COMMENTARY*

direction, then the next. He conducts an inner dialogue first with Simiche, then with himself, in places with Krateia herself (805-6), and ends with an imagined epitaph to the couple's unhappy love. Thus inner thoughts achieve the effect of lively dialogue. This is almost 'stream of consciousness' long before the term. Probably the speech went on for another eleven verses before the choral interlude. The last visible word τρισαθλ[ι-, 'thrice wretched', seems to indicate that Thrasonides went on lamenting to the end. For its psychological introspection combined with its dramatic quality the passage can claim perhaps to rival such masterpieces as Medea's prevarications in Euripides' play of that name (Giacomoni, 1998, 104). Although we do not (yet) possess it in its entirety, the efforts of scholars have managed to piece back the fragments into a coherent whole for quite a significant number of lines.

Linguistically the speech, or what we can restore of it, contains many fireworks, such as οὐ χολᾷς; (806), τὸ τῆς σωτηρίας ἐπίσημον (807-8), ὁμόσε ταῖς ὀργαῖς τρέχειν (808), πλεονεξία (809), the tricolon in 811, and overall the effect of quickly rushing thoughts is achieved by short staccato sentences with rapidly changing syntax and perspective. The speech well illustrates Plutarch's remark in his comparison of Menander and Aristophanes that Menander can, in one passage, pull out all the stops, only to modulate his language quickly to 'normal' level; see Furley (2009, 19, 22-23).

All that said, we must not forget the comedy. I *think* on the basis of the hypothetical placing of O[9] (above) that Krateia was eavesdropping on the speech, so she becomes one of the audience here. Then the audience knew Thrasonides' troubles were imaginary. There is always this dramatic irony in Menander's theatre: the characters are unaware of the truth lying behind their predicament, but the audience are not; see Halliwell (2007). And, if the reconstruction of lines 814-16 resembles the truth, then Thrasonides may have imagined *faking* suicide to try to get his way with Krateia. An Ajax, a Haimon, a Iokastē, does not fake suicide. And perhaps above all, the dramatic situation lacks essential gravity. Here we have a brave mercenary soldier strutting and fretting on his own, very private, little stage. He even accuses himself in line 757 of being μικρόψυχος, lit. 'of small soul'. Tragi-comedy remains a useful term to describe Menander's work; cf. Carlesimo (2018, 70): 'una comicità del rovescio, che si lascia riconoscere squisitamente menandrea.'

The effective performance of this long speech would have required a gifted and spirited actor. For all we know, Menander may have composed with a specific actor in mind, as roles in films nowadays are often tailored to acting stars. We recall that it was towards the end of the fourth century that records of winning actors began to be kept (between 329 and 312 BC: Hughes (2012, 219)).

798 (790 Bl) This is Handley's division of the words and punctuation. He translates ' ... if she is angry with you, you're pathetic' (Handley, 1996). Handley's readings

Act Four 205

of this passage (387-403) were given in the context of a Graduate Summer School in Greek Drama at the Institute of Classical Studies in London. Handley avowed that 'they are not for publication in this form, whether by me or by anyone else'. Nevertheless his readings have been adopted by subsequent editions (Arnott, Blanchard) and perhaps he would, after all, be pleased. We are not quoting his version of the passage *in toto.* **Σιμίχη 'ξ]ελήλ[υθεν.** For the second half of the line Handley must be right that the words mean 'out comes Simiche' (Arnott 'Simiche's come out') and not *pace* Blanchard 'La voilà partie', as ἐξέρχομαι is *enter* in Greek drama, εἰσέρχομαι *exit* (sc. into a house). Also Simiche must *enter* in Thrasonides' imagination in order for him to have the imaginary exchange of words with her which follows. It is also possible that Simiche *does* enter as a *kōphon prosōpon* at this point and Thrasonides conducts the exchange with her. Simiche must be Krateia's nurse, or maid (Bonollo, 2019, 90). It would be natural for her to be sympathetic to Krateia's position (799). On Simiche here see Arnott (1996c, 337).

799-80 (791-2 Bl) Thrasonides echoes questions Simiche has put to him (in his mind), in a spirit of indignation: 'What's that you say? "*She's* suffered all manner of things?" Is it *her* part you're taking in all this? *I'm* only concerned with *myself* in my relationship with her? This is all *my* fault?' (for the importance of the emphases in constructing Menander's meaning, see Sommerstein (2013, 91)). Such 'shadow-boxing' in dialogue is also found in *Epitr.* 1062ff. where Smikrines echoes, and rejects, remarks made by Sophrone. That Krateia has suffered can hardly be denied. If our reconstructions are right, she has been plucked from home and hearth, has lost a brother (she thinks) and never thought to see her father again. One might say that Krateia has been 'trafficked', to use a loaded modern term. I believe line 792 is the first formulation of egocentrism in personal relations in European literature. Or rather, the first recognition that one should not only think of oneself, but of the other person and how they're feeling.

799 (791 Bl) The readings of the two manuscripts are slightly divergent (again) in this line, and one can juggle the elements in various way. I have adhered broadly to the reading of O³ which gives a quoted remark of Simiche's 'she has suffered everything' (i.e. all manner of things). Thrasonides does not wish to acknowledge, it seems, the traumatic experiences of Krateia in being taken as a prisoner of war, and, possibly, witnessing her brother's death. He thinks she should quickly fall in love with him as he has with her: it is fascinating that Menander recognizes the egoism in this way of behaving (800).

Handley takes this quite differently: writing τί, φήις, πέπονθε; he translates the sentence: 'Out comes Simiche, and you ask "How is she?" All you say is about her'. But I am not convinced τί πέπονθε naturally means merely 'how is she?' (πῶς ἔχει;) nor that φήις in the middle of this imagined dialogue with Simiche easily refers to the present speaker, Thrasonides (even if in 'Selbstgespräch'), rather than Simiche, who is the subject of λαλ[εῖϲ (the ending is, admittedly, supplemented). Thirdly, ὑπέρ as equivalent to περί occurs, but is rare. Although I believe Blanchard is not right in taking ἐξελήλυθεν to mean that Simiche has exited (whether really or in Thrasonides' mind), I agree with his understanding of the next words: 'Que dis-tu (sc. Simiche)? Elle a été victime en tout? C'est en sa faveur que tu parles?' Apart from anything else, all these uncertainties show the problems caused by an unpunctuated and unarticulated ancient text (two differing texts!).

801 (793 Bl) ἅπαν ἀτύχημα τοῦτ'; (first metr. ∪−∪∪−) 'It's [all] just bad luck?' Again, Thrasonides seems to be picking up words he puts in the mouth of Simiche; his answer seems to be 'don't I blame *him*?' meaning, presumably, Demeas: the father is surely in considerable measure responsible for Thrasonides' misfortune. ἀτύχημα is a very Peripatetic word meaning 'mischance', an ill not deliberately committed, distinguished from ἀδίκημα, 'injustice', see Valeria Cinaglia, 'Menander, Aristotle, Chance and Accidental Ignorance' in Sommerstein (2014a, 152-66).   ἐκεῖ[νον] must be Demeas. We have learned that Demeas and Krateia are (together) decided in refusing Thrasonides' suit and (presumably) going home (to Cyprus?); cf. Simplicius (above p. 3 ἀπῆλθεν). The other theoretical possibilities are: ἐκεί[νην, her, i.e. Krateia. Another ἐκεῖ[νον, Kleinias perhaps? Could it be that both men are vying for Krateia's love, as Charisios and Chairestratos do for Habrotonon's favour in *Epitr.*? Krateia has probably gone with her father to Kleinias' house now.   [μὴ] ψέγω; If we supplement like this ψέγω must be subjunctive. Theoretically we could write οὐ ψέγω; with the indicative as a simple questioning of fact: 'don't I find fault with him?'.

From this point on it seems that Thrasonides' speech changes from a kind of dialogue with Simiche to pure *Selbstgespräch*, with Thrasonides posing himself questions and answering them. How far the questions would reflect what Simiche might have asked is hard to gauge.

802 (794 Bl) ἕν ἐϲτι. Handley's division of ενεϲτι into ἕν ἐϲτι gives good emphasis: 'the *one* thing there is for you to do'. Cf. Men. fr. 276.8 Sandbach ἀλλ' ἕν ἐϲτί τι ἀγαθὸν ἀπ' αὐτῆϲ, 'but one good comes from her' (sc. a 'high maintenance' woman); Antiphanes 211.1 Kock ἓν γὰρ τοῦτό μοι / τὸ λοιπόν ἐϲτι, 'this is the one thing left for me'. Xen. *An.* 2.1.19 has εἰ μὲν τῶν μυρίων ἐλπίδων μία τιϲ ὑμῖν ἐϲτιν 'if your one hope is … ', followed by acc. + infin. construction, as here. Hdt. 1.8.4 has ἐν τοῖϲι ἓν τόδε ἐϲτί, 'one among which is … ', which has the same combination of cardinal + demonstrative pronoun. O^3 has no rough breathing over the first epsilon, but the scribe's use of the breathing is erratic. There may be an ink trace over the epsilon in O^8 but that might be the long leg of chi above it, too. However Turner's ἔνεϲτι, 'it is possible', is also completely sufficient in sense: 'But

Act Four   207

isn't it possible for you…?' Very difficult to call.

803 (795 Bl) **ταύτην ἀπολαβεῖν τοῦτ[ον].** Object first: '[sc. prevent] *him* from taking *her* away?'

804 (796 Bl) **πρόσθεν γενό[μενα ἀπ]ώ[λ]ε[σε** (with *script. plen.*), 'things past spoil one's life (sc. now)'. Another line which can be put together in a number of ways, depending on which (of the two) manuscripts one prefers. I favour O³ as it is usually more accurate. πρόσθεν is the reading of both manuscripts, O⁸ may have had τὰ before that. But if one wants to retain τὰ, πρόσθεν has to become πρόσθε and the omission of τὰ in O³ has to be overlooked. τὰ seems to me to be intrusive in the true tradition (it is missing in O³) and to represent a certain smoothing of the text. The general sense is not in doubt. Thrasonides is brooding on the fact that something which happened in the past (his killing of Krateia's brother or simply his *alazoneia*, or something of which no one is aware yet?) is now spoiling the present. **ἀπ]ώ[λ]ε[σε.** The letter trace in O³ was read by Austin as an alpha, but it is not like this scribe's alphas. In my opinion it is omega. Hence my conjecture ἀπώλεσε, 'ruins' (gnomic aorist), rather than Handley's ἀνατρέπει. The other traces are too slight to interpret.

805ff. (797ff. Bl) In the next section down to 812 Thrasonides is addressing himself in *Selbstgespräch*: ἀφήσεις (805), σοι (807), εἶ, γενοῦ (810), ζῆις (811), σε (812). Then there is a brief change to 3rd p.s.: τὸν τἀγαθὰ δόντα (814), before changing to 1st p.s. μοι (814), με (815). There is no way of telling how the speech proceeded down to the choral interlude at 824. This analysis shows the continuing variety in his speech, and also how he can view himself from the outside as well as engaging himself in dialogue. The lively monologue would have required a gifted and versatile actor.

805 (797 Bl) **ἀφήσεις;,** 'you'll let her go?' Probably in the sense 'you'll free her from bondage?' cf. *Dys.* 503, *Perik.* 982-83 (release of Doris from slavery) (Giacomoni, 1998, 98-99). On the other hand, ἀφίημι regularly has the formal sense 'divorce' in the context of marriage; e.g. Eur. *Andr.* 973. Thrasonides and Krateia are not of course married, but he had wanted to consider her his wife (line 40). Perhaps the word is deliberately ambiguous here: 'let her go' in two senses: from bondage, and from their quasi-marital relationship.

805-6 (797-98 Bl) **θέλ[εις, τά]λαν … ἑλ]κ[ύσαι;,** 'Poor fool, do you wish to move (sc. my hate with pity)?' The reconstruction of Krateia's (hypothetical) rejoinder to Thrasonides' ἀφήσεις; has exercised the brain power of editors and certainty is, on present evidence, unattainable. Maehler's reconstruction with θέλξεις, τάλαν at the end of 805 and ἀσχαλᾶις ('will you charm, poor wretch … ? You're distressed!') at the end of the next line, has found general acceptance among recent editors (Arnott, Blanchard), but one could object that both words are more suited to

208   CHAPTER 5. COMMENTARY

tragedy than comedy; they both occur, for example, in Eur. *IA* (142, 920-1 respectively). However, the rest of Thrasonides' speech here is hardly typical comic diction, either. Another possible objection to θέλξεις might be: can one *charm* a person with pity? θέλγω is otherwise used almost invariably with qualities such as love, desire, beguiling or deceptive words etc. I.e. a person's wits are *beguiled* by something attractive, seductive, when θέλγω is used. Just one example: Gorgias, *Enc. Hel.* fr. 11.62: the persuasive word 'seduces' Helen: αἱ γὰρ ἔνθεοι διὰ λόγων ἐπωιδαὶ ἐπαγωγοὶ ἡδονῆς, ἀπαγωγοὶ λύπης γίνονται· συγγινομένη γὰρ τῆι δόξηι τῆς ψυχῆς ἡ δύναμις τῆς ἐπωιδῆς ἔθελξε καὶ ἔπεισε καὶ μετέστησεν αὐτὴν γοητείαι. 'For divine incantations (which work) through words induce pleasure, relieve pain; when it meets with the imaginitive power of the mind the power of the incantation *enchants* and persuades and alters the mind by sorcery'. Having felt uncomfortable with Maehler's guesses here for some time, I now advocate a different course in both lines combined.

805 θέλ[εις. In first position theta is probably marginally more likely in O^3 than sigma (ἐρεῖς Handley), as there is a spot of ink above putative sigma which could belong to theta. Theta-epsilon and then possibly lamda are plausible but after that – obscurity. LSJ state that *comici* use the form ἐθέλω not θέλω, but forms of θέλω are in fact regularly found in Menander (as many as 63 instances in *TLG*); one could, alternatively, write 'θέλεις here with prodelision.   **[τά]λαν** is suited to a woman's speech (Krateia). See my note on this word in *Epitr.* 434, and Sommerstein (1995, 68-70). We may take it to mean 'you poor thing' here, said ironically. See Dedoussi (1964, 5), Bain (1984, 33-35, here 33). The traces are negligible and Handley's ἄπαν remains a possibility – one favoured by Blanchard.

806 ἐλ]κ[ύσαι, 'draw', 'attract', 'move'. A good example of ἕλκω used with emotions as object comes in *Sik.* 243-4 Blanchard: πολλήν τινα / τοῦθ', ὡς προσῆκ', εὔνοιαν εἵλκυσ', 'and this drew considerable favour, as was appropriate' (said of Stratophanes' speech to the informal assembly). Cf. Eur. fr. 567 (*Oineus*) τὴν δόξαν ἕλκει, '*attracts* opinion (opp. repels)'. Handley had already suggested ἕλξεις at the end of 805 (ἐρεῖς· ἕλξεις ἄπαν), but, as I said above, sigma after ερει- is not quite right. The construction θέλεις ... ἑλκύσαι; 'do you wish to draw?' has the advantage, in my opinion, of making much better sense of ὡς σεαυτόν. In Maehler's reconstruction one has to take τὸ μισοῦν with ὡς σεαυτόν, 'hatred *for* you': a very unlikely use of ὡς. Theoretically, I suppose, one could take οἴκτωι with ὡς σεαυτόν, 'pity for you', but the same objection applies. I take the construction now to mean 'do you wish to move by pity my dislike (of you) round to your side (lit. toward you)?' Cf. Dem. 22.59 ἐχθροὺς ἐφ' ἑαυτόν ἐ., 'to bring enemies over to one's side'. Here, ὡς (with a person), 'toward', would correspond to ἐπί in Demosthenes. The whole sentence would be an ironical dismissal of the idea: no chance pity will move Krateia in

Act Four 209

Thrasonides' favour. An interesting connotation of this might be the sense of ἕλκω, 'attract', as of a magnet, as Getas had said of Thrasonides in line **43**.

Maehler's ἀσχαλᾶις as a sentence in its own right would simply mean 'you are upset', 'dismayed', as in the *IA* line: ἐπίσταμαι δὲ τοῖς κακοῖσί τ' ἀσχαλᾶν (920), 'I am familiar with unhappiness in adversity'. Hardly a witty ripost to Thrasonides. Palaeographically there is very little here to go on. The trace in third position may be chi (Maehler) or kappa ([ἐλ]κ[ύσαι]).

Here we see, then, Thrasonides dismissing the hope that Krateia will pity him in his lonely despair. It seems from the scene in the Mytilene mosaic illustrating, a (perhaps feigned) suicide attempt by Thrasonides in act five, is anything to go by, it would seem that Krateia remained unrelenting to the end, until finally the unexpected appearance of her very-much-alive brother (?) cut the knot.

807 (799 Bl) τίς ὁ βίος σοι; Thrasonides turns from Krateia and considers his own life now, what it is worth. He finds that his valour on the battlefield is a useless thing in civilian life.

807-8 (799-80 Bl) τὸ τῆ[ς σ]ωτ[ηρ]ἰα[ς] / [ἐ]πίσημον, 'that badge of safety'. M. Maehler's decipherment of O^8 points to the emblem on Thrasonides' shield, which may have been mentioned explicitly before. Arnott (1996d, 38) comments: 'Thrasonides would be asking himself "What is the point of that device of 'safety' on your shield, if now you sink into despair so easily"?' I think the point is slightly different. He is asking himself 'What is the point of that badge of valour on your shield when it is of absolutely no service to you in this crisis?' His train of thought runs on that military valour is no use in affairs of the heart; one cannot charge at the emotions as one can at the enemy. We hear of other badges on warriors' shields: Alkibiades had, according to Plutarch, Erōs bearing a thunderbolt on his (*Life of Alkibiades* 16). Thebans inscribed clubs (originally Herakles') on their shields (Xen. *HG* 7.5.20). The Persian king is said to have had a golden eagle on a round shield as his *sēmeion* (Xen. *An.* 1.10.12). There is an anecdote about a Spartan who was accused of cowardice because he bore a life-sized fly as his emblem on his shield. He responded that it was to approach so close to the enemy that they could see the fly life-size (Plutarch *Mor.* 234c-d = *Apophth. Lak.* 41). Otherwise things like gorgons, snakes, lions or the symbol of the warrior's family are known as emblems. Clearly a warrior identified with his *episēmon*, which embodied his striving for valour. Menander used the adjectival form of the word elsewhere in fr. **459** K-Th (from *Psophodeēs*): ἐπίσημον οὖν τὴν ἀσπίδ' εἰς τὴν τοῦ Διὸς στοὰν ἀνέθηκαν ('a noteworthy shield'). Here τῆς σωτηρίας is an objective genitive: his shield bears a 'badge of salvation', i.e. one which guarantees its bearer salvation, and perhaps that of the side he is fighting for.

808 (800 Bl) εἴ τις ὁμ[ό]σε ταῖ[ς ὀ]ργαῖς [τρέχ]οι, 'if one could (only) charge full tilt at emotions!' Brilliantly supplemented by Handley (following Maehler's tenta-

210   CHAPTER 5. COMMENTARY

tive ὀργαῖς). ὁμόσε (from ὁμός) is used in combination with a number of verbs (τρέχειν, χωρεῖν, ἰέναι, ἔρχεσθαι, βαδίζειν) meaning 'go', 'run', 'march', to give the sense 'close with', 'join battle with' (+ dative); cf. Eur. *Or.* 808 χωρεῖν ὁμόσε τοῖς λόγοις θέλων, 'wanting to confront the argument face to face'. Thrasonides means: if only his prowess in battle was of some use to him in the game (or war) of love now. Handley takes the sense somewhat differently: 'If one runs to keep up with one's passions, is that selfishness, if one does that?' But I concur with Blanchard here: 'Si l'on pouvait courir à l'assault des sentiments … Mais c'en serait trop.' I assume Thrasonides is regretting his aggressive behaviour toward Krateia earlier in the play (or before the play begins), to which Krateia (conjecturally) refers in lines 609-10. This seems to have been part of Thrasonides' problems in love: the aggressive behaviour suitable to the battlefield is out of place in a relationship with a loved girl.

809 (801 Bl) **πλεονεξία τοῦτ'**, 'but that's asking too much' (Blanchard: 'Mais c'en serait trop' [no question mark]); Handley: 'is that selfishness?' LSJ s.v. define 'greediness, assumption, arrogance'. πλεονεξία is a very political word, the desire of the individual to have more than his fair share (Plato *Rep.* 359c5, Arist. *Pol.* 1282b29). As is typical of Menander, who had enjoyed a training in the Peripatos, a political word is used in the private domain. Here Thrasonides is acknowledging that one cannot battle the emotions, that is asking too much. As the poet Ted Hughes put it: 'What happens in the heart, simply happens' (from 'Child's Park' in *Birthday Letters* by Ted Hughes).   **εἴ[περ;**, 'but if?' Handley's supplement gives good sense (see note on 808). Thrasonides is asking himself what he knows to be an unrealistic question. The point is that behind it all is the contrast between behaviour in war and in love: Thrasonides wishes his valour in the former were of service to him now in this trickier combat with a girl.

809-10 (801-2 Bl) **ἁ]ρπάσαι βλ[έ]πων κτλ.** 'with rape and pillage in your eye no doubt you're the aggressor then (sc. on the battlefield). Now achieve valour by thought.' I do not see why editors have gone for Maehler's τῶι λογισμῶι here. **τότε** is clearly readable in O³ and O⁸ has nothing here. There is no reason why the abstract noun λογισμῶι should not stand without article (as in fr. 213 K-Th, below), and τότε surely gives the necessary foil to νῦν.   **ἁ]ρπάσαι βλ[έ]πων**, lit. 'looking to pillage'. βλέπω can be followed by a noun, adjective, or infinitive (as here), with adverbial force: Aesch. *Seven* 498 Θυιὰς ὥς, φόβον βλέπων 'looking frightful like a Thyiad', Aristoph. *Knights* 631 ἔβλεψε νᾶπυ 'looked sour (like mustard)'; *Birds* 1671 αἴκειαν βλέπων 'looking like one disgraced'; Alex. 97 ὀρχεῖσθαι μόνον βλέπων, 'looking only to dance'. The combination recurs in *Epitr.* 398 ὁ προσελθὼν εὐθὺς ἁρπάζειν βλέπει. Cf. *Asp.* 464 θανάτους βλέπεις; *Dys.* 147 φιλάνθρωπον β[λέπειν; *Epitr.* 900 βλέπει θ' ὕφαιμον, 'with bloodshot eyes'. English has exactly the same idiom: 'they'll be looking to score four hundred on this

Act Four 211

wicket'. Handley translates 'looking to sieze *her* is perhaps impulsive' (my italics), but I think we can take it in a more general sense of the warrior's impulse in battle. Blanchard: 'Car peut-être qu'avec l'air d'un pillard, te voilà hardi?' **λογισμῷι**, 'by reckoning up', 'calculation'. From λογίζομαι, 'calculate', the abstract noun denotes a cool, level-headed, rational thought process opposite to the ὀργαί mentioned antithetically in 800. Fr. 213 K-Th (from *Imbrioi*) extolls the virtues of λογισμός, saying that 'he who excels in rationality (ὁ λογισμῶι διαφέρων [no article, note!]) has it all'. Thrasonides means that he should now reckon up exactly where he stands in life – and end it all, having concluded that life is not worth living. **νῦν γενοῦ**. The reading of O[8] here – νυν – is clear, making Handley's τότε λογισμῶι συγγενοῦ, 'join up with sound good sense', unlikely.

811 **εὔψυχος**, 'brave', 'stout-hearted'. Thrasonides has not been εὔψυχος since Getas described him thus in line 34. There is perhaps also an echo of μικρόψυχον in 757 (Giacomoni, 1998, 101 n. 40).

811 (803 Bl) **ζῆις**, 'you live'. I cannot agree with Handley that ζηθ (for ζῆθι, a rare imperative 2nd p.s., 'live!') is the better reading in either papyrus. The reading of both seems to point toward ζης quite clearly. Thrasonides is viewing his life from now on dispassionately: a life of misery is left to him (as he imagines). Handley's ζῆθ' would give the sense of an imperative addressed by Thrasonides to himself: 'live abjectly!' and *that* would be the ὄνειδος ἀθάνατον that he would direct at Krateia. But, palaeographical reasons aside, I think it is better to think that Thrasonides is examining his present and future life without Krateia and persuading himself that suicide makes sense. **ἀ[πό]ρως ζῆις, ὀδυνηρῶς, [ἀσ]θενῶ[ς**. Such asyndetic sequences of adverbs, adjectives or verbs have the effect of piling on the pressure in an unremitting way. The number three is also often relevant ('tricolon'), and sometimes the elements grow in length for effect (not here). As I commented on ζῆις, the sentence is a depressed stock-taking by Thrasonides of his current life situation, not an exhortation to live in any particular way (ζῆθ' Handley, al.). Similar asyndetic runs (with verbs) can be found in *Epitr.* 199-200 (see Furley (2021)), *Dys.* 60. **[ἀσ]θενῶ[ς**. The only real handhold for this supplement of Maehler's is -εν.- in O[3].

812-13 (804-5 Bl) This extraordinary thought of revenge through suicide (whether feigned or not) finds an interesting literary precedent in Eur. *Hel.* 982-87. There Menelaus announces to the priestess Theonoe that, should she reveal his arrival to the murderous Theoklymenos, he will kill first Helen, then himself, on the tomb of Proteus (Theoklymenos' father), and together they will lie 'an undying pain to you, and a reproach to your father' (κεισόμεσθα δὲ / ἀθάνατον ἄλγος σοί, ψόγος δὲ σῶι πατρί). Here Thrasonides tells himself he must punish Krateia with an everlasting reproach: 'Despite being treated well she rejected the man who gave her good things'. The formulation reads like the epitaph on a tomb – but whose? If Thra-

212 CHAPTER 5. COMMENTARY

sonides kills himself, then it can only be on his, but the logic is that it should stand written on *her* gravestone. In the *Helen* passage just referred to, it is Proteus' tomb on which Menelaos and Helen will lie. Perhaps, as with curse tablets (which were commonly placed in graves) the grave itself carried magical potency in cursing, regardless of whose. If, on the other hand, Thrasonides wishes only to feign suicide (προσποιουμένωι in the next line) then a modern psychologist would call this the worst sort of blackmail: to try to force somebody's hand by threatened suicide. Can we excuse Thrasonides by saying 'Remember: this is a comedy'? Bearing the Mytilene mosaic in mind, which may well depict a feigned suicide, the answer is probably yes. I do not, however, think that Thrasonides' soliloquy here can be played for laughs. On the relevance of justice/injustice in love cf. Giacomoni (1998, 102-4), and on Menander's brand of humour Halliwell (2007).

812 (804 Bl) αὐτῆι. O³ has Η inserted before αυτη. This seems to be meant as a rough breathing, so αὑτῆι was probably meant: a 'reproach against herself', i.e. a reason why she should reproach herself. Turner originally transcribed as αὕτη, presumably intending the nominative thereby. Since ταύτηι is ruled out by metre, and αὕτη by syntax, the alternatives are αὑτῆι and αὐτῆι. The latter is *lectio facilior*, and is preferred by Austin (1966, 297).   καταλιπεῖν. This is the unequivocal reading of O⁸ whilst O³ seems to have had καταλείπειν. One would have thought the aorist aspect was better suited here.

812-13 (804-5 Bl) ὄν[ε]ιδος ... ἀθάνατον, 'an eternal accusation'. Austin (1966, 297) compares with Eur. *Ba.* 9 ἀθάνατον ... ὕβριν; still closer is the *Helen* passage mentioned above (987 ἀθάνατον ἄλγος). The blame which Thrasonides wishes to lay at Krateia's door can only be eternal, of course, if he really kills himself. A feigned death could only last for a few hours or days.

815 (807 Bl) αὐτὸν κτα]νεῖν με προσποου[μένωι μόνον, (with πῶς ο[ὐ]κ ἔ[σ]τι μοι in previous line) 'what's to stop me merely pretending that I've killed myself? Editors (M. Maehler, Arnott) have suspected a reference to the pretence of suicide by Thrasonides here. The Mytilene mosaic (from the fifth act) may show Getas demonstrating what Thrasonides has done to himself (viz. hang himself) to make Krateia relent. Maehler suggests for these lines e.g. κτα]νεῖν (or ἀνελεῖν) με προσποού[μενον / τὸν παῖδα π]έμψαι τοῦτον εἰ[ς τὴν οἰκίαν, 'if I pretend that I have killed (?)myself and send my servant here inside?' But με cannot be the reflexive pronoun 'myself', we must supply αὐτὸν (with με) at line beginning as an equivalent of ἐμαυτόν; cf. Aristoph. *Thesm.* 1117 ἐμὲ δὲ καὐτόν (sc. ἔρως εἴληφεν). There's a pretend death in *Asp.*, too (329ff.), as a way to trick Smikrines out of his inheritance. One might connect up this 'sending him' with the Mytilene mosaic which seems to show Getas demonstrating something to (?)Demeas and Krateia; perhaps he has been 'sent' by Thrasonides to demonstrate Thrasonides' 'suicide', which fails to effect a change of

Act Five   213

heart in Krateia. This would aptly illustrate the title 'Misoumenos', which is the wont
of the Mytilene mosaics. If Krateia was privy to this monologue of Thrasonides' as I
think, she will not have been moved by Getas' drama-play in act five, believing it was
all a pretence.

821 (813 Bl) τισπα[̣]η. Editors to date have tended to supplement τίς πάθηι *vel
sim.* here. But one could also imagine a supplement with 'sword': -]τι σπά[θ]η(ι),
taking this as a pointer to Thrasonides' contemplated suicide. σπ]άθην, 'sword', is
almost certainly mentioned in line 5 of unplaced papyrus fragment 2, and explicitly
in book fr. 3.

824 (816 Bl) τρισαθλ[ι-. Certainly a form of τρισάθλιος, 'thrice-unfortunate', probably applied by Thrasonides to himself, continuing in his self-pitying vein. Following
this in O^8 there is space before line 825 in which [ΧΟΡΟ]Υ̣ probably stood, as an
end-upsilon is discernible, and the spacing looks right.

Act Five

Scene One: Getas and ??

827 (819 Bl) τὸ φάρμ[ακον. Arnott suggested that Thrasonides took some drug
here to simulate death. Alexis' 'Mandrake-Eater' (Μανδραγοριζομένη) may have
included something similar – but I wonder whether *Romeo and Juliet* has not unduly
exerted its influence here? The Mytilene mosaic points rather to hanging. In line 3
of unplaced papyrus fr. 2 we might have a mention of wine,].οιν.[. Wine might be
seen as a 'medicine' for pains. In *Phasma* 26 and 27, there is mention of a φάρμακον
which might remedy Pheidias' malaise; Cusset & Lukinovich (2019) comment *ad loc.*
that the only occurrence of the word is in fr. 741 K-A = 518 K-T οὐκ ἔστιν ὀργῆς,
ὡς ἔοικε, φάρμακον. The idea of a *remedium amoris* is, of course, widespead in the
magical papyri, and Ovid wrote a book about it!

Scene Two: ?Sham suicide and Recognition (2)

829-919 There is a considerable gap in our knowledge of the text here. The scene
illustrated in the Mytilene mosaic must have stood here, as it is clearly marked 'act
five', and there does not seem to be another location. If that is true, and if the intuition
is correct that Krateia's brother made his appearance some time before 948, we may
infer that the absolute nadir in Thrasonides' fate, his attempted suicide, fell just before
the revelation that Krateia's brother was still alive and well. In the construction of
the play this is real brinkmanship! Unfortunately there is very little firm evidence to
go on but the facts as we know them – the evidence of the Mytilene mosaic, Krateia's

214 CHAPTER 5. COMMENTARY

change of heart – have to be accommodated. Moreover, it has to be said that it would be unusual in Menander's plots if the crucial turning points occurred in the fifth act, and not, as is common, in the fourth (Hunter, 1985, 40), although Zagagi (1994, 71) is right to point to exceptions (e.g. the recognition of Kichesias in *Sik.*).

948-58 Arnott (1996d, 39) suggests that these lines were spoken by Krateia's brother, who has made his surprising appearance. In Arnott (1996c, 344) he attributes this thought first to Guidorizzi. About the only positive piece of evidence we have that the brother appeared comes in line 960 where the plural διδόασι might have as its subject father+brother of Krateia, although Treu (1974, 176 n. 2) suggests that the plural could refer to Demeas with Krateia; that does not seem correct, however, as Krateia can hardly 'give' herself away. Krateia's brother would not be the only character who returns from the dead in Menander: Kleostratos in *Asp.* was thought dead in battle, but it was a mistake, as already announced by Tyche in the prologue. He returns in act four. We would know if we had the prologue of *Mis.* It seems to me there is next to nothing in the traces of 948-58 which points in the direction of Krateia's brother, or the relief of his relatives or explanation of his apparent death. I think, on the one hand, that it is essential that the dead relative discussed by Krateia and her father in lines 647-52 appear in the play to show that he is *not* dead; on the other hand, there are next to no textual handholds for his surprise reappearance.

953 ζηλοτυπ[. A form either of ζηλότυπος or ζηλοτυπία. Jealousy has not been a theme elsewhere in the extant remains of the play, and one wonders what its significance is here. There was a hint earlier that Getas was on the look out for a rival for Krateia's affections (619) and one might speculate that the two men, Thrasonides and Getas, had suspected that behind Krateia's aversion to Thrasonides lay the suit of another. In *Perik.* the theme is manifest: Polemon abuses Glykera in a fit of jealous rage having heard she has been seen kissing another man. At the end of the play, when that man has turned out to be Glykera's brother, he forswears such jealous attacks in the future (986-7). Could it be that Menander has reduplicated the theme here: the suspected rival turns out to be Krateia's brother? That does not seem likely as Krateia presumably knew her brother so she could not simultaneously have thought him dead, and had him as a suitor. Gregory of Nazianzus, *Carmina de se ipso* 1176.5, has a curious allusion to the jealousy of (plural) Thrasonideses:

> Ἀλλ᾽ οἱ καλοί τε κἀγαθοὶ συμποίμενες
> Φθόνῳ ῥαγέντες (ἴστε τοὺς Θρασωνίδας·
> Οὐ γὰρ φέρει παίδευσιν ἡ ἀγροικία)

> 'But the great and good fellow shepherds, torn by jealousy (you know all those Thrasonideses: brutishness does not lead to good breeding).'

Act Five   215

This might be a reference to brutish behaviour on the part of Thrasonides in our play, but it seems much more applicable to Polemon in *Perik.*; there Polemon brutishly cut off Glykera's hair. See introduction p. 6.

Scene Three: Happy Ending

959 ἄνθρ[ωπ'. Arnott (1996d, 39) argues that the most likely addressee here is Krateia's brother, who would be a stranger to Getas.

961 διδόασί σοι γυναῖκα, 'they give her to you as wife'. Webster in P.Oxy. 33, 1968, 52, was the first to point out that this plural seems to refer to Demeas and a further (male) member of Krateia's family: that can only be the long-lost brother, who has made his appearance. For a plural 'they give' referring to marriage cf. *Fab. inc.* 18 Blanchard (τοῖς δοῦσι). O² seems to have had a nu (wrongly) after διδόασι (διδόασιν), certainly not sigma.   γυναῖκα predicative: 'as wife'. If my guess for the missing words τὴν ἐρωμένην happened to be right, the point would be that the person so denoted – 'your lover' – changes status to a lawfully married wife. It is worth repeating that Krateia can only marry in an official sense now that she has recovered her citizen status through reunification with her father (an Athenian?).

962 προσευξάμην, presumably a prayer that Demeas would have a change of heart and give him Krateia's hand, as has now happened. Perhaps ταύτας θεάς *vel sim.* after the verb; the reading ταυ[is very indistinct. The temporal augment is facultative in Menander (so not προσηυξ-).

963 οὕτως ἀγαθὸ[ν] γέ[νοιτο]. This is a standard expression for 'bless my/your soul!' Perhaps σοι after the optative: 'Bless you!' Cf. *Ep.* 159 with my note.

964 οὐκ ἐξα[π]ατᾶ‹ι›ς; 'you're not deceiving me?' We have had no instances of Getas trying to trick or deceive his master Thrasonides yet in this play, but it was a standard motif in master-servant relations in comedy. In *Perik.* Moschion is constantly suspecting Daos of leading him up the garden path, and Daos in *Asp.* is a real trickster. Habrotonon's ruse in *Epitr.* is decisive in the plot.

965 Ἡρ[άκλεις], 'By Herakles!' (*mehercule*). Getas is beginning to get impatient at Thrasonides' further questioning. As far as he's concerned he's given Thrasonides the message, and that should be enough. He is returning to the cocky and rather insolent servant that he started out as, now that Thrasonides is out of danger.

968 Enough of line **969** survives to make it more or less certain that a form of βούλομαι was contained in Demeas' question. The rest is e.g. but it seemed to me that the question with ἄνδρα, 'as your husband', was preferable to e.g. Arnott's supplements, as being more specific.

969-70 These supplements are based on the assumption that Krateia has now discovered that what she thought to be the case was in fact all wrong. Unfortunately we cannot be more specific than that. The realization of error is, in other plays, a central feature of the plot: Knemon in *Dys.*, for example, realizes the error of his ways, as does Charisios in *Epitr.* Here, Krateia's change of heart was probably a more minor element of the plot – though all-important for Thrasonides! **πάπ‹π›α.** It is a curious feature that Menander manuscripts invariably write this word with one pi. That can only have been on the assumption that the first alpha was long. **ἀ[ν]α[λελύσθαι** (H-D. Blume's suggestion *per litt.*) '[to have been] undone', 'nullified'. **ἀναλύω** is the verb used to describe Penelope's undoing of the weaving (*Od.* 2.105, 109 etc.); Menander uses the passive participle once in the sense 'relax' (*Herois* fr. 5.1 Sandbach), but otherwise the predominant sense is 'undo', 'nullify' (astronomical), 'cancel' Dem. 21.218. Interestingly the middle voice is used for 'cancel faults' Xen. *HG* 7.5.18, **ἁμαρτίας** Dem. 14.34, which would be exactly the sense required here (in the passive). The upsilon seems to be generally short in the aorist passive of this verb. Otherwise some other verb, such as **ἀνατετράφθαι**, 'have been turned on their head', to indicate that Krateia thinks that Thrasonides' supposed crimes have been shown to be a chimaera.

971 ἐκπλεῖ γελῶσά γ' ἠπί[ως, 'she bursts out laughing gently'. **ἐκπλεῖ** is the only clear reading here, although editors have commonly changed this to **ἐκπλέα.** I take **ἐκπλεῖ** in the metaphorical sense of 'losing control' attested in e.g. Hdt. 3.155, also with a participle as here: **Κῶς οὐκ ἐξέπλωσας τῶν φρενῶν σεωυτὸν διαφθείρας;** 'How can it be that you were not out of your mind in destroying yourself?' (**ἐκλώω** Ion. for **ἐκπλέω**). Cf. Ael. fr. 240. The next two words **γελῶσά γ' ἠπίως** are anything but certain. If correct, they indicate that at that point Krateia laughed in a conciliatory manner, underlining the recognition that the ill she had thought of Thrasonides has turned out to be groundless. The laughter marks an emotional release of tension.

972 ἐφήδομ', 'I'm pleased with you'. Getas joins in with Thrasonides' happiness.

973 Now Demeas appears to confirm what Getas has already told Thrasonides.

974 καλῶς ποιῶν This is a standard expression for 'you do well to do so', or 'quite right too' (Germ. 'gut so').

974-6 Demeas does not beat about the bush but comes straight out with his declaration of betrothing Krateia to Thrasonides. However, the declaration is not quite so bald as it might sound, as that is what the two men had been frantically contesting in the previous act: Thrasonides had implored Demeas for the hand of his daughter and Demeas had insisted Thrasonides release her from the effective bondage in which she stood to Thrasonides. The marriage formula as uttered by Demeas here is the standard one, thus permitting confident restoration from parallel passages. In

Act Five 217

Perik. 1015-7 we find (Pat.) ταύτην γν[ησίων] / παίδων ἐπ' ἀρότωι σοι δίδωμι. (Pol.) λ[αμβάνω— / (Pat.) καὶ προῖκα τρία τάλαντα (for more parallels see my note there). If 'war has scattered' Demeas' family, it is quite fortunate that he still has two talents to give as Krateia's dowry. Thrasonides indicates, however, that he would be happy to take her without any dowry (976-77).

976 δύο τάλαντα προῖκ', 'a dowry of two talents'. On the basis of such figures (*Ep.*: 3 talents, *Perik.* 1017: 3, *Dysk.* 844: 3) Casson (1976) argued that Menander's characters belonged to the class of super-rich in Athens, but this has been relativized by Roselli (2011), for example. Rather, we should think of Menander's dowry-giving fathers as affluent but not super-rich. As in modern film 'romantic comedies', which tend to feature beautiful people in beautiful homes and locations, I believe Menander situates his marriages at the economic level of the desirably affluent rather than the stinking rich. That Demeas can produce, apparently without any hesitation, such a handsome dowry might surprise us given his previous lamentation of the ravages of war in his home country, but perhaps we should not press the point. At any rate, war had obviously not left him destitute, even if childless.

978 ἀντε[ιρημένους ταύτηι λόγους], 'all the objections she brought forward'. I imagine that the sentence continued with something like 'have been resolved of their own accord' (ἀπὸ ταὐτομάτου), but of course one cannot be sure λόγους is the missing word with πάντας. It would be a mistake to build too much on an e.g. supplement, but if this is correct it shows that it was what Krateia thought she knew that had poisoned her mind against Thrasonides, not what he had told her.

979 ἀπὸ ταὐτομάτου, 'of their own accord'. It is a cliché of Menander's New Comedy that apparently insoluble conundrums resolve themselves by chance discoveries and recognitions. See *Ep.* 1108 and *Perik.* 151 with my notes and for a complete study Vogt-Spira (1992). Here, we think, the fortuitous event is the appearance, alive, of Krateia's brother.

980 δεῖπνον ξένια κ[αὶ. Having given his consent to marriage and confirmed that the previous obstacles have been removed, Thrasonides turns immediately to the celebrations (meal, reception) which should mark his marriage. Something will be put off to the next day (ἐπ' αὔριον 984), but possibly not the marriage ceremony.

981 ἀλλ' εἰσί[ωμ]εν ...[. Into Thrasonides' house, that is, presumably. Kleinias does not seem to have a role in this last scene.

986 ἐστ' ἔνδο[ν. Blanchard *ad loc.* thinks this must be Krateia, but it could be anything, including equipment (torches etc.) for the celebration.

987 σὺ πρ[ό]φ[ερε], 'Bring [them/it] out!' Demeas seems to tell Thrasonides to fetch what he had said was inside his house (986 ἐστ' ἔνδον). That, then, cannot be Krateia (see previous note) as προφέρω would be the wrong verb (better e.g. ἐξάγω).

218   CHAPTER 5. COMMENTARY

988 μετέμελ' αὐτ[ῆι, 'she regretted'. This looks like a comment by Demeas on his daughter's change of heart, very similar to that of Pataikos about Glykera in *Perik.* 1007-10, and again 1025. In both these plays it is for the fathers at this point to speak for their daughters, who are now brides about to be given away. Katsouris (2014, 282), however, suggests that it is Thrasonides who 'regretted' (sc. his previous behaviour); in that case we would have to supplement μετέμελ' αὐτ[differently.

989 ἄψας δᾶι[δας, 'light the torches'. Burning torches were an essential concomitant of an ancient Greek wedding: they lit the nocturnal procession of the bride with accompanying persons from the father's house to the groom's. In the iconography Hymenaios is commonly depicted holding a burning torch; e.g. in the Attic red-figure pyxis in the Penn Museum (MS5462 early 4th c. BC) showing the wedding of Herakles and Hebe, led by Hymenaios holding a burning torch. In this case one wonders whence Demeas will process (from and to Thrasonides' house?) but perhaps we should not ask.

991 δειπν[After μηδέπω presumably a form of δειπνέω rather than δεῖπνον, e.g. δειπνεῖν, but one cannot be sure.

994-96 These formulaic lines can be supplemented by virtue of their recurrence in near-identical form in other plays: *Dys.*, *Sam.* At the end of the play, the playwright addresses his audience and asks for their applause, in Shakespearian manner. There are other moments in his comedy, too, when he addresses the audience, for example, when Agnoia in *Perik.* asks the audience to forgive the somewhat violent beginning to this play (167-171). Likewise, characters occasionally speak to the audience, for example, when Demeas appeals to the men in the audience (ἄνδρες 269) in his long monologue. This somewhat jocular involvement of the audience is a defining feature of comedy compared to tragedy, which never concedes directly that this is a play, watched by theatre-goers. On the one hand comedy is by definition 'less serious' and can cheerfully acknowledge it is an entertainment put on for the people. On the other, the comedy itself is closer to the reality known by the audience in their everyday lives, so that one can speak to the other without a massive breach of the dramatic illusion. Alkiphron relates how Glykera used to wait behind the scenes with fingers crossed and bated breath until the audience showed its appreciation of the play by clapping (ἕως ἂν κροταλίσῃ τὸ θέατρον 4.19.5 cf. Vox (2014)).

The scribe ends the play with a huge *asteriskos* in the left margin and a line under the last line, followed by the title and *kolophōn* which reads '*Thrason[ides* or *Misoumenos]* of Menand[er]. Good will to the rea[der] and the wri[ter] (= scribe)'. Clearly the play could also be called by its main character, who was also the hated man. I discussed in the introduction (1.2) how Thrasonides' emotional journey seems to be the main theme of the play. Clearly this is reflected in the title. It is, then, a little surprising that the Mytilene mosaic illustrating the 'hated man' does not contain

Act Five

Figure 5.3: The End of *Misoumenos* in P.Oxy. 2656 (O³)

Thrasonides: or could it be that he is the middle person?

The *kolophōn* is normally, I think, taken to wish goodwill for the reader and writer of this manuscript. However there are at least two other possibilities. The 'reader' could be the recipient of the play, but the term hardly suits a member of a theatre audience, and the writer could be Menander. On the whole, I consider that unlikely as Menander continued to be performed, not just read in a book. Also, the 'writer' is usually a *didaskalos* or *kōmōdos*. Or the 'reader' could be a person who read the exemplar out loud, and the 'writer' would be the scribe. I.e. the closing expression would refer to the two people involved in the process of copying by dictation, a common method of duplication, as we know (Skeat, 1956). The request for 'goodwill' would be a kind of recommendation by the authors of this particular manuscript. I.e. 'the reader and writer (sc. involved in the production of this manuscript) recommend themselves to the general public. For the expression, Blanchard (2016, 242) compares *P. Bouriant* 1.272-276 and *P. Rylands* I 58, *P. Bodmer* VIII. On the whole, I think this is most likely, particularly as 'reader' comes before 'writer'. This expresses the logic of dictation, whereas if the 'reader' were the/any reader of the manuscript henceforth, he might come *after* 'writer'.

Fragmentum dubium: P. Berol. 8450

This papyrus was first published by Wolfgang Luppe and Wolfgang Müller in 'Zwei Berliner Papyri zu Komödien', *Archiv für Papyrusforschung* 29, 1983, 5-8. They suggested that the fragment may come from *Sam.*, but the only handhold is the mention of a Chrysis in line 2. There is equally a Chrysis in our play, and one or two other things might fit *Mis.* better, too. In line 6 someone is said to be 'free' (if ἐλεύθερος rather than ἐλευθέριος). This is an issue for Krateia in *Mis.* but no one's freedom is at issue in *Sam.* In line 7 someone is tearing his/her hair, as Thrasonides is predicted to do by Getas in line 723 of *Mis.* (δράττεται). And, again, in line 10 someone 'has returned' (κατῆλθε), which is a very relevant theme if the brother returning is a correct theory about the plot of *Mis.* In line 11, if my supplement ἀνάγκας (written ἀνανκας) is right, the 'dire straits' (Germ. 'Zwangslage') applies well to Thrasonides' position when Krateia continues to reject him right up to act five. In line 14 '(be) unfortunate' (] ἀτυχει[) is thematized by Thrasonides in lines 29 and 801. Needless to say, these pointers do not amount to proof, but it seems to me that they make *Mis.* a rather better candidate than *Sam.* as placement. If the suggestion were ever to be proved, it might provide valuable confirmation that Krateia's brother did really return. The fragment would, on this suggestion, fit in the missing portion of the play in act five.

Book Fragments

Fr. 1
That Krateia was εὐτελές, 'cheap', we hear only here, but it might be rhetorical exaggeration here, expressing Thrasonides' vexation. The sentiment of the words goes well with lines 36ff., but there is no visible overlap in this vicinity. That Menander allows Thrasonides to formulate his problem so clearly here – that a girl has defeated him where no enemy did – surely reflects the core matter of the play. This is exactly the theme of *Misoumenos*. The irony of καταδεδούλωκ' is, of course, that technically Thrasonides did that to Krateia, whilst she has achieved exactly the opposite emotionally.

His name – Thrasonides – from θρασύς, brave, bold, goes some way to defining his 'profile', as does Polemon in *Perik.* Bonollo (2019, 95) compares Thrasonides' position here with that of Herakles in Soph. *Trach.*, where the hero, victorious over monsters and foreign tribes, succumbs to a woman (1061-2).

The information given after the direct quote is interesting, as it is completely missing in the extant portions of text: Thrasonides boasts about his military exploits; he demands a sword and is cross with (Getas) who, from good will, does not provide it; he gives gifts to the girl who hates him, he begs and cries, recovers somewhat. Unfortunately there is no certainty that these elements really appeared in the play; they might be the fruit of Epictetus' imagination.

Book Fragments   221

Fr. 2
See p. 142f.

Fr. 3
If the fragment occupies the first two *metra* of the line it is interesting that αἱ σπάθαι appears prosodically interchangeable with τὰ ξίφη, the more common word, although one would expect γέγονε in that case (and ἀφανῆ). There does not, however, appear to be any question of dialect in connection with the rarer word. The word might occur in line 429 of the play (but I doubt it), and certainly occurs in line 578, spoken by Syra, Kleinias' elderly serving woman. Also in *Perik.* 355, *Sam.* 659.

Fr. 4
Presumably this is Thrasonides lamenting to Getas about his miserable plight. **ψυχήν** seems to mean 'courage', or 'hope', here, nothing to do with 'life'. One feels tempted to connect with ἀναψύχω, 'refresh', e.g. φίλον ἦτορ *Il.* 13.84, but κἂν is καὶ ἂν with optative λάβοιμι. **νυνὶ γάρ** indicates that the speaker has no hope at present. The second sentence indicates that the speaker has no faith in just gods but that his experience (with Krateia) has taught him the opposite.

Fr. 5
One notes the variant title quoted by the *Suda*: Μισούμεναι, *The Hated Women*. There was in fact a play entitled *Misoumenē, The Hated Woman*, by Phoinikides, and the *Suda* seems to have confused the two here. If the scholiast is correct in his exegesis here, a 'Laconian key' is a kind of lock which was operated from the outside. If Thrasonides is speaking here he might be wishing he could lock Krateia *in* here, to stop her running away. He cannot be referring to a rival suitor, as that person could unlock the door from the outside (perhaps) and get *in* to Krateia.

Fr. 6
Arnott (1968) reduces this fragment to πάτερ, ἀπεκτάγκασι δ' οὔ, maintaining that the opening words in the *Suda*, μισοῦσι μέν, ὦ, are probably a corruption of the source's title Μισουμένωι, 'in the *Misoumenos*', and that Thrason's name in the various sources for this fragment is obviously a mistake for Thrasonides. Arnott says that it is uncertain whether the fragment contained Thrasonides' name at all. In his view the only sure point in all the citations is the bizarre form ἀπεκτάγκασι (3rd p. pl. pf. indic. act.) which Menander appears to have used, perhaps for metrical reasons.
If we are to go with the longer version reconstructed by Dobree (Blanchard), it would seem that Krateia is addressing Demeas (her father) and commenting on Thrasonides. As we have seen, there is some plot against Thrasonides in the play, which becomes

visible in the strange narrative of Getas in act three (567-73). This fragment may refer to this plot, indicating that whoever it is that is plotting against Thrasonides, has not succeeded in killing him (yet). However, it is also conceivable that it is the mysterious brother of Krateia speaking here and pointing out that 'they' (whoever they were) have not killed *him*, the brother (Webster, 1974, 166 n. 78). This obviously works better on Arnott's view of things, without μισοῦσι μὲν / Θρασωνίδην.

Fr. 7
It is a strange coincidence that a rare lexeme for 'sword' (fr. 3) which occurs in this play also serves as etymological root for another rare word occurring in this play, σπαθᾶν, 'boast'. Perhaps the origin was 'wave one's sword around' or some such. English 'vaunt', 'boast', is said to derive originally from Latin *vanus*, 'empty'. The use of these rare military terms must have lent the play a military air, particularly when bandied about by the mercenary Thrasonides.

Fr. 8
Somebody must have appeared ἐνερόχρως, deathly pale, in the play: Thrasonides presumably, in his despair. The ἔνεροι are those below the earth, the dead. Their colour is the opposite of warm and ruddy. Kraus (1971a, 4) suggested that the colour word may have applied to Thrasonides' appearance in the play, i.e. his mask.

Fr. 9
ἀπόκνιζε occurs twice elsewhere in comedy, once in Aristoph. *Ach.* 869 as 'pluck flowers', again in Sotades 1.23 'pluck off heads'. Since there is no context here, we have no idea what is being plucked or twisted off.

Fragmentum dubium
Meineke thought this quote more likely to belong to *Mis.* than *Hēr.*, as Leo thought. Hermeias quotes the passage to illustrate the Epicureans' disdain for erotic love. It stands next to another fragment which says that Kypris is greatly augmented by a well-filled belly. In favour of Leo's attribution to *Hēr.* one might say that the Getas in that play is more likely to have gone hungry in the past than the well-placed servant of Thrasonides, who is hardly likely to have gone hungry at the side of the successful mercenary. But slaves in comedy are traditionally greedy, so the Getas in *Mis.* might have expressed such a complaint, even to the face of his master.

Bibliography

Alpers, Klaus (ed.), 1981: *Das attizistische Lexikon des Oros*, vol. 4 of *Sammlung griechischer und lateinischer Grammatiker*, Berlin.

Andorlini, I. (ed.), 2009: *Greek Medical Papyri*, vol. II, Florence.

Arnott, W. Geoffrey, 1957: 'Split anapaests, with special reference to some passages of Alexis', *CQ*, 51 (n.s. 7), 188–98.

—, 1964: 'The confrontation of Sostratos and Gorgias', *Phoenix*, 18.2, 110–123.

—, 1968: 'A little less Menander (Misoumenos Fr. 13 Körte)?', *CR*, 18.1, 11–13.

—, 1996a: *Alexis: the Fragments. A Commentary*, Cambridge.

Arnott, W. Geoffrey (ed.), 1996b: *Menander. Edited with an English Translation in three volumes. Vol. II*, Loeb Classical Library, Cambridge, Mass.

—, 1996c: *Menander, volume II*, vol. 459 of *Loeb Classical Library*, Cambridge, Mass.

Arnott, W. Geoffrey, 1996d: 'Notes on Menander's Misoumenos', *ZPE*, 110, 27–39.

—, 1998: 'Menander, Misoumenos 152-59 Sandbach (552-59 Arnott)', *ZPE*, 122, 20.

Austin, Colin, 1966: 'Review of New Fragments of the Misoumenos of Menander by Eric G. Turner', *The Classical Review*, 16, no. 3, 294–298.

Austin, Colin (ed.), 1968: *Nova fragmenta Euripidea in papyris reperta*, Berlin, de Gruyter.

—, 1973: *Comicorum Graecorum Fragmenta in papyris reperta*, Berlin.

—, 2012: *Menander. Eleven Plays*, vol. 37 of *Proceedings of the Cambridge Philological Society. Supplementary Volume*, Cambridge.

Austin, Colin, Stigka, Efrosyni, 2007: 'Not Comedy but Epigram; 'Mr Perfect' in fr. com. adesp. *1036', *ZPE*, 161, 13–16.

Bader, Bernd, 1971: 'The ψόφος of the house-door in Greek New Comedy', *Antichthon*, 5, 35–48.

Bain, David, 1984: 'Female speech in Menander', *Antichthon*, 18, 24–42.

Barigazzi, A., 1965: *La formazione spirituale di Menandro*, Turin.

Barrett, W.S., 2007: *Greek Lyric, Tragedy, and Textual Criticism. Collected Papers of W.S. Barrett, ed. by M.L. West*, Oxford.

Bastianini, Guido, Casanova, Angelo (eds.), 2004: *Menandro. Cent' anni di papiri. Atti del convegno internazionale di studi. Firenze 12-13 Giugno 2003*, Florence.

Belardinelli, Anna Maria, 1989: 'Menandro, *Misumenos* A31-A37', *ZPE*, 78, 31–34.

Beroutsos, Demetrios C. (ed.), 2005: *A Commentary on the Aspis of Menander, Part One: Lines 1-298*, vol. 157 of *Hypomnemata*, Göttingen.

Blanchard, Alain, 2014: 'Reconstructing Menander', in: Fontaine & Scafuro (2014), 239–257.

Blanchard, Alain (ed.), 2016: *Ménandre. Tome III. Le laboureur, La double tromperie, Le poignard, L'eunuque, L'inspirée, Thrasyléon, Le Carthaginois, Le cithariste, Le flatteur, Les femmes qui boivent la ciguë, La Leucadienne, le Haï, La Périnthienne*, Paris, Les Belles Lettres.

Blume, Horst-Dieter, 1998: *Menander*, Darmstadt.

Blundell, John, 1980: *Menander and the Monologue*, vol. 59 of *Hypomnemata*, Göttingen.

Bonollo, Elena, 2019: 'Alcune osservazioni sui personaggi del *Misoumenos* di Menandro', *Prometheus*, 45.1, 89–103.

Brown, Mitch, 2016: *Menander Offstage*, Ph.D. thesis, Cincinnati.

Brown, P.G. McC., 1980: 'Review of E.G. Turner 'Lost Beginning'', *Classical Review*, n.s. 30, 3–6.

—, 1987: 'Masks, names and characters in the New Comedy', *Hermes*, 115, 181–202.

—, 1990: '*Misoumenos* A31-36', *ZPE*, 84, 8–10.

Carlesimo, Roberta, 2018: 'P.Oxy. LX 4025 e LXXIX 5199 ricongiunti (Menandro *Misoumenos*)', *ZPE*, 108, 67–70.

Cartlidge, Ben, 2016a: 'Heteroclisis in Menander and the Authorship of P.Ant. 15 (= fr. Com. Adesp)', *ZPE*, 199, 17–24.

—, 2016b: 'Menander, *Misoumenos* 42', *ZPE*, 199, 16.

—, 2017a: 'Menander *Epitrepontes* 807 and the suffix of the feminine perfect active participle in fourth-century Athens', *ZPE*, 201, 32–39.

—, 2017b: 'Menander *Misoumenos* 563 Arnott', *ZPE*, 203, 68.

Casanova, A. (ed.), 2014: *Menander e l'evoluzione della commedia greca: atti del Convegno internazionale di studi in memoria di Adelmo Barigazzi nel centenario della nascita (Firenze, 30 settembre - 1 ottobre 2013)*, Florence.

Casson, Lionel, 1976: 'The Athenian upper class and New Comedy', *TAPA*, 106, 29–59.

Chantraine, P., 1968: *Dictionnaire Étymologique de la Langue Grecque. Histoire des mots*, Paris.

Charitonidis, S., Kahil, L., Ginouvès, R., 1970: *Les mosaïques de la maison du Mé-*

BIBLIOGRAPHY

nandre à Mytilène, vol. 6 of *Antike Kunst, Beiheft*, Bern.

Cinaglia, Valeria, 2014: *Aristotle and Menander on the Ethics of Understanding*, Leiden.

Colantonio, Maria, 1976: 'Scene notturne nelle commedie di Menandro: Nota al Pap. Oxy. 2826', *Quaderni Urbinati di Cultura Classica*, 23, 59–64.

Copley, F.O., 1956: *Exclusus Amator. A Study in Latin Love Poetry*, Baltimore.

del Corno, D., 1970: 'The Oxyrhynchus Papyri Volume 33. London 1968', *Gnomon*, 42, 250–261.

Cosmopoulos, Michael B. (ed.), 2003: *Greek Mysteries: the Archaeology and Ritual of Ancient Greek Secret Cults*, London, Routledge.

Cusset, Christophe, Lhostis, Nathalie, 2014: 'Usages de l'aparté dans quelques comédies de Ménandre', in: Pascale Paré-Rey (ed.), *L'Aparté dans le théâtre antique. Un procédé dramatique à redécouvrir*, Vincennes, 147–176.

Cusset, Christophe, Lukinovich, Alessandra (eds.), 2019: *Redécouvrir l'Apparition de Ménandre*, Paris.

Davis, Gregson, 1978: 'Ovid *Metamorphoses* 3.442f. and the prologue to Menander's *Misoumenos*', *Phoenix*, 32, 339–42.

Dedoussi, Christina, 1964: 'Studies in Comedy', *Hellenika*, 18, 1–10.

Dickey, Eleanor, 1995: 'Forms of address and conversational language in Aristophanes and Menander', *Mnemosyne*, 48, 257–71.

Diggle, James, 2007: 'Menander, «Misoumenos» 4f. and Catullus 45,25f.', *Eikasmos*, 18, 249–250.

Drago, Anna Tiziana, 1997: 'Due esempi di intertestualità in Aristeneto', *Lexis: Poetica, Retorica e Comunicazione nella Tradizione Classica*, 15, 173–187.

Dworacki, Sylwester, 1973: 'The prologues in the comedies of Menander', *Eos*, 61, 33–47.

Elderkin, G.W., 1934: 'The Curculio of Plautus', *American Journal of Archaeology*, 38, No. 1 (Jan. - Mar.), 29–36.

van Emde Boas, Evert, Rijksbaron, Albert, Huitink, Luuk, de Bakker, Mathieu, 2019: *The Cambridge Grammar of Classical Greek*, Cambridge.

Fantham, Elaine, 1975: 'Sex, Status, and Survival in Hellenistic Athens: A Study of Women in New Comedy', *Phoenix*, 29.1, 44–74.

—, 1986: 'ΖΗΛΟΤΥΠΙΑ: A brief excursion into sex, violence, and literary history', *Phoenix*, 40, 45–57.

Fantuzzi, Marco, 1982: 'Menander, *Misoumenos* A 4', *ZPE*, 48, 66.

Faraone, Christopher A., 2019: 'Cultural Plurality in Greek Magical Recipes for Oracular and Protective Statues', in: Ljuba Merlina Bortolani, William Furley, Svenja Nagel, ,Joachim Friedrich Quack (eds.), *Cultural Plurality in Ancient Magical Texts and Practices. Graeco-Egyptian Handbooks and Related Traditions*, Tübingen, vol. 32 of *Orientalische Religionen in der Antike*, 171–188.

Fontaine, Michael, Scafuro, Adele C. (eds.), 2014: *The Oxford Handbook of Greek and Roman Comedy*, Oxford.

Fortenbaugh, William W., Schütrümpf, Eckart (eds.), 2000: *Demetrius of Phalerum. Text, Translation and Discussion*, New Brunswick and London.

Frisk, H., 1970: *Griechisches Etymologisches Wörterbuch*, Heidelberg.

Frost, K.B., 1988: *Exits and Entrances in Menander*, Oxford.

Funke, Melissa, 2016: 'The Menandrian World of Alciphon's Letters', in: C.W. Marshall, Tom Hawkins (eds.), *Athenian Comedy in the Roman Empire*, London: Bloomsbury, 223–238.

Furley, William (ed.), 2009: *Menander Epitrepontes*, vol. 106 of *BICS Supplements*, London.

Furley, William, 2015: 'Textual notes on Menander's *Misoumenos*, taking in the most recently published fragments', *ZPE*, 196, 44–48.

Furley, William (ed.), 2021: *New Fragments of Menander's Epitrepontes*, London: University of London Press. PDF edition.

Gaiser, K., 1967: 'Menander und der Peripatos', *Antike und Abendland*, 13, 8–40.

García, Antonio López, 1987: 'Estudio preliminar del P. Mont. inv. 127: Comedia Nueva?', in: Sebastià in Janeras (ed.), *Miscellànea papirològica Ramon Roca-Puig en el seu vuitantè aniversari*, Barcelona, 177–179.

Gelzer, Thomas, 1996: 'Die Trimeter Fr. com. adesp. *1036 K-A und Menander', *ZPE*, 114, 61–66.

Giacomoni, Agnese, 1998: '"Dike e adikia" nel monologo di Trasonide (Menandro, *Misum*. P.Oxy. 3967)', *Quaderni Urbinati di Cultura Classica*, New Series, Vol. 58, No. 1, 91–109.

Goldberg, S.M., 1980: *The Making of Menander's Comedy*, London.

Gomme, A.W., Sandbach, F., 1973: *Menander: A Commentary*, Oxford.

Gould, John, 1973: 'Hiketeia', *Journal of Hellenic Studies*, 93, 74–103.

Green, Richard, Edwards, Mike (eds.), 2015: *Images and Texts. Papers in Honour of Professor Eric Handley CBE*, vol. 129 of *BICS*, London.

Grethlein, Jonas, 2020: 'Plato in therapy: a cognitivist reassessment of the *Republic*'s idea of Mimesis', *The Journal of Aesthetics and Art Criticism*, 78.2, 157–170.

Gärtner, Jan Felix, 2011: *Das antike Recht und die griechisch-römische Neue Komödie: Untersuchungen zu Plautus und seinen griechischen Vorbildern. Two volumes*, Habilitation, Leipzig.

Halleux, R., Schamp, J. (eds.), 1985: *Les lapidaires grecs*, Paris.

Halliwell, Stephen, 2007: 'What is there to laugh about in Menander?', *Dioniso*, n.s. 6, 198–213.

Handley, E.W. (ed.), 1965: *The Dyskolos of Menander*, London.

Handley, E.W., 1969: 'Notes on the *Theophoroumene* of Menander', *Bulletin of the Institute of Classical Studies*, 16, 88–101.

BIBLIOGRAPHY

—, 1970: 'The Conventions of the Comic Stage and their Exploitation by Menander', in: E. G. Turner (ed.), *Ménandre*, Vandœuvres-Genève, vol. XVI of *Fondation Hardt Entretiens*, 3–26.

—, 1990: 'The Bodmer Menander and the comic fragments', in: E.W. Handley, A. Hurst (eds.), *Relire Ménandre*, Geneva, 123–148.

—, 1996: 'A bow at a venture: Menander *Mis.* 387-403', Institute of Classical Studies. Graduate Summer School in Greek Drama 8-12 July 1996.

—, 2002: 'Acting, action and words in New Comedy', in: Pat Easterling, Edith Hall (eds.), *Greek and Roman Actors. Aspects of an Ancient Profession*, Cambridge, 165–88.

—, 2006: 'Dialogue with the Night (PAnt 1.15 = *PCG* VIII 1084)', *ZPE*, 155, 23–25.

Henry, W.B., Parsons, P.J., Prauscello, L., 2014a: '5198 Menander *Misoumenos* 123-54 Sandbach/523-54 Arnott', in: *Papyri Oxyrhynchi*, London, vol. LXXIX, 97–111.

—, 2014b: '5199 Menander *Misoumenos* 352-65 Sandbach/753-66 Arnott', in: *Papyri Oxyrhynchi*, London, vol. LXXIX, 111–114.

Hoffmann, W., Wartenberg, G., 1973: *Der Bramarbas in der antiken Komödie*, Berlin.

Hughes, Alan, 2012: *Performing Greek Comedy*, Cambridge. Ch. 11 on New Comedy.

Hunter, R.L., 1985: *The New Comedy of Greece and Rome*, Cambridge.

Jacques, J.M., 1974: 'Le début du Misouménos et les prologues de Ménandre', in: *Musa Iocosa: A. Thierfelder zum 70. Geburtstag*, New York, 71–79.

Jaekel, S. (ed.), 1964: *Menandri sententiae. Comparatio Menandri et Philistionis*, Leipzig.

Kassel, R., Austin, C. (eds.), 1983-2001: *Poetae Comici Graeci. 8 Volumes*, Berlin.

Katsouris, A.G., 1980: "Ὁ κοινὸς ἐχθρὸς πόλεμος. Menander *Misoumenos* 234', *Dioniso*, 51, 237–245.

—, 1985: 'Menander's *Misoumenos*. Problems of Interpretation', *Dodone*, 14, 205–229.

—, 2014: 'Methods of humanization and sympathy especially in reference to the traditional odd characters', in: Casanova (2014), 277–290.

Koerte, A., Thierfelder, A. (eds.), Third edition 1953-1955: *Menandri quae supersunt*, Leipzig. Pars prior: reliquiae in papyris et membranis vetustissimis servatae. Pars altera: reliquiae apud veteres scriptores servatae.

Korhonen, Tua, 1997: 'Self-concept and public image of philosophers and philosophical schools at the beginning of the Hellenistic Age', in: *Early Hellenistic Athens: symptoms of a change*, Athens, vol. 6 of *Papers and Monographs of the Finnish Institute at Athens*, 33–101.

Kraus, Walther, 1971a: 'Zu Menanders Misumenos', *Rheinisches Museum*, 114, 1–27.

—, 1971b: 'Zu Menanders Misumenos', *Rheinisches Museum*, 114, 285–86.

Krieter-Spiro, Martha, 1997: *Sklaven, Köche und Hetären. Das Dienstpersonal bei Menander. Stellung, Rolle, Komik und Sprache*, vol. 93 of *Beiträge zur Altertumskunde*, Stuttgart.

Kühner, Raphael, Gerth, Bernhard, 1966: *Ausführliche Grammatik der Griechischen Sprache*, Darmstadt.

Kumaniecki, C., 1965: 'Ad *Misumeni* Menandreae nuper reperta fragmenta observationes aliquot', *Eos*, 55.1, 57–58.

Lape, Susan, 2003: *Reproducing Athens. Menander's Comedy, Democratic Culture, and the Hellenistic City*, Princeton.

—, 2006: 'The Poetics of the "Kōmos"-Chorus in Menander's Comedy', *AJP*, 127.1, 89–109.

Lelli, Immanuel, 2007: 'Paroemiographicum Menandreum (*Mis.* 303)', *ZPE*, 159, 28.

MacCary, W. Thomas, 1969: 'Menander's Slaves: Their Names, Roles, and Masks', *Transactions and Proceedings of the American Philological Association*, 100, 277–294.

Maehler, M., 1992: 'P.Oxy. 3967', in: *The Oxyrhynchus Papyri. Vol. 59*, London, 59–70.

Mastronarde, Donald J., 1990: 'The Skene Roof, the Crane, and the Gods in Attic Drama', *Californian Studies in Classical Antiquity*, 9.2, 247–294.

Mayser, Edwin, 1906: *Grammatik der griechischen Papyri aus der Ptolemäerzeit. Mit Einschluss der griechischen Ostraka und der in Ägypten verfassten Inschriften*, Leipzig.

McC.Brown, P.G., 1981: 'Two notes on Menander's *Misoumenos*', *ZPE*, 41, 25–26.

McClure, Laura, 2003: 'Subversive laughter: the sayings of courtesans in Book 13 of Athenaeus' *Deipnosophistae*', *AJP*, 124.2, 259–294.

Meineck, Peter, Konstan, David (eds.), 2014: *Combat Trauma and the Ancient Greeks*, New York.

Merkelbach, Reinhold, 1966: 'Über die Handlung des Misumenos', *RhM*, 109, 97–108.

Mynors, Sir R. A. B. (ed.), 1990: *Vergil Georgics*, Oxford.

Mülke, Chr., 2002: 'Solons politische Elegien und Iamben', *Beiträge zur Altertumskunde*, 177.

Naiden, F.S., 2006: *Ancient Supplication*, Oxford.

Nervegna, Sebastiana, 2013: *Menander in Antiquity: the Contexts of Reception*, Cambridge; New York: Cambridge University Press.

Newiger, H.-J., 1961: 'Prokeleusmatiker im komischen Trimeter?', *Hermes*, 89,

BIBLIOGRAPHY

175–84.

Nünlist, René, 2002: 'Speech within speech in Menander', in: *The Language of Greek Comedy*, Oxford, 219–259.

Orth, C. (ed.), 2009: *Strattis, Fragmente*, Berlin: Verlag Antike.

Parsons, P.J., 1996: 'ΦΙΛΕΛΛΗΝ', *Museum Helveticum*, 53, 106–115.

Pernigotti, Carlo, 2008: *Menandri Sententiae*, vol. 15 of *Studi e testi per il Corpus dei papiri filosofici greci e latini*, Florence: L. S. Olschki.

Pfeiffer, R., 1978: *Geschichte der Klassischen Philologie. Von den Anfängen bis zum Ende des Hellenismus*, München[2].

Philippides, Katerina, 2019: 'Remarks on the performance of Menander's comedies in the Athenian theater of Dionysos', *Logeion*, 9, 301–334.

Powell, J.U. (ed.), 1925: *Collectanea Alexandrina*, Oxford.

Pritchett, William Kendrick, 1974: *The Greek State at War. Part I*, Berkeley and Los Angeles: University of California Press.

Pötscher, W., 1994,1995: 'Die Struktur der Hikesie', *WSt*, 107,108, 550–75.

von Reden, Sitta, 1998: 'The commodification of symbols: reciprocity and its perversions in Menander', in: C. Gill, N. Postlethwaite, R. Seaford (eds.), *Reciprocity in Ancient Greece*, Oxford, 255–278.

Roselli, David Kawalko, 2011: *Theater of the People. Spectators and Society in Ancient Athens*, Austin: University of Texas Press.

Ross, W.D., 1936: *Aristotle's Physics*, Oxford.

Rubenbauer, H., 1912: *Der Bau des jambischen Trimeters bei Menander*, Tübingen.

Scafuro, Adele C., 2014: 'Menander', in: Fontaine & Scafuro (2014), 218–238.

Schmid, W., 1919: 'Menandros-Glykera', *Wochenschr. f. Klass. Phil.*, 166.

Sisti, Francesco, 1973-74: 'L'inizio del *Misoumenos* e il cosidetto prologo posticipato', *Helikon*, 13-14, 485–491.

Sisti, Francesco (ed.), 1985a: *Menandro, Misumenos*, Genoa.

Sisti, Francesco, 1985b: 'Un verso del *Misoumenos* Menandrea in Nonio', *Studi Noniani*, X, 303–304.

Skeat, Theodore Cressy, 1956: 'The use of dictation in ancient book production', *Proceedings of the British Academy*, 42, 179–208.

Smyth, Herbert Weir, 1976[10]: *A Greek Grammar. Revised by Gordon M. Messing*, Cambridge Mass., Harvard U.P.

Sommerstein, Alan H., 1995: 'The language of Athenian women', in: F. De Martino, A.H. Sommerstein (eds.), *Lo spettacolo delle voci*, Bari, ii 61–85.

—, 2013: 'Samian Questions', *ZPE*, 185, 91–99.

Sommerstein, Alan H. (ed.), 2014a: *Menander in Contexts. Proceedings of a Conference in Nottingham in July 2012*, London.

—, 2014b: *Menander Samia*, Cambridge.

Stephanou, Damaris, 2006: *Darstellungen aus dem Epos und Drama auf kaiserzeitlichen und spätantiken Bodenmosaiken. Eine ikonographische und deutungsgeschichtliche Untersuchung*, vol. 40 of *Orbis Antiquus*, Münster.

Stephens, Susan A., Winkler, John J., 1995: *Ancient Greek Novels. The Fragments*, Princeton.

Studniczka, Franz, 1918: *Das Bildnis Menanders. Sonderdruck aus dem 21. Bande der Neuen Jahrbücher für das Klassische Altertum, Geschichte und Deutsche Literatur*, Wiesbaden.

Thomas, R.F., 1982: 'Menander *Misoumenos* A28-A29', *ZPE*, 45, 175–76.

Traill, Ariana, 2007: 'Notes on Menander *Perikeiromene* 715-717 and *Misoumenos* 698-9', *ZPE*, 159, 43–44.

—, 2008: *Women and the comic plot in Menander*, Cambridge: Cambridge UP.

Treu, Ursula, 1974: 'Neues Licht auf die Vorfabel von Menanders 'Misumenos'?', *ZPE*, 14, 175–177.

Trundle, Matthew, 2004: *Greek Mercenaries. From the Late Archaic Period to Alexander*, London.

Turner, E.G. (ed.), 1965: *New Fragments of the Misoumenos*, vol. supplement no. 17 of *Bulletin of the Institute of Classical Studies*, London.

Turner, E.G., 1968: 'P.Oxy. 2656, 2657', in: *The Oxyrhynchus Papyri. Vol. 33*, London, 15–65.

Turner, E.G. (ed.), 1970: *Ménandre*, vol. 16 of *Entretiens sur l'antiquité classique. Fondation Hardt*, Fondation Hardt.

Turner, E.G., 1973: *The Papyrologist at Work*, vol. no. 6 of *Greek, Roman and Byzantine Monographs*, Durham, North Carolina.

—, 1978: 'The lost beginning of Menander, *Misoumenos*', *Proceedings of the British Academy*, 63, 315–331.

—, 1979: 'Menander and the New Society of his Time', *Chronique d' Égypte*, 54, 106–126.

—, 1981: 'P.Oxy. 3368-3371. Menander, *Misoumenos*', in: *The Oxyrhynchus Papyri. Vol. 48*, London, 1–21.

—, 1982: '*Misoumenos* A 40/1', *ZPE*, 46, 113–116.

Vogt-Spira, G., 1992: *Dramaturgie des Zufalls. Tyche und Handeln in der Komödie Menanders*, vol. 88 of *Zetemata*, Munich.

Vox, Onofrio, 2014: 'Il Menandro di Alcifrone', in: Casanova (2014), 247–258.

Webster, T.B.L., 1960: *Studies in Menander. Second edition*, Manchester.

—, 1969: *Monuments Illustrating New Comedy (Second Edition)*, vol. 24 of *Supplement of the Bulletin of the Institute of Classical Studies*, London. First edition, *BICS* Supplement no. 11, 1961.

—, 1973: 'Woman hates soldier: a structural approach to New Comedy', *GRBS*, 14.3, 287–299.

BIBLIOGRAPHY

—, 1974: *An Introduction to Menander*, Manchester and New York.

White, J.W., 1909: 'The iambic trimeter in Menander', *Classical Philology*, 4, 139–61.

Zagagi, Netta, 1986: 'Notes on P. Köln 203', *ZPE*, 62, 38–40.

—, 1994: *The Comedy of Menander. Convention, Variation and Originality*, London.

—, 2004: 'The dramatic function of 'speaking back into the house' in Menander's *Dyskolos*', *ZPE*, 148, 99–113.

Zanetto, Giuseppe, 2014: 'La tragedia in Menandro. Dalla paratragedia alla citazione', in: Casanova (2014), 83–103.

Index of Main Passages Cited

Aeneas Tacticus
  18.6, 121
Aeschylus
  Ag.
    335, 118
    1072ff., 180
  PV
    113, 117
Alexis
  fr. 147.2 Arnott, 115
  Krateia, 172
Alkiphron
  2.13, 113
  2.27.1, 119
  4.19.5, 218
Antiphon
  First Tetralogy, 146
  2.8, 134
  1.4-5, 177
Apollonius Dyscolus
  De constr.
    I 41.10, 130
Archilochus
  fr. 128 W, 121
Aristainetos
  1.17.12-14, 157
  1.17, 30, 192
  1.22.13-14, 130
  1.22.21, 141
Aristophanes
  Ach.
    419, 115
  Frogs
    19-20, 157
  Knights
    84, 118
  Plut.

    Schol. 1098, 116
  Thesm.
    2, 120
    905, 173
    1065, 113
Aristophanes of Byzantium, *see* Syrianus
  ap. Eustath.
    971.45, 173
Arrian
  Diss. Epict.
    4.1.19, 154

Carmina convivialia
  PMG fr. 7.3 Page, 166
Catullus
  45.25f., 115
Chariton
  Kall.
    2.6.1, 113
    3.7, 129
    3.11, 123
    4.7.7, 113, 117
Choeroboscus
  In Theodos. can.
    p. 176.40-177.3 Hilgard, 122
Choricius Rhet.
  decl.
    42.1.1, 5, 138
Clemens Alex.
  Strom.
    2.15, 8
Com. fr. adesp.
  498 K-A, 120

Demosthenes
  36.32, 180
  Against Conon

54.8-9, 146
De fals. leg.
302.7, 176
[Demosthenes]
In Neaeram
59.46, 133
59.103, 133
Diogenes Laertius
Vit. Philosophorum
3.20, 3
7.130, 6, 115
Duris
FGH 76 F 14, 159

T.S. Eliot
The Love Song of J. Alfred Prufrock,
200
Epictetus
Diss.
4.1.19, 119, 121
Eratosthenes Scholastikos
Anthologia Graeca
5.242.9, 121
Erōtika Adespota
P. Michael. 4 col. i.21, 116
Euripides
Alk.
690, 194
Androm.
227, 118
El.
578, 173
First Hippolytos, 170
fr. 567 (from *Oineus*), 131
Hel.
557, 173
982-87, 211
Her.
1-8, 114
557, 173

722, 171
1015, 115
1303f., 161
IA
opening scene, 112
487, 177
920, 209
1370, 172
1403, 138
IT
727ff., 148
Med.
364-409, 180
507-8, 177
Or.
808, 210
951-2, 167
Eustathius
Comm. ad Hom. Od.
2.249.9, 121

Gregory Naz.
Carmina de se ipso
1176.5, 6, 214

Herodotus
3.155, 216
Hesiod
Theog.
35, 120
Homer
Il.
24.12, 199
Ted Hughes
Birthday Letters
Child's Park, 210

Lexicon Symeonis
s.v. ἐνθύμημα, 170
Lukian
Dial. Mer.

INDEX OF MAIN PASSAGES CITED

10, 17
13, 5
Hermotimos, 120
Philops.
14, 117
Pseudo-Lukian
Amores
8.14.8, 117

Machon
140 Gow, 186
fr. 12.168-173, 192
Maximus Soph.
Dialexeis
20.5.c2, 142, 202
Menander
Asp.
opening scene, 111, 125
35, 160
73, 122
286-87, 114
294-5, 124
328-9, 158
334-5, 129
372-3, 165
Dys.
88-89, 132
Epitr.
144, 120
345-7, 134
436-7, 174
457, 132
873-900, 194
908ff., 184
fr. 54 K-A, 165
fr. 298.3-4, 200
fr. 678 K-Th, 113
fr. 741 K-A, 213
Georg.
17, 116

32-33, 158
58-59, 129
fr. 3, 198
Her.
50-51, 137
Imbrioi
fr. 213 K-Th, 211
Kōneazousai, 122
Perik.
159, 124
162-171, 143
361ff., 145
492, 132
506-7, 191
516ff., 128
533-37, 114
1015-17, 216
1028, 19
jealousy in, 214
Phasma
26 and 27, 213
Psophodeēs
fr. 459 K-Th, 209
Sam.
18, 25
65-76, 123
555-6, 132
Sik.
5ff., 3, 176
141ff., 148
144, 130
286, 173

Nonius Marcellus
387.33 Mercier, 133

Orus
fr. 35 = *Mis.* fr. 6, 164
Ovid
Met.

236   *INDEX OF PASSAGES CITED*

3.442-3, 115
3.455-6, 139

Papyri
  P.Ant
    1.15 = *PCG* VIII 1084, 112
  P.Oxy.
    2826, 118
    3371, 113
  P. Mont. inv. 127, 153
PGM
  IV.3141-2 Preisendanz, 131
Phaedrus
  V 1, 139
Philo
  De congr. erud. gratia
    vol. 3 61.4 Wendland, 120
Phoinikides
  Misoumenē, 221
Photius
  Lex.
    ς 429, 5
Phronto
  Anth. Pal.
    12.233.3, 113
Plato
  Gorg.
    451e1-5, 166
  Symp.
    174e7-8, 182
    220a6-c3, 120
Plautus
  Amph.
    882, 172
  Curc., 25
  Mer.
    3, 112
Plutarch
  Apophth. Lak.
    Mor. 234C-D, 209

De cup. divit.
  Mor. 524F, 117
  4 (525A), 114
Comparison of Aristophanes and
    Menander
  Mor. 853-4, 29
Life of Demetrios
  7.4, 15
  10.3, 25
  16-17, 25
[Plutarch]
  Vit. X Orat.
    842a, 11
Pollux
  Onom.
    4.143f., 175
Porphyry
  Abst.
    1.34, 150

Simplicius
  Comm. in Aristotelem Graeca
    7.708.11 Diels, 116
Solon
  fr. 13.7-10, 167
Sophocles
  Aias, 15
  OC
    324ff., 171
  Trach.
    1061-2, 220
Stoic. Vet. Frg.
  III n. 716, 6
Strattis
  fr. 3 K-A, 141
Suda
  Μένανδρος, 139
Syrianus
  Comm. in Hermog.
    II 23 , 29

INDEX OF MAIN PASSAGES CITED

Theodoridas
    fr. 10.1-4 Snell, 114, 115
Theophrastus
    Char.
      15, 185
Theophylactus
    Ep.
      24.4-5, 182
Thucydides
    2.27, 175
    5.57.1, 116

Vergil
    Georg.
      1.335, 134

Xenophon
    Kyr.
      1.2.12, 121

Index of Greek words

ἀγαθός
    βέλ[τιον], 203
    οὕτως ἀγαθὸν γέ[νοιτο], 215
    ἀγαθόν, 167
ἀγαπάω
    ἀγαπᾶτε, 144
    ἀγαπῶ, 191
    ἠγάπησα, 191
ἀγορεύω
    εἰπεῖν, 138
    εἶπασ', 155
    ἐρεῖ, 136
ἀγροικία, 6
ἄγω, 148
ἀγωνιάω
    ἀγωνιῶ, 182
ἀδελφός, 8
ἄδηλος
    ἄδηλον, 200
ἄιδω
    ᾖσεν, 167
    ᾖσ', 165
ἀηδής, 138
ἀθάνατος
    ἀθάνατον, 211, 212
Ἀθηνᾶ
    μὰ τὴν Ἀθηνᾶν, 10, 130
ἄθλιος
    ἀθλιώτερον, 114
αἱρετός
    αἱρετώτερον, 118
αἰτέω
    αἰτῶ, 188
αἰτία
    αἰτίαν, 139
αἰχμάλωτος, 3, 15, 176
    τῆς αἰχμαλώτου, 128

ἄκουσμα, 167
ἄκρος
    ἄκρως, 138
ἀλίσκομαι
    ἁλοῦσ', 178
ἄλλος
    ἄλλον, 114
ἀλύω
    ἀλύονθ', 198
ἀμέλει, 138
ἄμεμπτος
    ἀμ[έμπ]τως, 166
ἄμιλλα, 178
ἀμφοτερίζω
    ἀμφοτερίσας, 115
ἀναγκαῖος
    ἀναγκαίαν, 139
ἀνακρούω
    ἀνακρούσει, 121
ἀναλαμβάνω
    ἀναλήψομαι, 158
ἀναλύω
    ἀ[ν]α[λελύσθαι], 216
ἄνοικτος
    ἄνοικτον, 147
ἀναφέρω
    [ἀνενε]γκεῖν, 158
ἀνήρ, 191
    ἄνδρ', 166
ἀνθρώπινος
    ἀνθρωπίνως, 188
    ἀνθρώπινον, 132
ἄνθρωπος, 165, 185
    ἀνθρώπων, 114
    ἄνθρ[ωπ'], 215
    ἄνθρωπον, 136
    ἡ ἄν[θρωπος], 192

INDEX OF GREEK WORDS 239

ἀνοίγνυμαι
　see ἄνοικτος, 147
ἀντελεέω
　τὸν ἀντελεοῦνθ᾽, 193
ἀντιλέγω
　ἀντε[ιρημένους], 217
ἀντίπαλος
　ἀντίπαλον, 8
ἄνω κάτω, 115
ἀξιόω
　ἀξιῶ, 188
ἄξων
　ἄξονες, 160
ἀπαίρω
　ἀπῆρα, 126
ἀπαλλάττομαι
　ἀπαλλάγηθ᾽, 158
ἀπαμφιέννυμι
　ἀπαμφιεῖ, 200
ἀπαξάπαντα, 181
ἄπας
　ἁπάντων, 180
ἀπάτη
　ἀπάτην, 153
ἄπειμι, 161
ἀπέρχομαι
　ἀπῆλθεν, 4
ἄπιστος
　ἄπιστον, 164
ἄπληστος
　[ἄπληστε], 197
ἀποδείκνυμι
　ἀποδείξας, 129
ἀποκναίω
　ἀποκναίεις, 122
ἀποκνίζω
　ἀπόκνιζε, 222
ἀπόκρισις, 192
ἀποκτείνω
　ἀπεκτάγκασι, 10

ἀπολαμβάνω
　ἀπολαβεῖν, 206
ἀπόλλυμι
　[ἀπ]ώ[λεσε], 207
　ἀπολεῖ, 120
　ἀπόλωλε, 177
Ἀπόλλων
　Ἀπόλλω, 192
　Ἄπολλον, 114
ἀπολυτρόω
　ἀπολυτροῦν, 188
ἀπολύω
　ἀπέλυσ᾽, 192
ἀπομιμέομαι
　ἀπεμιμήσατο, 29
ἄπορος
　ἀ[πό]ρως, 211
ἀποτρέχω, 169
ἀπροσδόκητος
　ἀπροσδόκητον, 151
ἅπτω
　ἅψας, 218
　ἅψατ᾽, 202
ἀργία
　[ἀργ]ίαν, 197
ἁρμόττω
　ἡρμόσαμεν, 202
ἁρπάζω
　[ἁ]ρπάσαι, 210
Ἄρτεμις
　νὴ τὴν Ἄρτεμιν, 163
ἄρχω
　ἄρχοντα, 164
ἀσθενής
　ἀσθενῶς, 211
ἀσχαλάω
　[ἀσ]χα[λᾶις], 207
ἀσχημονέω
　ἀσχημονήσω, 201
ἄτοπος

240 INDEX OF GREEK WORDS

ἀτοπώτερον, 169
ἄτοπα, 132
ἄτοπον, 194
ἀτυχέω
    ἀτυχῶ, 124
ἀτύχημα, 206
αὐθαδία
    αὐθαδίας, 185
αὐτόνομος, 141
αὐτόφωρος
    ἐπ᾽ αὐτοφώρωι, 174
ἀφίημι
    ἀφήσεις, 207
    ἀφῆκε, 3
ἀφοράω
    ἀφορᾶι, 190
Ἀφροδίτη
    Ἀφροδίτης, 113
Ἀχαρνεύς
    Ἀχαρνεῦ, 120

βαδίζω
    βαδιοῦμ᾽, 168
    βαδίσαι, 135
βάρβαρος, 192
βασιλεύς, 25
βίος, 209
    βίον, 156
βλέπω
    βλέπει, 195
    βλέπων, 210
βοάω
    βοήσεται, 194
    βοῶντος, 190
βουλεύω
    βουλεύσεται, 194
βούλομαι
    βουλόμενον, 200
    τί βουλόμενος, 123
    τί βούλεται; 148,160

βραχύς
    βρα[χέως], 153
βρόχος
    βρόχ-, 202

γὰρ δή
    σὺ γὰρ δή, 113
γελάω
    γελῶσα, 216
γῆ
    γῆν, 161
γίγνομαι
    γεγενημένον, 147
    γενομένη, 176
    γενομένης, 151
    γενοῦ, 211
    γενό[μενα], 207
    γενόμενον, 172, 193
γιγνώσκω
    [γνοῦσα], 184
γράμμα
    γράμματα, 16, 148
Γραῦς, 169
γρῦ, 186
γύναιον
    γύναι᾽, 165
γυνή
    γυναῖκα, 129, 153, 188, 215

δαΐς
    δᾶι[δας], 218
δακρύω
    δακρύει, 197
δακτύλιον, 160
δεῖ, 181
δείκνυμι
    δεῖξαι, 140
    δειξ.[, 169
    δέδειχα, 169
δεινός

INDEX OF GREEK WORDS

δεινόν, 153
δειπνέω
  δειπν[, 218
δεῖπνον, 217
δεσπότης
  δε[σπότ]ης, 164
δεῦρο, 198
  δεῦρ᾿, 148
δήπου, 136
διατρίβω
  διατρίβων, 120
δίδωμι
  διδόασι, 214, 215
  δός, 149
  δώσει, 180
  ἐδέδοτο, 165
διηγέομαι
  διηγεῖ, 140
δοκέω
  δοκῶ, 194
δοκιμάζω
  δοκιμάσει, 180
δούλη
  δούλην, 129
δράττομαι
  δράττεται, 195
δρύϊνος, 120
δύναμαι
  δυναί[μην, 155
  δυναίμην, 172
  δυνήσομαι, 200
δύο, 217
δύσποτμος
  δυσποτμώτερον, 114
δυστυχής
  ὦ δυστυχής, 122

ἑαυτόν, 198
ἐγκαταλείπω
  ἐγκαταλίπηις, 190

ἐγκράζω
  ἐγκραγών, 121
ἐθέλω
  θέλ[εις], 207
  θέλωσιν, 163
εἰκάζω
  εἰκάζειν, 181
εἰκός
  εἰκότως, 126
εἰμί
  ἔστω, 199
  ἦσθα, 126
  ὄνθ᾿, 170
  ὄντως, 170
εἴπερ
  εἴ[περ], 210
εἴρω
  εἴρει, 187
εἷς
  οὐδ[ὲ ἕν], 164
  ἕν, 160, 206
εἴσειμι
  εἰσιών, 147
  εἰσί[ωμ]εν, 217
  εἰσίωμεν, 178
εἰσέρχομαι, 145, 196
εἰσφέρω
  εἰσενέγ[κατε], 160
εἰσφορέω
  εἰσφορῶν, 162
εἶτα, 166
ἑκατέρωθε, 152
ἐκπλέω
  ἐκπλεῖ, 216
ἔκτοπος, 185
ἐλεέω
  ἐλεεῖν, 193
ἐλεινός
  [ἐλειν]ά, 186
ἐλευθερία

242 INDEX OF GREEK WORDS

ἐλευθερίαν, 129
ἕλκω
    ἑλκύσαι, 208
Ἑλληνικός
    Ἑλληνικόν, 193
ἐμαυτόν, 168
ἐμμανής
    ἐμμανέστατα, 117
ἐμπειρία
    ἐμπειρίαι, 196
ἐμφανίζω, 201
ἐναργής
    ἐναργῶς, 170
ἔνδον, 123, 195, 217
ἐνερόχρως, 222
ἐνθύμιος, 170
ἐνταῦθα
    ἐντ[αῦ]θ', 164
ἔντονος
    ἔντονον, 172
ἐντυγχάνω
    ἐντετυχηκώς, 188
ἐξάγω
    ἐξαγε[, 197
ἐξαίσιος
    ἐξαίσιον, 130
ἐξαπατάω
    ἐξαπατᾶις, 215
ἔξειμι
    ἐξιτητέον, 119
ἐξέρχομαι
    ἐξ[έρ]χ[εται], 195
    ἐξῆλθεν, 174, 203
    'ξελήλ[υθεν, 205
ἔξωθεν, 165
ἐπαγορεύω
    ἐπείπας, 135
ἐπανάγω
    ἐπανάξω, 171
ἐπίσημον, 209

ἐπιστροφή
    ἐπιστροφήν, 194
ἔρανος
    εἰς ἔρανον, 162
ἐράω
    ἐρωμένην, 117
    ἐρῶντα, 115
ἔρχομαι
    ἐλήλυθας, 125
ἐρωτικός
    ἐρωτικαί, 114
ἔσχατος, 128
ἕτοιμος
    ἕτοιμον, 158
εὖ, 202
εὔδηλος, 184
εὐπρεπής
    εὐπρεπῶς, 179
εὐπροσήγορος, 144
εὑρίσκω
    εὑρεῖν, 153
εὐτελής
    εὐτελές, 220
εὔχομαι
    εὔξασ[θαι], 152
εὔψυχος, 126, 211
ἐφεστρίδιον, 19, 159
ἐφήδομαι
    ἐφήδομ', 216
ἐχθές, 124
ἐχθρός, 175
ἔχω, 173
    σχών, 166
    ἔχει, 193
    ἔχειν, 117
    ἔχω, 194
    ἔχων, 135
ἕως, 162

Ζεύς

INDEX OF GREEK WORDS 243

Ζεῦ, 151
   μὰ Δι᾽, 156
   μὰ Δία, 152
   τὸν Δία, 133
   ὦ Ζεῦ, 173
ζηλοτυπία, 6
   ζηλοτυπ[, 214
ζητέω
   ζητοῦσι, 151
   τὸν ζητούμενον, 6
ζῶ
   ζώντων, 180
   ζῆι, 156
   ζῆις, 211
   ζῆν, 179

ἡγέομαι
   ἡγησάμην, 170
ἤδη, 135
ἥκιστος
   ἥκιστ, 177
ἥκω, 128
   ἥκεις, 150, 167
   ἥκων, 188
Ἥλιος
   νὴ τὸν Ἥλιον, 185
ἡμεῖς, 177
ἡμέρα
   ἡμέρας, 149
ἤπιος
   ἠπίως, 216
Ἡρακλῆς
   Ἡρ[άκλεις], 215

θάτερος, 166
θέλγω
   θέλξ[εις], 207
θέλω, *see* ἐθέλω
   θέλεις, 208
θεός

θεοί, 163
θεούς, 144
θεοῖς, 137
μὰ τοὺς θεούς, 119
θηρίον
   θηρί᾽, 162
θρίξ
   τῶν τριχῶν, 195
θυγάτριον, 198
θύρα
   θύραν, 121, 169
   τὴν θύραν, 149
θύω
   θύσαιμι, 137

ἱκετηρία
   [ἱ]κετη[ρ]ίαν, 176
   ἱκετηρίαν, 155, 156
ἱμάτιον
   ἱμάτια, 129
ἰχνεύω
   ἰχνεύων, 151

καθεύδω
   καθεύδεις, 122
καθοράω
   καθορᾶν, 124
κακοδαίμων
   κακόδαιμον, 192
κακός
   κακόν, 201
κακότης
   κακότητος, 151
καλέω
   κ[εκλήσει], 151
καλός
   καλῶς ποιῶν, 216
κάμπτω
   κάμπτεις, 167
καρτερέω

καρτερεῖν, 172
καταβαίνω
καταβήσ[ομαι], 145
κατάδεσμα
κατ[αδ]έσματ᾽, 202
καταδουλόω
καταδεδούλωκ᾽, 13, 220
κατάκειμαι, 135
κατάκειται, 195
κατακόπτω
κατακόψεις, 195
καταλείπω
καταλιπ[ών], 161
καταλιπεῖν, 212
κατέλειπον, 164
κεῖμαι
κειμ[ένων], 183
κελεύω
κελεύσω, 168
κηδεμών, 123
κοινός, 175
κόπτω
κόψαντι, 149
κόψασα, 169
κοτύλη
πρὸς κοτύλας, 161
κράζω
κέκραγα, 135
κράσπεδον
κράσπεδ᾽, 19, 159
Κρά[τεια], 152
κράτος, 16
κροτέω
κροτοῦσαν, 161
κρύπτω
κρύπτων, 168
κτείνω
[κτα]νεῖν, 212
κ[τα]νεῖν, 194
κυβερνάω

αὐτὸν κυβερνᾶν, 144
Κύπρος
Κύπρου, 175
παρὰ [Κύπρου], 150
κύριος
κυρία, 133
κυρίως, 180

λαβρώνιον
λαβρώνια, 160
λαλέω
[λα]λεῖς, 175
λαλῶ, 186
λαμβάνω, see ὕπνος
[εἰ]λη[μμ]έ[νου], 178
λαβεῖν, 185
λαβών, 153
λάβ᾽, 169
λάμβαν᾽, 175
λάφυρα
λαφύρων, 25, 128
λέαινα, 192
λέγω, see ἀγορεύω
λέγουσα, 156
τὸ λεγόμενον, 119
λήιζομαι
λεληι[σμ]έ[νου], 178
λῆρος, 168
λῆψις
λήψεων, 183
λίθος
λίθον, 199
λογισμός
λογισμῶι, 210
λυπέω
τὸ λυποῦν, 128
λυπρός
λυπρά, 202
λύρα
λύρας, 186

INDEX OF GREEK WORDS 245

λυτρόομαι
    λυτρούμενος, 150
    λυτρωσάμενος, 3
λωποδύτης
    λωποδύτας, 145

Μαγνῆτις
    ὦ Μαγνῆτις, 131
μακάριος, 124
    μακάριον, 157
    ὦ μακάρι᾽, 124
μανθάνω, 172
μαντεύομαι
    μαντεύεθ᾽, 181
μάρτυς
    μάρτυρα, 175
μέγας
    τὰ μέγιστ᾽, 124
μέθη, 201
μεθίημι
    μ[εθε]ί[ς], 199
μέσος
    ἐς μέσον, 199
μεσόω
    μεσούσης, 116
μεταμέλω
    μετέμελ᾽, 217
μετέχω
    μετέχεις, 113
μέχρι, 116
μιαρός, 168
    μιαρόν, 140
μικρόψυχος
    μικρόψυχον, 198
μισέω
    μισεῖ, 131
    μισεῖσθαι, 6
    μισούμενος, 112
    μισοῦσι, 10
μῖσος, 4, 130

μόνος
    μό[νον], 160
    μόνον, 212
Μυσός, 165

νομίζω
    νομίζω, 129
νοσέω
    νοσεῖ, 138
    νοσοῦντα, 138
νόσος
    νόσον, 199
Νύξ
    ὦ Νύξ, 113

ξένια, 217
ξένος, 17
    ξένε, 149
ξίφος, 154

ὀδύνη
    ὀδύν[ας], 202
ὀδυνηρός
    ὀδυνηρῶς, 211
οἶδα
    εἰδέναι, 181
    ἴσθι, 158
οἰκεῖος
    οἰκεῖον, 8
οἶκος
    οἴκοθεν, 175
οἴομαι
    ᾠόμην, 173
οἴχομαι
    οἴχεται, 180
ὀκνηρός
    ὀκνηρῶς, 181
ὀκτώ, 149
ὅλος
    [ὅλ]ως, 198
    ὅλως, 170

INDEX OF GREEK WORDS

ὁμοθυμέω
    ὁμοθυμεῖ, 140
ὁμόσε
    ὁμ[ό]σε, 209
ὄνειδος, 212
ὄνομα
    τοὔνομ᾽, 151
ὄνος, 186
ὁράω
    ἰδεῖν, 157, 173
    ὁρᾷς, 145
    ὁρᾶν, 166
    ὁρῶ, 170, 173
ὀργή
    ὀργαῖς, 209
ὀρεύς
    ὀρεῖ, 189
ὀρθός
    ὀρθῶς, 193
ὄρος
    ὄρει, 189
οὐ γάρ;, 157
οὗτος, 174
οὑτοσί, 149
ὄψις
    ὄψιν, 165, 173

πάθη
    πάθας, 149
παιδισκάριον, 13
παῖς
    παῖ, 174
πάλιν, 151, 167, 190
πανταχῆι, 193
πάξ, 152
πάππα
    πάπ‹π›α, 216
παρά
    πάρ᾽, 166
παράβασις

    see παρέκβασις, 142
πάρειμι
    [πάρ]εσθ᾽, 195
    παρ[ών], 175
    παρῆσθας, 123
παρεισφορέω
    παρεισφορῶν, 162
παρέκβασις
    παρεκβάσει, 142
παρέρχομαι
    παρελθών, 195
παρθένος
    παρθένον, 191
παρίημι
    παρῆις, 140
παροράω
    παρορωμένωι, 137
πᾶς
    παντός, 153
    πάντες, 144
πατήρ, 175
    [πατ]ήρ, 186
πάτρα
    πάτρ[ας], 177
παχύς, 165
πειράομαι
    πειρώμεθα, 133
περαίνω
    ἐπεράνω, 149
περιβάλλω
    περιβάλλειν, 175
περιμένω
    περίμεν᾽, 122
περιπατέω
    περιπ[ατ-, 145
    περιπατῶ, 115
περιτίθημι
    περιθείς, 129
περιτρέχω
    περιδραμοῦμαι, 182

INDEX OF GREEK WORDS

περιφέρω
    περιφέρεις, 199
πηνίκα, 183
πιαίνω
    πιαῖνον, 149
πίνω
    πίνει, 164
    πίνων, 167
πίπτω
    [π]εσ[εῖν], 196
    πεσών, 121
πλάνη
    πλάνης, 196
πλεονεξία, 210
πλουτέω
    πλουτεῖν, 166
πόθεν, 195
ποθέω
    ὦ ποθούμενος, 173
ποιέω
    ποεῖς, 174
    ποησ[, 170
    ποιεῖν, 200
    ποήσεις, 153
πόλεμος, 175
πόλις
    τὴν [πόλιν], 182
πολύς
    πλείστων, 183
    πολλά, 198
    πολλῶι, 133
    πολύ, 157
πόνος
    πόνον, 137
πρᾶγμα
    πράγματα, 198
πρᾶος, *see* πραΰς
πραΰς, 144
πρίν, 196
προίξ

προῖκ', 217
προσεύχομαι
    προσευξάμην, 215
πρόσθεν, 207
    εἰς τὸ πρόσθεν, 152
προσποιέομαι
    προσποου[μένωι], 212
προφέρω
    πρ[ό]φ[ερε], 217
πυνθάνομαι
    πυ[θόμενος], 150
πῦρ, 195

ῥέω
    ἔρρει, 187

σθεναρός
    σθεναρώτερον, 166
σκηνή, 8
σκότος
    σκότους, 136
σπαθάω
    σπαθᾶν, 5, 222
σπάθη
    [σπ]άθην, 213
    σπάθαι, 221
    σπάθας, 149
    τὰς σπάθας, 169
σπείρω
    ἔσπαρκε, 175
σπένδω
    σπείσονθ', 161
σπεύδω
    σπεῦδε, 146
στέγω
    στέγειν, 199
στέλλω
    στέλλει, 167
στενωπός
    στενωπῶι, 115

248 INDEX OF GREEK WORDS

στραβός, 139
στρατιωτικός
    στρατιωτικῶς, 5, 145
    τὸ στρατιωτικόν, 138
στρατόπεδον
    ἐν στρατοπέδωι, 125
συκάζω
    συκάζει, 140
συμβαίνω
    τὸ συμβεβηκός, 189
συμβολή
    τὰς συμβολάς, 168
συμπεριπατέω
    συμπεριπατήσω, 187
σύν, 153
συνάχθομαι, 163
σύνοιδα
    σύν[οισθα], 178
σφόδρα, 138
σχεδόν, 116
σωτήρ, 151

ταλαιπωρός
    ταλαιπωρόν, 156
τάλαν, 197, 208
τάλαντον
    τάλαντα, 217
τᾶν
    ὦ τᾶν, 137
τάττω
    τάττομαι, 126
ταὐτόματον
    ἀπὸ ταὐτομάτου, 217
ταχύς
    τοῦ ταχέως, 182
τέκνον, 173
τηθία, 173
τηλοῦ
    τηλ.[, 177
τηρέω

τηρῶ, 133
τίθημι
    [θ]ήσει, 156
    θεῖναι, 155
    θήσεται, 169
τιμάω
    τιμᾶν, 144
τίς
    μετὰ τίνων, 164
τοιοῦτος
    [τοιαῦτα], 175
    τοιαῦτα, 162, 167
    τὸ τοιοῦτον, 181
τοῖχος, 136
τότε
    τότ᾽, 172
τράχηλος
    τράχηλον, 157
τρέμω
    τρέμων, 181
τρέπω
    τρέπωσι, 162
τρέχω
    [τρέχ]οι, 209
τρισάθλιος
    τρισαθλ[ι-], 213
    τρισαθλιώτατον, 180
τροπαῖος
    Ζεῦ τροπαῖε, 151
τροπή
    τροπαί, 152
τρόπος
    κατὰ τρόπον, 132
τυγχάνω, 169
    τυγχάνεις, 175
τύχη
    ἀπὸ τύχης, 3

ὑπαίθριος
    ὑπαιθρίωι, 117

INDEX OF GREEK WORDS 249

ὑπεράστειος, 138
ὑπερεντρυφάω
    ὑπερεντρ[, 137
ὑπερπαίω
    [ὑπερ]πέπαικε, 155
ὕπνος
    ὕπνον λαμβάνω, 120
ὑποκάθημαι
    ὑποκαθήμενον, 157
ὑπονοέω
    ὑπονοεῖς, 132, 147
ὗς, 165, 189
ὕφασμα
    ὑφασμάτων, 159
ὑφοράω
    ὑφορᾶι, 190
ὕω
    ὕοντα, 133

φαίνομαι
    φαν[είς], 173
φάρμακον
    φάρμ[ακον], 213
φημί, 135
    φήις, 172, 180
φθείρω
    ἔφθαρμαι, 201
φθόνος, 6
φιλέλλην, 144
φιλέω
    φιλῶ, 191
φιλοβασιλεύς, 144
φίλος
    τοῖς φίλοις, 156
    φιλτάτη, 191
    φίλτατε, 137
φιλοσοφέω
    φιλοσοφῶν, 119
φοβερός
    φοβερόν, 152

φορέω
    φ[ορε]ῖ[ν], 199
φροντίζω
    φρόντισον, 182
φροντίς
    φροντίδες, 114
φυλόν, 140

χαίρω
    χαῖρε, 195
χαμαί, 121
χάρις
    χάριν, 153
χειμών
    χειμῶνος, 25, 118
χρή
    ἐχρ[ῆν], 177
χρόνος
    διὰ χρόνου, 125
χρύσιον
    χρύσια, 160

ψέγω, 206
ψιθυρισμός, 158
ψοφέω
    ψοφεῖν, 184
ψυχή
    ψυχήν, 199, 221

ὧδε, 198

Lightning Source UK Ltd.
Milton Keynes UK
UKHW020400090222
398380UK00002B/164

9 781905 670970